GUARDIANS
OF LETTERS

GUARDIANS OF LETTERS

Literacy, Power, and the Transmitters
of Early Christian Literature

Kim Haines-Eitzen

OXFORD
UNIVERSITY PRESS
2000

OXFORD
UNIVERSITY PRESS

Oxford   NewYork

Athens   Auckland   Bangkok   Bogotá   Bombay   Buenos Aires   Calcutta
Cape Town   Chennai   Dar es Salaam   Delhi   Florence   Hong Kong   Istanbul
Karachi   Kuala Lumpur   Madrid   Melbourne   Mexico City   Mumbai
Nairobi   Paris   Sâo Paulo   Shanghai   Singapore   Taipei   Tokyo   Toronto   Warsaw

and associated companies in
Berlin   Ibadan

Copyright © 2000 by Kim Haines-Eitzen

Published by Oxford University Press, Inc.,
198 Madison Avenue, New York, New York 10016

Oxford is a registered trademark of Oxford University Press.

Library of Congress Cataloging-in-Publication Data
Haines-Eitzen, Kim.
Guardians of letters : literacy, power, and the transmitters
of early Christian literature / Kim Haines-Eitzen.
p.   cm.
Includes bibliographical references and index.
ISBN 0-19-513564-4
1. Christian literature, Early — Rome — History and criticism.
2. Transmission of texts — Rome.   3. Scribes — Rome.   I. Title.
BR67.2.H35 2000
270.1 — dc21   00-021072

9 8 7 6 5 4 3 2 1
Printed in the United States of America
on acid-free paper

PREFACE

This book and the scribes on whom it focuses have been my steady companions for the last several years, and thus I feel a certain loss at releasing them. At the same time, I am relieved to find closure and eager to turn my attention to new projects. Both my reluctance and relief find resonance in the words of ancient scribes and authors, who acknowledged that "the word once sent, never returns," and simultaneously expressed the pure joy of completing a written text. I began to formulate the questions that drive this study while collating manuscripts for the International Greek New Testament Project. Who were the scribes that copied early Christian texts, I wanted to know. How might their handiwork (i.e., their copies) shed light on their identity, their training, their location, their social and religious proclivities? I hope that the chapters that follow offer at least the beginnings of answers to these questions.

One of the welcome pleasures of finishing this project is the opportunity to thank those who have contributed to it in a variety of ways. I owe special gratitude to my tireless advisor, Bart Ehrman, and those professors at the University of North Carolina, Chapel Hill, and Duke University who served on my committee when this book was in its dissertation form: Elizabeth Clark, Dale Martin, Paul Meyer, and John Van Seters. I also thank David Parker at the University of Birmingham, who graciously agreed to serve long-distance on the committee. Although his name does not appear within the pages that follow, David Halperin's inspiring seminars as well as his advice to me as a graduate student deciding on a course of study — do what you love to do — have remained an important guide throughout my transitions from master's student to doctoral student, from graduate school to life as an assistant professor.

Above all, I want to thank the people and the institution with whom I most closely associated during the actual research and writing of my dissertation: Ross Kraemer and Robert Kraft at the University of Pennsylvania welcomed me into the academic community in Philadelphia. For their generosity in reading drafts of certain chapters, in providing me with library privileges and internet services, and in taking such a keen interest in my work, I am truly grateful. Mention of these practical supports, however, does not begin to capture the warmth and kindness they have shown me. At Penn, I also found wonderful fellow graduate students, who similarly welcomed me into their midst. I especially thank Debra Bucher, Jill Gorman (at Temple), Shira Lander, Susan Marks, Beth Pollard, and Sarah Schwarz. To the members of my dissertation writing group — Max Grossman (now at the University of North Carolina, Greensboro) and Jonathan Klawans (now at Boston University) — I offer thanks for reading very early drafts and for sharing with me the often lonely experience of dissertation writing.

For my newest set of colleagues and friends at Cornell University, I give thanks. I have been pleased to find such a rich and rewarding intellectual life here. Thanks also go to my students, who have heard me chatter on about ancient scribes and who respond with fascinating and lively questions. Their interest has fueled my continued work on this project and reminded me of the relevance of research on a subject that sometimes seems arcane and remote.

I am particularly grateful to my family and friends, who have been terrifically supportive and understanding of my preoccupation with this project. My parents, Joe and Elaine Haines, have probably contributed to this book more than they realize: my mother taught me how to stick with a project until it was finished; my father, without his or my knowing it, instilled in me a love of languages and a fascination with history and religion. My sister, Kris Haines-Burnham, knows the ups and downs of academic life and offered me endless support and encouragement. Two very close friends, Jane Kenyon and Anne Vial, were writing their dissertations at the same time; with them I shared countless concerns, insecurities, and joys. Finally, I thank my partner and best friend, John Haines-Eitzen, who has lovingly accompanied me for the last ten years. I am immensely grateful for his willingness to give up a tenured position so that I could pursue my passion for the ancient Mediterranean world, for his emotional and financial support, and now for his help and companionship in making our commuting between Ithaca and Philadelphia not only viable but also enjoyable and fulfilling. My son, Eli, arrived just as this book was being copyedited; for the many ways in which he has enriched my life in such a short time, I give thanks.

Chapter 2 appeared in a modified form in the *Journal of Early Christian Studies* 6 (1998) 629–646. I thank the Johns Hopkins University Press for permission to include the chapter here.

Ithaca, New York   K. H.-E.
September 1999

CONTENTS

ABBREVIATIONS

For the names of Greek and Latin writers and their works, I have followed the abbreviations found in Liddell-Scott-Jones' *Greek-English Lexicon*, the *Oxford Latin Dictionary*, and the *Oxford Classical Dictionary*. For papyrological publications I have followed the abbreviations in E. G. Turner, *Greek Papyri: An Introduction*, and J. F. Oates, R. S. Bagnall, et al., *Checklist of Editions of Greek Papyri and Ostraca*. Abbreviations not found in the *JBL* stylesheet or those used with frequency are as follows.

AJP	*American Journal of Philology*
BAG	*A Greek-English Lexicon of the New Testament*, ed. W. Bauer, W. Arndt, and F. W. Gingrich (Chicago: University of Chicago Press, 1979)
BGU	*Aegyptische Urkunden aus den Staatlichen Museen zu Berlin, Griechische Urkunden* (Berlin, 1895–)
CIL	*Corpus Inscriptionum Latinarum* (Berlin, 1862–)
CPR	*Corpus Papyrorum Raineri*, vol. 1, ed. C. Wessely (Vienna, 1895)
CQ	*Classical Quarterly*
CSEL	*Corpus Scriptorum Ecclesiasticorum Latinorum* (Vienna: C. Gerodi, etc., 1866–)
GCS	*Die griechischen christlichen Schriftsteller der ersten drei Jahrhunderte* (Leipzig: J. C. Hinrichs, 1899–)
GRBS	*Greek, Roman, and Byzantine Studies*
ILS	*Inscriptiones Latinae Selectae*, ed. Hermannus Dessau, 3 vols. in 5 parts (Berlin: Weidmannos, 1892–1916)
JEA	*Journal of Egyptian Archaeology*
JRS	*Journal of Roman Studies*
LCL	Loeb Classical Library
LSJ	H. G. Liddell, R. Scott, and H. Stuart Jones, *A Greek-English Lexicon* (Oxford: Clarendon, 1968)

Liste   Kurt Aland. *Kurzgefasste Liste der griechischen Handschriften des Neuen Testaments* (New York: de Gruyter, 1994)

MPER   *Mitteilungen aus der Sammlung der Papyrus Erzherzog Rainer* (Vienna, 1887–1897)

MSB   C. H. Roberts, *Manuscript, Society, and Belief in Early Christian Egypt* (London: Oxford University Press, 1979)

NewDocs   Greg Horsley, *New Documents Illustrating Early Christianity*, vols 1–7 (McQuarie University, 1981–1994).

OCD   *The Oxford Classical Dictionary*, ed. N. G. L. Hammond and H. H. Scullard (Oxford: Clarendon Press, 1970)

OLD   *Oxford Latin Dictionary*, ed. P. G. W. Glare (Oxford: Clarendon, 1982)

PG   *Patrologia Graeca*, ed. J. P. Migne (Paris: Migne, 1857–1866)

PIR²   *Prosopographia Imperii Romani Saec. I.II.III.*, 2d ed., 5 vols., ed. E. Groag, A. Stein, and L. Petersen (Berlin: de Gruyter, 1933–1970)

PL   *Patrologia Latina*, ed. J. P. Migne (Paris: Migne, 1844–1865)

P.Oxy.   *The Oxyrhynchus Papyri* (London: Egypt Exploration Fund, 1898–)

RE   *Paulys Real-Encyclopäudie der classischen Alterthumswissenschaft* (Stuttgart: J. B. Metzler, 1893)

Repertorium Kurt Aland, Ed., *Repertorium der griechischen christlichen Paypri*. Vol. 1: *Biblische Papyri* (New York: de Gruyter, 1976); vol 2: *Kirchenväuter Papyri* (New York: de Gruyter, 1995)

SC   *Sources Chrétiennes* (Paris: Les Editions du Cerf, 1943–)

ZPE   *Zeitschrift für Papyrologie und Epigraphie*

GUARDIANS
OF LETTERS

INTRODUCTION

Around the year 170 C.E., a resident of Oxyrhynchus in upper Egypt sent a friend a request for copies of several literary works:

> Make and send me copies of books 6 and 7 of Hypsicrates' *Characters in Comedy*. For Harpocration says that they are among Polion's books. But it is likely that others, too, have them. He also has prose epitomes of Thersagoras' work on the myths of tragedy.

Unfortunately, the writer's name and identity have been lost. It does appear, however, that the request was sent to another literary-minded Oxyrhynchite who knew where the books might be obtained, for the letter proceeds in a new hand as follows:

> According to Harpocration, Demetrius the bookseller [ὁ βυβλιοπώλης] has them. I have instructed Apollinides to send me certain of my own books which you will hear of in good time from Seleucus himself. Should you find any, apart from those which I possess, make copies and send them to me. Diodorus and his friends also have some which I do not have. (*P.Oxy.* 2192)

This letter provides a glimpse into some of the social networks of Graeco-Roman Egypt. Even in the midst of a society characterized by restricted literacy, book trades were alive and well among circles of literate friends.[1] The instance of this letter suggests that in Oxyrhynchus, a thriving urban center in upper Egypt, a cluster of individuals could be found who had the ability and leisure to read and write. These individuals traded books among themselves and perhaps resorted to the services of local bookshops when necessary. At the same time, while the exchange provides a window into literary circles in upper Egypt, it offers little by way of details. The letter remains silent about several matters that the senders and recipients knew well, including the identity of the persons who would prepare the copies of these books and the process they would follow in doing so.[2]

Some sixty years earlier, on 20 October 111 C.E., a contract was drawn up in Oxyrhynchus that indicates the distribution of slaves belonging to a certain deceased Tiberius Julius Theon, a wealthy Roman citizen who had an estate in Oxyrhynchus. Both the form of the contract and the hand in which it was written suggest that this was a private agreement. It appears, further, that the recipients of these slaves were Theon's two sons, Tiberius Julius Theon and Tiberius Julius Sarapion, and his grandson Tiberius Julius Theon, who was to receive his deceased father's portion. Although the entire papyrus is not preserved, the passages that survive contain lists of slaves and in certain cases an accompanying occupation or skill.

> We, Tiberius Julius Theon, former strategus of the city and archidicastes, and Tiberius Julius Sarapion his brother, and Tiberius Julius Theon his nephew, one of the class of victors at the sacred games who are exempt from taxation, agree with one another that we have divided among ourselves out of the slaves left by Tiberius Julius Theon, former hypomnematographus and gymnasiarch, father of Theon archidicastes and of Sarapion, grandfather of Theon victor at the sacred games, those mentioned below; that there have fallen to the share of Tiberius Julius Theon, former strategus of the city and archidicastes, Heron scribe [γραμματέα], . . . Heraclas amanuensis [προχειροφόρον], . . . Ammonas notary [νοτάριον], . . . ; and to Julius Sarapion his brother, Demas amanuensis [προχειροφόρον], . . . Epaphrys notary, Agathys notary [each νοτάριον], Sarapas notary [νοτάριον], . . . Eucaerus notary [νοτάριον]. (P.Oxy. 3197)

The titles and positions of the deceased Tiberius Julius Theon and his sons indicate both their wealth and their prestige. As gymnasiarch, probably of Alexandria, Tiberius Julius Theon was a prominent and powerful official. It should not surprise us, then, that his estate required many slaves; indeed, the contract suggests that upward of fifty-nine slaves were involved.[3] The slaves whose occupations are mentioned consist of five notaries, two amanuenses, one scribe, a repairer, a cook, and a barber. That a large estate should demand specialized and skilled slaves who were able to write contracts, keep various records, and maintain the archives is not surprising; what is significant is that the slaves in administrative roles are the ones (with only three exceptions) whose occupations are singled out for mention. This suggests that these slaves were in a category above other domestic slaves. Although we learn nothing about precisely what these occupations entailed, this contract invites a preliminary hypothesis: in the hierarchy of slave occupations, administrative and clerical slaves were given a distinctively high rank.[4]

In a setting far from Oxyrhynchus and some two hundred years after the agreement was drawn up by Theon's descendants, Eusebius of Caesarea composed his *Ecclesiastical History*. As is well known, Eusebius devoted the sixth book to a "biographical account" of the life of Origen. Defending Origen's orthodoxy and his philosophical virtuosity, Eusebius "casts the Christian theological Origen in the stereotypical guise of a Hellenistic holy man."[5] One of the ways that Eusebius defends Origen is by emphasizing both Origen's zeal for the study of scripture and his prolific production of scriptural commentaries. The description of Origen's working environment is particularly instructive.

> From that time also Origen's commentaries on the divine Scriptures had their beginning, at the instigation of Ambrose, who not only plied him with innumerable verbal exhortations and encouragements, but also provided him unstintingly with what was necessary. For as he dictated there were ready at hand more than seven shorthand-writers [ταχυγράφοι], who relieved each other at fixed times, and as many copyists [βιβλιογράφοι], as well as girls trained for beautiful writing [κόραις ἐπὶ τὸ καλλιγραφεῖν ἠσκημέναις]; for all of whom Ambrose supplied without stint the necessary means. (HE 6.23)

The historicity of this story aside, Eusebius has illustrated the means by which ancient writers, at least those with exceptional resources, composed. Throughout antiquity, poets, novelists, and commentators relied upon the system of patronage for financial support; patrons provided writers with the freedom to devote themselves to their craft.[6] Ambrose provided just such support for Origen.[7] Eusebius's story further specifies the kinds of secretaries, copyists, and calligraphers that Ambrose placed at the service of Origen. Shorthand writers were commonly employed in households or public settings to write contracts, letters, or memoranda that were dictated to them. Copyists could be found both in private settings, as in this story, as well as the more public settings of libraries and book shops. Most striking is Eusebius' mention of the female calligraphers; the fact that Eusebius includes these women without comment suggests that he found their presence neither unusual nor remarkable. What Eusebius finds commonplace, however, demands our attention.

In the mid–second century, the Christian author Hermas tells the story of a vision he had on the road to Cumae. An "ancient lady," whom he had seen in a vision just a year before, reappeared to him reading aloud from a little book. The dialogue between the "ancient lady" and Hermas went as follows:

> She said to me, "Can you take this message to God's elect ones?" I said to her, "Lady, I cannot remember so much; but give me the little book to copy." "Take it," she said, "and give it back to me." I took it and went away to a certain place in the country, and copied everything, letter by letter, for I could not distinguish the syllables [μετεγραψάμην πάντα πρὸς γράμμα οὐχ ηὕρισκον γὰρ τὰς συλλαβάς]. So when I had finished the letters of the little book it was suddenly taken out of my hand; but I did not see by whom. (Shep., vis. 2.1.3–4)

Some fifteen days later the "knowledge of the writing was revealed to Hermas." A "beautiful man" appeared to Hermas and asked him if he knew the woman from whom he had received the book. Hermas confidently replied, "The Sibyl." Hermas was told he was quite wrong, that the "ancient lady" represented the church. Later, another vision came to Hermas:

> The ancient lady came and asked me if I had already given the book to the elders. I said that I had not given it. "You have done well," she said, "for I have words to add. When, therefore, I have finished all the words they will be made known by you to all the elect. You will therefore write two little books and send one to Clement and one to Grapte. Clement then will send it to the cities abroad, for that is his duty; and Grapte will exhort the widows and orphans; but in this city you will read it with the elders who are in charge of the church." (*Shep.*, *vis.* 2.4.2–3)

The story of Hermas and the "ancient lady" illumines the transmission and dissemination of early Christian literature and offers an instance for reflecting on the intersection of literacy and authority in the early church. In the narrative of the vision, Hermas himself—evidently a Christian with intimate connections to ecclesiastical leaders in the church of Rome—is responsible for the copying of these sacred texts as well as for their dissemination. Although the anonymous Muratorian Canon claims that Hermas was the brother of the bishop of Rome, nowhere is Hermas described as a scribe or copyist by profession; the most we learn about Hermas in *The Shepherd* is that he is a slave.[8] And yet Hermas can assure his readers/hearers that he received these words from the divine "church" herself. Thus, the transmission and dissemination of the sacred books proceeds according to ecclesiastical instruction. Moreover, Hermas simultaneously ascribes power to texts and maintains a power over the texts.

These four illustrations—the letter about the book trade at Oxyrhynchus, the contract distributing administrative slaves, Eusebius's story about Origen's scribes, and Hermas' vision of the ancient lady—are variously helpful for a study of the scribes who copied Christian literature during the second and third centuries. The contours of the present analysis are shaped by two central questions: Who were the scribes that copied Christian texts during the second and third centuries? And what role(s) did these scribes play in the (re)production, transmission, and interpretation of these texts? In the chapters that follow, we will return to the stories with which we have begun, for they contribute to our understanding of the background in which Christianity composed and transmitted its own literature and ascribed authority to its literature and church leaders. In the pre-Constantinian milieu, we should imagine an exchange of various Christian texts ("orthodox" and "heretical") not all that unlike the portrait of our book traders at Oxyrhynchus. The papyri of early Christian texts imply just such a private network: physical features such as handwriting, marginal notes, and collections of disparate and various texts in a single codex suggest that copies were made by and for individuals or, at the very least, for individual churches during the second and third centuries.

Perhaps more than the other stories, the contract among Theon's descendants offers a glimpse of scribes working in a rather different sphere: that of administration. Yet there are indications in the evidence from antiquity that these very same scribes—who were trained to prepare documents, contracts, letters, and so on—could be called upon to copy literary texts.[9] Moreover, that wealthy Christians, say at Oxyrhynchus, may have had their slaves copy Christian and non-Christian texts for them should at least be considered plausible. However we understand early Christian language of slavery, we should not imagine or suppose that in reality Christians attempted to abolish or even reform the system of slavery in antiquity.[10]

What perhaps unites the four stories more than anything else is the incomplete picture of the roles and positions of scribes in antiquity that they each provide. The letter about the book trade does not specify how the copying of books will proceed nor does it mention who will do the copying; the contract among Theon's relatives provides no elaboration of occupations related to administration; Eusebius fails to remark on the precise social, religious, and economic identity of the scribes in the service of Origen; and Hermas simply suggests that he himself, a Christian slave or freedperson who is apparently closely tied to the bishop of Rome, is to copy the sacred texts. While slaves and freed scribes were most frequently the copyists of literary texts — indeed, an outward sign of one's extensive education and socioeconomic standing was the ability to avoid reading and writing by owning or employing scribes for these tasks[11] — Hermas does not tell us that he is a professional scribe. Thus, each of the portraits provides facets to a social history of scribes, but none is sufficient alone.

If we stand back and look at these stories from a different angle, they provide occasion for commenting on the texture and role of literacy in antiquity. More precisely, a study of the roles and function of early Christian scribes contributes to discussions about ancient literacy by focusing on a particular social, religious, and ideological context. The most significant and comprehensive study on the subject of literacy in antiquity is William Harris's *Ancient Literacy*.[12] Harris combined literary, inscriptional, and papyrological evidence from the ancient world with modern anthropological and sociological studies to show that the preconditions (e.g., an extensive network of schools) necessary for mass literacy were not present throughout antiquity. He argued on this basis that "we must suppose that the majority of people were always illiterate."[13] Harris estimated that at no point in the period from the invention of the Greek alphabet to the end of the Roman Empire did literacy exceed 10–15 percent of the entire population, women and slaves included.

Although the work of Harris has dismantled the notion that there existed widespread literacy and education in antiquity,[14] we would do well to look more closely at the levels and function of literacy among those at the lower ends of the class spectrum.[15] It is clear that while the scribes of the Roman Empire operated at a number of different socioeconomic levels and within a variety of social and cultural contexts, scribes can most often be found among slaves — who, according to Roman law, were forbidden to own anything — and lower to middle-class professionals.[16] An outline of the range of scribal roles and contexts coupled with investigation of scribes' status in the Roman Empire can further our understanding of the levels and functions of literacy in antiquity. While both the use and meaning of the terms "status" and "class" for describing social stratification remain debated among scholars of the ancient Mediterranean, both terms are important for understanding scribal roles: "status" carries with it a certain flexibility and fluidity that permits us to look beyond the more simple economic classifications of scribes to their function within various ancient contexts; the economic connotations associated with the term "class" allow us to explore the role and function of literacy for those who were not members of the wealthy elite segments of the population.[17] Once we begin to look closely at issues of status, class, economics, and education as these relate to second-and third-century scribes and in particular the work of scribes in the early Christian context of text reproduction, we are led into the intersection of texts, power, authority, and ideology in ways that have remained largely unexplored until now.

THE STUDY: EVIDENCE AND METHODOLOGY

In the Mediterranean world of the second and third centuries C.E., scribes could be found at nearly all levels of society, performing a range of functions. It is quite clear that scribes were normally literate, but no generalizations can be made about their degree of literacy. Nor can generalizations be made about their class, for in the Roman period, scribes could be found at various socioeconomic levels (with highest concentrations among slaves and freedpersons). Yet for all their ubiquity, Roman-period scribes seldom received recognition for their work; neither ancient sources nor modern scholarship has paid them much attention as a social group. To be sure, scholars have studied scribes of earlier and later periods;[18] presented various detailed studies on handwriting, writing positions, the materials used, and the forms of ancient books;[19] analyzed the confusing and contradictory data on Jewish scribes;[20] given attention to the official and literary scribes of Roman Egypt;[21] examined the emergence and development of ancient libraries and the book trade;[22] and offered histories of the book arts.[23] Such related studies can certainly aid the investigation of Graeco-Roman scribes. But there are no comprehensive social histories of scribes in the second and third centuries C.E.

In part the lack of scholarly attention to scribes may be due to certain assumptions that frequently manifest themselves in treatments of the transmission of literature in antiquity. Nowhere is this more striking than in Robin Lane Fox's study of literacy and power in early Christianity. After comparing the little we know about Jewish and Christian scribes, Lane Fox concludes that "scribes did not command particular respect among Christians because, at first, the oral prevailed over the Christian written; texts were not sumptuous nor supreme symbols of Christian identity, let alone a source of pollution for hands which touched them; *if Jewish scribes did indeed do more than merely copy, Christian scribes did not.*"[24] The assumption that Christian scribes — or even that scribes more generally (with the exception of Jewish scribes) — merely copied texts may well contribute to the lack of attention to scribal roles, for if these scribes served only the mechanical function of text reproduction this can be summarized in a sentence or paragraph at most.

The question of the roles of scribes who copied texts, particularly in the context of early Christianity, is at the fore of the discussion throughout the present study. For Lane Fox and others notwithstanding, it has become increasingly clear that scribes were readers embodied in social, cultural, and religious contexts and that their contexts did shape their (re)production of texts.[25] As Zetzel has put it for the Latin context,

> the readers, critics and scribes of Latin texts in antiquity were not machines, and they were not even monks or professional copyists. They were intelligent and thinking people, who read and copied books because they had an interest in them, not because it was their job. And because they understood what they read and wrote, they inevitably affected the texts in accordance with their own ideas.[26]

We will return again to the ways in which scribes (re)formed and (re)created texts in the process of copying them, the extent to which they had liberty to do so, and the implications of their modifications in the chapters that follow. The rationale for this study begins with the recognition that books were manufactured and shaped by the scribes who copied them, and therefore it is of utmost importance that we learn as much about these scribes as possible. As Roger Stoddard reminds us, "Whatever they may do, authors do not write books. Books are not written at all. They are manufactured by scribes and other artisans, by mechanics and other engineers, and by printing presses and other machines."[27]

The lack of detailed studies on the roles and status of scribes in Roman antiquity may well be due to other reasons; indeed, a number of problems seriously complicate such a study. The first and most significant difficulty concerns the nature of our evidence and the methods used to study it. The bulk of our evidence for ancient scribes derives from papyri found in upper Egypt and provides valuable information regarding administrative or official scribes in the various districts of nomic Egypt. Our Greek and Latin literature, while containing some information about these public administrative scribes, offers evidence for a rather different type of scribe — the scribe, stenographer, secretary, and/or copyist in the employment of various authors. We must continually ask, therefore, how typical the evidence from Egypt is and, further, whether the evidence from the towns and villages from upper Egypt can tell us about Egypt more generally. The diversity of opinions on precisely this issue alerts us to the complexities involved. Roger Bagnall, for example, questions whether the evidence of cities like Hermopolis, Antinoopolis, Oxyrhynchus, and Arsinoe were typical of other towns and villages.[28] C. H. Roberts argued that the evidence from Egypt can be used for more generalizing conclusions: "the evidence of hands written outside Egypt, both documentary and literary, is by now sufficient to show that the Egyptian hands are, in general, not local or provincial types, but the standard hands of the Greco-Roman world."[29]

E. G. Turner, on the other hand, claimed that "documents found at Avroman, Dura-Europus, Qumran, and Engedi shake the comfortable assumption of an earlier day that Greek documentary handwriting at any given date took a standard form throughout the Graeco-Roman world."[30]

Other problems compound those of the comparative use of evidence. We must, for example, address the correlation between evidence deriving from literature penned by members of the upper classes (especially in an urban center such as Rome) and evidence from elsewhere in the empire. Additionally, our evidence contronts us with the multiplicity of languages in the Roman Empire. Different cultural, social, and religious contexts required different languages; scribes in many cases had to be bilingual, even trilingual, to remain professionals in a diverse world. Willy Clarysse, for example, has shown that in papyri from Tebtunis documentary texts were in Greek, "while most of the religious and literary material consists of demotic and hieratic fragments."[31] The multilingual Mediterranean world complicates any discussion of literacy and education, for many may have been literate in one language but not in another.[32]

Since the problems of evidence and methods are serious and cannot be dismissed easily, it may be useful to outline briefly the sources we do have at our disposal for a study of the scribes of early Christian literature as well as the general contours of scholarly discussion that relates to these sources.

Ancient Literature

Throughout Greek and Latin literature from the Graeco-Roman world we find scattered references to scribes. Not coincidentally, many of these references relate to scribes in a particular arena — namely, the production, (re)production, and dissemination of literary texts. Here we find various types of secretaries, from notaries and record keepers to shorthand writers and secretaries who took dictation.[33] These scribes are rarely named, and we are given little information as to their precise status and location in society.[34] In the literary corpus, we also find references to the active book-trade industry in which literary scribes had a large part, since they were typically employed to copy books for booksellers.[35] It is also in our Greek and Latin literature that we learn about the ancient libraries, particularly those at Alexandria and Athens;[36] occasionally these discussions of libraries include mention of copyists. We also find the presence of private copyists in our literature. Private copyists included such persons as slaves employed by upper-class persons, or even the freedmen and slave servants in the house of the emperors or wealthy estate-owners.

The scholarly treatments of the transmission of Greek and Latin literature have relied precisely on such literary evidence, but they have typically provided an inadequate treatment of scribes.[37] L. D. Reynolds and N. G. Wilson's *Scribes and Scholars*, still considered a classic study, nowhere offers a discussion of those who copied the texts. In their section on antiquity, Reynolds and Wilson mention scribes only three times in passing:

The form of the book made this necessary, since a text written on the back of a roll would have been very easily rubbed away, and perhaps the surface of the papyrus contributed to the formation of this convention, since scribes always preferred to use first the side on which the fibers ran horizontally.

Scholars had not merely determined what the text of Homer should be, but succeeded in imposing this text as standard, either allowing it to be transcribed from a master copy placed at the disposal of the public, or alternatively employing a number of professional scribes to prepare copies for the book market.

We hear nothing of a book trade at Rome before the time of Cicero. Then the booksellers and copyists (both initially called *librarii*) carried on an active trade, but do not seem to have met the high standards of a discriminating author, for Cicero complained of the poor quality of their work. (Q. F. 3.4.5, 5.6)[38]

When Reynolds and Wilson do speak of scribes, their attention is on those who were in the service of exceptional writers such as Cicero. Yet we have only to recall the letter with which we began (*P. Oxy.* 2192), which nowhere suggests that the senders and recipients of the letter have the remarkable resources that Cicero had at his disposal, to know that there were circles of literate readers in contexts quite different from those of Cicero.

Even more recent treatments offer the same problems: Elaine Fantham's *Roman Literary Culture*, for example, begins with an enticing introduction entitled "Toward a Social History of Latin Literature." At the outset, however, Fantham's understanding of "social history" excludes scribes: "I see as important aspects of any literary work its *author* in his social and political setting, its *recipients* and their culture, and the *medium or nature of its presentation*."[39] Nowhere do we find attention to the very persons we might wish to know more about in a "social history" of Latin literature: the scribes.[40] In fact, scribes are treated cursorily with the following statements later in the book:

Booksellers had to produce each copy of a text individually, and must have done a lot of work to order; if they kept a master copy, they could always employ their scribes to copy new texts from it, whether by eye or dictation. But, of course, these scribes were Greeks, trained to copy Greek, and it is a mistake to assume that current Latin works were regularly copied for sale.[41]

So much for scribes employed in the shops of booksellers. Fantham informs us they were Greeks and trained to copy Greek, but nothing further. And what about private copyists? Fantham continues,

The burden was on an author to forward his own work to those he wanted to read it, and Cicero was exceptionally lucky that he could simply commission his friend Atticus to supply copies of his new compositions, for Atticus was one of the very few men at Rome who kept professional scribes and could produce multiple copies of a text for himself or his friends. It seems that Crassus, a great man of business, also kept trained copyists, and Plutarch reports that he directed their education, even teaching them himself (Plut. *Crass.* 2.6), but Crassus's main interest will have been the production of accurate contracts and accounts. Any busy public man needed scribes to draft his contracts or legal agreements, but when at leisure they could be set to copying a Latin manuscript.[42]

Here Fantham states that there were professional scribes, few people owned them, and that some of them may have been able to produce both legal documents and copy literary texts. Such is the extent to which this recent study of literary culture deals with scribes.

Fantham's study illustrates that little has changed since the work of Reynolds and Wilson: the treatment of the production, circulation, and transmission of ancient literature depends primarily upon literary evidence. Unfortunately, such evidence is partial at best; it offers glimpses of library scribes only filtered through an upper-class lens.

Papyri

Any treatment of Graeco-Roman period scribes necessarily must take into account the corpus of papyrological remains, which offers our most abundant evidence for ancient scribes but is not without difficulties.[43] Within this enormous body of evidence, deriving primarily from Egypt, various kinds of papyri provide insight into different types of scribes, but almost all of these scribes move in an arena quite different from the scribes we find in Greek and Latin literature. Among the extant papyri, there are letters and petitions addressed to official scribes, which provide clues into the range of responsibilities entrusted to various regional and royal scribes. There exist numerous contracts, sale agreements, and receipts in which scribes are variously mentioned. In addition, our evidence includes archival materials from individual scribes, which yields information about the range of activities involved in the occupation of scribes.[44] In contrast to the nameless literary scribes, these official scribes are named, and it would be possible to produce a history of the different official scribes in Egypt, much like the study of the *basilikos grammateis* published by John Oates.[45]

As should be clear, this evidence pertains most directly to the context of Roman-period Egyptian bureaucracy. One of our tasks (in chapter 1) will be to analyze the extent to which this evidence is useful for understanding the roles of scribes elsewhere in the Roman Empire as well as to discuss the relationship between official, bureaucratic scribes and those scribes who copied literature. It is rather striking that papyrologists who study this material rarely suggest that the "official" scribes we find in "documentary papyri" may also have copied literature. Although exceptions can be found to this tendency — C. H. Roberts, for example, remarks that "the same scribe might copy manuscripts for a living and himself be a frequent writer of letters . . . , or a slave might be trained to make copies of literary works for his owner and at the same time keep his owner's memoranda and accounts"[46] — most papyrological discussions revolve around the bureaucratic hierarchies, legal proceedings, agricultural life, social structures, economics, and so forth.[47] Perhaps, then, a more fruitful exploration can be found among the "literary papyri" (i.e., copies of ancient literature).

The literary papyri — consisting of copies of known or unknown literary works (prose, poetry, etc.) — do not offer the same kind of information about the scribes who copied them as the documentary papyri.[48] Although there are some extant colophons in which the owner of the copy is named,[49] we have almost no names of literary scribes from the second and third centuries. Moreover, subscriptions tell us very little about the scribe who produced the copy.[50] Therefore, the most useful facet of the literary papyri, at least for a study of scribes, is the physical features of these papyri themselves. For example, the handwriting styles can provide insight into the skill and level of education of various scribes. In some cases it appears that persons copying literary texts had only minimal education.[51] In other cases, however, papyri exhibit a high degree of education (as evidenced in scholarly marginal notes) and a practiced book-hand (which implies that the person was a scribe by profession). We have some papyri that give us an indication of how scribes learned to write.[52] School texts — in which relatively unpracticed hands copied lines over and over again, and/or practiced writing by breaking words down into syllables — provide useful points of comparison.[53] In addition to the clues that handwriting provides, we can use features, such as critical markings, marginal notes, abbreviations, spelling and grammatical errors, to aid in our search for ancient copyists.

The discipline of papyrology has traditionally focused most closely on the "documentary papyri," leaving the copies of ancient literature to Greek and Latin textual critics.[54] This bifurcation of the papyri has indeed led to the bifurcation of the field of papyrology: while those who study documents devote their time to reading, editing, and understanding these documents, those interested in ancient literature use the papyri to aid in the reconstruction of critical texts or editions. What falls by the wayside in both endeavors is attention to the scribes who were responsible for producing copies of ancient literature.[55]

Archaeology

In addition to the evidence from literature and papyri, we will need to take into account archaeological finds that help shed light on the roles of scribes. Our most abundant source of archaeological material consists of inscriptions. As we shall see, the epigraphic record is especially significant in offering glimpses of female scribes. We shall also have opportunity to discuss the archaeological evidence for ancient "scriptoria," particularly as some think has been discovered at Qumran.[56] In addition, the portraits from Pompeii depicting writing implements and materials, as well as various persons involved in reading and writing, can shed further light on the status of scribes and the demographics of ancient literacy.[57] Various funerary depictions can provide clues to the identity of writers and scribes in antiquity.[58] As important as these depictions may be, they can only serve to supplement what we learn from textual evidence for scribes; for, as Parássoglou laments, "we lack even a single representation of an ancient Greek or Roman professional scribe, a person, that is, whose task was the multiplication of literary texts."[59]

Early Christian Evidence

The evidence for scribes in early Christianity is similar to that pertaining to scribes more generally and consists essentially of references in early Christian literature and our earliest Christian papyri. The only literary reference from the second and third centuries to a scribe copying a Christian text is found in the story of Hermas with which we began. We have some evidence for the use of secretaries in the first century among early Christian letter writers, and the evidence for copyists and the dissemination of literature becomes increasingly abundant once we move into the fourth century; but the second-and third-century sources remain largely silent.[60] Such silence may in itself be a useful guide, for the letter among certain literate book readers in Upper Egypt shares this silence—a silence that presumes a common sensibility and understanding. Is it not possible then that the Christian sources are silent about copying because the same mechanisms (i.e., the same types of scribes) were involved in copying and transmitting Christian literature as those operative for Graeco-Roman literature more broadly? This may well explain why Christian sources become less silent at the very same time that the processes of textual transmission take on a peculiarly Christian form (i.e., the model of Christian monastic scriptoria).

The earliest Christian literary papyri provide a wealth of indirect clues for the scribes who copied this literature during the second and third centuries.[61] The papyri can be used for three types of evidence: the physical form of the manuscripts,[62] the scribal habits that they exhibit,[63] and the scribal modifications of the texts themselves.[64] For example, features such as the codex form, the size of margins and letters, and the type of handwriting are often used to determine the social location for which a particular manuscript was copied. Since some of our earliest manuscripts contain a rather motley collection of Christian texts (and several are written on the recto or verso of non-Christian texts), some scholars have argued that these texts were copied for private use.[65] Other texts, however, contain reading aids in the margins and exhibit comparatively large letters, suggesting that these were public manuscripts, perhaps used in a church setting.[66] These features are only seldom used as indicators of the social location of the scribes themselves.[67] In addition to such features, when we are able to determine the very readings that individual scribes create in the process of copying a text, we are brought closer to the ideological, social, and religious identity of these scribes.

Given the extensive text-critical work on early Christian literature, it is rather surprising that no one, until now, has presented a comprehensive study of the scribes responsible for transmitting this literature in the earliest period. Studies of the text of the New Testament abound, but nowhere is there a thorough treatment of those who preserved these texts by copying them. In part, this stems from the isolation in which scholars traditionally have worked: those who look closely at the physical features of manuscripts, often pay little attention to the textual readings of the manuscripts themselves; those who study textual history and criticism, often do so without concern for physical features or scribal habits. One might suppose that in the numerous manuals of textual criticism of the New Testament, we would find an exploration of scribes. Not one of our standard manuals of New Testament textual criticism, however, offers anything approaching a thorough treatment of the scribes who copied early Christian literature during the second and third centuries. Kurt and Barbara Alands' *The Text of the New Testament* simply offers a cursory summary: "All manuscripts must have been copied privately by individuals in the early period. . . . The earliest Christian scriptorium may have been in Alexandria about 200."[68] Bruce Metzger's treatment offers more detail on the practice of scribes, but produces a summary similar to the Alands: "In the earlier ages of the Church, Biblical manuscripts were produced by individual Christians who wished to provide for themselves or for local congregations copies of one or more books of the New Testament."[69] What is called for is an integrative approach: an approach that combines attention to the physical features with textual issues and literary resources. While the disciplines of textual criticism, paleography, and codicology should remain distinct entities, a study of the scribes who copied early Christian literature must take into account both clues from the physical features of the earliest Christian manuscripts as well as from the texts themselves. As D. C. Parker has argued, "the individual text must be taken seriously as a physical object. . . . I am impatient of a textual criticism that discusses variant readings but not the scribes who made them, textual history but not the manuscripts in which it is contained. It would be unwise to confuse textual criticism with paleography and codicology. There are in fact different skills to each of these disciplines. But it is necessary to study a text in conjunction with its material representatives."[70]

In the chapters that follow, I will adopt precisely such an integrative and comparative approach to the sources of evidence we have at our disposal: ancient literature (and Christian literature more precisely), papyri (both "documentary" and "literary"), and archaeological evidence. When we juxtapose physical features with textual features, Graeco-Roman literary sources with Christian, and Egyptian evidence with evidence from elsewhere in the empire, we are brought closer to the scribes who copied ancient literature. However multifaceted and complicated the social history of ancient scribes — and, in particular, the scribes who copied early Christian literature — we can be sure of at least one constant: ancient scribes were a necessary, indeed indispensable, part of Roman-period Mediterranean society in which few people learned how to read and write. Their social status should be interpreted not only in terms of their education and their wealth (or lack of it) but also in terms of their function. In other words, their social power should be understood in light of restricted literacy.

THE STUDY: ARGUMENT AND STRUCTURE

The central theses of the present study are that the scribes who copied early Christian literature were also the users of this literature and that these scribes formed private networks for the transmission of early Christian literature during the second and third centuries. Stated negatively, this means that Christians do not appear to have hired professional scribes, nor were Christian scriptoria in existence during the second and third centuries. In this respect, the Christian context of text transmission differs somewhat from the larger Graeco-Roman milieu in which there normally existed a distinction between scribes and users (i.e., scribes prepared copies for authors, readers, and so forth). The significance of the argument for scribes as users emerges when we look closely at the function of these early Christian scribes, who performed not only a conservative task (reproducing written texts) but also a creative one (rewriting, i.e., modifying and correcting, these texts in the process of copying them).

That the scribes who copied early Christian texts were theologically invested in the texts they (re)produced, and worked from within private networks of friendships and acquaintances, illumines the intersections between texts and authority as well as literacy and power in early Christianity. Herein lie the broader implications of this study: through the lens of early Christian scribes, we approach doctrinal debates, controversies over texts and their interpretations, contests over canonization, and the means to enter into such debates, controversies, and contests through the powerful medium of writing. The work of early Christian scribes highlights the importance of texts in early Christianity and the ability to manipulate the very words of these texts when necessary; furthermore, such manipulations illustrate how scribes staged a certain power over the texts they copied.

To demonstrate these theses, I have organized the study into two unequal halves. In the first half, I focus on the identity of the scribes who copied early Christian literature. I begin with ancient scribes more generally: Who were ancient scribes? What was their social status? How did one become a scribe? How do female scribes fit into the portrait of Graeco-Roman scribes more generally? And, most specifically, what can we know about the identity and status of the earliest copyists of Christian literature? These questions will drive the discussion in the first half. The last two chapters focus, respectively, on two questions: How does the form of the earliest Christian papyri shed light on the circumstances in which these texts were copied during the second and third centuries, and to what extent did copyists of early Christian literature possess control or power over their texts?

Chapter 1 casts a wide net over the evidence for Graeco-Roman scribes. Because of such complexities and also the limitations of this project, I will not attempt to present a comprehensive study of Graeco-Roman scribes; indeed, to do so would require a separate study altogether. Rather, the aim of this chapter is fourfold: to assess the primary evidence for Graeco-Roman scribes in order to determine as far as possible the variety of scribes; to outline the tasks, roles, and functions of these scribes; to analyze the work and status of ancient scribes in the social context of limited literacy; and to discuss how the evidence for scribes in early Christian literature fits with the portrait of Graeco-Roman scribes. We shall find that some of our early Christian evidence conforms with what we find in Greek and Latin literature and papyri; at other times, however, the picture of the copyists of early Christian literature that emerges from our sources looks markedly different from that of Graeco-Roman scribes. For instance, while the task of copying was viewed with antipathy by Greek and Latin writers, and scribes were almost always slaves or freedpersons, the Christian evidence neither denigrates the task of copying nor explicitly identifies copyists as slaves or freedpersons. Moreover, as I have already indicated, Christian literary evidence points us to the conclusion that the copyists of early Christian literature were also the users of this literature. This conclusion, as we shall see, is corroborated by close analysis of the second-and third-century Christian literary papyri and has significant implications for our understanding of the roles that scribes played in early Christian text transmission.

Chapter 2 discusses the presence of female scribes in antiquity and then utilizes this discussion as a backdrop for an analysis of the early Christian evidence for female copyists. The primary aim of this chapter is to contextualize Eusebius's comments we noted earlier regarding Origen's female calligraphers. To accomplish this we will overstep the temporal boundaries of this study, for in both earlier and later periods female scribes appear with some frequency. Most of our attention will be focused here upon Latin inscriptions that date primarily to the three centuries preceding the work of Origen. Although in many ways female scribes parallel closely their male counterparts, they also differ in some respects; female scribes, for example, typically worked in private settings for female owners. Such differences both justify the inclusion of a chapter on female scribes and enhance our understanding of the complexity of scribal identities and roles in antiquity.

Once we have a map of the range of scribes, a thorough discussion of copyists in early Christian literature, and an exploration of the presence of female scribes, we will turn in chapter 3 to the earliest Christian papyri to determine what a materialist and sociohistorical approach to these artifacts can tell us about the copyists who produced them. The central theme of this chapter is that of the education and training of ancient scribes who copied early Christian literature. Since we have no direct evidence for how Christian scribes in particular were trained, I juxtapose the evidence for ancient scribal training with the evidence of our earliest Christian papyri, focusing specifically on three characteristics that shed light on the education and training: handwriting, the use of abbreviations, and the presence and nature of harmonizations. These features point both to a training geared toward multifunctionality as well as an education — broadly construed — in early Christian texts.

The overarching theme of chapters 4 and 5 is that of scribal production and formation of early Christian texts. In chapter 4, I discuss the relationship between the social, historical, and cultural context of particular scribes and the form of the manuscripts they produced. I begin with a discussion of text transmission and dissemination in ancient libraries, public book shops, and the private book trade. The greater portion of the chapter is then spent on the nature of early Christian text transmission, for which we have some evidence in early Christian literature. Beyond literary references, I use various features in our earliest manuscripts to discuss how the forms provide clues to the context in which the various scribes worked and the context for which they produced their copies. I focus in particular on one third-century Christian codex that contains a rather disparate collection of texts, copied by six different scribes over a period of some years. A close analysis of this particular codex, coupled with other papyrological and literary evidence, suggests a private network of scribes quite similar to the network implied in the letter requesting copies of books with which we began.

The fifth chapter investigates the extent to which scribes had control over their texts, and includes the more general question of the extent to which ideology played a role in the scribal production of texts. I begin by looking at attitudes toward scribes and the freedom they were permitted in copying ancient literature rather broadly. Then I turn once again to our earliest Christian papyri. I address the notion of "sacred text" and how this appears to have affected the freedom scribes had with their copies and the evidence for ideologically influenced scribal alterations. The central thesis of this chapter is that scribes in different contexts were permitted varying degrees of freedom, which allowed them to (re)form and (re)produce their texts in the process of copying them. It is these manipulations of the texts that scribes during the second and third centuries felt permitted to make that will lead me into the intersection between literacy and power in early Christianity.

When scribes modified the texts, whether they recognized it or not (and I suspect they did not), they were exerting a certain power over the text and a power over the community that received it. Throughout this study, I will use the term *power* in multiple ways: (1) to describe the actions of scribes who undertook to (re)form the texts they copy; (2) to illuminate the results of scribal modifications; and (3) to assess the web of relations (ecclesiastical, communal, and/or individual) and discourses (e.g., about doctrine) at play in the work of scribes.[71] Scribes occasionally did more than "merely" copy texts; they appear to have "corrected," "corrupted," and "controlled" the texts. During the second and third centuries the church hotly debated the limits and contents of the Christian canon; moreover, controversies over canon were interwoven with issues of "heresy" and "orthodoxy." Scribes entered into such debates at least to a limited degree by preserving certain texts and not others. Their choices affected both the shape of the canon and the texts that local communities used. Even more significantly, their preferences for particular readings, which occasionally affected the meaning of the text significantly, left an indelible stamp on the textual history of the books within the canon. Particularly fascinating is the fact that during this period Christians were ascribing ever greater authority to their various written gospels, letters, acts, apocalypses, and theological treatises (as opposed to the oral teachings of Jesus and his disciples, for instance); alongside the freedom scribes appear to have taken with their texts, the notion of "inviolable scripture" — following from an earlier "scriptural consciousness" — began to be attached to specifically Christian works.[72]

Two Caveats

Every study requires boundaries and limitations. It should be apparent that I have found it necessary to limit this study and have done so in ways that may not be readily understandable to the reader. First, I have chosen to limit my analysis of early Christian papyri to second- and third-century papyri of *specifically* Christian texts. I have not distinguished, of course, between canonical and noncanonical Christian texts, since issues of canon were far from decided in the second and third centuries. But I have not included papyri of the Septuagint or Old Greek translation of the Hebrew Bible. It may well be that these would offer a point of comparison for a later study, but since my intent is to represent what we can know about the copyists of early Christian literature, I have focused on the texts that are undeniably Christian. The issue of how to distinguish Jewish copies of the Septuagint from Christian is a thorny one and has depended to a large degree on the characteristics of the *nomina sacra* and codex form. As we shall see, however, even these criteria are not without problems. Furthermore, much of the discussion that follows concerns only the most extensive early Christian papyri; indeed, many of our second- and third-century papyri are so fragmentary that their value for our investigation is limited. Since I have attempted to combine the evidence of physical features (e.g., handwriting and abbreviations) with textual ones (e.g., harmonizations and intentional modifications), it has been important to focus upon the most extensive papyri, for these offer both types of evidence.

And second, and perhaps more problematic, I have not begun my study with the Jewish background from which Christianity emerged. I begin instead with Graeco-Roman scribes more generally because of the nature of the social history of early Christianity. Our evidence suggests that throughout the second and early third centuries, Christians did not have the means or the inclination to teach people how to read and write. At the same time, Christianity was becoming ever more separate from Judaism and developing its mission to "pagans." We should suppose, then, that the copyists of early Christian literature were probably pagan converts who already knew how to write when they converted to Christianity. Our earliest Christian manuscripts, as we shall see, support such a hypothesis. To be sure, certain scribal customs may have originated in the Jewish environment of the early church; for example, C. H. Roberts has advanced the controversial argument that the Christian practice of contracting sacred names (such as God, Lord, Jesus, and Christ) originated in the early Jerusalem church, whose reverence

for the divine Name emerged from the Jewish environment.[73] Yet while a reverence for the divine Name may have been rooted in Judaism, the *nomina sacra*
evident in our earliest manuscripts share little similarity with the treatment of the
Tetragrammaton in Jewish manuscripts of the period. Rather, as some scholars
have suggested, it appears that the *nomina sacra* provided a means for copyists to
differentiate Christian manuscripts from Jewish. This is not to say, however, that
the evidence from Judaism will be ignored, for we will find occasionally that
evidence from Jewish contexts will enhance our understanding of the practices
of scribes in early Christianity.

This study finds its appropriate niche in the intersection between textual criticism,
the history of manuscripts, and social history. Crucial to my conceptualization of
the present project has been the work of Roger Chartier; particularly important
is his call for cultural historians to take seriously the physical forms of manuscripts,
to attend to "the crossroads of textual criticism, the history of the book, and
cultural sociology," and his notion of "communities of readers" (influenced by
both Stanley Fish's construal of "interpretive communities" and Brian Stock's
"textual communities").[74] My principal concern is with ancient scribes, particularly
those who copied Christian literature during the second and third centuries —
their identity and their social, cultural, and ideological contexts. Yet the project
is also an attempt to view manuscripts not simply as collections of readings from
which scholars can extract the "original" texts, but as artifacts that provide clues
to the flesh-and-blood human beings who produced them. Our explorations will
take us well into the social and ideological history of Christianity in its earliest
centuries; interwoven with the identities and roles of scribes are the central themes
of heresy and orthodoxy, persecution and martyrdom, and the development of
ecclesiastical hierarchies and institutions, all of which were accompanied by the
emergence of a "textual culture" in the course of the third century.[75] The debates
over issues of doctrine and praxis that occupied the early Christian church indeed
all found their way into the textual arena. Finally, the broad concern of the study
is one that belongs in the realm of cultural and social history, for I am interested
in understanding what it meant to be literate and live in a society with restricted
literacy, what it meant to transmit written materials and modify them as one saw
fit, and what it meant to be conveyers of cultural and religious meaning in a
preprint society.

1

"I COPIED EVERYTHING LETTER BY LETTER"

Locating the Copyists of Early Christian Literature

The laborious is not necessarily the noble. There are many things that are laborious, which you would not necessarily boast of having done; unless, you actually thought it glorious to copy out stories and whole speeches in your own hand.

Laboriosum non statim praeclarum. Sunt enim luta laboriosa, quae si faciatis, non continuo gloriemini; nisi etiam si vestra manu fabulas aut orationes totas transscripsissetis gloriosum putaretis.

— *Rhetorica ad Herennium* 4.6

I took [the little book] and retreated to a certain place in the country, and copied everything letter by letter, for I could not find the syllables.

ἔλαβον ἐγώ, καὶ εἴς τινα τόπον τοῦ ἀγροῦ ἀναχωρήσας μετεγραψάμην πάντα πρὸς γράμμα· οὐχ ηὕρισκον γὰρ τὰς συλλαβάς.

— Hermas, *The Shepherd, vis.* 2.1.4

Who copied Christian texts during the second and third centuries? A seemingly simple question occupies us for the duration of this chapter and the next. Since we have little direct literary evidence from Christian texts with which to answer this question, in this chapter we will begin with a broader question: Who copied texts in the Graeco-Roman world? As we shall see, the complex interplay of literacy, class, and status in the Graeco-Roman world alerts us to the possibility that even this question itself requires nuance; indeed we will have to consider both who was able to copy texts and who did copy texts. According to the first-century B.C.E. anonymous author of the *Rhetorica ad Herennium*, the task of copying was not an honorable one; this suggests that those who were able to copy texts did not necessarily do so. In fact, we will see throughout this chapter the resources — namely, a wide range of slave and freed scribes — that permitted elites to avoid writing, and in particular copying.[1] At the same time, the story of Hermas indicates that we cannot assume that only professional scribes copied texts. Hermas, in the only passage that depicts copying in second-century Christian literature, attaches no stigma to copying these sacred texts; to be sure, Hermas identifies himself as a slave at the opening of *The Shepherd*, but he does not indicate that he is a scribe.

The juxtaposition of these two passages suggests that locating early Christian scribes may be more complex than it appears. Indeed, any rubrics used for classifying the range of scribes in the Graeco-Roman world are fraught with problems: professional vs. nonprofessional, public vs. private, literary vs. documentary, or administrative officials vs. literary copyists—none of these dichotomies of classification is entirely satisfactory. The problems of classification, however, may well be one of our important clues to the roles and functions of ancient scribes, for it will become clear that scribes varied in their level of education and training (the subject of the following chapter); moreover, individually they were most often multifunctional and multicontextual. In this chapter, I will outline the range of scribes, utilizing what may seem a rather simplistic system of classification; I will then problematize these classifications by illustrating the ways in which scribes often transgressed the boundaries of their designated function. One set of boundaries, found particularly in the writings of elite authors, is the demarcation of a low-class/status scribal profession in contrast to the upper-class ability to avoid copying literary texts, but in this chapter, we will also pay close attention to the boundaries of different scribal professions—again, usually demarcated in literary texts—and the occasions on which scribes crossed these boundaries.[2] I begin with those who seem to have been primarily occupied in copying literary texts: literary copyists. Then, I move to the opposite end of the spectrum, to administrative officials who held scribal titles. After locating "literary" and "administrative" scribes, I problematize the distinction by looking at the ways in which scribes crossed such boundaries. Next, I look closely at a category of scribes that has very often been overlooked: nonprofessional scribes who did not have a scribal training, and did not hold scribal titles, but undertook to copy literary texts.

Against the backdrop of Graeco-Roman scribes, I finally consider the Christian context by discussing not only the literary evidence we have from early Christian texts but also the economic texture of early Christianity and the processes of conversion during the second and third centuries. This chapter will highlight both the similarities and differences between the scribes who copied early Christian texts and those who copied Greek and Latin literature more generally. More precisely, I argue that when early Christian texts that refer to copying are set within the milieu of Graeco-Roman scribal practices, what emerges is a picture of private copyists, and sometimes nonprofessionals, who were responsible for producing the earliest copies of Christian literature.

PUBLIC PROFESSIONAL SCRIBES

Before turning to literary copyists, it may be useful at the outset to define the terms of my subheading. *Public* and *professional* are not terms easily applied to the ancient Graeco-Roman context. By the term *professional* I mean to include all persons who were scribes by occupation and held scribal titles indicating this occupation. This is not to suggest that these persons were *only* involved in scribal tasks, for it remains unclear the extent to which some of these scribes also had other unrelated jobs (as we find in the analogy to modern notaries public). Although the modern use of *professional* often connotes a person who receives remuneration for a particular task, this is not the case for all the scribes I designate as "professionals": administrative scribes in upper Egypt, for example, were not paid; nor is it clear that slave-scribes always received pay for their work. The root of the English term *professional* is the Latin *professio*, which designated an "occupation" or "calling." Typically this noun was used for such occupations as doctors and grammarians.[3] Additionally, the word *professor* designated someone with advanced education and training, such as a teacher of rhetoric.[4] Scribes, as we shall see in chapter 3, did not have advanced education, nor was the term *professio* applied to their occupation; the term remains useful, however, for it captures the notion of an occupation in which one is primarily engaged.

Likewise, the term *public* requires some comment. I use *public* to locate the literary scribes who worked in the contexts of bookshops and "public" libraries, as well as scribes who held recognized public and official administrative scribal positions.[5] This usage corresponds well to ancient understandings of public settings as well as the use of the term *publicus* to designate slaves that held various public administrative positions.[6]

Literary Copyists

The work of literary copyists — those persons employed primarily for the task of copying literary texts in public settings — was necessarily intertwined with the ancient book trade, a subject we shall return to in more detail later. Defined quite loosely, the "book trade" consists of the transmission — production, (re)production, and dissemination — of literature, either in public settings or through private means.[7] All forms of the book trade, of course, required persons who would prepare the copies — most frequently called *librarii*. Not surprisingly, given the demand for literary texts that only emerges within the Roman period among Latin writers, the Greek term βιβλιογράφος is not used with any frequency.[8]

Literary copyists worked in two public settings in the second and third centuries, the bookshop and the public library. In its earliest occurrences, the noun *librarius* is quite ambiguous: it could designate a bookseller, copyist, or bookshop. Catullus, in the mid-first-century B.C.E., appears to offer our earliest literary evidence for *librarii* as booksellers: in response to the gift of a "dreadful and accursed book" (horribilem etsacrum libellum),Catullus writes, "for let the morning come — I will run to the shelves of the booksellers, gather together Caesii, Aquini, Suffenus, and all such poisonous stuff, and with these penalties I will pay you back" (nam, si luxerit, ad librariorum curram scrinia, Caesios, Aquinos, Suffenum, omnia colligam venena, ac te his suppliciis remunerabor) (Catullus

14.12–20).[9] It is quite likely that these shop owners (*librarii*) themselves produced copies of documents — petitions, contracts, and so forth — before there existed a demand for copies of literature. Indeed, Phillips has plausibly suggested that "before the book trade existed, a *librarius* was a copier of documents; he did not make any copy except on demand and did not retain extra copies of a document unless he had a reason to do so."[10]

Epigraphic evidence offers a good counterpart to Catullus's identification of a *librarius* as a bookseller. We find, for example, the following funerary inscription on a marble tablet from Rome: "P. Cornelius Celadus, a librarius from outside the Trigemina gate; lived 26 years" (P. Cornelius Celadus librarius ab extra porta Trigemina vix. an xxvi) (*CIL* 6.9515 = *ILS* 7751). During the second century B.C.E., the Emporium of Rome was located just outside the Porta Trigemina, and over time it extended south from this gate; the Emporium — "the wholesale market of Rome" — would have been a likely location for a bookshop.[11] Inscriptionary evidence such as this is notoriously difficult to date, and the most we can say with assurance — given what we know about commercial activity outside the Trigemina gate and the popularity of the name Celadus from the first century B.C.E. to the first century C.E. — is that this inscription offers evidence roughly contemporaneous with Catullus. Furthermore, Celadus is typically a slave name; the fact that we find it here combined with the abbreviated praenomen P. and the nomen Cornelius suggests that this was a freedman.[12]

Soon after Catullus, we find named *librarii*/booksellers with increasing frequency: the Sosii brothers carry the works of Horace; Dorus sells (according to Seneca) both Cicero's and Livy's works, Pollius Quintus Valerianus, Secundus, and Trypho sell Martial's epigrams.[13] During the first century C.E., the Greek borrowed term *bibliopola* is also used by Latin authors to designate booksellers, perhaps in the wake of the emergence of the use of *librarii* to designate private copyists.[14] If we can take the writings of Aulus Gellius as testimony, by the time we reach the second century C.E., bookshops were a commonplace, at least in the city of Rome, and they were often the site of public readings and literary discussions.[15] The extent to which we should understand any of these booksellers as analogous to "publishers" in the modern sense of the word remains a subject of debate. Although the passage from Catullus implies that booksellers had ready-made copies on hand, copies of literature were normally produced on demand (i.e., for a particular customer) and therefore a bookseller only needed an exemplar on hand from which to make the copies requested.[16] Indeed, the work of booksellers did not begin to approach mass reproduction or distribution of literary works. As Starr suggests, "each bookdealer made the copies he sold. . . . If a bookshop owner in a provincial city sold a copy of a book, it implies that he had made that copy, not that he had bought a large number of copies from a Rome-based distributor."[17]

When exactly *librarii* as copyists became distinguished from booksellers is not entirely clear, though we can assume that once there was a market for literature booksellers would have employed copyists to prepare the copies, either through dictation or by copying an exemplar.[18] A late ancient commentary on Horace, *Epistulae* 1.1.55, seems to suggest the presence of multiple copyists: "dictated is the term properly applied to what is dictated by a *librarius* to his slaves" (dictata propria dicuntur quae pueris a librario dictantur).[19] While the term *puer* here could be translated as "young boys," "slaves" seems more accurate given the context and the fact that most scribes were slaves. As to the historicity of the scenario preserved in this passage, it should be recognized that this commentary is quite late, perhaps as late as the fifth century C.E., and may well superimpose a later system of copying onto the earlier period. The scenario of multiple copyists does not appear in the context of Roman-period references to booksellers. Still, it is logical to suppose that originally the proprietors of the shops were also the copyists and that it was only later, once the public book trade was more established and had more of a market, that these shop owners employed *librarii* to prepare copies for their shops. Phillips attributes this shift in the demand for books to the "spread of education and the increasing number of Latin texts available for educational purposes (not to mention the steady demand for the Greek classics). In that way certain *librarii* ceased to be just copyists of texts on demand and became *bibliopolae*."[20] By the time of Horace, the book trade had established itself so that books were not only made for local customers but at least occasionally also for "shipment abroad" (*Ars* 343–6).

In addition to the context of bookshops, we can turn to another public context of text transmission: ancient "public" libraries. Despite the recent interest in the emergence of public libraries in the Graeco-Roman world, we still have much to learn about how these libraries operated and in what sense they were truly "public."[21] Public libraries appeared first in Alexandria, then Athens, and finally in Rome.[22] According to Pliny, the first public library in Rome was established by Asinius Pollio in the first century B.C.E. (*NH* 7.30.115).[23] Soon after Pollio, Augustus built two more public libraries, the first attached to the temple of Apollo on the Palatine between 36 and 28 B.C.E., and the second built in the Porticus Octaviae.[24] After the example of Augustus, "public libraries" in Rome emerged with even greater frequency so that by the fourth century there were some twenty-eight in existence. The extent to which we should call these libraries "public" is important but one not directly relevant to our concerns with scribes. Anthony Marshall's comments should suffice: "the new imperial libraries, although housed in state buildings, were not so much Carnegie-style institutions, 'public' in the modern sense, as the Emperor's libraries generously thrown open to his *amici* and urban *clientes* as a form of patronage."[25]

We know little about the staff of these libraries, but the librarians, as well as the slaves who made copies, arranged the collections, and generally performed clerical functions, seem to have been either among the administrative personnel of the *familia Caesaris* or *servi publici*.[26] Suetonius provides an added piece of information, for he indicates that when the Octavian library was destroyed by fire, "Domitian sent his *skilled copyists* to Alexandria itself for replacements."[27]

That copyists were sent rather than booksellers sought out, may well suggest that the commercially produced selection was too limited.

Although bookshops and "public" libraries were clearly in existence in the second century C.E., it should be noted that private modes of transmission of literature were still alive and well.[28] We will turn to the private channels momentarily, but I wish to highlight their existence within the discussion of public contexts. Our sources suggest, indeed, that if "a Roman could acquire a text through those private channels, there was no reason for him to buy from a bookdealer. Neither Cicero nor Pliny, for instance, two of our major sources for the circulation of literary texts, ever mentions going to a bookshop."[29] The examples of Cicero and Pliny the Younger, separated by some 150 years, provide evidence of the continuation — at least for those who could afford it — of the use of private *librarii* for the copying of literary texts.

The impetus behind private commerce in books was usually an individual's desire to build up a personal library. Lucian's well-known diatribe against the ignorant book collector suggests that some sought copies of book to increase status:

> You expect to get a reputation for learning [παιδεία] by zealously buying up the finest books, but the thing goes by opposites and in a way becomes proof of your ignorance [ἀπαιδευσίας]. Indeed, you do not buy the finest; you rely upon men who bestow their praise hit-and-miss, you are a godsend to the people that tell such lies about books, and treasure-trove ready to hand to those who traffic in them. Why, how can *you* tell what books are old and highly valuable, and what are worthless and simply in wretched repair — unless you judge them by the extent to which they are eaten into and cut up, calling the book-worms into counsel to settle the question? As to their correctness and freedom from mistakes, what judgement have you, and what is it worth? [ἢ πόθεν γάρ σοι διαγνῶναι δυνατόν, τίνα μὲν παλαιὰ καὶ πολλοῦ ἄξια, τίνα δὲ φαῦλα καὶ ἄλλως σαπρά, εἰ μὴ τῷ διαβεβρῶσθαι καὶ κατακεκόφθαι αὐτὰ τεκμαίροιο καὶ συμβούλους τοὺς σέας ἐπὶ τὴν ἐξέτασιν παραλαμβάνοις; ἐπεὶ τοῦ ἀκριβοῦς ἢ ἀσφαλοῦς ἐν αὐτοῖς τίς ἢ ποία διάγνωσις;] (*Ind* 1)

While Lucian offers testimony to one motivation behind book collecting — as a display of status or position, more commonly books were sought by those who wished to read and own, and perhaps also lend, literary works. Our most abundant evidence for the private literary scribes/copyists who transcribed literature for private readers is found in the letters of Cicero, evidence that has received much attention from scholars.[30] We will turn to the evidence of Cicero and Atticus' private copyists shortly, but first we should discuss public professional scribes in a context quite far removed from our bookshops and libraries.

Public Scribal Officials and Administrative Scribes

The public administrative scribe was one of the most ubiquitous officials in the second-and third-century Graeco-Roman world. In contrast to the scribes we have just noted, administrative scribes did not normally hold the Latin title *librarius*, but *scriba*; in Greek, the most common title was γραμματεύς.[31] The papyri from upper Egypt attest a wide range of roles for various γραμματεῖς: villages had scribes in charge of official archives (γραμματεῖς καταλογεῖου), scribes who oversaw financial and agricultural workings (γραμματεῖς μητροπόλεως; κωμογραμματεῖς), scribes who worked in temples (ἱερογραμματεῖς), and so forth.[32] There were public scribes on hand to prepare legal documents (petitions, receipts, etc.) for private individuals (γραμματεῖς). In essence, scribes worked at every level of the administration of upper Egypt, with the βασιλικὸς γραμματεύς being one of the highest-level officials and the γραμματεύς, who may have worked in the office of the βασιλικὸς γραμματεύς or any other administrative office, one of the lowest.[33]

Comparable to the scribal officials of Egypt are the Roman *scribae* — the public governmental officials ("scribes") who worked in the offices of the magistrates, held high-level official positions in the courts or army or were assistants to prefects.[34] The *scribae* clearly held a higher status than the *librarii*/literary copyists mentioned above. Indeed, like the scribal officials of upper Egypt, *scribae* were considered honorable — in Cicero's words, "the order (of the scribes) is honourable, for to the good faith of these men are entrusted the public laws, and the sentences of the magistrates" ([scribarum] ordo est honestus, quod eorum hominum fidei tabellae publicae, periculaque magistratuum committuntur) (Cicero, *Verr.* 3.79.183). Also like other high-level scribal officials, *scribae* did not usually prepare the legal documents or letters or copies of various memoranda themselves; they had, as we shall see momentarily, copyists and clerks who worked for them.[35]

Were these public administrative scribes able to copy literary texts, and, if so, did they ever do so? When one reads discussions of the administrative workings of the Roman Empire, these questions are rarely posed. But they are at the fore of the discussion here, for I am interested in precisely those scribes who copied literary texts. In the next several pages, I will explore answers to these questions; I begin with an illustrative story.

In the year 184 C.E., a certain Petaus from the village of Karanis on the northern edge of the Fayum was appointed as the village scribe for the village of Ptolemais Hormou, located some forty kilometers to the south and east of Karanis.[36] Since village scribes were part of the "liturgical system" of Graeco-Roman Egypt, in which officials were nominated to office based on their assets and were required to dip into their own pockets to defray expenses or make up deficits, we often find village scribes (and others) contesting their nomination; in addition, it became customary for village scribes like Petaus to be appointed to villages other than their own to avoid fraud or favoritism while in office (such as passing over their friends for nomination to other offices).[37] Like other village scribes — κωμογραμματεῖς — Petaus was responsible for overseeing the financial and agricultural administration of the village, and his extant archive illumines the range of responsibilities: assessing landownership, administering and processing census returns, dealing with uncultivated land, transporting grain, and so forth.[38] In May 184, Petaus was forced to respond to some complaints that had been lodged against a certain Ischyrion, a native of Ptolemais Hormou who was serving as village scribe for Tamais, another village in the Fayum. We do not know exactly who lodged the complaints against Ischyrion, but among the accusations was the claim that he was incompetent because he was illiterate (ἀγράμματος).[39] Particularly striking is Petaus' response: Ischyrion is not ἀγράμματος because he has signed (ὑπογράφειν) all of the documents that were sent from his office to the στρατηγός and other officials (*P.Petaus* 11.35–37).

What Petaus fails to mention in his response is that he himself was in a similar situation. Among the documents found in Petaus' archive are seven on which he adds in his own hand his signature along with the standard formulaic ending of a petition: on four he adds, Πεταῦς κωμογρα(μματεὺς) ἐπιδέδωκα ("I, Petaus, village scribe, have submitted [this]"); and on three others, Πεταῦς ἐπιδέδωκα ("I, Petaus, have submitted [this]").[40] In all of these subscriptions the writing is "stiff, awkward, uneven, kept on the line with obvious effort. Petaus is totally without skill as a writer. He is indeed not a writer at all in any proper sense, but a man copying a model or repeating it from memory."[41] If there was any doubt as to Petaus' skill as a writer, we find certainty in the much discussed scrap on which he practices his handwriting. On this papyrus, Petaus practices his signature over and over, a total of twelve times: Πεταῦς κωμογρα(μματεὺς) ἐπιδέδωκα (*P.Petaus* 121).[42]

> Starting with a form prepared by someone for his guidance, he produced in four successive lines reasonably correct if rough copies. In the fifth line he overlooked the initial vowel of the verb, and from that point through seven more copies of the signature he invariably omitted the vowel. The error was repeated so often because from line 5 on he was using his own copy as a model. He was unable to introduce a correction at any point because he could not read what he wrote, and we understand in consequence why his papers have nothing from his hand except one formula.[43]

The story of Petaus, a barely literate village scribe in upper Egypt, highlights one of the points I wish to make about scribal officials. Throughout the empire various officials held scribal titles and positions that gave them a certain level of prestige as well as power. To be sure, this is more prominent in Egypt, where scribes from Pharaonic times were "a highly respected class of skilled professionals."[44] Their social power notwithstanding, however, at least some of these scribes were not highly literate.

If we return once again to the Roman-period notion with which we began — that writing/copying by hand was not a respected occupation — we are less surprised to find scribal officials who are not highly literate (like Petaus). Furthermore, when we survey the hundreds of papyri and pertinent literary references, we find that these officials did not in fact need to write, for they had various secretaries, notaries, clerks, shorthand writers, and record keepers at hand. Petaus himself had scribes who prepared the documents and copies of the documents for his office; we can recall the official Tiberius Julius Theon from the previous chapter who had at his disposal notaries and secretaries; similarly, a high-level official in Panopolis had many secretaries who wrote on his behalf;[45] *scribae* had clerks and secretaries and copyists who worked for them. We do not find that these high-level officials were required to copy documents, much less literary texts, in their own hand. At the same time, however, we should not suppose that these scribal officials were *invariably* unable or disinterested in copying literary texts; as we shall see below, there is evidence to suggest that on occasion these public scribes did copy literary texts.

Thus far we have considered two ends of the spectrum of public scribes: those that were involved directly in copying literary texts and those who held public scribal titles but did not write or copy literary texts. Rather conspicuously, the evidence for the former is almost entirely found in Latin literature while the latter are found predominantly in papyrological and epigraphic evidence. Furthermore, the *librarii* are typically slaves and freedpersons, while the public scribal officials were men of at least some means and prestige.[46] We have not considered, however, the most ubiquitous scribe of all: the public or private secretarial scribe. In the discussion that follows, the term *private* may be viewed as somewhat problematic since some of the scribes who prepared documents or petitions or wrote letters for illiterate persons could actually be found at work "in the street" (i.e., out in public). Turner, in fact, calls these public scribes: "The public scribe, seated 'in the street', as the phrase goes in contracts."[47] What I have in mind, however, is private in the sense of individually hired, contracted, or employed. The scribes I will describe here were either hired on an individual basis to prepare private documents, write personal letters, take down dictation, keep records, and so forth or were private and personal slaves who worked for their masters.

PRIVATE SECRETARIAL SCRIBES

In an increasingly text-centered culture, scribes were integral to financial administration, legal proceedings, maintenance of the army, imperial and provincial administrative offices, as well as a necessary resource for the inhabitants of the empire who either could not read and write (and therefore needed a scribe to prepare a document or letter for them), did not have the training to prepare formulaic contracts, petitions, and so forth, or they were too busy or considered it too demeaning to write themselves. Elite and sub-elite households required various secretaries, clerks, stenographers, and record keepers. The private slave *a manu* in elite households was occupied with taking down letters from dictation or providing more general clerical functions.[48] The illiterate farmer in upper Egypt who wished to lease land required a written document and often hired a scribe to prepare the document.[49] Written correspondence between illiterate or barely literate friends and family necessitated the use of a scribe, though it is notoriously difficult to determine the writers of extant papyrological letters, since the use of scribes for writing letters was so common that these scribes did not identify

themselves in the letters.[50] Contracts or agreements of sale demanded an experienced professional scribe to prepare the initial draft. As Raffaella Cribiore writes,
"While multiplication of copies was the regular work of scribes, drafting a text
ex nihilo was a specialized task that only few could perform. The distinction
between copying and composing is spelled out in a contract of Roman Egypt
for the hire of scribes to work in a government bureau for the purpose of drafting
population lists on the basis of records of preceding years. Those who drafted
new texts were paid at a higher rate than those who merely copied."[51] Much can
be learned about the roles of private secretarial scribes by looking closely at the
most well known and plentiful source for these scribes: the letters of Cicero.

Throughout Cicero's letters to Atticus, we meet with various *librarii* in the
service of both Atticus and Cicero. Atticus, as is widely known, made available
to Cicero numerous copyists. According to Cornelius Nepos, Atticus had a large
number of copyists (*plurimi librarii*), as well as some even more specialized highly
educated slaves (*pueri litteratissimi*) (*Att.* 13.3). The primary responsibilities of these
librarii was to write down letters that were dictated to them and to prepare copies
of letters and other writings. Although Cicero writes his letters in his own hand
quite frequently early on in his correspondence with Atticus — indeed, in one of
his early letters he opens with "I do not think you have ever read a letter of
mine that I myself had not written" (*Att.* 2.23) — his later letters no longer draw
attention to the fact that he has not written the letters himself.[52] The following
passages provide a sampling of the use of *librarii* for correspondence:

> The fact that my letter is by the hand of a scribe will show you how busy I
> am [Occupationum mearum vel hoc signum erit, quod epistula librarii manu
> est]. (*Att.* 4.16)

> I read him a letter, not in your own hand, but in that of your scribe [Eique
> legi litteras non tuas, se librarii tui]. (*Att.* 6.6)

> Let the hand of my scribe be a sign that I am suffering from inflammation of
> the eyes, and that is the cause of my brevity [Lippitudinis meae signum tibi
> sit librarii manus et eadem causa brevitatis]. (*Att.* 8.13)

> Therefore I did not even dictate it to Tiro, who can follow whole sentences,
> but syllable by syllable to Spintharo [Ergo ne Tironi quidem dictavi qui totas
> περιοχὰς persequi solet, se Spintharo syllabatim]. (*Att.* 13.25)

In this last passage, we should note the point of contact with Hermas' comments
about copying letter by letter; Hermas, it would appear, does not even have the
ability of Cicero's less well-trained copyists, since he can only copy letter by letter
(*Shep.*, *vis.* 2.1.4).

Although we find Cicero and Atticus' *librarii* most frequently involved in
writing letters, they fulfilled a wider range of functions. Throughout Cicero's
letters, it is quite clear that the *librarii* were responsible for making copies of letters

as well as other literary works. This explains Cicero's remarks to Atticus: "I will send the book to you as soon as it is copied out by the copyists" (Quem librum ad te mittam, si descripserint librarii) (*Att.* 12.14); "So I have sent the book to Musca to give to your copyists, for I want it to be put into circulation" (Itaque misi librum ad Muscam, ut tuis librariis daret. Volo enim eum divulgari) (*Att.* 12.40; and similarly, *Att.* 12.44). Equally explicit, however, is that the *librarii* had diverse tasks: Cicero asks Atticus to send him some copyists to prepare title pieces for some of the books in one of his libraries (*Att.* 4.4a); *librarii* are asked to make corrections in copies (*Att.* 12.6a; 13.44); and *librarii* act as messengers, or letter carriers (*Att.* 13.29), and as readers (*Att.* 16.2). Cicero's secretary Tiro appears to be in a different category from most of these *librarii* in terms of the fondness that Cicero had for him.[53]

The wide range of roles that these *librarii* seem to have played is an important feature and stands in contrast to the *librarii* who were employed in bookshops or public libraries and the scribal officials, who seem to have had more narrowly defined roles; another striking difference between the copyists employed in book-shops and libraries and Cicero's copyists is that the latter are so frequently named: Hilarus, Pharnaces, Salvio, Antaeus, Philotimus, Spintharus, Alexis, and of course Tiro — a list of named *librarii* that is unlike any other found in Latin literature of the Roman period. The fact that these copyists were named may well suggest that the relationship between them and Cicero and Atticus was more personal that that of a copyist to a bookseller.

The closest point of contact between Cicero's copyists and the literary scribes in public contexts (in contrast to scribal officials) is that of class. In all the cases we have discussed so far, *librarii* are either slaves or freedmen. I offer just a few examples: the bookseller Secundus, mentioned by Martial, is a freedman;[54] the staff of the public libraries in Rome were imperial slaves; the copyist Philotimus is a freedman;[55] and Tiro himself is a freedman. Inscriptionary evidence corrobo-rates the portrait of private slave or freed secretarial scribes.[56] That the scribes who prepared copies of literary texts, took down dictated letters, or were responsible for distributing copies of these letters were from the slave and freed classes should not surprise us, for we can recall the stigma attached to such labor. No matter how indispensable these scribes were, they were not members of the upper classes.[57]

By all accounts, the resources and contexts for literary text transmission we have discussed so far (both in the public settings of bookshops and libraries and in the case of Cicero and Atticus) were exceptional.[58] Indeed, our discussion has focused almost entirely on Rome. Yet the general contours of book transmission that I have outlined so far — the occasional use of bookshops and libraries and the more frequent recourse to private copyists — appears to resonate with processes elsewhere in the empire. The letter among book readers in upper Egypt, as well as a host of other indicators, suggests the existence of avid readers in locations quite different and far removed from Rome (*P.Oxy.* 2192). Although these readers do not mention a library, they do indicate that a bookseller (Δημήτριος ὁ βυβλιοπώλης) could be contacted for copies; furthermore, the letter implies that turning to friends and acquaintances was the most viable, favorable, and productive option. Such literate readers — found in the very households that had the financial means and leisure to support reading habits — normally had secretaries who could be used for such a purpose.

The distinct impression one gets from reading secondary literature on the book trade and on the papyrological remains is that there was a wide divide between the scribes involved in copying books and those who were involved in preparing documents or letters. Furthermore, the traditional distinction between documentary and literary hands — with the former being cursive, speedily written, highly abbreviated, and often formulaic and the latter written in bilinear, evenly spaced, slow, clear, and careful hands — appears to suggest that the functions, domains, and abilities of administrative scribes were vastly different from those of literary scribes.[59] In the preceding pages, I have deliberately replicated the prevailing dichotomy between literary and documentary scribes; this classification, however, is too simplistic, as I will demonstrate in the following pages. When we look closely at both the literary evidence for the private book trade and papyrological materials that illumine private scribal roles, in fact, we find that private scribes — either slaves or freedpersons who were privately employed or scribes who were hired on an as-needed basis — were able to prepare *both* the documents or letters that were commonly needed and to copy a literary text when (more occasionally) called upon.

MULTIFUNCTIONAL SCRIBES

A variety of clues suggests that scribes who were normally involved with preparing nonliterary documents could also write or copy literary texts and apparently did so; additionally, those who usually copied literary texts could produce and copy documents. As we have seen, the *librarii* at the service of Cicero and Atticus did more than copy texts; they took down letters from dictation (probably in shorthand form), edited texts, and kept various records and even copies of letters. Professional scribes who worked in the civic offices of Athens may well have "moonlighted" on the side producing lead curse tablets.[60] In the first century C.E., a certain Chariton of Aphrodisias, who identifies himself as the clerk or secretary (ὑπογρα- φεύς) in the office of a lawyer named Athenagoras, also appears to have written the literary text *Chaereas and Callirhoe*. The opening of the text is as follows:

> My name is Chariton, of Aphrodisias, and I am clerk to the attorney Athena- goras. I am going to tell you the story of a love affair that took place in Syracuse.
>
> Χαρίτων Ἀφροδισιεύς, Ἀθηναγόρου τοῦ ῥήτορος ὑπογραφεύς, πάθος ἐρωτικὸν ἐν Συρακούσαις γενόμενον διηγήσομαι. (1.1)

Particularly interesting here is the term ὑπογραφεύς, "one who writes under another's orders, secretary, amanuensis" (*LSJ*). This is precisely the character who appears in so many papyrological documents as one whose basic function was to verify the contents of a document and write a subscription on behalf of someone who was illiterate.[61] Again, we find correlation with the story of Hermas, who similarly crosses boundaries: in Hermas' *The Shepherd*, it is Hermas — a slave or freedman — who is responsible for composing and copying the book.[62]

The existence of mixed archives — archives in which both documents and copies of literature have been found — also points toward scribes who were multifunctional. Although E. G. Turner correctly noted the rarity of finding literary texts in documentary archives — "when we look through some of these archives we cannot but be struck by the fact that works of literature are rarely included among them"[63] — more recent studies have highlighted the cases where literary texts do appear in what seem to be predominantly documentary archives.[64] Among such archives, we find evidence that literary texts were at least occasionally copied in government offices,[65] that individual scribes could copy both an administrative document and a literary text,[66] and that tax clerks could sprinkle "some Callimachus among the names of a huge tax-register."[67] P. W. Pestman has offered an interesting explanation for how the scribes at Kerkeosiris, where a mixed archive has been found, managed to get a copy of a literary document such as the *prostagmata* (royal decree) found there:

> The procedure may have been that an authentic text circulated among the village scribes in a given district and that each of them in turn first made a copy for his own use and then sent the original to the next village scribe. This is, however, rather complicated and time consuming and one wonders if the procedure could have been simpler. Now we know that all the village scribes of the Fayum often had to go to the capital Krokodilopolis, in order to present, for example, their administrative records. . . . At such gatherings the central government of the Fayum had an ideal opportunity to get in touch with Menches and the other village scribes. It could give them all kinds of information and orders and communicate the royal *prostagmata* which the scribes could, all of them, easily copy on the spot, in Krokodilopolis.[68]

That administrative or documentary scribes could also produce literary texts, and on occasion did so, thus seems quite clear. This offers an explanation of the well-known phenomenon of reused papyri, on which one side contains a document and the other a copy of a literary text. If, as Turner tentatively suggested, administrative offices saved official documents as scrap paper, these could then be used to copy literary texts at a later date: "after a time the keepers of the records in Alexandria sold their documents as scrap-paper to the bookshops in Alexandria, who then turned out cheap copies on the verso. But the natural explanation is that the officials in whose offices these documents were compiled . . . retained possession of them, and reused them for copying texts in which they were interested."[69]

These are just a few examples of the evidence we have for scribes producing both documents and literary texts. The picture that begins to emerge is of the multifunctionalism of scribes. This should not surprise us, for the Graeco-Roman world had few readers of literature, and it would be difficult for a scribe to make a living solely by copying texts. Rather, professional scribes had to diversify their abilities: they were required to write letters when someone hired them to do so; if they were slaves, their master might have them take down letters or draw up documents, but at another time copy a literary text; and if they worked in an administrative office, they might offer other services on the side. Such multifunctional scribes are perhaps most visible in a private context (i.e., a context in which they were slaves or freedpersons working for one master, or in a context where they hired their services out to individuals), but we also find them in more public settings.

Thus far, all of the scribes we have considered were in some sense "professional": they appear to have had scribal occupations. Literate elites and sub-elites resorted to the services of these scribes, as did the majority of the inhabitants of the empire who could not read or write. We may well think that we have answered one of our initial questions: "who copied texts in the Graeco-Roman world?" We have not, however, exhausted the possibilities, for we must consider the possibility that at least on occasion copies of literary texts were not made by professionals at all, but by literate people who simply wished to have a copy of a literary text and proceeded to make the copy themselves.

NONPROFESSIONAL COPYISTS

"In ancient Rome copies were made by professionals, many of whom were slaves."[70] So concludes the most recent study of the writing habits among the elites and sub-elites of Rome. But while the practice of utilizing slaves as copyists may well be typical of Roman elites, there is evidence to suggest that some copies of literature were not made by professionals at all, but rather by the users of the texts themselves. As Raffaella Cribiore has pointed out in her work on Graeco-Roman Egyptian papyri, "sometimes literate people, the readers themselves, copied their own books."[71] The juxtaposition of these two statements highlights the partiality of our evidence: Roman literary evidence offers an illustration of practices among urban elites, while the Egyptian papyri yield glimpses of broader segments of society. Indeed, when we look closely at the literary papyri themselves, it becomes clear that there were nonprofessionals (i.e., those who were not scribes by occupation) involved in writing, as well as in copying literary texts more specifically. It is often possible to distinguish professionally produced copies from nonprofessionally produced: the former, for example, usually have the stichometric markings that were used to calculate the scribe's pay.[72] The fact that some copies do not have these stichometric markings leaves the door open to the possibility that these copies may not have been produced by professional scribes. There are also, to be sure, degrees of professionalism: some scribes were clearly more experienced and more skilled than others. Yet what concerns us most here is not the degree of professionalism, but the question of whether the people copying literary texts were scribes by trade (by occupation) or not.

A most obvious example of nonprofessionals are school children who produced copies of literature as part of their curriculum.[73] More pertinent, however, are the cases where authors indicate that they produced a copy themselves. Cicero appears to make copies of his own correspondence in his own hand, for he begins a letter to L. Papirius Paetus sometime during 46 B.C.E. as follows: "I have just taken my place at 3 o'clock, and have written a copy of this letter to you in my notebook" (Accubueram hora nona, cum ad te harum exemplum in codicillis exaravi) (Cicero, *Ep.ad Fam.* 9.26). Although Cicero quite frequently appears to *compose* letters in his own hand, nowhere else does Cicero suggest that he produces *copies* in his own hand. Yet that clearly seems to be the implication here. That nonprofessional scribes did copy texts is corroborated by the existence of literary papyri that do not manifest the characteristics of a professionally produced copy.[74]

Before turning to our early Christian evidence, it may be useful to summarize what we have covered so far. We have seen that literature was copied and disseminated through two public means — the bookshop and the library. Public administrative officials held scribal titles, but only rarely appear to have copied literary texts. The clerks, secretaries, and scribes who worked in the offices of these officials, the scribes at the disposal of writers such as Cicero, and the various secretarial slaves in large households provided the most widely used means of obtaining literary texts. Indeed, as we shall see later, utilizing private means (i.e., private scribes) was the favored method of obtaining a text because there was more control over the copying process. There is no doubt that hiring a copyist independently to copy a text was expensive; cheaper, though it required that you had economic means to begin with, was using your own slave or freedperson. A last option, which was uncommon and undesirable among elite Romans but at least occasional among middle- or lower-class readers, was simply to copy the text for oneself. This, of course, was the least expensive method of obtaining a text, though it required that one was able to read and write and willing to undertake the task.

EARLY CHRISTIAN LITERATURE

Each of the models for text transmission we have discussed so far finds resonance in our earliest Christian literary references to writing or copying practices. Already in the mid–first century in the well-known case of Tertius, we find a parallel to the relationship between Cicero and the scribes to whom he dictated letters. In the closing of Paul's longest epistle, we find the following statement: "I, Tertius, the one writing this letter, greet you all in the Lord" (ἀσπάζομαι ὑμᾶς ἐγὼ Τέρτιος ὁ γράψας τὴν ἐπιστολὴν ἐν κυρίῳ) (Rom 16:22). Here we have a first century clue to the use of scribes, or secretaries, by Christians.[75] It is quite clear from this passage and others that Paul used the services of secretaries in the production of his letters. On several occasions, Paul calls attention to the fact that he is writing in his own hand (2 Thess 3:17; 1 Cor 16:21; Phlm 19; Col 4:18), and he also mentions his large handwriting as indicative of his own hand (Gal 6: 11).

For the period with which we are most interested here — the second and third centuries — we have one passage in Christian literature that depicts copying, a passage with which we began this chapter. While on the road to Cumae, Hermas meets the lady he has encountered before in a vision, and she instructs him to take the book she is reading and copy it. Hermas at first objects that he will not be able to remember everything in the book. So the lady gives the book to Hermas, and he does as she asks:

> I took it and after having departed to a certain place in the country, I copied everything letter by letter, for I could not distinguish [literally, find] the syllables.
>
> ἔλαβον ἐγώ, καὶ εἴς τινα τόπον τοῦ ἀγροῦ ἀναχωρήσας μετεγραψάμην πάντα πρὸς γράμμα· οὐχ ηὕρισκον γὰρ τὰς συλλαβάς. (Shep., vis. 2.1.4)

Later the "knowledge of the book" is revealed to Hermas by the lady; she then adds some words to the books and instructs Hermas to

> write two little books and send one to Clement and one to Grapte. Clement then shall send it to the cities abroad, for that is his duty; and Grapte shall exhort the widows and orphans; but in this city you shall read it yourself with the elders who are in charge of the church
>
> γράψεις οὖν δύο βιβλιαρίδια καὶ πέμψεις ἐν Κλήμεντι καὶ ἐν Γραπτῇ. πέμψει οὖν Κλήμης εἰς τὰς ἔξω νουθετήσει τὰς χήρας καὶ τοὺς ὀρφανούς. σὺ δὲ ἀναγνώσῃ εἰς ταύτην τὴν πόλιν μετὰ τῶν πρεσβυτέρων τῶν προϊσταμένων τῆς ἐκκλησίας. (Shep., vis. 2.4.3)

In this story, Hermas himself acts as copyist for sacred texts and is responsible as well for their dissemination. Hermas is nowhere described explicitly as a scribe or copyist; the only information about him is found at the very beginning of the book: "The one who brought me up, sold me to to a certain Rhoda at Rome. After many years I made her acquaintance again and began to love her like a sister" (Shep. vis. 1.1.1). Although this introductory statement indicates that Hermas was a slave, the fact that he lost touch with Rhoda, his owner, may indicate that he had been sold or freed. If so, we have a story in which a slave or freedman, who does not identify himself as a scribe by profession or trade, undertakes to copy texts. Whether this story is entirely fictional or contains a kernel of historical "reality" is of less concern for us than the fact that it offers a representation of the means by which texts were copied and disseminated: a nonprofessional reader/ user copies existing literary texts.

A striking parallel to the depiction of Hermas here can be found in the story of Jacob in the book of Jubilees:

> And [Jacob] saw in a vision of the night, and behold an angel was descending from heaven, and there were seven tablets in his hands. And he gave (them) to Jacob, and he read them, and he knew everything which was written in them, which would happen to him and to his sons during all the ages. And he showed him everything which was written on the tablets. And he said to him, " . . . Do not fear, because just as you have seen and read, thus will everything come to pass. But you write down everything just as you have seen and read (it)." And Jacob said, "O Lord, how will I remember everything that I read and saw?" And he said to him, "I will cause you to remember everything." And he went up from him and he woke up from his sleep and he recalled everything that he had read and seen and he wrote down all of the matters which he had read and seen. (Jubilees 32:21–26).[76]

Like Hermas, Jacob is not a trained professional scribe; furthermore, he shares the same hesitation: "how will I remember everything?" Unlike Hermas, however, Jacob *understands* what he has read, and he does not copy by exemplar but by being given divine powers of recollection. Though the significance of such differences between these texts will have to be saved for a later study, the Jacob story provides yet another portrait, however imaginary, of nonprofessionals who copy texts.

In some ways the story of Hermas stands between the paradigm of slave-scribe in the broader Graeco-Roman context of scribal transmission of literature and the nonprofessionals who occasionally undertook to copy a text: like many Graeco-Roman scribes, Hermas is a slave, but the fact that Hermas is not described as a scribe by trade corroborates evidence for nonprofessionals behind some copies of ancient literature. Most intriguing of all is that the story represents Hermas, a slave/freedman who prepares these copies (but is not necessarily a professional scribe), as having close connections to the leaders of the church: he is to read the copy of the little book with the elders (πρεσβυτέρων) of the church in Rome. This point deserves emphasis, for such a scenario finds support in the early Christian papyri themselves, as we shall see later. The picture that emerges from *The Shepherd* is one of private copying — either by a professional slave-scribe who does not identify himself as such or by a nonprofessional — and of a certain degree of intimacy between the copyists and church leaders.

Once we move into the fourth century, our Christian literary evidence for copying practices and text dissemination increases dramatically. At the turn of the fourth century, Eusebius of Caesarea composed his *Ecclesiastical History*, which has two key references to copyists. The first pertains to the time of Zephyrinus (Bishop of Rome, ca. 198–217 C.E.). Recording the words of an unknown author, Eusebius writes against a certain adoptionist sect:

"There was a certain confessor, Natalius, not long ago but in our own time. He was deceived by Asclepiodotus and by a second Theodotus, a banker. These were both disciples of Theodotus the cobbler, who was first excommunicated by Victor, who, as I said, was then bishop, for this way of thinking, or rather of not thinking. . . . " We would add to this some other words of the same author on the same persons, which runs as follows: "They [i.e., Asclepiodotus and Theodotus, the banker] have not feared to corrupt divine Scriptures, they have nullified the rule of ancient faith, they have not known Christ, they do not inquire what divine Scriptures say, but industriously consider what syllogistic figure may be found for the support of their atheism. . . . And that I do not calumniate them in saying this any who wish can learn, for if any be willing to collect and compare with each other the texts of each of them, he would find them in great discord, for the copies of Asclepiades do not agree with those of Theodotus, and it is possible to obtain many of them because their disciples have diligently written out copies corrected, as they say, but really corrupted by each of them. Again the copies of Hermophilus do not agree with these, the copies of Apolloniades are not even consistent with themselves, for the copies prepared by them at first can be compared with those which later on underwent a second corruption, and they will be found to disagree greatly. . . . They cannot even deny that this crime is theirs, seeing that the copies were written in their own hand [ὁπόταν καὶ τῇ αὐτῶν χειρὶ ᾖ γεγραμμένα], and they did not receive the Scriptures in this condition from their teachers, nor can they show originals from which they made their copies." (HE 5.28)

The scenario that is presented here is again quite plausible in light of what we know more generally about scribes in the ancient world.[77] In this story there is no indication that the disciples of Asclepiades or Theodotus are copyists by trade, but they appear to have enough education and desire to copy out the teachings of their teachers and make copies of Scripture. The representation of multiple copyists (here in the form of disciples) occurs again in Eusebius when he describes the resources that Ambrose placed at the disposal of Origen.[78] According to Eusebius, as Origen "dictated there were ready at hand more than seven shorthand-writers [ταχυγράφοι], who relieved each other at fixed times, and as many copyists [βιβλιογράφοι], as well as girls trained for beautiful writing [κόραις ἐπὶ τὸ καλλι-γραφεῖν ἠσκημέναις]" (HE 6.23). The multiple copyists depicted here in the service of Origen have often been taken as suggestive of a scriptorium in the "catechetical school" at Alexandria; the question of when and where Christian scriptoria emerged is notoriously thorny, but any argument for their existence in the early third century is entirely dependent upon Eusebius.[79] As we shall see in the chapter 4, however, there is no evidence in the earliest Christian papyri to corroborate the existence of a scriptorium in the third century C.E.

By the middle of the fourth century, Christian sources are brimming with references to text transcription and dissemination. The increase of material on text transmission may well have to do with Constantine's conversion, but may also be a byproduct of the emergence of asceticism and monasticism, for we find that these movements effected a change in the notion of a scribe/copyist as low class: copying texts, and writing more generally, becomes an ascetic practice that raises one's religious stature.[80] We learn of Christians who are copyists by trade; the case of Hieracas is particularly noteworthy, for he is identified by Epiphanius as a καλλιγράφος, the same term used to describe Origen's female copyists:

> After . . . Mani's . . . sect, there arose one Hieracas by name, from whom the Hieracites derive. He lived in Leontopolis in Egypt, had a sound elementary education, was well versed in all the pagan subjects, and mastered as well medicine and the other sciences of the Egyptians and Greeks, to which he doubtless added astrology and magic. For he was quite skilled in many disciplines, including exegesis, as his writings show. He had a perfect mastery of the Egyptian language (for the man was Egyptian) but also knew Greek well enough, being of a most keen intelligence. He was in fact a Christian, but he did not persevere in the Christian way of life; he slipped, fell, and ran aground. To put it plainly, he memorized the Old and New Testament, and in commenting on them he taught doctrines which he got from his own empty ideas, things which he considered true and which suggested themselves to him. . . . Now some say of him that he lived for over ninety years and that until the day of his death he practiced the copyist's art (for he was a copyist), for he retained his eyesight. (*Panarion* 67.1.1–4; 67.7.9)[81]

Like Hieracas, a certain Scetian scribe is identified as a scribe: "They told of the abbot Silvanus that he had a disciple in Scete named Marcus, and he was of great obedience, and also a writer of the ancient script."[82] In addition to references to Christian scribes — albeit in Hieracas' case one considered heretical by Epiphanius — we find in the fourth century a new prominence of books, readers, and copyists in the literature on the desert fathers.[83] Furthermore, it goes without saying that writers such as Jerome, Rufinus, and Augustine had plenty of uses for copyists, particularly in the establishment of their monastic libraries. By the time we reach the turn of the fifth century, we even hear of booksellers carrying Christian books. Sulpicius Severus' *Life of St. Martin*, for example, found its way into the eager hands of booksellers: "Paulinus, a man who has the strongest regard for you, was the first to bring it to the city of Rome; and then, as it was greedily laid hold of by the whole city, I saw the booksellers rejoicing over it, inasmuch as nothing was a source of greater gain to them, for nothing commanded a readier sale, or fetched a higher price. This same book, having got a long way before me in the course of my traveling, was already generally read through all Carthage, when I came into Africa" (*Dialogues* 1.23). But with Jerome, Augustine, and Sulpicius Severus, we have gone beyond the context with which this study is concerned — the pre-Constantinian milieu.

The fact that we do not have an abundance of information, let alone details, regarding the copyists involved in reproducing Christian texts prior to the fourth century is itself instructive. Recall the request for books among the circle of readers in upper Egypt—"Make and send me copies of books . . . "—which does not specify who would produce the copies. The most plausible explanation for the silence in our letter and in our early Christian sources is that the authors knew quite well who would produce copies. Most property owners or members of the sub-elites who would have wanted copies of texts had at least some slave or freed clerks, copyists, or secretaries in their service. They may well have used these workers to produce copies, for as we have seen even those slaves who were normally occupied with financial, administrative, or clerical work could be called upon to copy a literary text when the situation demanded it.

There is no reason to suppose that literate Christians who wished for copies of literature had substantially different resources from those of other literate folk in the empire. Although for many years the accusations of Celsus—that Christians were all of lower classes—were taken at face value by scholars, more recent studies have looked closely at prosopographic evidence to demonstrate that Christians appear to have come from a broader range of classes (although perhaps in the early centuries very few were from the most elite classes).[84] It is quite plausible to suppose that the wealthy women who owned homes and supported Paul had slaves or freedpersons who provided clerical service to them. It is also quite possible that some scribes, either as part of whole households or individually, converted to Christianity, and when they did, they may well have provided the secretarial help necessary for writing letters as well as copying and disseminating them.[85]

In addition, we have seen instances where nonprofessionals, literate persons who wanted a copy of a text and who possessed enough reading and writing ability could undertake to copy a text. This is evident in various literary papyri as well as in literary references. And this is precisely the model assumed by our only literary Christian source that illustrates text reproduction and transmission: in *The Shepherd*, Hermas himself could copy the desired texts. While he may have been a slave or freed clerk, and certainly he must have possessed some kind of training to produce the written text of *The Shepherd*, nowhere does he indicate his occupation in the text. Yet more striking is that he stands in close proximity to church leaders in Rome. Hermas, in marked contrast to our post-third-century sources, illustrates the private modes of text copying and transmission that were operative for Christianity's earliest centuries. In the chapters that follow, we will find support for this argument in our earliest Christian papyri, which illumine the private (and occasionally nonprofessional) identity of the scribes who copied early Christian literature, the private network of scribes who transmitted and disseminated this literature, and the close connection between these scribes and church leaders. For now, we turn to the role of female copyists in Roman antiquity and early Christianity, in an effort to expand our exploration of the scribes who copied early Christian literature.

"GIRLS TRAINED FOR BEAUTIFUL WRITING"

Female Scribes in Roman Antiquity and Early Christianity

As [Origen] dictated there were ready at hand more than seven shorthand-writers [ταχυγράφοι], who relieved each other at fixed times, and as many copyists [βιβλιογράφοι], as well as girls trained for beautiful writing [κόραις ἐπὶ τὸ καλλιγραφεῖν ἠσκημέναις].

— Eusebius, *HE* 6.23

. . . most of the available theories of reading, writing, sexuality, ideology, or any other cultural production are built on male narratives of gender.

— Teresa de Lauretis, *Technologies of Gender*

The complex portrait of Graeco-Roman scribes offered in the previous chapter conspicuously, and deliberately, failed to address an important dimension in the social history of scribes: the question of gender. All of the scribes we have explored thus far have indeed been male. Our investigations may well have seemed complete, for scholars have largely overlooked the presence of female scribes in the inscriptionary and literary evidence from the Graeco-Roman world. In omitting female scribes from the discussions of the transmission of ancient literature, scholars, on one level, simply replicate their disinterest in scribes more generally; if scribes are "mere copyists" they hardly deserve extensive treatment. As we shall see, however, there is an additional facet to the scholarly neglect of female scribes; the lack of an awareness of the extent to which there is evidence for female scribes has resulted in misunderstandings of the ancient literary references to female scribes. It is unfortunate that there has been such a lack of scholarly attention to female scribes, for it has obscured the role that women played in the production, transmission, and dissemination of literature and has erased their presence from the historical record. The goal of this chapter is to make the female scribes of antiquity visible again and to offer some hypotheses regarding their role in the (re)production of early Christian literature. Devoting a chapter to female scribes should not be taken to imply that women who were involved with the transmission of literature were somehow essentially different from the men involved in similar pursuits; rather, the present focus on female scribes simultaneously remedies the failure to recognize even the existence of female scribes in treatments of the transmission of literature in antiquity, furthers our discussion of ancient scribes more generally, and contributes to the history of women in antiquity.[1]

The following passage from Eusebius serves as a useful point of departure for a discussion of female scribes in early Christianity. While it is somewhat ambiguous whether this passage pertains to Origen's situation at Alexandria or that at Caesarea, the latter is perhaps more likely. According to Eusebius, it was in 232 C.E. that Origen left Alexandria for Caesarea (*HE* 6.26) and *HE* 6.19 makes it explicit that Origen was still in Alexandria.

> At that time also Origen's commentaries on the divine scriptures had their beginning, at the instigation of Ambrose, who not only plied him with innumerable verbal exhortations and encouragements, but also provided him unstintingly with what was necessary. As [Origen] dictated there were ready at hand more than seven shorthand-writers [ταχυγράφοι], who relieved each other at fixed times, and as many copyists [βιβλιογράφοι], as well as girls trained for beautiful writing [κόραις ἐπὶ τὸ καλλιγραφεῖν ἠσκημέναις]; for all of these Ambrose supplied without stint the necessary means. (*HE* 6.23)

This passage preserves an instance of multiple scribes in the service of one early Christian author — Origen. Shorthand writers, as we have seen, were commonly employed in households or public settings to write contracts, letters, or memoranda that were dictated to them.[2] Copyists could be found both in private settings and in the more public settings of libraries and bookshops. What interests me here, however, is the mention of female calligraphers.

The fate of Eusebius' record is worth highlighting: it suffers not only at the hands of ancient writers but also those of modern scholars. The first erasure of Eusebius' record takes place already with Jerome, for Jerome claims that Ambrose offered Origen, "seven or more short-hand writers (*notarii*) . . . and an equal number of copyists (*librarii*)" (*Vir.Ill.* 61). What has happened to the "girls trained in calligraphy"?

Modern attempts to restore Eusebius' account offer little consolation, for these illustrate the ease with which scholars are able to domesticate ancient texts that are somehow unpalatable. Interpretations of Origen's female calligraphers have illustrated all too well — to use de Lauretis' notion — how studies of "cultural production" in antiquity rely upon "male narratives of gender."[3] For example, Albert Schramm approves the notion that these girls are the precursors to the modern "type-writing girls" in his 1903 study of stenography in the ancient church.[4] Ancient and modern readers of Eusebius have not only effaced the presence of "female scribes" but also offered interpretations that once again uphold a certain "phallic-centered" orthodoxy and sensibility. Nowhere is this more striking than in G. H. Putnam's account of Eusebius: "Eusebius speaks of young maidens whom *the learned men* of his time employed as copyists."[5] Putnam's remarks imply that it was a commonplace for women copyists to work for men; the evidence we explore in this chapter, however, indicates precisely the opposite: when we find female copyists they almost invariably work for female masters.

The difficulty with all of these interpretations is parallel to the interpretations of the roles of scribes in the transmission of ancient literature more generally. As I pointed out in the introduction, scholars have largely neglected ancient literary scribes because of the assumption that they were "mere copyists," who provided only a mechanical reproduction of texts. In our last chapter, we shall have opportunity to fully explore the evidence that opposes the notion of scribes as "merely" copyists. But the scholarly comments on Origen's female scribes have an additional assumption at work, one that further obscures the roles of these female copyists: scholars presume a modern parallel and claim that these female calligraphers were mere secretarial help, and more importantly, they frame their discussions in terms of an implicit gender hierarchy.

Other modern interpretations of Eusebius' comments about Origen's female calligraphers are simply mistaken, as I will show in this chapter. Colin Roberts's remark, for example, in the early 1960s — that Eusebius' comment represents "the earliest known instance of woman's *invasion* of the book trade"[6] — is problematized by the appearance of female scribes centuries before Origen. Later, in Roberts's *Cambridge History of the Bible* entry on the transmission of early Christian literature (an article still widely quoted), Roberts explains Eusebius' account as "the first reference on record to the employment of women *stenographers*."[7] As we shall see both epigraphic and literary evidence offer a direct challenge to Roberts's stance. The claim that Origen's female calligraphers were somehow novel or unique misreads the evidence.

Eusebius' illustration or "representation" of the means by which ancient writers, particularly those as fortunate as Origen, composed and transmitted their work, offers no indication that the presence of "girls trained in calligraphy" was unusual or remarkable. But what Eusebius takes for granted, requires us to ask: What, precisely, did these female calligraphers do? To what extent *were* women involved in the transmission of literature in antiquity? Were the "girls trained in calligraphy" a common feature of ancient life? How were these girls trained? Did ancient women occasionally hold *professional* positions as scribes, secretaries, record keepers, copyists, and shorthand writers? If so, can we determine precisely which women participated in the transmission of literature? Were they urban or rural? slave, freed, or free? upper or lower class? young or old? Furthermore, what are the implications of women's involvement for our understanding of the transmission of literature in antiquity? And finally, the question at the fore of my discussion here, is it possible that some of our earliest Christian manuscripts were copied by women?

ROMAN-PERIOD EVIDENCE FOR FEMALE SCRIBES

Most of the evidence for female scribes in the Roman period is epigraphic. We have at least eleven Latin inscriptions from Rome itself that identify women as "scribes."[8] In these inscriptions we meet with Hapate, a shorthand writer of Greek who lived twenty-five years (*CIL* 6.33892 = *ILS* 7760); Corinna, who was a storeroom clerk or scribe (*cell[ariae] libr[ariae]*) (*CIL* 6.3979); and Tyche, Herma, and Plaetoriae, all three of whom are identified as amanuenses (*CIL* 6.9541; *CIL* 6.7373; *CIL* 6.9542). We also find four women who are identified by the title *libraria*, a term, as we have seen, that not only denoted a clerk or secretary but also more specifically a literary copyist. Among those identified as *librariae* is Sciathis Magia, a *libraria* who died at the age of eighteen (*CIL* 6.9301); Pyrrhe, simply identified as a *libraria* (*CIL* 6.9525 = *ILS* 7400); a freedwoman who remains nameless in the inscription, but is identified as a *libraria* (*CIL* 6.8882); and Vergilia Euphrosyne, another freed *libraria* (*CIL* 6.37802). In some cases, we know about the women in the inscriptions from other sources. For example, a certain Grapte is identified in one inscription as the amanuensis of Egnatia Maximilla—a woman who, according to Tacitus (*Ann.* 15.71), accompanied her husband, Glitius Gallus, when he was exiled by Nero (*CIL* 6.9549 = *ILS* 7397). Furthermore, we know that this Egnatia Maximilla had a substantial personal fortune, which was taken away from her, according to Tacitus, when she went into exile; it should not be surprising, therefore, that she had her own personal amanuensis.

In addition to these Latin inscriptions, two Greek inscriptions are useful: an inscription from Tralles identifies a woman as a γραμματεύσασα;[9] and an inscription located near the gymnasium at Pergamum identifies, among the girls who were successful in the contests, one girl who wins in καλλιγραφία.[10] It is here that we find a rather close connection with Eusebius' record, for this inscription suggests similarly that there were "girls trained for beautiful writing."[11]

What information can we glean from our collection of Latin and Greek inscriptions? First, class. At least six "scribes"—four amanuenses, the writer of Greek shorthand, and one *libraria*—in the Latin inscriptions appear to refer to women who were slaves. Two inscriptions quite clearly refer to freedwomen, both of whom are *librariae*. With the remainder, we cannot be sure whether the women are slaves or freedpersons. In five of the inscriptions, approximately half, it appears that the husbands—or, more precisely, the *contubernales*—of these scribes and secretaries set up the inscription on their behalf.[12] None of these inscriptions, perhaps not surprisingly, records children of these women, perhaps, as Natalie Kampen and others have suggested, "because of the tendency to commemorate more frequently women who die young than those who die in middle and old age."[13] That these women seem to be either slaves or freedwomen resonates perfectly with what we know about *librarii* more generally: as we saw in chapter 1, with the exception of high-level officials who held scribal titles, scribes in the Graeco-Roman world were normally slaves or freedpersons.[14]

With the exception of the shorthand writer in Greek and the storeroom clerk, it is difficult to determine precisely the nature of these female scribes' work. It may be that those identified as *a manu* or *amanuenses* were, as Susan Treggiari has suggested, "employed primarily for writing letters, as personal secretaries, while *librariae* had more general clerical functions."[15] Unfortunately, however, the evidence itself does not provide this information. Furthermore, when we compare the titles of our female "scribes" to their male counterparts (the *notarius*, the *librarius*, and so forth), whom we have already discussed, we find that these "scribes" did more than clerical work; they are not infrequently involved in the copying of literature.[16]

It is also worth noticing that all of these inscriptions derive from urban areas. Is this simply the result of the serendipitous survival of evidence? Or is it perhaps indicative of the locations where female scribes more generally were to be found?[17] When we note the uniformly urban context of the inscriptions, and the absence of evidence for female scribes in rural contexts — for which our evidence is admittedly less than adequate — or the papyri from the towns of upper-Egypt, the urban context becomes meaningful. It seems most likely that there were more female scribes in urban settings. Support for this point can be found in the fact that these inscriptions, when they are specific on this point, indicate that these female scribes worked for female masters. Such a scenario is particularly plausible in an urban setting. Urban elite women in the Roman period were usually literate; moreover, we would expect them to have the means to employ scribes.[18] In this light, the appearance of female scribes in urban contexts employed by upper-class women becomes quite sensible. We should be cautious, however, in supposing that female scribes worked only for women, for Eusebius' account presents a different urban scenario.

The existence of female scribes in urban contexts in the service of upper-class women is supported by two — and so far as I have been able to determine, the only two — literary references to female scribes outside of Eusebius. First, according to Suetonius' account of Vespasian, when Vespasian's wife (Flavia Domitilla) died, "he resumed his relations with Caenis, freedwoman and amanuensis of Antonia [*Antoniae libertam et a manu*], and formerly his mistress" (*Vesp.* 3). This anecdotal description of Caenis fits well with the information from our Latin inscriptions: a freedwoman who was employed as an amanuensis by another woman.

The second literary reference requires more careful analysis. In his well-known Book Six of the *Satires*, Juvenal catalogs with characteristically ruthless mockery the ways of wives. In the following passage he satirizes the well-to-do-lady who idles away her days unjustly punishing her slaves if her husband rejects her sexual advances.

If the husband has turned his back upon his wife at night, the *libraria* is done for. The slaves who dress their mistresses will be stripped of their tunics; the Liburnian will be accused of coming late, and will have to pay for another man's [i.e., the husband's] drowsiness; one will have a rod broken over his back, another will be bleeding from a strap, a third from the cat; some women engage their executioners by the year. While the flogging goes on, the lady will be daubing her face, or listening to her lady-friends, or inspecting the widths of a gold-embroidered robe. While thus flogging and flogging, she reads the lengthy Gazette, written right across the page, till at last, the floggers being exhausted, and the inquisition ended, she thunders out a gruff "Be off with you!" (*Satires* 6.475–485)

Crucial for my purposes is the very beginning of the passage where Juvenal indicates that the lady's *libraria* will suffer her mistress's temper. Scholars have been loath to translate this term as "clerk," or "scribe," or even less "copyist" and have rather argued that here the term *libraria* is essentially the same as *lanipendia*, the slave who was responsible for weighing and doling out the wool to the slave wool-workers. For example, Ramsay's translation in the Loeb Classical Library edition of Juvenal translates *libraria* here as "wool-maid." The scholarly reluctance appears to derive at least in part from the scholia gloss in which the term *libraria* is replaced with *lanipendia*. According to E. Courtney's commentary on the Satires, Σ—which represents the scholia preserved in P (the main manuscript used for the LCL text)—understood the use of *libraria* as the equivalent of *lanipendia* (the one "who weighs out the *pensum* to the female slaves").[19] John Ferguson likewise adopts the *lanipendia* interpretation, but admits that this interchange occurs no-where else: "*libraria* . . . the servant who weighs out the wool for the workers, only here in literature, elsewhere called *lanipendia*."[20] The *OLD*, however, does not suggest such an interchange of terms, and the *OCD* notes that no scholia on ancient Latin literature are earlier than third century (s.v. "Scholia"). Furthermore, scholars have argued that the context supports the interchange of *lanipendia* for *libraria*. And finally, some have pointed to etymological reasons for the gloss: it is possible that *libraria* derives not from the root *liber*, meaning book, but from *libra*, a unit of weight, and hence leads to the interpretation of "one who weighs out the wool" (i.e., the *lanipendia*).[21]

Each of these arguments, however, is problematic: scholia on ancient literature must be assessed on an individual basis, since it is just as possible that a scribe or copyist has mistakenly—intentionally or unintentionally—glossed a word, as that he (or she) has preserved a good reading; additionally, extant scholia date to several centuries after Juvenal. Furthermore, there is nothing in the context that inherently suggests one interpretation over another: we know that *libraria* were among the personal servants of wealthy women, and this passage appears essentially to produce a list of various slaves. And finally, most problematic in my opinion, is that if *libraria* means *lanipendia* in this passage, it would represent the sole instance in all of Latin literature where this interchange is made.[22] Essentially, there are no controls on such a replacement, and therefore I would argue that Juvenal also attests to female slaves who were trained as clerks, secretaries, or copyists, and were in the service of female masters.

To the inscriptions and literary references we can add one final piece of Roman period evidence for female scribes—an early second-century marble relief from Rome that preserves an illustration of a female record keeper or clerk. The woman is seated on a high-backed chair and appears to be writing on some kind of a tablet; she faces the butcher who is chopping meat at a table. While one may well wonder whether the image could be read differently—perhaps, for example, the male figure is in the employment of the seated female—such a reading pushes at the limits both of what is contextually plausible (e.g., does it seem likely that a *butcher* worked *for* a clerk or book keeper?) and sensible in light of other reliefs that depict both butchers and various other merchants with clerks at their employment.[23] It strikes me as particularly interesting that among the few Roman-period visual illustrations of scribes or clerks one depicts a woman.[24] Furthermore, it suggests that the employment of female scribes was not exclusively restricted to female employers, for here we have a vivid portrait of a female scribe working for a male butcher. It may well be, as some have suggested, that *librariae* could do "freelance" work beyond the household in which they were primarily employed.[25]

That some women, or girls, of slave and lower class were trained as clerks, secretaries, and shorthand writers seems clear from the evidence I have just discussed. These women must have had a certain degree of literacy and training, which, as we shall see in the chapter that follows, they probably received by apprenticeship, training with a tutor in the household in which they worked, or by attending a "public" school. But have we found any clear indication that female scribes were involved in copying literary texts? Although nowhere is this task specifically mentioned, we cannot rule out this possibility for several compelling reasons. As I have said, the masculine counterparts to our female scribes, the male *librarius* in particular, are frequently found to denote male slaves and freedpersons who did copy texts. Furthermore, as I will show, there is explicit evidence for women copying texts within the context of the rise of monasticism in early Christian ascetic circles.

Before turning to the late-ancient context of women's monasticism, I want very briefly to point out that the Roman evidence is not anomalous in the history of the Mediterranean and Ancient Near East. For our purposes it will be sufficient simply to list some of the earlier evidence:[26] at Mari, we know of some ten female scribes by name;[27] at Sippar, the cloister of the celibate *naditu* women attests fourteen female scribes, who appear to have instructed some of their own women as scribes;[28] a Neo-Assyrian (ca. 744–612) personnel list mentions six female scribes;[29] in Middle and New Kingdom Egypt, we find the title "female scribe" on ostraca and seals;[30] in Theban tombs, there are depictions of women seated with scribal implements under their chairs, and scholars have argued that the connection between the women and the items under their chair is not arbitrary but rather suggests that these women were involved in scribal tasks;[31] and a 26th Dynasty tomb also attests the title "female scribe."[32] These examples, not exhaustive of the available evidence, show that the Roman period evidence accords well with what we find in earlier periods: not only do we find the attestation of "female scribes"; they also appear to have used their skill to serve other women;[33] furthermore, as with the Roman evidence, female scribes appear to have been slaves or at the very least low-class women.[34] Scholarly reluctance to read this evidence as suggestive of women's involvement in scribal professions also parallels treatments we have seen of Eusebius and Juvenal. Some scholars, for example, have argued that those identified as "female scribes" in the depictions from Egypt actually represent women cosmeticians, perhaps an interpretation more palatable to some modern historians who cannot fathom the appearance of women in a realm traditionally occupied by men.[35] While this evidence is admittedly earlier than the period with which we are concerned, when we couple this evidence with the references to Christian women copying texts in the fourth century and beyond, we find that Eusebius' comments become sensible.

FEMALE SCRIBES IN EARLY CHRISTIANITY

It is in the period after Eusebius' description of Origen's scribal resources that we find our clearest evidence for women copying texts. With the rise of Christian monasticism, references to women learning how to read and write as well as copying texts become increasingly frequent.[36] In the illustrations of women as copyists that follow, we will admittedly overstep the second-and third-century boundaries of the present study. The goal of doing so is not to suggest that the models of later centuries can apply to an earlier period, but simply to demonstrate not only that female scribes and copyists existed before Eusebius' account of Origen's female calligraphers (as we have just seen) but also afterward.

Melania the Younger

In the mid-fifth-century hagiographic account of Melania the younger (ca. 383–439), Gerontius describes her religious zeal as follows:

> The blessed woman read the Old and New Testaments three or four times a year. She copied them herself and furnished copies to the saints by her own hands.
>
> Ἀνεγίνωσκεν δὲ ἡ μακαρία τὴν μὲν παλαιὰν καὶ καινὴν διαθήκην τοῦ ἐνιαυτοῦ τρίτον ἢ τέταρτον, (καὶ) καλλιγραφοῦσα τὸ αὐταρκες παρεῖχεν τοῖς ἁγίοις ἐκ τῶν ἰδίων χειρῶν ὑποδείγματα. (Life 26)[37]

In this passage it is not entirely clear whether Melania furnished these copies for use in her monastery for women, or whether they were intended for both her monastery for men and the one for women.[38] The use of τοῖς ἁγίοις may suggest that her copies were intended for an audience beyond the women in her monastery. We know from other texts that some ascetic women did provide books for men. For example, Marcella figures prominently as a book owner and book lender throughout Jerome's letters (e.g., *Ep.* 47 and *Ep.* 49, 4), and Eusebius also records that Juliana supplied Origen with Symmachus' works (*HE* 6.17).[39] Particularly significant is the term that is used here to describe Melania's copying: καλλιγραφοῦσα. We can recall Eusebius' use of the very same verb to describe Origen's female calligraphers. Lest we think that "beautiful writing" was only used to describe the work of female scribes, however, we should recall also that Epiphanius identifies Hieracas as a καλλιγράφος; additionally, this is the term used in Constantine's request of fifty copies of "sacred scripture" and no gender is specified there (*de Vita Const.* 36). That this term could be used to denote *copying* underscores the problem of modern interpretations of Eusebius. Furthermore, Gerontius' story indicates that he found it plausible that women in monasteries in fifth-century Palestine indeed copied texts.

One of the fascinating aspects of this passage is the inversion of the paradigm of scribe as low class; here Melania's copying is used precisely to show her ascetic devotion (i.e., to raise her "status"). There is clearly much here that deserves attention, for in one sense the use of "writing" to elevate one's status harkens back to the Pharaonic Egyptian setting; we find, indeed, in the late antique and early medieval context a reemergence of a "scribal class" — loosely construed — within the context of Christian monasteries and the rise of Christian scriptoria. Yet it seems to me that the passage regarding Melania's copying has more to do with the intersection of asceticism, theological disputes, and reading/writing that emerges on different levels and in different forms in fourth-century Christianity. It is in the fourth century that the varied forms of ascetic Christian life become problematic within circles of orthodoxy; simultaneously, texts take on a new relevance for debates of heresy and orthodoxy, as well as for ascetic life. These texts required careful commentary and interpretation so as to constrain the increasing variety of ascetic forms of life. The intersection of bodies and texts is one we shall return to in chapter 4, for it emerges as a matrix for a third-century Christian "miscellany."

Caesaria the Younger

That monastic women in late antiquity copied texts is supported by the somewhat later account of Caesaria at her convent in Arles.

> [When Caesarius'] sister, holy Caesaria [the Elder], mother of the monastery, passed on to the rewards of Christ . . . she was succeeded as mother [superior] by Caesaria [the Younger], who is still alive. Her work with her companions is so outstanding that in the midst of psalms and fasts, vigils and readings, the virgins of Christ beautifully copy out the holy books, having their mother herself as teacher.
>
> *Non multo igitur post monasterii matrem germanam suam Caesariam sanctam, ad praemia Christi migrantem . . . succedente eidem quae nunc superest, Caesaria matre, cujus opus cum sodalibus tam praecipuum viget, ut inter psalmos atque jejunia, vigilias quoque et lectiones, libros divinos pulchre scriptitent virgines Christi, ipsam magistram habentes. (Vita Caesarius* I.58)[40]

This testimony, from sixth-century Gaul, suggests the similar practice of monastic women copying scriptures as the account of Melania's life. Furthermore, this passage fits well with what we know about Caesaria's rule for the nuns at Arles more generally, for the rule included the requirement that "no nun be allowed to enter who does not learn letters."[41] As for the processes of instruction, it appears that the abbess herself taught the women how to copy texts.

"Thecla" and the Codex Alexandrinus

A third, and my final, illustration brings us closer to early Christian manuscripts and approaches the existence of female scribes from a different angle. Interlaced with the history of the fifth-century Codex Alexandrinus winds a rather mysterious and provocative tradition. Cyril Lucar, patriarch of Constantinople who sent this codex to Charles I in 1627, attached a note to the beginning of the codex that reads as follows:

> This book of the sacred scriptures, New and Old Testaments, according to the tradition we have, has been written by the hand of Thecla, the noble Egyptian woman, approximately 1300 years ago, shortly after the council of Nicea. The name of Thecla had been written at the end of the book, but because of the annihilation of the Christians in Egypt by the Muslims, other books of the Christians are similarly in disrepair. And so the name of Thecla was torn off and destroyed, but the memory and the tradition are observed recently.

> *Liber iste scripturae sacrae N. et V. Testament, prout ex traditione habemus, est scriptus manu Theclae, nobilis foeminae Aegyptiae, ante mile et trecentos annos circiter, paulo post concilium Nicenum. Nome Theclae, in fine libri erat exaratum, sed extincto Christianismo in Aegypto a Mahometanis, et libri una Christianorum in similem sunt reducti conditione. Extinctum ergo est Theclae nomen et laceratum, sed memoria et traditio recens observat.*[42]

What can we make of Cyril's record? He suggests that before the end of the manuscript was destroyed, the name of a scribe "Thecla" was written in a final colophon. Indeed, there are a number of leaves missing at the end of the second epistle of Clement, the last text in the codex.[43]

In addition to Cyril's memorandum, we find an Arabic note, dated to the thirteenth or fourteenth century, on the second page of the table of contents at the very beginning of the codex. This marginal note reads, "They say that this book was written by the hand of Thecla, the martyr."[44] Sir Thomas Roe, who delivered the manuscript from Cyril to Charles I, appears to have received two different stories from Cyril.[45] In the letter of 30 January 1624 to the Earle of Arundell, Roe writes: "By his [i.e., the patriarch's] means, I may procure some books, but they are indeed Greek to me: one only he hath given me, for his majesty, with express promise to deliver it; being an autograph Bible entire, written by the hand of Tecla the protomartyr of the Greeks, that lived in the time of St. Paul; and he doth aver it to be true and authentic of his own writing, and the greatest antiquity of the Greek church." In his letter of 27 February 1627 to the Archbishop of Canterbury, however, he writes about the same manuscript: "The letter is very fair, a character I have never seen. It is entire, except the beginning of St. Matthew. He [i.e., the patriarch] doth testify under his hand that it was written by the virgin Tecla, daughter of a famous Greek, called Αβγιεριενος, who founded the monastery in Egypt upon Pharaos tower, a devout and learned maid, who was persecuted in Asia, and to whom Gregory Nazianzen hath written many epistles. At the end whereof, under the same hand, are the epistles of Clement. She died not long after the council of Nicea. The book is very great, and hath antiquity enough at sight."[46]

Most scholars have simply dismissed the tradition of "Thecla" as scribe of Alexandrinus. Indeed, beyond the Arabic note, Cyril's memorandum, and Roe's comments about the tradition, there is no concrete evidence whatsoever to support the tradition of "Thecla," whoever she may have been, as the scribe of this codex. But the evidence does raise questions: Did the codex in its original form contain a colophon that named a female scribe? Or did an oral tradition somehow emerge that associated this codex with "Thecla"? Indeed, we know that Thecla, the "legendary heroine" of the Apocryphal Acts quickly became a monument and model for women ascetics. Some Christians, even some who did not take up the ascetic life, found it desirable to name their daughters "Thecla."

What strikes me as most significant in the Thecla-Alexandrinus tradition is that nowhere is the plausibility of a female scribe questioned. Indeed, even Wettstein, in his *Prolegomena ad Novi Testamenti* of 1730, suspected the work of a female scribe. Why? Because, he said, the codex was so full of mistakes! (Imperitior fuit librarius, vel ut cum aliis suspicor libraria femina.)[47] Lest we find Wettstein's reasoning persuasive, I should add that the monks at St. Catherine's in Sinai at the end of the nineteenth century, proudly displayed a Psalter that they claimed was written by "Thecla," and when all of its twelve leaves were carefully examined ("under a microscope"), they were found to be completely error-free.[48] Other explanations for the Thecla tradition have been offered: Tischendorf apparently considered as a possibility that the Thecla referred to was the Thecla with whom Gregory of Nazianzen corresponded, but this would have been earlier than Alexandrinus can properly be dated; Tregelles sought an explanation in the fact that in the New Testament the extant text began with the lectionary reading of Matthew 25:6, the lesson in the Greek church for the festival of St. Thecla, but this does not take into account that the Arabic numeration, which is itself later than the Arabic note about Thecla, begins with the number 26, "so that the twenty-five leaves now lost must have been still extant when that note was written."[49] Although we cannot definitively link this codex with a female scribe, the emergence and maintainance of such a tradition suggests the plausibility of female copyists in a way similar to Eusebius' lack of comment regarding the gender of Origen's copyists.

When the Thecla-Alexandrinus tradition, for which we have only late attestation, is seen in light of Origen's calligraphers, Melania's calligraphic copying, Caesaria who trained her virgins to produce beautiful copies, as well as the evidence for female scribes more generally in the Mediterranean world, the suggestion that some of our earliest Christian manuscripts may have been copied by women becomes conceivable and, indeed, quite plausible.[50] Such a proposal has implications for our understanding of the transmission of literature in antiquity, and early Christian texts in particular, as well as our knowledge about the roles of women in the transmission of literature. Our attention to the ancient representation of women as scribes in this chapter indeed restores not only Eusebius's account but also an aspect of the history of women that has all too often been overlooked and a facet to identity and role of ancient scribes and copyists. The assumption that women were not involved in the transcription and transmission of literature is shown to be false by the range of evidence presented in this chapter; in addition, the claims that Origen's calligraphers were unique or that female copyists commonly worked for the "learned men" (i.e., male writers) are problematized by close investigation of the evidence.

In the last two chapters, we have focused on the question of "identity": Who were ancient scribes? In what contexts did they work? What did their positions entail? These questions have been important for locating ancient literary scribes and the scribes who copied early Christian literature more specifically. When we compare the roles of female scribes to their male counterparts, we find many similarities and some significant differences. First, the tendency that emerges in both cases is one of gender separation: normally female scribes worked for female masters, and males scribes worked for male masters. But this appears as a tendency, not a rule, as we see in the cases of Origen's calligraphers and the girl who worked in a butcher shop. Like male scribes, female scribes were involved in a variety of tasks, from record keeping to copying literary texts. What strikes me as a significant difference, however, is that we do not find (not surprisingly) women holding official scribal positions; to the contrary, all of the evidence (with the possible exception of the record keeper in the butcher shop) for female scribes places them in private contexts.

Why is it important to understand the "identities" of ancient scribes and the scribes who copied early Christian literature more specifically? The answer to this question will only fully emerge in chapters 4 and 5, when we discuss the evidence that indicates how scribes—as readers and writers who were embodied socially, culturally, and religiously—played an integral role in the (re)production and (re)creation of early Christian literature. For now, we turn to an issue closely related to scribal identities: the education and training of scribes.

"FOR I COULD NOT FIND THE SYLLABLES"

The Education and Training of Early Christian Scribes

Ignoramus and knave, leave the old [reading], and do not change it!

— Codex Vaticanus, marginal note at Hebrews 1:3

As for the Latin books, I don't know which way to turn; they are copied out and sold so full of mistakes.

— Cicero, *Ep.Q.Fr.* 3.6

Inscribed in the margins of the fourth-century Codex Vaticanus are the words of one scribe to another: "Ignoramus and knave, leave the old [reading], and do not change it!" (ἀμαθέστατε καὶ κακέ, ἄφες τὸν παλαιόν, μὴ μεταποίει).[1] For the purpose of this chapter, I am particularly interested in the first epithet that this disgruntled scribe hurls at his predecessor: ignoramus. Does this simply yield a glimpse of an irritated (and no doubt exhausted) scribe? That copying was considered manual labor is clear from the comment in *Rhetorica ad Herennium*, which we discussed at the outset of chapter 1 and where the task of copying is described as *laboriosum* (4.6). We could also note the various colophons attached to manuscripts from a variety of periods: "He who does not know how to write supposes it to be no labour; but though only three fingers write, the whole body labours"; "Writing bows one's back, thrusts the ribs into one's stomach, and fosters a general debility of the body"; "As travellers rejoice to see their home country, so also is the end of a book to those who toil [in writing]"; and "The end of the book, thanks be to God!"[2]

Or does the marginal note in Codex Vaticanus contain a clue to the educational levels of ancient scribes? To be sure, we have a number of Greek and Latin literary authors who complain about the lack of good copies just as Cicero does in the quotation above.[3] Furthermore, the fictional story of Hermas implies a rather meager education, for Hermas indicates he copied the sacred texts "letter by letter" because he "could not find the syllables" (μετε-γραψάμην πάντα πρὸς γράμμα οὐχ ηὑρισκον γὰρ τὰς συλλαβάς) (*Shep.*, *vis.* 2.1.4). Similarly, Cicero was forced to break down phrases and even words into syllables for a less well trained *librarius* (*Att.* 13.25). But will the accumulation of ancient complaints about uneducated scribes or apologies of individual copyists provide a balanced picture of the scribes' education and training? Probably not. If we want to determine the extent to which ancient scribes were educated, or how they were trained, we have two sources that take us beyond the passing comments of authors: 1) the corpus of literary and papyrological evidence regarding education in general and the training of scribes in particular, and 2) the copies of literature that scribes produced.

The previous two chapters were concerned with the broad contours of scribes' identities and status in the Graeco-Roman world. We saw that scribes in this period defy scholarly attempts to categorize scribes and to generalize about a "scribal class"; while scribes are concentrated in the slave and lower classes, they are also found in higher classes. Their tasks are not easily defined or classified, since many scribes — especially private scribes — seem to have often been multi-functional, crossing the lines of administrative and literary work with some frequency. This chapter continues the discussion of scribal identities and functions by looking closely at the education and training of scribes. Throughout, I will use the terms "education" and "training," respectively, to designate a general course of schooling (i.e., that may have taken place in a "public" school or a private context) in contrast to a particular technical component designed to teach scribes a specialty. In the case of the copyists of early Christian literature, I will further give attention to evidence that may indicate that the scribes had a specifically Christian "education" (to the extent that they were acquainted with other Christian texts or may have been aware of liturgical or catechetical rites). What emerges from the literary and papyrological evidence corroborates the multifarious portrait in the previous chapters: the degree of education and training among scribes of this period varies from the illiterate[4] to the well-educated,[5] from the poorly trained copyist[6] to the experienced calligrapher.[7] Moreover, physical features of our literary papyri — and occasionally our documentary papyri — support the notion of multifunctional scribes. Into the evidence for scribal education and training — as found in our literary and papyrological sources — we can then set our earliest Christian papyri, which provide an important counterpart to the Christian literary evidence we discussed in chapter 1 and offer our only source for the education and training of the scribes who produced them. The central argument of this chapter is that the scribes who copied early Christian literature were multifunctional scribes who were educated and trained through private channels. Additionally, it appears that in some cases the copyists of early Christian literature may have had a more specialized "education" in early Christian "texts," for their copies occasionally betray knowledge of other Christian literature as well as various liturgical practices.

LEARNING TO WRITE IN GRAECO-ROMAN ANTIQUITY

The unusual case of Petaus notwithstanding, the basic function of a scribe in antiquity was writing. This is true not only for the freed and slave scribes but also for those nonprofessional copyists who on occasion acted as scribes. Numerous scholars have studied the Graeco-Roman educational systems as well as the specific education in writing;[8] for our purposes it will suffice simply to outline the various models of education that existed. Some scribes apparently learned how to write in the private context of the household *paedagogium* or the "public" context of a "school." What is meant by both "public" and "school" is, of course, somewhat problematic, as the wide ranging scholarly definitions attest. Sites of instruction — in reading, writing, and literature — could indeed be found in public places, such as in a portico on the edge of the forum or even "in or practically in the street."[9] Ancient schools, however, were clearly not "public" in the same sense as, for example, modern American public schools, where public funds are used to provide equal opportunity for education; as Harris puts it, "what was lacking . . . in most communities throughout the Greek world was the will to allocate public or philanthropic funds to schooling for the children of the poor."[10] Cribiore defines "school" simply as the activity of instruction, "rather than in terms of the identity of the person teaching, the student-teacher relationship, or the premises where teaching takes place."[11] While Cribiore is correct in not limiting the definition of "school" to a particular location, the distinction between instruction in homes versus in a more public setting remains helpful. In maintaining the differentiation between public and private forms of instruction, we borrow Quintilian's own distinction between the two (*Inst.* 1.2.1).

However we understand the terms "public" and "school," it goes without saying that the slave and freed scribes did not normally progress to the highest levels of the curriculum (i.e., the study of rhetoric); this was reserved for a select few, as Harris and others have so clearly demonstrated.[12] Dorothy Thompson has made similar claims with respect to the training of scribes in Ptolemaic Egypt: "although scribes and others working within the royal administration may have acquired a knowledge of Poseidippus and Callimachus, it was of little practical application."[13] And A. D. Booth's study of the education of slaves in first-century Rome draws similar conclusions: "The training of slaves in clerical skills, termed *litterae communes* in later antiquity . . . , was uncontroversial. But liberal study was properly the preserve of the freeborn upper-class."[14] While there is some evidence that some scribes were given a specialized, technical training to prepare them to fulfill a rather specialized task or occupation, our evidence for such technical training is mostly indirect.

Channels of Education and Training

For those who both desired and had financial resources for education and training — either for their children or slaves — a number of channels existed for learning how to write. Although it is quite clear that Marrou and others overestimated the existence of a widespread network of schools in the Hellenistic and Roman periods, it goes without saying that there were schools throughout Graeco-Roman antiquity, particularly in urban areas. Quintilian implies precisely this when he compares the benefits of public schooling with those of private tutoring: "This therefore is the place to discuss the question as to whether it is better to have him educated privately at home or hand him over to some large school and those whom I may call public instructors" (Hoc igitur potissimum loco tractanda quaestio est, utiliusne sit domi atque intra privatos parietes studentem continere an frequentiae scholarum et velut publicis praeceptoribus tradere) (*Inst.* 1.2.1). The comments of other ancient writers also point to the existence of schools, however "physically makeshift" the setting for these schools.[15] We still have much to learn about the precise modes of teaching as well as the structure of the curriculum in these schools, but we can be certain that the elementary levels included the basic, but distinct, tools of reading and writing.[16]

Who attended these schools? Our literary sources, which predominantly refer to the schools in Rome, suggest that the sons, and occasionally the daughters, of the elite were sometimes sent off to these schools.[17] As to whether slaves — and we are particularly interested in slave-scribes — attended schools, our evidence is insufficient to make a definitive statement. That slaves were sent to these schools seems to be the assumption behind Petronius' fictional freed Hermeros' statement regarding his teacher: "our master used to say, 'Are all your things safe? Go straight home; do not look around you; and do not abuse your elders'" (dicebat enim magister: Sunt vestra salve? recta domum; cave, circumspicias; cave, maiorem maledicas) (*Satyricon* 58.13). Furthermore, Martial suggests that slaves or freeborn boys attended these schools, and his comments are particularly interesting to us because he suggests that *notarii* had schools: "may no teacher of bookkeeping or shorthand be surrounded by a larger gathering" (nec calculator nec notarius velox maiore quisquam circulo coronetur) (10.62.1–5). Unfortunately, we cannot be entirely sure whether Martial's comments pertain to slaves or to freeborn boys, since the term *capillati* can refer to either, but his offhand remark about the circles of students surrounding the teachers of shorthand provides a glimpse into forms of specialized training.[18] If we cannot be certain that slaves to any great extent attended these public schools, we can look to other channels of education; before turning to these, however, we would do well to consider briefly the possibility that those who were involved with transcribing Christian texts could have been educated in the Graeco-Roman schools.

The views Christians held on schools as found in literary sources of the second and third centuries are notoriously contradictory.[19] Although Clarke, citing the examples of Origen, Basil, and Gregory of Nazianzus, claimed that "it was quite common for Christians to study under non-Christian teachers,"[20] there is some evidence that some Christians may have withdrawn their children from the Graeco-Roman schools. The most well known evidence for Christians' hostility to schools and schoolteachers is found in Celsus' claim, quoted by Origen, that Christians turn children against teachers:

when they [Christians] get hold of the children privately, and certain women as ignorant as themselves, they pour forth wonderful statements, to the effect that they ought not to give heed to their father and to their teachers . . . that the former are foolish and stupid, and neither know nor can perform anything that is really good, being preoccupied with empty trifles. . . . And while thus speaking, if they see one of the instructors of youth approaching, or one of the more intelligent class, or even the father himself, the more timid among them become afraid, while the more forward incite the children to throw off the yoke, whispering that in the presence of father and teachers they neither will nor can explain to them any good thing . . . *but that if they wish they must leave their father and their instructors . . . that they may attain to perfection.*

ἐπειδὰν δὲ τῶν παίδων ἰδίᾳ λάβωνται καὶ γυναίων τινῶν σὺν αὐτοῖς ἀνοήτων,
θαυμάσι᾽ ἄττα διεξιόντας, ὡς οὐ χρὴ προσέχειν τῷ πατρὶ καὶ τοῖς διδασκάλοις
. . . καὶ τοῦ μέν τε ληρεῖν καὶ ἀποπλήκτους εἶναι, καὶ μηδέν τῷ ᾽ὄντι καλὸν
μήτε ἰδέναι μήτε δύνασθαι ποιεῖν, ὕθλοις κενοῖς προκατειλημμένους. . . . καὶ
ἅμα λέγοντες, ἐὰν ἴδωσί τινα παριόντα τῶν παιδείας διδασκάλων καὶ
φρονιμωτέρων ἢ καὶ αὐτὸν τὸν πατέρα, οἱ μὲν εὐλαβέστεροι αὐτῶν διέτρεσαν·
οἱ δ᾽ ἰταμώτεροι τοὺς παῖδας ἀφηνιάζειν ἐπαίρουσι, τοιαῦτα ψιθυρίζοντες, ὡς
παρόντος μὲν τοῦ πατρὸς καὶ τῶν διδασκάλων οὐδὲν αὐτοὶ ἐθελήσουσιν, οὐδὲ
δυνήσονται τοῖς παισὶν ἑρμηνεύειν ἀγαθόν . . . εἰ δὲ θέλοιεν, χρῆναι αὐτοὺς
ἀφεμένους τοῦ πατρός τε καὶ τῶν διδασκάλων . . . ἵνα τὸ τέλειον λάβωσι.
(*Contra Celsum* 3.55)

Celsus' comments hint at Christians turning their children away from schoolteachers; and Origen's reply does not deny this, but rather embraces it:

if we turn [our hearers] away from those instructors who teach obscene comedies and licentious iambics, and many other things which neither improve the speaker nor benefit the hearers . . . we are not, in following such a course, ashamed to confess what we do. ·

εἰ μὲν γὰρ ἀποτρέπομεν διδασκάλων διδασκόντων τὰ ἰάμβων, καὶ ὅσα ἄλλα,
ἃ μήτε τὸν λέγοντα ἐπιστρέφει, μήτε τοὺς ἀκούοντας ὠφελεῖ . . . οὐκ
αἰσχυνόμεθα ὁμολογεῖν τὸ πραττόμενον. (*Contra Celsum* 3.58)

Christians in the second century also lambaste schoolteachers. Hippolytus, for example, suggests that those who are schoolteachers by trade should find a different occupation, and Tertullian claims that schoolmasters "border on idolatry" (Hippolytus, *Apost.Trad.* 2.16.13; Tertullian, *de Idol.* 10). The attitudes of Hippolytus and Tertullian may well have been shared by other Christians, and it is possible that such views had an effect on the use of Graeco-Roman schools among Christians. At the same time, if no Christians were enrolled in the Graeco-Roman schools or sent their slaves to these schools, and there were no Christian schoolteachers, Celsus' claims carry no weight, and Hippolytus and Tertullian would have no need to lambaste schoolteachers; indeed their very hostility indicates that some Christians *were* involved with these schools. Hippolytus's statements only make sense, in fact, if there were schoolteachers who had converted to Christianity. Furthermore, it may well be that such converts were occasionally involved in the copying of early Christian literature. As we shall see below, Christian papyri manifest a distinct dual influence between literary and documentary styles of writing, and we know that schoolteachers were able both to copy literary texts (as evidenced in the school papyri) and prepare documents and letters.[21] Moreover, the titles held by schoolteachers—especially, διδάσκαλος and πρεσβύτερος—are particularly prominent in the nascent hierarchies of early Christian churches.

The extent to which slaves—and importantly for us, slave-scribes—were enrolled in Graeco-Roman schools, as well as the ambivalence toward these schools felt among some Christians, is still uncertain, and we would do well to consider other channels of training and education. We do not have to look far to find other possibilities: scribes, in fact, could be trained in the homes of their elite masters, either by a tutor or in the *paedagogium*.[22] The Latin term *paedagogium* derives from the Greek παιδαγωγεῖον, which referred to a "room in a schoolhouse in which the παιδαγωγοί waited for their boys."[23] Although the *paedagogium* was clearly linked to some context of education or training, we still know quite little about its precise purpose; most of our evidence suggests that the slaves who were trained in the household *paedagogium* were being trained to prepare and serve food.[24] With respect to the extent and function of the *paedagogia*, Forbes clearly overstated the extent to which these provided primary education to slaves: "The Romans had in mind larger objectives, of preparing slaves worthy to become freedmen in responsible and trusted positions as chamberlains, bookkeepers, secretaries, or procurators. Hence the slaves were undoubtedly taught reading, writing, and arithmetic; indeed they got much the same kind of basic education that free boys did, besides specific training in various duties of the dining room."[25] Though the evidence for *paedagogia* is slim—particularly the extent to which these "schools" trained slaves as secretaries or scribes—the private training of slaves in clerical skills appears to have taken place primarily in the homes of the wealthy. Much of our evidence for private training is literary.

According to Plutarch, Crassus took a keen interest in training his slaves: "so many and so capable were the slaves he possessed—readers, scribes, silversmiths, stewards, table-servants; and he himself directed their learning, and he took part in it himself as a teacher" (τοσούτους ἐκέκτητο καὶ τοιούτους, ἀναγνώστας, ὑπογραφεῖς, ἀργυρογνώμονας, διοικητάς, τραπεζοκόμους, αὐτὸς ἐπιστατῶν μανθάνουσι καὶ προσέχων καὶ διδάσκων) (Plutarch, *Crass.* 2.6). Similarly, Plutarch suggests that the elder Cato bought slaves, had them taught by a slave-teacher, and then sold them at a higher price: "he used to lend money to those of his slaves who wished it, and they would buy boys; then, after training and teaching them, at Cato's expense, they would sell them again" (ἐδίδου δὲ καὶ τῶν οἰκετῶν τοῖς βουλομένοις ἀργύριον. οἱ δ᾽ ἐωνοῦντο παῖδας, εἶτα τούτους ἀσκήσαντες καὶ διδάξαντες ἀναλώμασι τοῦ Κάτωνος μετ᾽ ἐνιαυτὸν ἀπεδίδοντο) (Plutarch, *Cat.Ma.* 21.7).[26] While the latter instance does not mention exactly what the slaves were taught, in both of these cases, Plutarch indicates that the slaves were trained in the household itself. This is precisely the same scenario as we find in Cornelius Nepos' remarks on Atticus' slaves:

> He had slaves that were excellent in terms of utility, although mediocre in personal appearance; for there were among them very highly educated boys [i.e., slaves], some excellent readers and many copyists; there was not even a footman who was not expert in both of these accomplishments. In the same way, other artisans who were required for the management of the house were of first rate quality. Nevertheless, he did not possess a slave who was not born and trained in his house, which is a sign not only of his self-control but also of his thrift.

> *Usus est familia, si utilitate iudicandum est, optima; si forma, vix mediocri. Namque in ea erant pueri litteratissimi, anagnostae optimi et plurimi librarii; ut ne pedisequus quidem quisquam esset qui non utrumque horum pulchre facere posset; pari modo artifices ceteri, quos cultus domesticus desiderat, apprime boni. Neque tamen horum quemquam nisi domi natum domique factum habuit; quod est signum non solum continentiae, sed etiam diligentiae.* (Nepos, *Atticus* 13.3–4)

This passage illumines the multifunctionality of slaves—at least in Atticus' household—as well as the existence of mechanisms for training these slaves in the house itself. It appears that even "footmen" had a certain multifunctionality; the implication of this passage is that when necessary these footmen could be called upon as readers or copyists. Furthermore, Nepos suggests that in-house training was the least expensive means of training and education of slaves. Atticus may well have been exceptional in having so many slaves who were trained to read and copy literary texts, but his in-house private training was not unique. In addition to the information we glean from Plutarch on Crassus and Cato, Cicero identifies himself as the *magister* of Tiro (*Fam.* 16.3.1).[27] The question of what Cicero means by this is somewhat ambiguous; the association of Tiro with the shorthand-writing system called *Notae Tironianae* is still a subject of debate, although it is worth noting that Cicero indicates that he himself could and did write in shorthand (Cicero, *Att.* 13.32).[28] It is most likely that Cicero undertook to give Tiro a broad education and training in skills that were probably designed to meet Cicero's own needs—taking down letters from dictation, making copies of letters, editing texts, keeping records and copies of various letters and literary texts, and so forth.

Again, it might be helpful to consider our only piece of Christian evidence regarding trained shorthand writers, copyists, and calligraphers in light of the information we have for in-house training. As we have already seen, Eusebius recounts the resources that Ambrose placed at the disposal of Origen, both in Alexandria and later in Caesarea: "more than seven shorthand-writers [ταχυγρά-φοι], who relieved each other at fixed times, and as many copyists [βιβλιογράφοι], as well as girls trained for beautiful writing [κόραις ἐπὶ τὸ καλλιγραφεῖν ἠσκημέν-αις]" (*HE* 6.23). This passage implies a similar scenario to what we find in the case of Atticus, for Atticus makes his supply of clerical staff available to Cicero. It may well be that Origen's shorthand writers, copyists, and calligraphers were trained in the in-house system of hiring tutors or perhaps some type of *paedagogium*. Ambrose certainly appears to have had the financial means to offer such training to his slaves; moreover, we may well hypothesize that these slaves, as part of Ambrose's household, were also converts to Christianity. We still have much to learn about the identity of Ambrose himself. Origen says that Ambrose was "honoured and well-received by numerous cities" (*Ex.Mart.* 36), and Jerome claims that Ambrose was a deacon in the church, well-endowed financially, and well-educated (*Vir.Ill.* 56). Trigg, while admitting that we do not know precisely what Ambrose's occupation was, provides the following summary: "Ambrose, a wealthy and cultured Alexandrian. Ambrosius was a householder whose entire family, including his wife Marcella, also became Origen's friends."[29] However we might construe the precise class and status of Ambrose, his resources are particularly sensible given his urban setting, first in Alexandria and later in Caesarea. Indeed, the evidence for *paedagogia*, or in-house educational methods more generally, pertains to urban environments — where the concentration of elites for whom "a degree of written culture was a social necessity" — demanded more slaves trained in clerical skills.[30]

In addition to the evidence for private in-house training and education of slaves, a third channel of clerical education offered a specialized training: apprenticeship.[31] The most useful evidence for apprenticeship of this nature is found in a papyrus letter dated 155 C.E. in which an ex-kosmetes of Oxyrhynchus sends his slave to a shorthand writer for two years:[32]

> Panechotes also called Panare, ex-cometes of Oxyrhynchus, through his friend Gemellus, to Apollonius, writer of shorthand, greeting. I have placed with you my slave Chaerammon to be taught the signs which your son Dionysius knows, for a period of two years dating from the present month Phamenoth of the 18th year of Antoninus Caesar the lord at the salary agreed upon between us, 120 silver drachmae, not including feast-days; of which sum you have received the first instalment amounting to 40 drachmae, and you will receive the second instalment consisting of 40 drachmae when the boy has learnt the whole system [τοῦ παιδὸς ἀνειληφότος τὸ κομεντάρ[ι]ον ὅλον], and the third, the remaining 40 drachmae, you will receive at the end of the period when the boy can write and read faultlessly from all kinds of prose [τοῦ παιδὸς ἐκ παντὸς λόγου πεζοῦ γράφοντος καὶ ἀναγεινώσ[κον]τος ἀμέμπτως]. If you make him perfect within the period, I will not wait for the aforesaid limit; but it is not lawful for me to take the boy away before the end of the period, and he shall remain with you after the expiration of it for as many days or months as he may have done no work. (*P.Oxy.* 724)

A number of features of this apprenticeship contract are particularly interesting. First, it is clear that a slave is being sent to apprentice with a shorthand writer, whose own son is also trained in the skill of shorthand writing; this contract, therefore, supports the notion that both slave and free were apprenticed as means of education and training.[33] Second, it appears that Chaerammon is not only to learn the specific signs involved in writing shorthand but also to be fluent in reading and writing — with the implication perhaps that he will use his knowledge of the shorthand signs to read with better understanding and to write with this system of signs. And third, it is not insignificant that the owner of Chaerammon formerly held a high-ranking position with the gymnasium in Oxyrhynchus;[34] we would be hard pressed to imagine that many who were less wealthy or of lower standing would be able to afford the cost of apprenticeship as well as the length of time it appears this slave would be occupied simply in education and training — up to two years.

The Processes of Learning to Write

Now that we have surveyed the various settings and channels of education and training of scribes, it will be helpful to fill in something of the precise processes involved in learning to write. Literary sources offer various descriptions of the procedure: Quintilian's account suggests that children should have letters cut into a board so that they can trace their outlines with a pen (*Inst.* 1.1.27). After practicing the letters, a child can then proceed to writing out words and copying verses (*Inst.* 1.1.34–35). Seneca offers a somewhat different process: first the child learns to write the letters by having their hand held and guided by the teacher's hand. Then follows the copying of verses that "are placed in front of them" (*Epist.Moral.* 94.51). Interestingly, both Quintilian and Seneca attest to a progression from practicing letter forms to the copying of a literary exemplar.[35] This progression is corroborated by the extant school texts on papyri, ostraca, or wooden tablets from Graeco-Roman Egypt, as Raffaella Cribiore's recent study has demonstrated.[36]

One further method of instruction, which we might imagine was yet less common than the preceeding methods, involves the instruction of children by their parents. Jerome, for example, combines the methods of both Quintilian and Seneca, in his famous letter to Laeta about the education of her daughter: "as soon as she begins to use the style upon the wax, and her hand is still faltering, either guide her soft fingers by laying your hand upon hers, or else have simple copies cut upon a tablet, so that her efforts confined within these limits may keep to the lines traced out for her and not stray outside of these" (*Ep.* 107.4). This passage implies that Laeta herself might play a direct role in teaching her daughter how to read and even write. This may well explain the striking similarities in writing styles that Cribiore finds between the papyri written by a certain Aurelia Charite in the early fourth century and that written by her mother.[37]

School exercises, which may derive from any of the channels of instruction we discussed above, can be classified, but not always with certainty, as products of children's school curriculum or as scribal exercises.[38] Among all of these elementary exercises the range in ability and level of training is wide, although in general the scribal exercises seem to be marked by a greater attention to detail; as Cribiore has shown "practicing individual letters appears to have been a favorite scribal exercise."[39] It is worth noting, however, that the examples she brings of such scribal exercises date from the fourth to eighth centuries, well beyond the time frame with which we are concerned here. One wonders if many of the examples she brings of scribes practicing capital letters may not reflect a later time period when the transmission of literature was properly in the domain of monastic scriptoria and the difference in handwriting between book hands and documentary hands becomes even more distinct.

There are two important points worth highlighting about the school exercises. First, as Cribiore has shown, after children learned their letters, they proceed to copy a text graphically (i.e., without much if any comprehension of the material they were copying).[40] This may well be the implication of Hermas' attempt to find the syllables: he cannot understand (i.e., cannot read with understanding) the text, but he can copy it all the same.

The second point we can derive from these exercises concerns the precise handwriting that students were taught. The traditional differentiation between "book hands" and "documentary hands" has long been a commonplace among papyrologists. According to this classification, a "book hand" is "a handwriting in capitals strictly or roughly bilinear, usually made slowly . . . normally for the writing of books."[41] Turner used the term *bilinear* to describe those hands in which each letter (with the exception of φ and ψ) seems "to have been placed between an upper and a lower line notionally present to the scribe as he wrote, and these 'notional parallels' determined the height and size of the letters."[42] Other definitions of the book hand share essentially the same characteristics as Turner's: according to Roberts, it manifests, "clarity, regularity, and impersonality," aims at beauty and legibility;[43] for Thompson, the literary hand is "that which professional scribes would employ in writing books for the market."[44] Documentary hands, by contrast, have been characterized as "a cursive writing that flowed swiftly and smoothly over the papyrus; individual letters seldom received full articulation, and the scribe's nubbed pen remained in contact with the surface of the papyrus, producing a chain of letters joined together in ligature."[45] Furthermore, much has been made of the differences between literary and documentary papyri in terms of abbreviations: according to the standard view, when scribes copied literary texts they avoided abbreviations (e.g., for numerals or words), while when producing or copying documents they routinely used abbreviations to quicken the writing and simultaneously save space.[46] Although on two extremes of a spectrum a hastily and highly abbreviated document will look entirely different from a literary text copied by a careful and slow strictly bilinear hand, when one begins to look more closely at the range of papyrological remains, it becomes clear that many of our papyri (literary copies and documents alike) fall somewhere along the range between a literary and a documentary hand. As Cribiore points out, "Between [literary and documentary hands] there is an almost infinite range of different levels, and sometimes it is difficult to decide whether a hand belongs to one or the other category."[47] We will discuss further the issue of how the hand that was used was influenced by the function of the text itself in chapter 4; here it will suffice to point out that the frequent overlap in literary and documentary styles points us again toward scribes who were offered a general training geared toward multifunctionality. As we shall see momentarily, it is precisely in the overlap between documentary and literary that we can locate all of our earliest Christian papyri.

Such an overlap is also what we find in the hands of schoolchildren, who seem to have been taught a semicursive writing that aimed in part at legibility as well as regularity.[48] Scribes at more advanced levels worked even more for fluency and regularity. It appears that schoolchildren, and scribes at the earliest levels, were taught a multifunctional basic hand, very close to the hand we find in the private letters.[49] It is only with advanced training that those who were to become professional scribes would learn a cursive writing (that aided speed) and/or the careful strictly bilinear hand that book dealers might wish to exhibit in their commercial copies. Such advanced writing practices may well have been taught by apprenticeship, as the letter regarding Chaerammon's apprenticeship suggests above. We might also consider the more advanced, but still not professional level, scribal exercises that may simply represent scribes learning the trade while on the job.[50] Yet it is worth remembering that such specialization appears to have taken place after the student had at least the ability to write a semicursive, all-purpose hand. Indeed, all the evidence points to a correlation between the levels of accomplishment attained in writing and the ability to traverse between "literary" and "documentary" forms of writing comfortably. The case of the third-century C.E. Timaios' letter to Heroninos, "who worked in the central administrative office of a wealthy estate owner," is particularly illustrative: "Timaios tells Heroninos that he needs to take care of a certain matter in a hurry and to emphasize this, he writes in the margin two verses from the beginning of *Iliad* 2: 'All the other gods and men, lords of chariots, were sleeping the whole night through, but Zeus could not have sweet sleep.' Although Timaios writes the body of his letter in a relatively fast cursive, he employs well-separated, upright, and bilinear letters for the Homeric quotation."[51] Once again we are pointed toward the multifunctionality of scribes.

Conclusions

Before turning to the earliest Christian papyri themselves to see what clues they yield concerning their producers, it may be useful to summarize our discussion so far. The channels of education and training, both for freeborn children and slave-scribes, were multiple: public schools of various types, private in-house training, and apprenticeship for an advanced specialized training. The choice of instructional context was dependent partly upon economic considerations, but even more so on the intended function of the student. The schools appear to have taught elementary levels of reading and writing skills that would prove to be useful even to those students who did not progress to the highest level of the schools or to those who would go on to a specialized scribal training. It is logical to suppose that the large households found it most efficient to hire a tutor of some type to train simultaneously several slaves in clerical skills; furthermore, in this type of private training and education the master had control over the content and form of training and could intervene in the process (as Crassus seems to have done). The supply of shorthand writers, copyists, and calligraphers that Ambrose places at the disposal of Origen are particularly sensible in light of in-house training. Apprenticeship provided a form of technical training for those who would function in a specialized capacity; it is probable, for instance, that the scribal hands at the extreme ends of our documentary and literary spectrum were the product of such a specialized technical training. Finally, scribes who were most accomplished at writing—however they were trained and regardless of whether they were professional or nonprofessional—were able to use their abilities for a wide range of purposes and functions and to alter their handwriting according to the particular task at hand. It is indeed a mistake to think that a simplistic statement—such as "literary scribes wrote in the formal book hand, but government *scribae* wrote in documentary and cursive scripts"—is sufficient to describe the abilities of ancient scribes, particularly given what we know about the precise methods of instruction.[52]

With the discussion of the previous chapters in mind, as well as our more recent survey of the education and training of scribes, we can turn to our earliest Christian papyri to see what clues they might yield regarding the identities of their producers.

A MATERIALIST AND SOCIOHISTORICAL APPROACH TO EARLIEST CHRISTIAN PAPYRI

Christian papyri from the second and third centuries provide our most important— albeit indirect—source for the scribes who copied them, and it goes without saying that they have not lacked for scholarly attention.[53] One of the themes that has run throughout much of the scholarly discussions is that of the apparent unique qualities of early Christian papyri. We shall have opportunity in chapter 4 to investigate the "unique" features that have been most widely discussed— the codex form of these early papyri and the presence of *nomina sacra*—although it is worth remarking here that the argument that both the codex and *nomina sacra* features are particular to Christian papyri relies at least in part upon a circular argument: unquestionably Christian papyri appear to be predominantly in codex form and contain the *nomina sacra*; hence, the codex form and *nomina sacra* are used to identify texts as Christian.[54] For now, I am concerned with the handwriting and use of abbreviations in early Christian papyri—two other features that have been described as "unique" to Christian papyri. Colin Roberts, for example, described the hands as "reformed documentary" in an attempt to account for why these hands show similarities to both documentary hands and literary.[55] Others have variously described the hands of these papyri as "informal uncial," or the scribes as not highly professional or committed to "calligraphic production."[56] Similarly, scholars have pointed to the use of abbreviations in these Christian papyri—a feature not typically found in literary papyri more generally—as a feature of difference and uniqueness.[57]

We do not have to look far, however, to problematize the notion that Christian texts are entirely unique.[58] Striking similarities can be found between the handwriting of individual Christian papyri and literary copies of the classics: for example, the hand of the third-century P^{45} closely resembles that of a third-century copy of Homer's *Iliad* and a copy of Euripides' *Cresphontes*.[59] The use of abbreviations for numbers in early Christian papyri, however, stands in tension with the fact that this feature is not found in most classical papyri, particularly those that are professionally produced. It becomes clear that both the handwriting and use of abbreviations require further investigation, and in what follows I will suggest that these features point us toward the multifunctional scribes who were responsible for copying many classical texts and, more specifically, all of the early Christian texts.

Handwriting and Abbreviations

We would do well to have in mind two different, but related, spectrums: first, the spectrum between literary and documentary styles of writing, and second, the spectrum of variations of skill, expertise, and level of training. While there is some truth to the contrast between a "book hand" and a "documentary hand"—as I summarized them above—there is a tremendous range and overlap between the two styles: there are copies of literature written in "documentary hands"; documents written in "literary hands"; and most of our literary papyri exhibit a broad spectrum of hands on the continuum between a documentary cursive and a literary capital. Furthermore, we might add to the dichotomy, the "chancery hand"—which uses few ligatures, "is clear, legible, and possesses a high degree of calligraphic beauty"—that was often used for writing official decrees.[60] According-ing to Roberts's analysis, second-century Christian texts "employ what is basically a documentary hand" with an effort at literary style.[61] When we limit ourselves to specifically Christian texts and include the Christian papyri from the third century, we may continue to locate them on the spectrum between literary and documentary hands, but they appear toward the literary end of the spectrum. Take, for example, our lengthiest early Christian papyri—P^{45}, P^{46}, P^{47}, P^{66}, P^{75}, P^{72}, the Egerton Papyrus 2, the Michigan papyrus of *The Shepherd*, and *P.Bodmer* V—all of which exhibit features that resemble documentary hands (such as letters produced cursively, or ligatured letters)[62] but are most closely parallel to copies of literature in their legibility and clarity.

The influence of documentary and literary styles is also apparent in the use of abbreviations for numerals in Christian papyri, as I indicated above. Turner and others, of course, have observed that the numeral notation and abbreviations found in documentary papyri are also "found in copies of the sacred scriptures";[63] literary copies by contrast, at least those that were professionally written, almost always write out numbers in full.[64] In our earliest Christian papyri, we find scribes who are accustomed to using abbreviations for numerals, but also seem just as comfortable using the written out form. Even within particular papryi, there is little consistency.[65] A few examples will suffice to illustrate this point. P^{45} normally writes out numbers in full (e.g., Mk 6:39, 43, 44; 8:19, 21; Lk 9:28), but occasionally the scribe uses an abbreviated form (Mk 8:19; Lk 10:17; and perhaps Jn 11:7). P^{47} routinely uses documentary abbreviations for numbers, but can occasionally write out the number in full (e.g., Rev 11:14, 15; 12:4). P^{66} uses abbreviations for numerals on just two occasions (Jn 5:5; 6:70);[66] in every other instance the scribe writes the number out in full (e.g., Jn 1:36, 39; 2:1, 6; 4:35; 6:9; etc). By contrast, the scribe of P^{75} uses abbreviations for numerals frequently. It is particularly instructive to compare the same passage in P^{75} and P^{66} to see how these scribes differ in their use of numeral abbreviations: at John 1:36, for example, P^{75} uses B instead of the δυo found in P^{66}; again at John 2:6, P^{75} writes B η Γ instead of the full form found in P^{66}, δυo η τρις. Other examples could be adduced, as well as scholarly discussion on this issue. For example, regarding P^{64} Peter Head writes: "A further important factor is the use in P^{64} of abbreviated symbols to represent numbers (frag. 3 verso line 2: ιβ for δωδεκα). This is not found in either the Greek literary manuscript tradition or in Jewish manuscripts of the Greek Old Testament (where numbers were written in full), but it is characteristic of early Christian manuscripts from Egypt."[67] These examples illustrate the presence of numeral abbreviations that occur in all of our early Christian papyri, indicating once again the overlap between documentary and literary styles.

That early Christian papyri are influenced by both documentary and literary styles does not make them unique, for copies of classical literature exhibit the same influences.[68] The difference, rather, is a question of degree: stated negatively, while there are no Christian papyri that are free from a dual influence, there are classical papyri that have no similiarities whatsoever to documentary practices.[69] More simply and to the point, all of our early Christian papyri manifest both features that are normally found in documents and those that are usually found in copies of literature. I am here stating somewhat differently what Roberts has already pointed out with respect to the second-century Christian papyri: "Works of secular literature are also written in such hands [i.e., those that manifest a dual influence], but there is not the same preponderance of them."[70] Before drawing conclusions about the evidence of handwriting and abbreviations for the scribes of early Christian papyri, it is worth discussing our second spectrum: the continuum of level of skill, expertise, and training.

Classifying hands simply on the basis of style is admittedly highly problematic. "Beautiful," "elegant," "lovely" — the use of such words to describe ancient hands are unavoidably bound to modern, and individual, notions of aesthetics and style.[71] This is not to say, however, that the ancients were unaware of variations in aesthetic quality or levels of professionalism. Indeed, Diocletian's Edict betrays precisely such an awareness: "To a scribe for best writing (scriptori in scriptura optima), 100 lines, 25 denarii; for second quality writing (sequentis scripturae), 100 lines, 20 denarii; to a notary for writing a petition or legal document (tabellanioni in scriptura libelli bel tabularum), 100 lines, 10 denarii."[72] We might with some certainty be able to link Diocletian's identification of "best writing" to an example such as the Hawara Homer, but most of our literary papyri will prove to be more difficult to classify.[73] The same is true for Christian papyri, with one significant exception: there are no second- and third-century Christian papyri that exhibit the highly calligaphic features of the best literary hands, such as that found in the Hawara Homer, whose strict bilinearity, regularity, and formality suggests a highly trained scribe specializing in the art of copying books. To be sure, we can locate some hands that appear to be well trained and practiced among our early Christian papyri: the hands of P[46] and *P.Bodmer* V (Protevangelium Jacobi), for example, avoid ligatures, approach bilinearity, and maintain regularity—features that seem to indicate practiced and capable scribes. Kenyon considered P[46] second only to the Chester Beatty Numbers and Deuteronomy in terms of style: "The script . . . is far more calligraphic [than P[45]] in character, a rather large, free, and flowing hand with some pretentions as to style and elegance, upright and square in formation, and well spaced out both between the letters and between the lines."[74] Michel Testuz, editor of *P.Bodmer* V described the writing as "magnificent, very dark, vertical and square. . . . It is graphically very stylistic, and the scribe is at home with the preoccupation of making the height of each letter equal to its width as much as it is possible."[75]

On the opposite end of the spectrum, we might locate the inexperienced, awkward, and irregular hand of P[72], a third-century copy of 1 and 2 Peter and Jude that is found, quite interestingly, in the same codex as *P.Bodmer* V. I will devote an extensive discussion to this particular papyrus in chapter 4, for it is a portion of a third-century codex that has much to say about the role of scribes in the transmission of early Christian literature. Here I simply wish to point out that the copyist of P[72], more so than any other copyist of an early Christian text, appears to be an inexperienced copyist of literature, perhaps an inexperienced writer altogether: the writing is irregular with respect to the character of individual letters, the spacing between letters, and the size of letters.[76] We would be hard pressed to see in this particular example the work of a professional scribe; it may well be that we here have an instance of a nonprofessional copyist. Within the two extremes of P[46] or *P.Bodmer* V and P[72], we find the remainder of our earliest Christian papyri, all of which manifest to varying degrees regularity and legibility.[77]

Along both of the somewhat different spectrums I have just described we can locate Christian copies in the middle. This is not to say that the middle space is *unique* to Christian texts, but rather that Christian texts appear to be different in that they are *only* located in the middle range. What significance does this have for our study of the scribes who produced these copies of Christian texts? It seems to me most plausible to conclude from these data that the scribes who copied early Christian literature were multifunctional scribes, who were equipped with general skills in writing but did not have a specific training or extensive experience in copying literary texts. Given our literary evidence for the presence of such scribes as well as the evidence we have for the education and training of such scribes, the fact that Christian papyri (as well as many classical papyri more generally) all exhibit the influences of documentary and literary styles indicates scribes who were either comfortable with and experienced in both styles or trained in more general styles of writing that could be adapted in rather simple ways to different tasks; it seems to me that the latter scenario is more likely since had these scribes had extensive training in literary book hand, their hands would have manifested this training. Since experience, by its very definition, is based upon practice, we might well suppose that the earliest copyists of Christian literature were trained professional scribes, whose multifunctionality may well have been suited best for a private context. We might imagine here the scribes who, like those employed by Cicero and Atticus, worked in homes to provide clerical help. Although we still have much to learn about the handwriting exhibited in the private letters from upper Egypt and these may well shed further light upon private scribes, I do not think it coincidental that our early Christian papyri often exhibit similarities to the hands we find in private letters — hands that strive for legibility, clarity, and occasionally regularity (at least when written by well practiced scribes). Campbell Bonner offered such a connection for the scribe of the Michigan *Shepherd*: he notes that the "scribe's practice was not very regular either in the number of lines allowed for a page or in the number of letters making a line," but also goes on to suggest that "the writer was evidently an accomplished scribe, but it may be that his skill was acquired in professional letter writing rather than in the copying of books."[78]

There is one important exception, however, to this portrait of multifunctional scribes: the scribe of P[72] does not manifest the characteristics of an experienced or highly trained scribe; rather the scribe here appears to be a nonprofessional copyist. As we shall see momentarily, there are also indications that this particular scribe was a Christian, for embedded within the text that this scribe preserves are hints of a specific knowledge of early Christian liturgical "texts."

Harmonizations

We may well wonder if there are indications in our earliest Christian papyri that the scribes had a specific "education" or "training" in Christian literature. Is there, for example, evidence that these copyists were familiar with Christian texts beyond the very text they were copying? A more general question may be posed: to what extent do the copies of early Christian literature provide evidence that the scribes who produced them were themselves Christians? One feature of early Christian papyri that may shed light on the degree to which these scribes were trained and educated, as well as the possibility that they had a specifically Christian education is the presence of harmonizations in these copies.[79] It is commonly asserted that "harmonizations between different texts" are "particularly frequent."[80] In what follows, I will argue precisely the opposite: when we look closely at our *earliest* Christian papyri, we find very few instances of "harmonizations between different texts"—an argument that has the support of historical developments in early Christianity, as well as the advantage of particularly highlighting the few instances where we do find "harmonizations between different written 'texts'." At the outset, however, several definitional and methodological issues deserve consideration.

First, the question of definitions. According to the standard definition, "harmonizations" are deliberate changes to the text that are motivated by a desire to make the passage conform either to a remote parallel passage, to a passage close in context, or to customary usage.[81] Such classifications, however, are not without problems for our period. How indeed should we imagine harmonizations to remote parallels taking place? According to Metzger, "Since monks usually knew by heart extensive portions of the Scriptures . . . the temptation to harmonize discordant parallels or quotations would be strong in proportion to the degree of the copyist's familiarity with other parts of the Bible."[82] More recently, Harry Gamble has offered a similar explanation:

> In addition to the general liability of scribes to error, early Christian texts held some particular inducements, especially to intentional changes. For example, the often closely parallel accounts among the Gospels led many a scribe to harmonize the text of one with the text of another. Inexact quotations of Jewish scripture in Christian texts were often conformed to the Septuagint.[83]

Such an explanation of harmonistic tendencies presents several problems if we apply it to the earliest period of text transmission, apart from the obvious fact that "monks" were not responsible for the transmission of texts during the second and third centuries.[84] We do have evidence for Christians, such as Origen, Didymus, and Antony, who memorized "extensive portions" of scripture;[85] but we would do well to ask in the earliest period of text transmission what would have constituted "Scripture." This comes to the heart of the problem of restricting remote harmonizations to biblical passages. There is no reason to suppose that a scribe who harmonizes a text only does so by parallels to other biblical texts, for indeed the whole question of what constitutes "biblical" in the second and even third centuries remains open. Canonization was in fact a process of long duration and intense debate; the list of what texts a scribe may have known well or even have memorized was contingent upon geographic location, doctrinal and perhaps personal predilections, and the availability of texts.[86] Finally, the assumption that a scribe would have at hand several copies of different texts and be able to compare similar passages, or even collate manuscripts, is an assumption based in part on evidence from a later period and in part on exceptional cases such as Tatian.[87] A restricted definition of "harmonizations" limits our understanding of the identities and roles of the scribes who copied Christian texts; in the discussion that follows, I have expanded the definition of "harmonizations" to include not only parallels to written texts but also parallels to oral "texts."[88]

Serious methodological issues compound the problems of definitions. Most importantly, if we want to determine where individual scribes of individual papyri harmonized their text in the process of copying, we must distinguish between a scribe *creating* a new reading and a scribe simply *copying* a reading that was already in his or her exemplar. Fortunately, there are ways to determine with some degree of confidence when an individual scribe *creates* a reading, and for our purposes of understanding the identities of the copyists of early Christian literature, this distinction will be particularly crucial. In 1965 Colwell presented a study of the scribal tendencies of three early papyri as an initial step toward defining a method for assessing scribal habits.[89] Using Tischendorf's eighth edition[90] as the collating *apparatus criticus*, Colwell noted every "singular reading" contained in these papyri. For Colwell, a singular reading was "a reading which has no Greek support in the critical apparatus of Tischendorf's 8th Edition."[91] His preliminary study of P^{45}, P^{66}, and P^{75} provided just enough information to demonstrate the fruitful results of such a study, particularly for the discipline of New Testament textual criticism.[92] Colwell's results roused the interest of several other text critics who have now demonstrated both the value of Colwell's initial work and the exciting possibilities for understanding the history of the New Testament through research on scribes and their texts.[93] What Colwell and others used for furthering the quest for the original text of the New Testament also proves to be useful for our own investigation of the scribes who preserved our earliest copies of Christian texts.

Equipped with Colwell's methods, we can return to harmonizations. Given the fluidity of "canon" during the second and third centuries, as well as the problems with superimposing later monastic developments on an earlier period, it should not be surprising that we find very few examples of "harmonizations to remote [i.e., biblical] parallels" in our earliest Christian papyri. The *infrequency* of the practice has been demonstrated by both Colwell and Royse.[94] Royse's more recent and extensive indentification of remote harmonizations in the six extensive third-century New Testament papyri — P^{45}, P^{46}, P^{47}, P^{66}, P^{72}, and P^{75} — highlights precisely the infrequency of the practice. A review of his identifications shows that even the few instances he finds of remote harmonization are often questionable. For example, Royse finds the following instances of remote harmonization in P^{46}: "The addition at He 7:2a agrees with Gn 14:20 LXX, and the addition at He 5:10 agrees with Ps 110:4 LXX (as cited in He 5:6). The plural θυσιας at He 13:15 agrees with the plural found at He 9:9, 10:1, and 10:11. At 1 Cor 11:24a the transposition agrees with the parallels at Mt 26:26, Mk 14:22, and Lk 22:19 in having τουτο εστιν. The substitution at 1 Cor 16:15 gives απαρχη της ασιας, thus agreeing with Ro 16:5."[95] However, we might questions these identifications. Why should we see the addition of αυτω at Hebrews 7:2a as a harmonization to Genesis 14:20? Could the simple addition of a dative pronoun perhaps better be explained as a scribal idiosyncrasy? If this scribe indeed wished to harmonize this passage to the "parallel" in Genesis 14:20, why did he or she not change the verb (εμερισεν to εδωκεν) as well? The second of Royse's "remote harmonizations" — the addition of συ ει at Hebrews 5:10 — seems to be far better explained by the immediate context: the scribe has just copied the phrase συ ει ιερευς (a quotation from Ps 110:4) four verses prior. Why assume this is going back to Psalms rather than the immediate, or very close, context, particularly when we do have evidence of the tendency among our earliest scribes to harmonize to the context? Similarly, we could question his identification of four remote harmonizations in P[66]: (1) At John 6:69 the scribe of P[66] has substituted ο Χς ο αγιος του θυ for the simpler ο αγιος του θεου, and Royse sees this as a harmonization to John 11:27 and Matthew 16:16; (2) at John 13:1a P[66] reads ηκει instead of ηλθεν, which Royse sees as a harmonization to John 2:4 (which reads ουπω ηκει η ωρα μου); (3) at 10:16 the scribe of P[66] substitutes συναγαγειν for αγαγειν and Royse suggests that this "may have come about because of the συναγομενος συναχθη-σεται of the parallel in Mic 2:12 LXX, or was perhaps occasioned by συναγαγη in the similar passage at Jn 11:52";[96] and (4) in John 18:38c the transposition ευ[ρισκ]ω αι[τι]αν εν αυτω for ευρισκω εν αυτω αιτιαν, Royse suggests may be harmonization to Luke 23:4.[97] I fail to see why the addition at John 6:69 should be explained as a harmonization to Matthew 16:16 (if the scribe wanted to harmonize why not include "living"?). It is true that the scribe has created a parallel to a later passage in John, but this may suggest no more than that the scribe was familiar with the whole of his text. Royse's second harmonization classified as "remote parallel" seems to be better explained by the fact that the scribe has simply recalled something from earlier in the text he is copying. The third example suggests again that the scribe is familiar with the whole of the Gospel of John and so can import something from later. Royse found at most five instances of harmonizations to remote parallels — Luke 3:22 (to Mt 3:16 in ‫א‬); Luke 8:21 (to Mt 12:48); Luke 12:31 (to Mt 6:33 ‫א‬); John 6:5a (to Mt 14:15 and Mk 6:36); and John 6:5b (to Mt 14:15 and Mk 6:36) — although he admitted that two of these are doubtful. In fact, if we look at these instances closely, each of them can be called into question. At Luke 3:22 and 12:31, the scribe appears to have a reading that *coincidentally* matches that found in the parallel texts in the MS ‫א‬ (the first involves the rather simple addition of the definite article before πνευμα and the second consists of an omission of the possessive αυτου. At Luke 8:21 we should question whether P75's substitution of the singular αυτον for αυτους indeed can be called a remote harmonization. It is true that the parallel text at Matthew 12:48 makes it quite explicit that Jesus answers one person, but the Lukan passage uses a passive form of the verb (and therefore leaves ambiguous the identity of the messenger[s]). Finally, it should be noted that the last two "remote harmonizations" are found in a fragmentary portion of P[75]. Royse has reconstructed the passage in such a way that it conforms to parallel passages, though it is not clear to me (from the facsimile) that this is accurate. V. Martin and R. Kasser, in fact, do not offer this reconstruction.[98] Indeed, I would argue that in P^{46}, P^{45}, P^{66}, and P^{75} we find almost no clear and certain instances of remote harmonization.

In P^{45}, a copy of the Gospels and the book of Acts, I would agree with many of Royse's indentifications of remote harmonization. According to Royse, harmonizations to parallel passages occur a total of eleven times in this papyrus: Matthew 20:31a (to Mk 10:48 = Lk 18:39); Mark 8:10 (to Mt 15:39); Mark 8: 12a (to 1 Cor 1:22); Luke 9:30 (to Mt 17:3 and Mk 9:4); Luke 10:11a (to Mt 10:14 and Lk 9:5); Luke 11:12 (to Mt 7:9); Luke 12:7b (to Mt 10:30); Luke 12: 24a (conflation of Mt 6:26); Luke 12:24b (to Mt 6:26); Luke 12:51 (to Mt 10: 34); and Luke 13:30 (to Mt 19:30 and Mk 10:31).[99] For the most part, Royse's classificiation of these singular readings as harmonizations is compelling. It is worth noting, however, that the first two of these are found in fragmentary portions of P^{45}; the change found in Luke 11:12 replaces a hapax legomenon (ᾠόν) with a word that appears frequently in the texts this scribe is copying (ἄρτον);[100] and the harmonizations in Luke 12:24a and 12:24b (which Royse counts as separate harmonizations) should probably be classified as one. If we take these points into account, we are left with just seven apparent harmonizations to other early Christian texts. Yet even here the question of definitions is of utmost importance, for with the exception of a possible harmonization to 1 Corinthians 1:22 at Mark 8:12a, all of the parallels are found within the very texts that the scribe is in the process of copying. This may well only suggest that the scribe of P^{45} is familiar with the texts he/she is in the process of copying, as well as the possibility that this scribe refers back and forth between texts in the same codex. But in what sense are these truly "remote"?

If the "remoteness" of the harmonizations in P^{45} can be called into question, however, there remains one papyrus whose remote harmonizations deserve careful consideration. Indeed, demonstrating that scribes harmonized their texts *infrequently* during the second and third centuries has the paradoxical advantage of highlighting the occasions when they do harmonize their texts. In proportion to the quantity of text in P^{72}, the frequency of harmonization is rather high. Royse found six instances of harmonization to remote parallels. What is particularly striking in this copy is the number of harmonizations that appear to be influenced by "liturgical" usage of "texts." Here we would do well to think of "texts" as oral ones, heard in the context of early Christian services.[101] For example, at Jude 24a the scribe of P^{72} replaces φυλάξαι with the στηρίξαι that appears in the "doxology" of Romans 16:25. The textual problems of the Roman "doxology" (Rom 16:25–27) are well-known and may well indicate the use of this passage in liturgical contexts; in P^{47} the passage occurs at the end of chapter 15, in other witnesses we find it at the end of chapter 14, and in other witnesses it appears both at the end of chapter 14 and chapter 16.[102] Again at Jude 25b, the scribe appears to be influenced by the text of Revelation 5:13 when adding αὐτῷ δόξα κράτος τιμή, even though the word order is slightly different. Also interesting is the addition that P^{72}'s scribe makes at 2 Peter 1:20: instead of προφητεία γραφῆς (prophecy of scripture) the scribe here writes προφητια [προφητεια] και γραφη.

Royse attributes this to the influence of 2 Timothy 3:16 (which reads πᾶσα γραφή); this suggestion, however, seems rather tenuous. Is it not more likely that the apparent distinction that this scribe has in mind—prophets and scripture—came from both literary and liturgical customs of the second and third centuries?[103] We begin to see just a glimmer of the possibility that this scribe was a member of a Christian community, whose participation in church services is evident in the text. We find support for this in a number of harmonizations that Royse—mistakenly in my opinion—identifies as harmonizations to "general usage." For example, at 1 Peter 3:7c the scribe of P[72] replaces the simple ζωῆς with ζοης εωνιου (ζωῆς αἰωνίου). Not only is the latter extensively attested, we know that it was embedded within liturgical hymns and prayers used by the early church.[104] For example, in the *Didache* we find that the prayer that is to be said after the Eucharist includes the following phrase: καὶ ζωὴν αἰώνιον διὰ τοῦ παιδός σου ("and life everlasting through your son") (10:3). Similarly, at Jude 24 the scribe replaces κατενωπιον (which only appears here, at Eph 1:4, and Col 1:22) with απεναντι (which appears here and four other times). Although Royse accounts for this substitution as a harmonizing to general usage, this seems somewhat problematic because απεναντι only occurs two more times in the New Testament than κατενωπιον. It is indeed the case that if we look more broadly at the texts early Christians were using (especially the LXX), we find απεναντι occurring with far more frequency. It seems more likely to me, however, to suppose that since we have already found a trend in the P[72] to harmonize according to possible liturgical or oral practices, this is another case of such an alteration, for Jude 24 contains a "benediction."

We have devoted an extensive discussion to harmonizations in the earliest Christian papyri because they have often been used to argue that scribes frequently harmonized their texts; moreover, they can provide a clue to the specific education of these scribes when "education" is construed rather broadly. The fact that we find so few harmonizations to remote parallels in our earliest six extensive papyri of New Testament texts should not be pressed too far, since abundant evidence for harmonistic tendencies in the same period can be found elsewhere, for example, the work of Tatian, Justin, and the Gospel of the Ebionites. Indeed, harmonistic tendencies are evidenced in such early Christian texts as well as in early versions of the New Testament.[105] The *infrequency* with which these particular scribes harmonized their texts may well not offer us concrete evidence for their knowledge of early Christian texts, but it does have the distinct advantage of emphasizing the cases where remote harmonizations are evident. The scribe of P[72], in particular, appears to have knowledge of early Christian liturgical practices and harmonizes the text according to such remote "texts" (here, an oral "text") with some degree of fluency and frequency. The scribe's handwriting, moreover, leads us to conclude that we have an instance of a private, nonprofessional, Christian who undertook to copy certain Christian texts.

Other Features

It may well seem that we could turn to other features to investigate further the education and training of the scribes who produced our early Christian papyri. Indeed, we might observe "errors" that these scribes produced: itacistic readings, orthographic mistakes, grammatical blunders, or omissions and additions due to eye skips. Turner, for example, suggested that itacisms could be used to determine the education of the scribe; Youtie, however, argued that itacisms should properly be considered phonetic spelling variations based on pronunciation and not on the abilities of the scribe.[106] We still know far too little about pronunciations in various ancient locales to utilize itacisms as evidence for the education and training of scribes. Perhaps we could examine the ways in which our scribes attempted to smooth out their texts, eliminate unnecessary words, and "correct" the grammar.[107] What we find, however, is that the scribes who copied early Christian literature produce to varying degrees all of the "errors" to which scribes more generally were susceptible. Exhaustion, lack of concentration, eye skips — such were the common causes of "errors." These features may well indicate something of a scribe's care, or perhaps occasionally a scribe's experience, but they offer little to indicate the level of education and training among these scribes; we stand to learn far more from the features of handwriting, abbreviations, and harmonizations.

Any scholarly endeavor necessarily involves some disappointment: we may suppose, expect, or hope to find certain results in the course of research. Since highlighting what we do not find in the course of our research is often helpful, by way of concluding this chapter, I wish to discuss briefly a pattern that I had hoped would emerge from the data of Christian papyri. In the early stages of my research, I looked closely for patterns of characteristics in the early Christian papyri; in particular, I was interested in whether there was a correlation between handwriting (and abbreviations), harmonizations, and "errors." I wondered whether more professional and calligraphic hands might exhibit fewer remote harmonizations and more nonsensical readings (with the implication that the scribe was highly professional, and perhaps hired by a Christian to copy, but not a Christian and therefore uninterested in the text itself and unaware of other early Christian texts); on the other hand, I thought I might find unprofessional hands that produced more remote harmonizations and fewer errors (here with the implication that a private Christian who was not a professional scribe copied the text, fully cognizant of other Christian texts and equipped with a desire to produce a good "error-free" copy).[108] The first pattern did not emerge with any consistency. The latter pattern emerged quite clearly, but only in one manuscript: P^{72}. In this text, we seem to have the work of a nonprofessional Christian who has a particular investment in the text: an inexperienced hand, several harmonizations that appear to be influenced by Christian liturgy, and "errors" that are due largely to the influence of Coptic.[109]

The fact that consistent patterns do not emerge, however, serves to suggest once again the tremendous range in the abilities, training, education, and experience of the scribes who copied these texts. As we have seen in this chapter, scribes were trained through a variety of channels and their educational levels varied quite widely. Various channels of education can be gleaned from early Christian literary sources regarding the training and educational levels of scribes: Hermas' account suggests he cannot read with comprehension but is able to copy graphically; the staff of writers that Ambrose placed at the disposal of Origen seem far more specialized and highly trained. Features of literary papyri manifest similarly a range of experience and ability. What is striking about our earliest Christian papyri is that they all exhibit the influences of literary and documentary styles, and they all seem to be located in the middle of the spectrum of experience and level of skill. The scribes who produced these copies fit well into the portrait of multifunctional scribes — both professional and nonprofessional — whose education entailed learning how to write a semicursive style. With the exception of P^{72}, we did not find abundant evidence that the scribes who copied early Christian literature had extensive knowledge of other Christian texts; this is not to say, of course, that they did not know of other texts, but that if they did, we do not have evidence for this knowledge in their copies. We will return to our exceptional P^{72} again in chapter 4, for we have only begun to investigate its clues. An ancient author may well have lambasted it as "poorly written" or "full of mistakes," but for our purposes it illustrates the possibility that nonprofessional Christian scribes were responsible for some of our earliest copies of Christian literature.

"MAKE AND SEND ME COPIES"

Private Scribal Networks and the Transmission of
Early Christian Literature

Make and send me copies of books 6 and 7 of Hypsicrates' *Characters in Comedy*, for Harpocration says that they are among Polion's books. But it is likely that others, too, have them. He also has prose epitomes of Thersagoras' work on the myths of tragedy.

    — *P.Oxy.* 2192

Please send me Brutus' *Epitome of the Annals of Caelius*, and get Panaetius' *On Foresight* from Philoxenus.

    — Cicero, *Att.* 13.8

We send you, just as you requested, the letters of Ignatius, which were sent to us by him, and others, which we had with us. These are attached to this letter, and you will be able to benefit greatly from them.

    — Polycarp, *Phil.* 13.2

To my dearest lady sister in the Lord, greating. Lend the Ezra, since I lent you the little Genesis. Farewell from us in God.

    — *P.Oxy.* 4365

That early Christian texts were composed, reproduced, and disseminated during the second and third centuries cannot be disputed. Furthermore, the fact that soon after *The Shepherd* of Hermas was written, apparently in Rome, we find papyrus copies of the text in upper Egypt, quotations in Clement of Alexandria and Irenaeus of Lyon, and some forty years later a mention in the Muratorian Canon testifies to the widespread circulation of at least some early Christian texts.[1] Early Christian texts indeed betray an active exchange of literature — letters, Gospels, accounts of martyrdoms, and so forth — between churches and between individuals, and we do not need to look far to find out precisely how these texts made their way from one church to another:

Christian letters are replete with references to friends or associates who served as couriers (Rom 16:1; 1 Cor 16:10; Eph 6:21; Col 4:7; 1 Pet 5:12; 1 Clem 65.1; Ign, *Phil* 11.2 and *Smyr* 12.1).[2] It appears that such exchanges of texts began with a simple request: "make and send us copies of the letters of Ignatius" the church at Philippi must have requested of Polycarp. Similarly, the fourth-century writer who asks for "the Ezra" offers us a glimpse into the processes of text circulation.[3] Such requests were the impetus behind the copying of classical literature more generally, as the requests of our anonymous letter writers in upper Egypt and Cicero illumine. Classical and Christian literature alike appear to have circulated by the agency of social networks.

Yet while we can be confident that early Christian texts were reproduced and disseminated, we know little about the more precise circumstances, modes, and contexts of their transmission. Were there, for example, centralized efforts to orchestrate the production of multiple copies of texts? If so, where were multiple copies produced? Was a degree of control maintained over the production of copies of Christian texts? If so, to what extent and by whom was it enforced? Or was early Christian literature transmitted along more private, individual, local, and perhaps even random channels? To what extent indeed was the transmission of early Christian literature dependent upon relationships and communications between churches and individuals? And what role did scribes play in the transmission of early Christian literature? Could scribes select the texts they wished to copy? Or were they simply assigned a text, or hired to copy a text, by some higher level authority in a church? Did scribes communicate among themselves about the copying of early Christian literature? To what extent did scribes operate from within a social network that was different from the networks between churches and individuals? These questions drive the discussion in this chapter, which marks a distinct shift in our exploration of the scribes who copied Christian literature during the second and third centuries.

My concern in this chapter is to trace the channels by which early Christian literature was transmitted and disseminated. I shall be less interested in the scribes themselves than in the relationships between scribes, the intersection between the scribes as producers and the readers/hearers as users, and the social networks behind the transmission of early Christian literature. The argument of this chapter is that social networks among early Christians provided the framework by which Christian literature was transcribed, transmitted, and disseminated. More precisely, I argue that the scribes who copied early Christian literature did so from within private scribal networks.

Behind these arguments lie scholarly debates over the nature of early Christian text transmission, and it may be worth outlining the contours of such debates at the outset. Discussions over the transmission of early Christian literature during the second and third centuries, as we shall see throughout this chapter, have generally proceeded along a fairly strict dichotomy between arguments for central-ized efforts to produce Christian literature in the controlled environment of a "scriptorium" and arguments in favor of the private, fluid, and local channels of individualized production of early Christian literature. Interwoven with this dichotomy is a further contrast between the actual modes of transcription: in a scriptorium, the theory goes, scribes would usually copy by dictation, while in a private setting, scribes would produce a copy from a visual exemplar.[4] In its most widely used context (the monasteries of the Middle Ages) the term "scriptorium" denoted the "writing room" where multiple scribes copied literary — biblical, sacred, and secular — texts. David Diringer's definition is representative of standard understandings of "scripture": "In the most important abbeys and monasteries a 'writing room' or *scriptorium* was assigned to the scribes, who were constantly employed in transcribing, not only service-books for the choir and the church, but also books for the library and the monastery school, and even lay books."[5] Medieval monastic scripture per se, found possibly as early as the fifth-century monasteries under the influence of Rufinus, operated according to a set of rules and guidelines, which included conventions of script, punctuation, and abbreviations, and provided careful monitoring and correcting of the work of scribes.[6] Some scholars have, as we shall see, argued for the existence of such Christian scripture already in the second and third centuries, and they have based their arguments in large part upon features from our earliest Christian papyri. It is these features that will occupy our attention in the second portion of this chapter. Here I wish simply to point out that the debate between the existence of early Christian scripture and individualized modes of text transmission hinges upon the interpretation of our evidence; furthermore, the controversy has serious implications for our understanding of the degree to which early Christian texts were controlled in the earliest period of their circulation. Such implications will be the subject of the next chapter. For now, we turn more closely to the nature of Christian text transmission during the second and third centuries.

THE PRIMACY OF INDIVIDUAL AND PRIVATE CHANNELS OF TEXT TRANSMISSION

It began with a simple request. The church at Philomelium, a town not far from Antioch in Pisidia, asked the church at Smyrna to send a written account of the events surrounding the martyrdom of Polycarp, the bishop of Smyrna in the middle of the second century.[7] The Smyrneans did not waste time in preparing the account: Marcianus (ὁ ἀδελφός) composed the account, and Evarestus (ὁ γράψας) did the actual writing (*Mart.Poly.* 20.1–2).[8] As scribe, Evarestus's function may well be best understood as similar to that of Tertius, the writer of Paul's letter to the Romans: "I Tertius, the writer of this letter, greet you in the Lord" (ἀσπάζομαι ὑμᾶς ἐγὼ Τέρτιος ὁ γράψας τὴν ἐπιστολὴν ἐν κυρίῳ) (Rom 16:22). Likewise, at the conclusion of Polycarp's letter to the Philippians, extant only in Latin, we find acknowledgment of the scribe: "I have written to you through Crescens, whom I commended to you when I was present with you and now commend again" (Haec vobis scripsi per Crescentem, quem in praesenti commendavi vobis et nunc commando) (*Phil.* 14.1). Returning to our story, the

Smyrneans dispatched the text relating Polycarp's martyrdom to the church at Philomelium with the following instructions: "when you have heard these things, send the letter to the brethren further on, so that they also may glorify the Lord, who takes his chosen ones from his own servants" (μαθόντες οὖν ταῦτα καὶ τοῖς ἐπέκεινα ἀδελφοῖς τὴν ἐπιστολὴν διαπέμψασθε, ἵνα καὶ ἐκεῖνοι δοξάζωσιν τὸν κύριον τὸν ἐκλογὰς ποιοῦντα ἀπὸ τῶν ἰδίων δούλων) (*Mart.Poly.* 20.1). We do not know precisely how or when the Philomelians passed on the text for we lose track of its journey for some time; when we pick up the traces of its movements later on, however, we find that the church at Philomelium must have complied with the request. As we shall see, copies of this text soon circulated quite widely. The initial stage of writing is strikingly a group effort: a circle of readers and writers at Smyrna prepare a written text and send it to the Philomelians, who in turn pass it on to other "brethren."

We can trace the life of this text via an even more detailed route, which begins with a relationship — apparently a teacher-student relationship — between Polycarp and Irenaeus (μαθητοῦ τοῦ Πολυκάρπου). When Irenaeus was just a boy in Smyrna, he used to go to Polycarp's house and listen to him speak. Later, in Irenaeus' letter to Florinus quoted by Eusebius, Irenaeus recalls how "the blessed Polycarp sat and disputed, how he came in and went out, the character of his life, the appearance of his body, the discourses he made to the people, how he reported his intercourse with John and with the others who had seen the Lord, how he remembered their words, and what were the things concerning the Lord which he had heard from them" (ὁ μακάριος Πολύκαρπος, καὶ τὸν προόδους αὐτοῦ καὶ τὰς εἰσόδους καὶ τὸν χαρακτῆρα τοῦ βίου καὶ τὴν τοῦ σώματος ἰδέαν καὶ τὰς διαλέξεις ἃς ἐποιεῖτο πρὸς τὸ πλῆθος, καὶ τὴν μετὰ Ἰωάννου συναναστροφὴν ὡς ἀπήγγελλεν καὶ τὴν μετὰ τῶν λοιπῶν τῶν ἑορακότων τὸν κύριον, καὶ ὡς ἀπεμνημόνευεν τοὺς λόγους αὐτῶν, καὶ περὶ τοῦ κυρίου τίνα ἢ ἃ παρ' ἐκείνων ἀκηκόει) (*HE* 5.20).[9] Irenaeus "listened eagerly" to these things, and recorded them not in writing, but in his heart. As disciples were prone to do, however, Irenaeus no doubt did collect, perhaps later in his life, records related to his first teacher, Polycarp,[10] for we find the following passage at the conclusion of the *Martyrdom of Polycarp*:

> These things Gaius copied from [the writings of] Irenaeus, the student of Polycarp, and he [i.e., Gaius] also had lived with Irenaeus. And I, Socrates, copied [it] in Corinth from the copies of Gaius. Grace be with you all. And again I, Pionius, wrote from what had formerly been written, after searching for it, according to a revelation [i.e., vision] of the blessed Polycarp that appeared to me . . . and I gathered it together when they had already been worn out with age.
>
> ταῦτα μετεγράψατο μὲν Γάϊος ἐκ τῶν Εἰρηναίου, μαθητοῦ τοῦ Πολυκάρπου, ὃς καὶ συνεπολιτεύσατο τῷ Εἰρηναίῳ. ἐγὼ δὲ Σωκράτης ἐν Κορίνθῳ ἐκ τῶν Γαΐου ἀντιγράφων ἔγραψα. ἡ χάρις μετὰ πάντ-ων. Ἐγὼ δὲ πάλιν Πιόνιος ἐκ τοῦ προγεγραμμένου ἔγραψα ἀναζητῆσας

αυτά, κατὰ ἀποκάλυψιν φανερώσαντός μοι τοῦ μακαρίου Πολυκάρπου . . .
συναγαγὼν αὐτὰ ἤδη σχεδὸν ἐκ τοῦ χρόνου κεκμηκότα. (Mart.Poly.
22.2–4)

The authenticity and date of this colophon to the *Martyrdom of Polycarp* have been
subject to extensive debate.[11] I will not rehearse those debates here because what
interests me is not whether the precise information it preserves is historically
accurate nor whether it should be dated to no earlier than the fourth century;
rather, what interests me is that it illustrates an active scribal network, probably
over a period of time. A relationship between Irenaeus and Polycarp began the
network. Subsequently, an apparently close relationship (given the detail of the
colophon that they lived together) between Irenaeus and Gaius, acting as scribe
or copyist, leads to further copies; an implied relationship—though nothing
suggests that it was more than an impersonal connection—between Gaius and
Socrates, yet another scribe, results in more copies; and finally, Pionius, another
scribe, apparently obtained a copy from Socrates from which he then made his
copy. The connection between Pionius and Socrates is left ambigous in the
quotation above, but appears more explicitly in the thirteenth-century Moscow
manuscript of the *Martyrdom of Polycarp*, which concludes: "And again I, Pionius,
wrote from the copies of Isocrates [Socrates]" (ἐγὼ δὲ πάλιν Πιόνιος ἐκ τῶν
Ἰσοκράτης ἀντιγράφων ἔγραψα). We appear to have a scribal network—a web,
if you will—that hinges first upon Irenaeus but subsequently upon relationships
between scribes. Such a network is remarkably similar to the circle of readers in
upper Egypt who correspond about obtaining copies of books; here, however,
we are drawn into the role of scribes beyond simply copying: their relationships
(or links or connections) were integral to the reproduction and circulation of
early Christian literature.[12]

Such circles of acquaintances, friends, and companions who participated in
the dissemination of early Christian literature confirms and correlates well with
what we know more generally about text transmission in the Graeco-Roman
world. We may recall our discussion from chapter 1 regarding contexts and modes
of book transmission. Although by the second century C.E. libraries and bookshops
had emerged as settings in which literary texts were reproduced and from which
one could either consult or procure a copy, private settings remained the primary
mode of circulation.[13] If one wished to acquire a copy of a text, the most valuable
resource was a circle of literate friends: Cicero could borrow books from Atticus,
Philoxenus, or his brother Quintus (*Att.* 2.3; 8.11; 13.8; 13.31);[14] Terentius Iunior
could turn to Pliny for books (*Ep.* 8.15.1); and our network of readers in upper
Egypt provides further examples of solicitation of copies from friends (*P.Oxy.*
2192).[15] Though beyond the time frame, we might also recall Jerome's correspondence, which illuminates well a circle of readers/friends who loaned each other
texts even in the late fourth and early fifth centuries. In the center of that circle,
we find Marcella, who is perhaps the most prominent book owner and book
lender throughout Jerome's letters (e.g., *Ep.* 47, 3; *Ep.* 49, 4). In each of these

situations, copies of literature appear to have been produced in direct response to a reader's request for a copy of a book. By and large, copies were made individually and as needed.[16] This point is worth emphasizing, for throughout this chapter we are concerned not only with the circumstances surrounding the reproduction of texts but also with the mechanics involved in doing so.

Our literary evidence is quite uniform in depicting the prominence of private channels of transmission. This has not prevented some scholars, however, from invoking medieval scriptoria in their discussions of the ancient circumstances of text transmission. T. C. Skeat, for instance, referred to "the mass-production scriptoria of the big publishers of the ancient world, such as Atticus."[17] It is quite true that Cicero's letters betray several copyists at work for Atticus who appear on some occasions to have produced multiple copies of Cicero's works (e.g., *Att.* 5.6a; 12.40; 13.23); in addition, Cicero's letters indicate that Atticus had "library copyists" (*librarioli*) sufficient to spare.[18] Cicero's letters, however, offer nothing even approaching "mass-production," and while we might *infer* that there was a "scriptorium" (literally, a writing room) where several scribes worked simultaneously, we have no evidence for a scriptorium per se. Cicero, like most authors in the ancient world, produced several copies not because he wished to "publish" them in the modern sense of the word (i.e., make them widely available for purchase to people *with whom he had no contact*), but rather because he may have wished for copies for his own libraries or for copies to be sent to friends and acquaintances. As William Harris puts it, "the primary way of distributing books was not in any case by means of a trade of any kind, but through gifts and loans among friends."[19]

It has similarly been assumed by some scholars that large centers of intellectual activity — such as Alexandria and Pergamum, which had the largest libraries in antiquity — probably had scriptoria. Diringer, for example, claims that "the libraries of Alexandria, Pergamum, and so on, probably had *scriptoria* similar to those of the medieval monasteries."[20] Yet again, we are faced with the problem of evidence, for there is nothing to suggest that these libraries had specific writing rooms, nor is there secure evidence that the work of multiple scribes who produced copies was overseen, controlled, and carefully corrected. Interestingly enough, serious attempts have been made to identify one of the rooms at Qumran as a "scriptorium." Reasons for this have included the oblong shape of the room, reconstructions of what appear to have been long tables or benches, the discovery of three inkwells, and, of course, the numerous scrolls found in caves nearby.[21] None of these arguments is unproblematic, and given the lack of any comparable archaeological finds, it seems unwise to impose medieval monastic practices on first-century Palestine.[22] Even if we cannot identify a room as a "scriptorium" at Qumran, however, it does appear that there were scribes (possibly at Qumran) who produced the copies of biblical texts and "sectarian" literature found among the Dead Sea Scrolls; when we turn shortly to our early Christian context, we will need to ask, then, where and when do we find a parallel to Qumran among Christians.

Our literary evidence points to the prominence of private circulation of classical texts, and archaeological evidence for this period fails to provide conclusive evidence for "scriptoria" per se. The reproduction of a particular text almost invariably began with a simple request for a copy—a request that may have been sent to a friend, an acquaintance, or the author himself.[23] But what about papyrological evidence? Can, and do, our literary papyri offer support for the private transmission of literature? Or do literary papyri provide some evidence for centralized and controlled "scriptoria" of some kind? To be sure, as mentioned in chapter 3, certain features in our literary papyri have been used to indicate something of the context—commercial bookstore, library, or private—in which and for which particular extant papyrus copies were made, but little progress has been made on this front.[24] We still are unable to link with certainty extant papyri to geographic locations, to draw up profiles of regional scribal practices, or to associate papyri with any supposed "scriptorium," although this has not prevented efforts in this direction. Nowhere indeed has papyrological evidence been used more problematically to argue for the existence of scriptoria than in studies of our earliest Christian papyri.

THE MYTH OF CHRISTIAN SCRIPTORIA IN THE SECOND AND THIRD CENTURIES

Despite literary evidence for the private reproduction, transmission, and circulation of both classical and Christian literature, some scholars have been surprisingly unwilling to relinquish the notion of Christian scriptoria during the second and third centuries. To be sure, most would probably agree with Metzger's summary:

> In the earlier ages of the Church, Biblical manuscripts were produced by individual Christians who wished to provide for themselves or for local congregations copies of one or more books of the New Testament. . . . When, however, in the fourth century Christianity received official sanction from the State, it became more usual for commercial book manufacturers, or scriptoria, to produce copies of the books of the New Testament.[25]

Yet while scholars might agree in theory with Metzger's general assessment of the transmission of early Christian literature, in practice arguments for second- or third-century Christian scriptoria continue to be made. As we shall see, the rather emphatic claims of G. Zuntz are still influential: "The conclusion is almost inescapable that already in the latter half of the second century the Alexandrian bishopric possessed a scriptorium, which by its output set the standard for the Alexandrian type of Biblical manuscripts."[26] These arguments have almost invariably been based upon various features of the earliest Christian papyri. Given that our evidence points quite uniformly to the norm of private copying and transmission of literature, it is worth emphasizing at the outset that such arguments *in favor* of scriptoria—or similar carefully controlled and orchestrated environments for the reproduction of texts—bear the burden of proof. However well we may understand the temptation among scholars of early Christianity in particular to draw parallels with later monastic scriptoria, such arguments hinge upon interpretations of papyrological evidence — interpretations that, as we shall see, are uniformly problematic.

In the pages that follow, my intent is not to argue in absolute terms that no Christian scriptoria of any kind existed in any place in the Graeco-Roman world during the second and third centuries, nor do I wish to imply that early Christian literature had only two mutually exclusive means of transmission (centralized scriptoria or individualized copying). Rather, my task in the pages that follow is simply to demonstrate that we have no secure evidence of early Christian scriptoria, and that what remains constantly before us are circles of readers and scribes who transmitted Christian literature individually and privately.

Calligraphy

One of the features that has been used to argue for early Christian scriptoria is that of the handwriting found in certain papyri. Both Fee and Colwell argued that the "calligraphy" in P^{66}, particularly when coupled with the high percentage of corrections in this copy (see below), draws us toward the conclusion of a scriptorium context behind this particular papyrus. Colwell was the first to make the argument: "P^{66} gives the impression of being the product of a scriptorium."[27] Fee agreed: "There are two features about the [manuscript] which point to this conclusion: the scribe's excellent calligraphy and the changes to the text made against a second *Vorlage*."[28] The assumptions operating behind such arguments appears to be that only scriptoria would require controlled, standardized, and high degrees of calligraphy, that scriptoria found in urban centers may have had the financial resources to afford the very best and most experienced scribes available, and that only in a controlled environment would manuscripts be corrected according to a second exemplar. The third assumption I will take up momentarily; for now, I will address the issue of calligraphy.

There are several difficulties with such "calligraphic" arguments for scriptoria. We might begin with questions: To what extent, in fact, do our early Christian papyri, P^{66} or any others, exhibit what might be called high levels of calligraphy? Is calligraphy only possible from a scriptorium environment? And what would be our control on such an argument? To begin to address these questions, we might recall, first, the discussion in chapter 3 of the characteristics of our earliest Christian papyri: while there is a spectrum of calligraphic quality exhibited among these, not one exhibits the strict bilinearity that we find in the most calligraphic of Greek literary papyri more generally; our earliest Christian papyri fall rather into a middle range on the spectrum between highly experienced, calligraphic, and strictly bilinear literary hands and the less specialized, and perhaps more inexperienced, hands that exhibit more of a cross between documentary and literary styles. There are indeed more calligraphic hands than that found in P^{66}, but even these do not require an explanation of a scriptorium context.[29] As we shall discuss below, some of the more "calligraphic" examples of early Christian papyri are found in what are clearly privately produced and privately used copies of Christian texts. Finally, the papyrus that Colwell and Fee chose to highlight — P^{66} — is a particularly problematic choice since (1) it is not, as I have stated, the most "calligraphic" or experienced hand found in the earliest Christian papyri, and (2) the closest parallel to its handwriting is not found in a literary text at all, but rather in a private early third-century letter.[30]

We have already seen that the form — and degree of experience — of the handwriting was dependent upon the content of the material, the function or destination of the text, as well as perhaps the financial resources of the person requesting the copy. It is due less to the context of copying than the intended use of the text. Furthermore, handwriting alone is a rather precarious feature upon which to rest arguments concerning the context in which a particular papyrus was produced; Fee and Colwell indeed are aware of this, and they point to another criterion in tandem with the argument of handwriting: the presence of corrections in the text. As I will presently show, however, this argument too is fraught with difficulties.

Corrections or Recensional Activity

Corrections can be found with some frequency in copies of both classical and Christian literature; they occasionally take the form of erasing the "mistakes," or more frequently placing dots around or lines through the "mistakes," and then writing the corrections in the text or margins. Manuscripts that exhibit a more specific type of correction — corrections that appear to have been made against a second Vorlage (i.e., that the scribe actually referred to a *different* exemplar in making the corrections) and appear to be "the result of deliberate critical work by an editor" — have traditionally been called recensions, or rather manuscripts displaying "recensional activity."[31] Both Fee and Colwell point to the presence of corrections in P^{66} as additional evidence for the likelihood that this copy was produced in a "scriptorium."[32] Fee, furthermore, emphasized that the corrections in P^{66} clearly demonstrated that a second exemplar was consulted; at the same time, he admitted that the nature of the "recensional activity" in this particular manuscript was not "guided by apparent controls," nor was it "scholarly" in nature.[33] Zuntz's extensive work on P^{46} similarly led him to the conclusion that this text showed the marks of recensional activity, and specifically here he had in mind scholarly editorial work that could be associated with a scriptorium in Alexandria.[34] For both P^{46} and P^{66} there are corrections made by the hand of the initial scribe as well as by other hands.[35]

What is behind the connection drawn by Zuntz, Colwell, and Fee between corrections, or the more specific "recensional"/editorial work, and a scriptorium environment in Alexandria? In a scriptorium, the logic runs, there would be more of an effort to control and correct; either the scribe would be required to correct his/her copy and/or the scriptorium's διορθωτής would undertake to correct the copy.[36] The presence of the initial scribe's corrections could be explained on the basis of the controlled environment of the scriptorium, while the appearance of the work of second or even third hands could be explained on the basis of a scriptorium's corrector (διορθωτής) or another scribe in the scriptorium.

Again, such arguments demand several questions. Most obviously, of course, does the fact that the initial scribe corrected his/her own work necessarily require the environment of a scriptorium? Is it not possible that a scribe of his/her own volition chose to correct the copy? Moreover, is a second corrector necessarily indicative of a controlled, scriptorium-like environment? The problem with the arguments advanced by Fee and others is that they have been advanced purely on the basis of uninformed "common sense," rather than on the grounds of a careful comparison with known data from the ancient world.

When we look at literary papyri more broadly, we find that often it is *the owner* of the manuscript who chose to add corrections or make annotations.[37] Hence, the explanation of a second hand is not necessarily dependent upon a scriptorium environment. Furthermore, the most common way that correctors identified themselves was by signing the end of the manuscript with a δι, an abbreviation for διορθωτέον, but this signature is not found in early Christian papyri. And strikingly, the signature can be found in documents as well as in literary papyri and therefore does not indicate a literary scriptorium proper.[38] Moreover, Turner notes that the process of correcting was "often carried out by *private individuals* to secure a reliable text."[39] Although they relate to correcting one's composition, rather than a copy, Quintilian's comments corroborate such a scenario: "the next point which we have to consider is the correction of our work, which is by far the most useful portion of our study: for there is good reason for the view that erasure is quite as important a function of the pen as actual writing. Correction takes the form of addition, excision and alteration" (Sequitur emendatio, pars studiorum longe utilissima. Neque enim sine causa creditum est stilum non minus agere, cum delet. Huius autem operis est adiicere, detrahere, mutare) (*Inst. Or.* 10.4.1).

Literary evidence confirms the evidence from papyri. It is quite clear from the few comments in literary sources regarding corrections that corrections did not require the environment of a scriptorium. Martial, for example, comments on correcting copies of his works himself: "You make me correct my little books with my own pen and hand, Pudens. Oh, how excessively you approve and love me, wanting to have an original of my trifles" (7.11). Likewise, Pliny attests to the ability of authors to correct copies of their works (*Ep.* 4.26.1). Although Cicero's letters indicate that it was normally the task of the *librarii* to proofread and correct, we should recall that the resources Atticus provided for him were exceptional (e.g., *Att.* 12.6a; 13.21; 13.23; and 13.44). Finally, and more specifically, the consultation of a second exemplar does not require the environment of a scriptorium; as Turner has put it, ancient authors were aware of the potential for mistakes in their copies "and adopted a routine to counter it: they themselves (or their secretaries) checked the copy to be used against another exemplar."[40]

Once we begin to look more closely at the practice of correction of literary papyri, either by the initial hand or by a secondary hand, the notion that corrections required a scriptorium environment appears to be a forced and unfounded interpretation of corrections in early Christian papyri. Indeed, it was the responsibility of the user of the manuscript—an author, a scholar, or simply an interested reader—to correct the copy, and this could be done by simply proofreading the copy, or possibly by also consulting a second exemplar. Even when one turned to a secretary or scribe to proofread the copy, there is no indication that such a process required a "controlled" environment of a scriptorium. We shall deal in the following chapter with the issue of control over texts, but for now it is worth pointing out that a simple dichotomy between scriptorium (control) private copying (freedom) will be insufficient for understanding the processes at work in the transmission of early Christian literature.

Stichometrical Markings

Ancient prose texts were not divided by chapters, and punctuation was left to the discretion of the scribe copying the text and in fact rarely employed. The problem naturally arose of how to calculate a scribe's fees for copying a particular text, without some kind of measuring system. Although poetic texts could be measured by verse, prose texts required a different measuring system and the one that was commonly employed was based upon στίχοι: a line that measured fifteen or sixteen syllables—approximately the same length as a hexameter verse.[41] The presence of stichometric markings in literary papyri has often been taken as indicative of a commercial context or even more specifically a scriptorium environment. Zuntz, for example, used the presence of these at the conclusion of Philippians in P[46] to contribute to his argument for a Christian scriptorium in the late-second century. He identified the second hand of the manuscript—that which added in page numbers and wrote the stichoi—as the "hand of the *ex officio* corrector who, still in the scriptorium, applied the finishing touches to the work of the scribe."[42] Although stichoi are only extant for Philippians, Zuntz extrapolates from the fact that the end of all the other epistles in the manuscript are defective, that stichoi were present at the conclusion of each epistle. Metzger's summary of stichometric practices also assumes the context of a scriptorium, but he also identifies a second explanation for these markings:

> Scribes *who were hired by a scriptorium* to do a certain piece of work would be paid in accord with the number of lines which they wrote. The standard length of line was originally a line of poetry, either a Homeric hexameter or an iambic trimeter. When prose works were copied, a line called a stichos, having sixteen (or sometimes fifteen) syllables, was frequently used as a measure for determining the market price of a manuscript. . . . The application of stichometric reckoning served also as a rough and ready check on the general accuracy of a manuscript, for obviously a document which was short of the total number of stichoi was a defective copy. On the other hand, such calcula-

tions were far from being foolproof safeguards to the purity of the text, for only longer interpolations or omissions would be likely to be disclosed by counting stichoi.[43]

There are, however, two problems with Metzger's summary and Zuntz's argument: stichometrical markings do not indicate exclusively commercial copies (i.e., copies produced by hired scribes),[44] and even more importantly a commercial environment means simply that the scribe was paid, not that the context was a scriptorium per se.[45] We can recall from chapter 3 that it is just as common that scribes were hired privately and paid privately; that is to say, it is not simply in the context of commercial booksellers that we find scribes being paid. Finally, Metzger's second explanation surely leaves open the possibility that stichometrical markings could be used to ensure that the text had been copied in its entirety (i.e., that lines were not lost); measuring lines, in other words, may well serve the purpose of preserving accuracy.[46]

Itacisms

Certain phonetic errors have also been used to argue for early Christian scriptoria; the principle errors used here are itacisms — common interchanges of vowels based on customs of pronunciation.[47] The logic is that scriptoria used dictation as the mode of producing copies:

> Here a lector (ἀναγνώστης) would read aloud, slowly and distinctly, from the exemplar while several scribes seated about him would write, producing simultaneously as many new copies as there were scribes at work. Although it increased production, dictation also multiplied the types of errors that could creep into a text. A particular source of trouble arose from the circumstance that certain vowels came to be pronounced alike.[48]

Although it may seem that such a connection between itacistic errors and dictation theory holds a certain plausibility, scholarship on reading practices has emphasized the degree to which reading aloud was the norm throughout antiquity.[49] The implications of this point for interpretations of itacistic errors — or even more broadly construed errors based on pronunciations — are quite obvious: "If in fact the scribe, while copying a manuscript visually, pronounced aloud each word as he read it in his exemplar, the sounds so produced must inevitably have influenced, or indeed determined, what he put on paper."[50] Once again, arguments for the existence of early Christian scriptoria are found problematic.

Critical Notes and Markings

A further and final criterion has been used to argue for the presence of a Christian scriptorium in second-century Egypt: the appearance of "critical signs" in copies of early Christian literature. "Critical signs or markings" are often found in the margins of literary papyri, and they are typically used to represent various kinds of annotations, corrections, additions, and so forth. Roberts has used the presence of such markings in a late second-century copy of Irenaeus' *Adversus Haereses* (*P. Oxy*. 405) to suggest a connection between this papyrus and a Christian scriptorium.[51] In this particular papyrus, a quotation from Matthew 3:16–17 is marked off in the margins by wedge-shaped brackets ⟪ ⟫). Drawing upon the work of Turner on scholars' texts — work that we have discussed above — Roberts argues that the presence of such marginal critical signs suggests the likelihood of a scriptorium at Oxyrhynchus in the second century.

Again, Roberts's arguments are not without problems. First, the presence of "critical signs" — if indeed the presence of these marginal marks can be taken as such — indicates more in this period about the reader or user of the manuscript than about the context in which it was produced. This is, furthermore, precisely Turner's argument about scholars' copies: they appear to be copies that were *used by* scholars. Nowhere does Turner suggest that they were commercial copies or that they were produced in scriptoria. In fact, if one peruses the collection in Turner's *Greek Manuscripts of the Ancient World*, it becomes rapidly clear that the copies of ancient literature that contain critical signs and marginal marks are those that were utilized by scholars for private use: the hands are not literary hands (such as we would expect in a scriptorium, and which seem to lie behind Roberts's arguments regarding the copy of Irenaeus), but rather more functional, cursive hands that commonly copied the commentary texts used by scholars.[52] Finally, Turner is quite deliberate and careful in using patterns of characteristics to suggest a scholarly text; Roberts, however, has utilized but one criterion to point toward a scriptorium.

Such are the arguments for Christian scriptoria in the second or third centuries that have been put forth by scholars of early Christian papyri. We cannot leave the discussion of Christian scriptoria, however, without reviewing two passages in Eusebius that have often been used to argue for Christian scriptoria in the third or early fourth centuries.

The Witness of Eusebius

In addition to characteristics from the earliest Christian papyri, scholars have pointed to two passages in Eusebius to suggest the existence of early Christian scriptoria. The first passage we have already seen on several occasions: Eusebius's comments regarding the staff in service of Origen, first at Alexandria and then at Caesarea. The whole question, indeed, of the catechetical school in Alexandria in the late second and early third century is fraught with numerous difficulties, most significantly that our evidence for the school is so scant.[53] However that may be, according to Eusebius's testimony, Ambrose placed in the service of Origen seven shorthand writers, as many copyists, and girls trained in calligraphy (*HE* 6.23). Eusebius furthermore makes clear that Ambrose supplied the financial support for the secretarial staff. It may well seem, as Gamble suggests, that we have here "Origen's scriptorium."[54] However, it may be worthwhile looking more closely at Eusebius's text in conjunction with our use of the term "scriptorium." Eusebius points out that the "more than seven short-hand writers" were scheduled to relieve "each other at fixed times" (χρόνοις τεταγμένοις ἀλλήλους ἀμείβοντες). Key here is the participial form of τάσσω, which means "fixed, prescribed, or regular" and especially the use of the verb ἀμείβω, which indicates precisely that these shorthand writers alternated with each other.[55] In other words, Origen — if we take Eusebius quite literally — did not have shorthand writers who simultaneously made seven or more copies of his sermons, commentaries, or theological treatises; rather, Eusebius's point here seems that Origen was extremely prolific and therefore required a secretarial staff around the clock.

This is not to say, however, that Eusebius does not suggest that Origen had multiple copyists and multiple calligraphers, who may well have transcribed works simultaneously. What I am saying is that we do not have clear evidence for a scriptorium per se here, and therefore arguments in favor of "Origen's scriptorium" must remain tentative at best. We should recall the analogy of Cicero and Atticus, which again does not require that we conjure up a notion of an scriptorium designed for "mass-production" of literary works. Given that the most common form of transmission of literature — even into the third-century — remained private and individualized we are reminded that any arguments *for* scriptoria bear the burden of proof, and we do not find incontrovertible evidence for such a controlled writing center in the time of Origen.

A final piece of evidence from Eusebius is used by nearly every scholar of early Christian literature for definitive evidence of an early fourth-century Christian scriptorium: Contantine's request for fifty copies of scripture. Although this is beyond the time period with which we are concerned — the second and third century — since it is so widely cited, it may be worthwhile to discuss briefly the passage. First, Constantine's letter to Eusebius:

> I have thought it expedient to instruct your Prudence to order fifty copies of the sacred Scriptures, the provision and use of which you know to be most needful for the instruction of the Church, to be written on prepared parchment in a legible manner, and in a convenient, portable form, by professional transcribers thoroughly practiced in their art. The chief financial officer of the diocese has also received a letter giving instructions that he should take care to provide everything necessary so that the copies can be completed. It will be for you to take special care that they be completed with as little delay as possible.

> πρέπον γὰρ κατεφάνη τοῦτο δηλῶσαι τῇ σῇ συνέσει, ὅπως ἂν πεντήκοντα σωμάτια ἐν διφθέραις ἐγκατασκεύοις εὐανάγνωστά τε καὶ πρὸς τὴν χρῆσιν εὐμετακόμιστα ὑπὸ τεχνιτῶν καλλιγράφων καὶ ἀκριβῶς τὴν τέχνην ἐπισταμένων γραφῆναι κελεύσειας, τῶν θείων δηλαδὴ γραφῶν, ὧν μάλιστα τήν τ' ἐπισκευὴν καὶ τὴν χρῆσιν τῷ τῆς ἐκκλησίας λόγῳ ἀναγκαίαν εἶναι γινώσκεις. ἀπεστάλη δὲ γράμματα παρὰ τῆς ἡμετέρας ἡμερότητος πρὸς τὸν

τῆς διοικήσεως καθολικόν, ὅπως ἅπαντα τὰ πρὸς ἐπισκευήν αὐτῶν ἐπιτήδια παρασχεῖν φροντίσειεν· ἵνα γὰρ ὡς τάχιστα τὰ γραφέντα σωμάτια κατασκευασθείη, τῆς σῆς ἐπιμελείας ἔργον τοῦτο γενήσεται. (de Vita Const. 36)

Eusebius's response to Constantine indicates that Contantine's instructions were immediately (αὐτίκα) followed and copies were prepared and sent to him "in magnificently and elaborately bound volumes of threefold and fourfold form" (ἐν πολυτελῶς ἠσκημένοις τεύχεσι τρισσὰ καὶ τετρασσὰ) (de Vita Const. 37). Precisely what Eusebius means in his description of the copies themselves remains highly debated: Does the "threefold and fourfold form" refer to the structure of the quires (i.e., the gathering of leaves in the codices)? Or to the columns of writing per page? Or, perhaps, to copies being sent three and four at a time? Although we are less concerned here with the form of these copies than with the claim that such a request required a scriptorium where numerous copies could be produced at once, the interpretation of "threefold and fourfold form" is crucial to the argument, so frequently made, that this passage indicates the presence of an early Christian scriptorium that had the resources (i.e., multiple scribes working from dictation) to produce so many copies so rapidly. We should recall that Pliny's remarks on the one thousand copies of Regulus's memoir did not require a "scriptorium" (Ep. 4.7.2). It seems to me, given the overwhelming evidence for private circulation and transmission of Christian literature — and we shall see at the conclusion of this chapter that this evidence continues into the early fourth century — that we should be cautious before assuming (1) that the mode of transmission of early Christian literature changed so abruptly and rapidly with the "conversion" of Constantine and (2) that the library at Caesarea necessarily had a working scriptorium with sufficient scribes to produce *rapidly* fifty copies of "sacred scripture."

EXCURSUS: *NOMINA SACRA* AND THE CODEX FORM

The two most extensively and widely discussed features of early Christian papyri are the *nomina sacra* and the codex form. Although the notion of early Christian scriptoria is not usually explicitly invoked in connection with these features, it is appropriate to discuss them here because they have been used to argue for some kind of centralized, or institutionalized, control over the production of early Christian texts during the second and third centuries. Martin Hengel, for example, used the codex form and *nomina sacra* to argue that "the circumstances and customs in the church in the second half of the first century and the first half of the second century do not seem to me to have been as diffuse and chaotic as people like to represent them today."[56] In what follows, I problematize this view by demonstrating (1) that while the *nomina sacra* are widespread in early Christian papyri, they are not used uniformly or consistently; and (2) that the codex form indicates more about the use of early Christian texts than about a supposed centralized orchestration of the transcription and transmission of early Christian literature.

One of the most discussed features of the early Christian papyri is the use of the *nomina sacra*.[57] Although these might properly be described as contractions, or in the earliest period suspensions,[58] they fall under the rubric of abbreviations. Stated briefly, the *nomina sacra* consist of contractions of "sacred" words: in the earliest stage, according to standard introductory treatments of the *nomina sacra*, θεός, κύριος, Ιησοῦς, and χριστός were contracted; later, contractions developed for *son, spirit, David, cross, mother, father, Israel, savior, man, Jerusalem,* and *heaven*.[59] All of our earliest Christian papyri exhibit the *nomina sacra*, and the effort to explain this fact has been vigorous. Roberts's voice has been quite influential for the view that the presence of the *nomina sacra* in early Christian papyri indicates some kind of centralized effort at the outset:

> Everything would fall into place were we to assume that the guidelines for the treatment of the sacred names had been laid down by the Church at Jerusalem, probably before A.D. 70; they would carry the authority of the leaders of the Church as the first Gospels must have done. The system was too complex for the ordinary scribe to operate without either rules or an authoritative exemplar; otherwise the difficulty of determining which was a secular, which a sacred usage would have been considerable even in a small community.[60]

Roberts here proposes that the system and use of the nomina sacra could not have developed without institutional and centralized authority. Given the evidence that indicates that books in antiquity circulated from one interested reader to another and that books were normally copied individually and by the interested party or by his or her scribe, we might wonder whether there is an explanation for the *nomina sacra* that would be sensible against the backdrop of private transmission. In what follows, I will suggest precisely such an explanation. When we look closely at the use of the *nomina sacra*, we find, in fact, that scribes during the second and third centuries are quite idiosyncratic in their application of the *nomina sacra*. While they appear to be aware of a tradition of treating divine names and words in a special way, they do not exhibit standardized and uniform contractions. It is precisely in the earliest period of text transmission that such *inconsistency* in the treatment of the *nomina sacra* is evident.[61] A few examples will suffice to demonstrate this point.

The scribe of P[45], for example, uses abbreviations for *nomina sacra* frequently, and most of them are well-attested in other early papyri: for *God, Lord, Spirit, father, Jesus, Christ, Son,* but not *heaven, man, David, Israel, Jerusalem,* or *mother*.[62] Yet the scribe of P[45] is hardly consistent in the form of the *nomina sacra*: while the scribe normally uses ιη for Jesus, on two occasions the scribe uses ιης (with no apparent reason for the switch); in addition, the scribe uses πρς and πς for πατρός interchangeably. Moreover, some of the *nomina sacra* in this manuscript are unique or rare: ιη (for Ἰησοῦς) is somewhat rare.[63] The πρ (for πατήρ) found in P⁴⁵ at Mark 9:24 is also not frequently used (though it does appear in P⁴⁶, P⁶⁶, and P⁷⁵) and π̄ς̄ for πατέρες appears to be unknown.[64] P⁴⁵ also appears on one occasion to consider ῡῑε̄ (for υἰε) a *nomen sacrum* for the scribe writes in a suprascript line above it.[65] Finally, we should note the apparent abbreviation for Christian: [Χρα]νους that appears once in this manuscript and nowhere else. Other abbreviations that Aland says are unique to this papyrus: σ̄ρ̄ν̄ and σ̄ρ̄ν̄αῑ (for σταυρόν and σταυρωθῆναι). Also, the abbreviation χ̄ρ̄ (for χριστός) is attested only in P¹⁸.

If P⁴⁵ demonstrates some inconsistency internally and exhibits some unique nomina sacra, with P⁴⁶ these traits are found far more frequently. Royse's comments on the P⁴⁶'s scribe's handling of the *nomina sacra* are important:

> The scribe appears to have difficulty understanding the abbreviations for nomina sacra which stood in his Vorlage, and accordingly often introduces an impossible form. In 2 cases (He 6:6 [αναστρες], 12:14c [κ̄ς̄]) the variation is just considered as orthographic, and in 4 cases (1 Cor 2:15 [π̄ν̄ς̄]; 2 Cor 7:1a [π̄ν̄ῑ], 10:7b [ο χρς̄]; Eph 4:15 [του χρ̄ῡ]) what the scribe writes happens (accidentally, it is clear) to be more or less sensical. But there are 5 cases of nonsense: He 12:24 [ῑη̄ς̄ χ̄ρ̄ς̄]; 1 Cor 2:14 [π̄ν̄ς̄], 3:1 [π̄ν̄ς̄], 4:21 [π̄ν̄ς̄], 15:24 [παρι and παρ]. The readings at 1 Cor 2:14, 3:1, and 4:21 are especially interesting, since there the scribe overlooked the distinctive endings and collapsed three distinct words into π̄ν̄ς̄ [with suprascript line].[66]

Royse's comments regarding the scribe's inability to understand the *nomina sacra* and lack of consistency can be further supported. The number of *nomina sacra* preserved in P⁴⁶ that are unique to this manuscript is quite large: ᾱῑμ̄ᾱ (for αἱμα!); π̄ᾱρ̄ῑ (for πατήρ [dat.]); π̄ν̄ω̄ν̄, π̄ν̄κ̄ο̄ς̄, π̄ν̄κ̄ο̄ν̄, π̄ν̄ῑκ̄ο̄ν̄ (for forms of πνεῦμα); σ̄τ̄ο̄ς̄, σ̄τ̄ρ̄ο̄ῡ, σ̄τ̄ο̄ῡ, σ̄τ̄ρ̄ω̄, σ̄τ̄ρ̄ν̄, εστ̄αν̄, εστ̄ρ̄αν̄, εστ̄ρ̄θ̄η̄, εστ̄ρ̄αῑ, συνεστ̄ρ̄αῑ, εστ̄ν̄, αναστρες (all for nominal and verbal forms of σταυρός); and ῡῑῡ (for υἱός [gen.]). That such *inconsistency* and *idiosyncracy* is found among our earliest manuscripts is significant, for it points toward a mode of transmission in which standardization and uniformity was not in existence.

Other examples of inconsistency can be found without difficulty. Our earliest extant New Testament papyrus (P⁵²), for example, appears to leave Ἰησοῦν uncontracted.[67] P⁴⁷ uses two rare abbreviations: ᾱθ̄ν̄ (for form of ἄνθρωπος)[68] and εστ̄ρ̄ω̄ (for verbal form of σταυρός). Although the scribe of P⁶⁶ appears to be quite familiar with the *nomina sacra*, again there is lack of consistency: while θεός, Ἰησοῦς, κύριος and Χριστός are *always* abbreviated, ἄνθρωπος, πατήρ, πνεῦμα, and υἱός are only sometimes abbreviated.[69] P⁶⁶ also has some unique *nomina sacra*: σ̄ρ̄ρ̄ο̄ῡ, σ̄ρ̄ω̄, εσ̄ρ̄αν̄, εσ̄ρ̄θ̄η̄, σ̄ρ̄ω̄σ̄ω̄, σ̄ρ̄ᾱτ̄ε̄, and σ̄ρ̄θ̄η̄ (all for variations on verb and noun forms of σταυρός). The Bodmer composite codex, which we shall discuss in depth below, exhibits numerous idiosyncrasies in the treatment of the *nomina sacra*. The following *nomina sacra* appear to be unique to this codex: ᾱν̄θ̄ς̄, ᾱν̄π̄ς̄, ᾱθ̄ῡ, ᾱν̄θ̄ν̄, ᾱν̄θ̄ο̄ν̄, ᾱθ̄ω̄ν̄, ᾱν̄θ̄ω̄ν̄, ᾱν̄ν̄ω̄ν̄ (for forms of ἄνθρωπος); δ̄ᾱῡῑδ̄ (with the overstrike, for Δαυίδ); δ̄ῡμ̄ῑ, δ̄ῡν̄ῑ, δ̄ῡῑν̄, and δ̄ν̄ῑν̄ (for forms of δύναμις);

θεω (written plene but with an overstrike); ιελμ, ιρσημ, ιυλμ, and ιυσλμ (for Ἰερουσαλήμ); ιηυς and ιηυν (for forms of Ἰησοῦς); ισαηλ and ισρηλ (for forms of Ἰσραήλ); κυριου, written plene but with an overstrike, and κον (for forms of κύριος); ουρν (for οὐρανόν); παρ, πτρα, πτρν (for forms of πατήρ); πντς, πναι, αγιω πνι, πνατικος, and πνατικας (for forms of πνεῦμα); υιος (with an overstrike), υις, υιν,[70] and υιων (with an overstrike) (all for forms of υἱός); and χσυ (for Χριστοῦ). Notice that in many of these instances the words are not in fact contracted or abbreviated; the scribes, however, clearly understand that these words are to be treated differently, for they include the overstrike. With P[75] the situation is similar to what has already become apparent: while θεός, Ἰησοῦς, χριστός, and Ἰσραήλ are always contracted, the forms are not consistent. For example, both ις with ιης are used for Ἰησοῦς; πρς and προς are used for πατρός; and contractions for σταυρός and σταυρόω are varied, including, for the latter, εστρωσαν with a suprascript line.[71]

Thus a sample of the *nomina sacra* found in some of our earliest Christian papyri is sufficient to demonstrate this inconsistency—both within individual papyri and between papyri—as well as the idiosyncrasies of forms.[72] Typically, as I have already indicated, explanations for such diversity have hinged upon the issue of dating: as Bell and Skeat put it, "such eccentricities are on the whole more likely to have occurred at an early period than later, when the system of *nomina sacra* had become more regularized."[73] The question that concerns us here is how we can correlate the notion of a inceptive centralized effort to implement a standardized treatment of sacred words (i.e., Roberts and others) with the apparent transition from an inconsistency and lack of uniformity in the second and third centuries to a consistent, standardized, and uniform use that emerges only in the fourth and later centuries. Given what we have already seen with respect to the modes of text transmission in early Christianity, the most plausible explanation for the spread of the *nomina sacra* but the lack of uniformity in their implementation is that of a network of scribes who communicated with each other (as we saw in the opening of this chapter) about the practice of copying early Christian texts. It must be conceded, of course, that such an explanation for the *nomina sacra* is based upon indirect evidence; yet it has the advantage of offering an explanation for the *nomina sacra* that is particularly sensible in light of what we know about the transmission of literature more generally. Furthermore, it also explains both the presence of the contractions and their inconsistencies and idiosyncratic use.

As with the *nomina sacra*, scholars have looked to the codex form as indicative of some centralized effort to transcribe and transmit early Christian texts. Skeat, for example, drew this conclusion:

the significant fact is that the introduction of the *nomina sacra* seems to parallel very closely the adoption of the papyrus codex; and it is remarkable that those developments should have taken place at almost the same time as the great

outburst of critical activity among Jewish scholars which led to the standardization of the text of the Hebrew bible. It is no less remarkable that they seem
to indicate *a degree of organization, of conscious planning, and uniformity of practice*
among the Christian communities which we have hitherto had little reason
to suspect, and which throws a new light on the early history of the Church.[74]

To counter Skeat's conclusion we might adduce evidence similar to that for the
nomina sacra, evidence that might point to a lack of uniform usage of the codex
form in early Christian papyri; here we could point out the second-century roll
of Irenaeus's *Adversus Haereses* (*P.Oxy.* 405) or the mention of scrolls in early
Christian texts.[75] The situation with the codex, however, is not the same as that
with the *nomina sacra*, for the codex appears to have been used consistently and
uniformly for Christian texts: quite strikingly, the proportion of Christian texts
on codices during the second and third centuries is near 100 percent, while for
classical texts the number of codices is scant (2.0–4.5 percent).[76]

What remains open for debate, however, is whether such a near universal
adoption of the codex in Christian circles of the second and third centuries
requires an explanatory appeal to a *centralized* effort and "degree of organization."
For our purposes, the origin of the codex form and the reasons for its adoption
by Christians is of less importance than the issue of the widespread use of the
codex among Christians.[77] Skeat, quite rightly, proposes that the organizational
effort would have taken place *between communities*, and we should avoid the notion
that "conscious planning" took place at some kind of inceptive stage; Roberts,
on the other hand, connects the use of the codex with the Roman church.[78]
Indeed, were we to imagine such an initial, centrally orchestrated effort, which
could only have been made by the upper echelons of church hierarchies, we
might do better to imagine an appeal toward the use of rolls rather than codices.
Rolls, especially the deluxe editions that were calligraphically written, were the
most prized forms of literature. Codices by contrast found their closest counterpart
in private notebooks and school tablets, not copies of ancient literature. Moreover,
our earliest Christian papyri are found in a single-column format (one column
of text per page), and Turner's extensive study of the codex form concluded
"that scribes who copied on a codex of papyrus in single column were aware
that they were writing a second-class book."[79] The reasons for the widespread
use of the codex form for early Christian texts may have been economic, religious,
practical, and/or doctrinal, but such explanations of use do not require appeals
to a centralized effort toward uniformity of practice.[80]

We have discussed thus far literary evidence that points to the predominance
of private transmission of early Christian literature as well as noted the problems
with arguments for early Christian scriptoria based on features of the earliest
Christian papyri. The story with which we began our investigation in this
chapter — the circles of readers/scribes who formed the networks that were responsible for the transmission of *The Martyrdom of Polycarp* — should continue to remain
in the foreground. It depicts a scenario of private networks of friends and acquain-

tances that is corroborated by our literary evidence more generally and is supported by our more indirect papyrological evidence. The remainder of the chapter presents a return to such networks by exploring closely one particularly intriguing third-century Christian codex that offers a window onto the scribal networks behind early Christian text-transmission.

PRIVATE SCRIBAL NETWORKS AND A THIRD-CENTURY CHRISTIAN MISCELLANY

Among the purchases that the Swiss banker Martin Bodmer made in the early 1950s was a small third- to fourth-century Greek codex containing an apparently disparate collection of Christian works.[81] The importance of this codex for the light it brings to bear on early Christian scribes, modes of transmission of literature, and the uses of early Christian literature, not to mention its importance codicologically, is entirely disproportionate to the scholarly attention it has received. It is particularly unfortunate that when the texts in this codex were published, beginning in the late 1950s, by Michel Testuz and later Victor Martin, it was only in a piecemeal fashion that obscured both the integrity of the codex as a whole and the wealth of information it offers.[82] Testuz concluded on the basis of its small size (just 14.2 × 15.5 cm) and various internal clues, which we shall explore shortly, that the codex was produced by Christians in Egypt, probably for the library of a wealthy member of their community.[83] More recently, James M. Robinson has argued for a connection between this codex and a "Pachomian monastic library."[84] There is much to support Robinson's claim, including the fact that the codex was found among a collection of literary works as well as copies of Pachomius' letters, that the entire collection of texts was found not far from the Pachomian headquarters, and that within Pachomian literature itself we find an attention to books and reading. It is in the *Rules*, for example, that we find the first mention of a Christian program for teaching people how to read: "Whoever enters the monastery uninstructed shall be taught first what he must observe; and when, so taught, he has consented to it all, they shall give him twenty psalms or two of the Apostle's epistles, or some other part of the Scripture. And if he is illiterate, he shall go at the first, third, and sixth hours to someone who can teach and has been appointed for him. He shall stand before him and learn very studiously with all gratitude. Then the fundamentals of a syllable, the verb, and nouns shall be written for him, and even if he does not want to, he shall be compelled to read" (*Rules* 139).[85] In what follows, I will attempt to unravel something of the mechanisms and networks that operated to produce the codex in its final form, as well as sub-networks that may have operated on an earlier level. We can begin with a description of the codex itself.

The codex contains eleven texts, which were copied by several different scribes. The texts appear in the following order: *Nativity of Mary* (= *Protevangelium of James*), the *Apocryphal Correspondence of Paul and the Corinthians*, the eleventh *Ode of Solomon*, the Epistle of Jude, Melito's *Homily on the Passover*, a fragment of a hymn, the *Apology of Phileas*, Psalms 33 and 34, and the two Epistles of

Peter.[86] With the exception of the *Apology of Phileas*, which cannot be dated before the time of Phileas' martyrdom (306–307 C.E.), all of the texts are dated on paleographic grounds to the third century. Since what will occupy us for most of the discussion following are the scribes behind this codex, it will be useful to present Testuz's summary of the codex in table 4.1.

Table 4.1. THE BODMER CODEX

	TEXT	PAGINATION	LINKS	COPYIST
1.	*Nativity of Mary*	1–49		A
			certain	
2.	*Apocryphal Correspondence*	50–57		B
			certain	
3.	11th *Ode of Solomon*	57–62		B
			certain	
4.	Jude	62–68		B
			certain	
5.	Melito, *Passover Homily*	1–63		A
			certain	
6.	Hymn fragment	64		A
			uncertain	
7.	*Apology of Phileas*	?–?		C
			certain	
8.	Psalms 33 and 34	?–?		D
			uncertain	
9.	1 and 2 Peter	1–34		B

Source: Michel Testuz, *Papyrus Bodmer VII–IX* (Cologny-Genève: Bibliothèque Bodmer, 1959).

According to Testuz, as we can see, the *Nativity of Mary*, Melito's *Homily*, and the hymn fragment were copied by the same scribe; the *Apocryphal Correspondence*, eleventh *Ode*, Jude, and 1 and 2 Peter by a different scribe; and the *Apology* and Psalms each by yet different scribes. Furthermore, as this chart indicates, Testuz was remarkably confident in securing the codicological links (see below) between texts in the codex; with the exception of the link between the hymn fragment and Phileas and that between the Psalms and 1 and 2 Peter, Testuz argued that the codex had been composed in this order. Testuz, unfortunately, offered little by way of paleographical and codicological analysis in his publications, so we must rely on the single plates that are published with each text.[87] In addition, it is unclear at what point he decided that the scribe of the *Nativity of Mary* was the same as that of Melito's *Homily* and the fragment of the hymn: he suggests this identification in his publication of this chart above, but in his publication of the texts themselves, he only remarks that the hands are "similar." Based on a close examination of the photographic reproductions available, however, it is clear that Testuz's identification of scribes and links is in need of correction and modification.

Turner offered a correction of Testuz's table in his *Typology of the Codex*. He argued that there were fully six scribes who produced the texts in the codex: scribe 1 copied the *Nativity of Mary*; scribe 2, the *Apocryphal Correspondence*, eleventh Ode, and Jude; scribe 3, Melito's *Homily* and the hymn fragment; scribe 4, the *Apology of Phileas*; scribe 5, Psalms 33 and 34; and scribe 6, the Epistles of

Peter.[88] Furthermore, on codicological grounds, Turner claimed that all the links between the texts in this codex are certain with the exception of the link between Jude and Melito.

Examination of the handwriting and textual characteristics confirms Turner's identification of scribal hands over that of Testuz. First to be considered is the hand of Melito's *Homily* and the hymn fragment. There is, to be sure, a noticeable similarity between this hand and that of the *Nativity of Mary*: they are the hands that in this codex most closely approach bilinearity, they are both well-written, regular, and experienced literary hands. At the same time, there are also significant differences. We can, for example, notice the distinct difference in style of sigmas: while in the *Nativity*, we find the scribe making the sigma (usually in the lunate form of a C, but not always) in two strokes, the scribe of the *Homily* and hymn fragment makes carefully executed sigmas (always lunate) without any gaps; omicrons in the *Nativity* are similarly made in two strokes, and often the gap is visible at the top and bottom, while in the *Homily* the omicrons appear as a full circle, with no gaps; likewise the thetas clearly show gaps in the top and bottom in *Nativity* while there are no gaps in the *Homily*. These few examples of paleographic differences may seem tedious, but they point to a significant difference between the scribe of Melito and that of the *Nativity*: the scribe who copied the *Homily* was a more experienced — particularly in the production of a formal literary hand — scribe than that of the *Nativity of Mary*.[89] We could point to other paleographic features or differences in the abbreviations of *nomina sacra* in support of the argument that there are two different scribes at work here: the punctuation markings in the *Nativity* are infrequent and when they do appear they are almost always in the form of a raised point, while by contrast in Melito, punctuation appears with some frequency and is almost exclusively in the form of an apostrophe; the scribe of the *Nativity* occasionally leaves a blank line between two lines of script (although the reasons for these are not always clear), while Melito contains not a single blank line; in the *Nativity*, the suprascript line over the *nomina sacra* appears as a simple straight line, while in Melito the suprascript line always has a hook on the left side; in *Nativity*, ιηρουσαλημ is not abbreviated, while in the Melito, it is always abbreviated, though the abbreviations vary in form. While the *nomina sacra* do not provide definitive proof of two different scribes, since individual scribes were not always consistent in their use of the *nomina sacra*, the fact that the *Nativity* and the Melito are *consistently* different in their treatment of ιηρουσαλημ contributes to the other factors that point to different scribes.

Such arguments seriously problematize Testuz's identification of the scribe who copied *Nativity* and that who copied the Melito and hymn. Similar arguments can be adduced in favor of different scribes for Jude and for the Epistles of Peter. Although it must be admitted that the photographic reproductions for these texts are more problematic than for the *Nativity* and Melito (the only plate provided of the Epistles of Peter is one in which the original hand was traced over), the paleographic data support a differentiation of scribes. Jude, which we discussed in chapter 3, is written in a hand that tends toward cursive. Letters, whenever possible, are made in one stroke (as opposed to the multistroke letter formation typically used in fine literary hands): α, υ, and η are particularly striking examples. Furthermore, this hand makes use of ligatures to join two letters without lifting the pen: ligatured λη and αι appear on the first page of the Epistle. By contrast, the Epistles of Peter are written in a hand that attempts to avoid (quite painstakingly) cursively formed letters and ligatures. Noticeable differences can be readily seen in the formation of the υ (here the standard uncial form Υ that required more than one stroke) and even more distinctly the α (which exhibits no trace of a cursive).

Since paleographic grounds alone may be insufficient to demonstrate that there were two different scribes at work on these texts, we can point to other features in support of this argument. Itacisms in both of these texts are, as they are in most papyri of this period, quite frequent. Yet they can occasionally be quite significant. The title to Jude appears at the very beginning of the epistle (separated from the *Ode of Solomon*, which concludes on the same page, only by a decorated line) and at the end: ιουδα επειστολη. In both cases the itacistic interchange ι/ει occurs to produce επειστολη instead of επιστολη. In the Epistles of Peter, by contrast, the interchange in the title is never made: the title appears (four times!) as πετρου επιστολη (at the beginning and end of the first and second Epistles). The consistency with which these scribes spell the titles is significant. We could furthermore point to significant differences in the treatment of the *nomina sacra*: in Jude, Ιησου Χριστου is always abbreviated as ιη̅υ χρ̅υ; by contrast at the very opening of 1 Peter, the scribe offers ι̅υ χρ̅υ (1 Pet 1:1, 2). It is not until the third verse that the scribe begins writing the three-letter abbreviation. Other examples of differences include: in Jude, δυναμε is not abbreviated (Jude 24), while in 1 Peter, it is (δυμ̅ι, 1 Pet 1:5); there are no breathing marks in Jude, while in 1 and 2 Peter, they appear with some frequency (see, e.g., 1 Pet 1:8, 13, 19; 2:23, 24; 3:4; etc); and there are no marginal notes in Jude, while marginal notes — a feature we will return to momentarily — appear frequently in 1 and 2 Peter (at 1 Pet 1:15, 22; 2:5, 9; 3:18; 4:1, 6, 8, 19; 2 Pet 2:1, 5, 8, 14, 22; 3:3, 15). Furthermore, the particular orthographic features that Testuz used to point toward a Coptic scribe around the region of Thebes — in particular the interchange of γ and κ (with the tendency to write κ where a γ is required) — is true of 1 and 2 Peter, but not of Jude.[90]

Careful attention to the details of the texts within this codex thus demonstrates, as Turner has also argued, that there were six scribes who participated in the production of the codex.[91] Before turning to the significance of this point, we would do well to consider briefly the links between the texts themselves, so as to ascertain the extent to which this is a single composite codex — a codex produced over time in precisely the order in which it is found — or perhaps some combination of two or more composites that were later joined together. The *Apocryphal Correspondence* begins in the same quire (gathering) as the conclusion of the *Nativity of Mary* and therefore the link between these texts is certain.[92] Since the *Apocryphal Correspondence, Ode of Solomon*, and Jude are quite clearly written by the same scribe, and each of the endings and beginnings of these texts fall on the same page, the links are here again certain.[93] Furthermore until the end of Jude, the pagination of the codex is continuous. With Melito, the pagination begins anew and since the first page or two is missing, it is unclear whether this text began in the last quire of Jude or in a new quire altogether. The fact that the Melito and hymn fragment is larger in size (page dimensions: 14.2 × 16 cm) than all the other texts in the codex may well support the notion that it may have originally been part of a separate composite or individual codex, but even this is not definite.[94] We must leave open the possibility that the join between Jude and Melito was not original. After Melito and the hymn fragment (which are unmistakably linked by quires), the links are varied: the *Apology* of Phileas begins in a new quire and contains new pagination, suggesting an insecure link;[95] Psalms 33 and 34 are linked securely to the *Apology*, for they begin in the same quire as the *Apology* concludes; the Epistles of Peter begin with new pagination, and Testuz's data regarding the quire gatherings here is insufficient to determine whether the link with the Psalms text is secure.[96] We may well, then, have before us a codex that was produced from earlier collections.

To understand the significance of a codex that was produced over time and that involved the hands of six different scribes, we can begin by tracing the life of this codex working backward from an anchorage point in the fourth century. The *Apology* cannot be earlier than 306/307 C.E., the date of the martyrdom of Phileas. If the join between the *Apology* and the Psalms is secure, then the Psalms text must be dated to the early fourth century as well. To these texts, then, were added a series of other older papyri, some in composite form (such as the opening four texts and the Melito and hymn fragment) and some in individual form (such as the Epistles of Peter).[97]

Such a production required connections to a library (that contained all of these papyri) or connections between the fourth-century anchor — according to Testuz, a Christian of some socioeconomic standing — and individuals, or possibly churches, who had these earlier copies of Christian works. Given the features of the codex as a whole, particularly its small size that suggests private usage rather than public reading, it is more likely that the anchor had a network of individuals who were able to provide these copies, than that churches were contacted. Furthermore, if all the papyri were in one library, we would be hard pressed to explain why such effort was taken to bind them into a single codex. The ability to obtain copies of such disparate works, produced by different scribes in different locations, required connections to individuals who had these copies, as well as, more indirect perhaps, links to the scribes who copied these texts. The closest and perhaps most direct connection may well have been to the copyists who produced the *Apology* and the Psalms texts. More distant connections could be traced between the anchor figure and the scribes who copied the remaining texts. Tracing, insofar as we are able, the relationships and personal links (here different from the codicological links we discussed above) that operated to produce such a codex highlights precisely the thesis of this chapter: the transmission of early

Christian literature was dependent upon the private channels of personal relationships and individual acquaintances.

We can go one step further in unraveling the scribal network behind earlier stages of the codex. Recall in our discussion of the codicological links above that we could not be secure, on codicological grounds, that the first four texts and the copy of Melito's *Homily* as well as the copies of Psalms texts and the copies of the Epistles of Peter were originally part of a composite codex. We have a significant clue, however, to a different type of link between the texts of the *Nativity*, Melito, and 1 and 2 Peter. The scribes of these three texts exhibit an unmistakable connection with each other: each of these scribes concludes with virtually the same colophon. Although colophonic endings to early Christian texts are not uncommon, the precise colophon used in the three texts in the Bodmer codex is unique. The *Apology*, for example, concludes with a common colophon: "Peace to all the saints" (ιρηνη τοις αγειοις πασει). A variety of other colophonic endings can be seen in the fourth-century Nag Hammadi codices: "Remember me also, my brethren, [in] your prayers: Peace to the saints and those who are spiritual" (at the conclusion of Nag Hammadi Codex II); "I have copied this one discourse of his. Indeed, very many have come to me. I have not copied them because I thought that they had come to you. Also, I hesitate to copy these for you because, perhaps they have (already) come to you, and the matter may burden you. Since the discourses of that one, which have come to me, are numerous" (conclusion of Nag Hammadi Codex VI); and "This book belongs to the fatherhood. It is the son who wrote it. Bless me, O father. I bless you, O father, in peace. Amen" (conclusion of Nag Hammadi Codex VII).[98] The colophon at the conclusion of the *Nativity*, Melito, and 1 and 2 Peter, by contrast, reads as follows:

ειρηνη τω γραψαντι και τω αναγινωσκοντι

Peace to the one who wrote [this] and to the one who is reading [it] (Nativity of Mary).

ιρηνη τω γραψαντι και τω αναγινωσκοντι και τοις αγαπωσι τον κν εν αφελοτητι καρδιας

Peace to the one who wrote [this] and the one who is reading [it] and to those who love the Lord in simplicity of heart (Melito's *Homily on the Passover*).

ειρηνη τω γραψαντι και τω αναγινωσκοντι

Peace to the one who wrote [this] and to the one who is reading [it] (ending of both 1 and 2 Pet).

The fact that the Melito colophon is longer than the other two does not detract from the verbatim similarities at the ending of the *Nativity* and 1 and 2 Peter. Such a similarity requires either that the scribes of these individual texts read the each other's colophons and/or that these scribes had some sort of personal connection or relationship that included discussions of scribal practices, including colophonic endings. Either of these scenarios establishes a link — written and/or personal, distant or close — between the scribes who participated in the production of a single early Christian codex. On a very small scale and through a rather specific instance, this argument illumines the scribal networks behind early Christian text transmission. The colophons here in the Bodmer codex also imply quite interestingly a link between the scribe — "the one who wrote" — and the reader — "the one who is reading." That they both receive a blessing of peace from the scribe may suggest that they are part of the same community.[99] Here we have a papyrological counterpart to the colophonic ending of the *Martyrdom of Polycarp*, which displays the manner in which relationships and interconnections between scribes/readers were vital to the reproduction and transmission of early Christian literature.

We cannot conclude our discussion of the Bodmer codex without remarking on the gathering of the particular, and apparently disparate texts, into one codex in the early fourth century. It may, at first glance, be particularly troubling to find the *Nativity of Mary* bound in the same codex as Melito's *Homily on the Passover*, for while the *Nativity* has often been invoked as representative of some form of "Jewish-Christianity," Melito's *Homily* has been noted for its trenchant hostility toward Judaism. The attribution of the *Nativity of Mary*, more commonly called the *Protevangelium of James*, to some form of "Jewish-Christianity," for example, has been made primarily on the basis of the extensive parallels drawn between Mary in this text and the portrayal of Hannah's birth to Samuel in the opening chapters of 1 Samuel and the emphasis on Mary's Jewishness in the text. Furthermore, the text appears to be popular early on among the Ebionites.[100] Melito's hostility to Judaism is apparent in his homily, which is one of the earliest texts that explicitly indicates the destruction of Jerusalem in 70 C.E. took place as punishment on "the Jews" for killing Jesus: "Therefore, O Israel . . . you forsook the Lord, you were not found by him; you did not accept the Lord, you were not pitied by him; you dashed down the Lord, you were dashed to the ground" (*Homily* 99).[101] The notion that the *Nativity* and Melito stand in stark contrast, however, may be more a problem with our own categories, for recent discussions of the *Nativity* and the whole phenomenon of "Jewish-Christianity" suggest that perhaps our identification of this text with such a milieu must be reevaluated; thus the discord between the *Nativity* and Melito's *Homily* in our text begins to disappear.[102] It may also seem surprising that "New Testament" texts were gathered into a codex with "apocryphal" material, but we should recall that discussions of canon continued well into the fourth century.

Victor Martin offered a rather general explanation for the collection of texts in the Bodmer codex: the texts are unified, he claimed, in belonging to the classification of theological literature; more specifically they deal with the question of orthodoxy versus heresy.[103] The advantage of this explanation is that it offers a theological consanguinity between, in particular, the *Apocryphal Correspondence* (which offers a response in the voice of Paul to questions of right belief versus wrong beliefs), Jude (which attempts to counter "false teachers"), and 1 and 2

Peter (which similarly deal with "false prophets"). Furthermore, several of the marginal notes in the Epistles of Peter, which we have already alluded to, seem to highlight this theme as a concern to the scribe (and by implication perhaps also to the reader or user of the copy). Since these marginal notes, which highlight themes throughout 1 and 2 Peter, are not written with any apparent regularity, we might conclude that they are meant to draw attention to the particular concerns of the scribe and/or user/reader of the manuscript. For example, we find the following marginal notes: περι γενος εγλεκτον βασιλιον ιερατευμα εθνος αγιον λαον ποησιν (at 1 Pet 2:9); περι ψεδοδιδασκαλοι (at 2 Pet 1:2); περι τεκνα καταρα (2 Pet 2:14).[104] Martin's explanation, however, has the disadvantage of being so general that one wonders what early Christian literature would *not* fit in the category of "theological literature," or what third and fourth century Christian writings are *not* concerned in some way with the questions of doctrine — particularly in the form of controversies over "orthodoxy" and "heresy." It seems most fruitful to conclude by highlighting a related but somewhat more specific theme that runs throughout this codex and may well shed light on the milieu in which and for which it was produced.

Perhaps the most pervasive theme in the texts gathered into this codex is that of the body — a theme that became so crucial for the early church with the emergence of a bewildering variety of ascetic choices. Contests over "bodies" and "texts" were, in fact, remarkably interwoven in the arena of early Christian theological debates. Did Christ have a real body? Does God have a body? Is there a resurrection of the flesh? Such were the questions that drove intense combat among patristic writers and desert monks.[105] Particularly significant is that while debates over the corporeality of Christ and God ensued, contests over the ascetic body — especially the bodies of virgins — were waged. The collection of texts found in the Bodmer codex dramatizes nicely the way in which contests over bodies, as they intersected with doctrinal competitions, found their way into the textual arena.

The *Nativity*, while primarily interested in the glorification of Mary, strives to demonstrate that Jesus was born in the flesh. At the birth the text reads, for example, "and [the child] went and took the breast of its mother Mary" (19:2). The narrative of the attendance of the midwife and Salome's appearance serves quite paradoxically both to affirm the materiality of the child and the birth and to indicate unquestionably the perpetual virginity of Mary: Salome, who greets the midwife just after the birth of the child, takes it upon herself to test the virginity of Mary by "putting forward her finger" (i.e., apparently by inserting her finger to test the intactness of the hymen) (19.3–20.1); soon afterward "an angel of the Lord" tells Salome to take the child into her arms, to touch him (αψε) (19.3), thereby fixing the material body of the child. The *Apocryphal Correspondence* depicts a Paul who must respond to those who deny the "resurrection of the flesh" (1.10) and who claim "that the Lord is not come in the flesh" (1.14). One of the themes in the 11th *Ode of Solomon* is that of the circumcision of the "Holy Spirit," language that speaks of a spiritualized notion of bodily flesh (11.2–3).

Jude and the Epistles of Peter share a concern with those who "defile the flesh" (Jd 8) and those "who indulge their flesh in depraved lust" (2 Pet 2:10), while simultaneously affirming Christ's sufferings in the flesh (1 Pet 4:1ff). Melito's *Homily* shares the concern over resurrection of the flesh (54). And the *Apology* of Phileas depicts in a striking way the proper outcome of purity of doctrine and of flesh — martyrdom; and the Psalms that are copied directly after the *Apology* follow directly from its themes: assurance of God's favor on the righteous (LXX, Ps 33:16), strength to the righteous who are sought and opposed (LXX, Ps 33:20), prayer for deliverance from persecution (LXX, Ps 34:17ff). The theme of persecution here encapsulates once again the close connection between themes of martyrdom and asceticism in the third and fourth century; it is precisely when persecution no longer presents a viable option for Christians (for all practical purposes martyrdom ends with the "conversion" of Constantine), that asceticism takes on a new meaning.[106] This transition, as well as the ensuing debates over the ascetic body, is captured well in the texts gathered in one codex — possibly the earliest Christian "miscellany"[107] — early in the fourth century.

Scribes and readers, interested members of Christian communities, formed networks that enabled the transmission of early Christian literature. That these networks were private and theologically (ascetically, socially, etc.) driven should seem clear by now. The Bodmer "miscellany" provides illumination of the process of transmission, the motivations and impetuses behind transmission, as well as doctrinal, theological, and social issues facing Christianity in the late third and early fourth centuries. The parallels between the portraits of text transmission as found in the colophons to the *Martyrdom of Polycarp*, the Bodmer codex, the letter between anonymous readers in upper-Egypt, and the requests for copies of literature that are embedded within Greek and Latin literature testify to the importance of social networks for the transmission of Christian, as well as classical, literature. Even more strikingly, nowhere do we find evidence that Christian "scriptoria" existed during the second or third centuries; rather, transmission of Christian literature, if we can trust the unified portrait our evidence provides, appears to have proceeded along the personal channels of friendships and acquaintances.

The significance of such private channels of text transmission in early Christianity will be developed extensively in the following chapter, which turns to the issues of control or power over texts, the degree to which texts were malleable, and the freedom that scribes had in (re)producing their copies. That texts were at the heart of how theological, social, cultural, and ideological debates were waged is demonstrated by the manner in which scribes and readers used texts as a means of entering into such controversies. Although, as we shall see, it would be unwise to assume that private channels of transmission permitted complete freedom to manipulate the texts themselves, and, by contrast, that scriptoria were the only settings in which control over texts were maintained, the arguments of this chapter will inform and guide the lines of inquiry and discussion in the chapter that follows.

"I AM THE GUARDIAN OF LETTERS"

Contested Readings, Authoritative Texts, and
Early Christian Scribes

I am the coronis, guardian of letters. The reed pen wrote me, the right hand
and the knee. If you should lend me to someone, take another in exchange. If
you should erase me, I will slander you to Euripides. Keep off!

— Third-century scribal colophon

New methods . . . authorize new ways of looking at texts, of inscribing texts
within "discourses" (a new term for intellectual historians), and of linking both
texts and discourses to their contexts.

—White, *The Content of the Form*, 185

Ancient texts were remarkably fluid. The "misinterpretation" and "misuse"
of written texts could not be prevented: the interpretation of literary texts
was and is unavoidably flexible and dependent upon the varied contexts of
readers.[1] Ancient authors knew well the potential for "miscarriage"; Horace
captures the risks of "publishing" succinctly, and his words — "the word once
sent, never returns" (nescit vox missa reverti) — resonated with other ancient
writers (*Ars* 389–90).[2] Clement of Alexandria feared that his text might fall
into the wrong hands (who would "misunderstand" his intentions), and
therefore he was reluctant to put words into written form (*Stromata*, preface).
But if ancient and modern texts share the multiple contests that ensue over
their interpretation and meaning, ancient texts have an additional fluidity and
flexibility: in the ancient context where texts were copied — reproduced —
by the hands of individual scribes, there was the unavoidable accident
of human error as well as the potential for deliberate modification —
(re)production — of texts. Human scribes may well have been the closest
thing to a modern xerox machine, but their handiwork did not approach
mechanical duplication.[3] Copying an exemplar meant producing a "resemblance" not an identity; as Michel Foucault has put it: "Resemblance has a
'model', an original element that orders and hierarchizes the increasingly less

faithful copies that can be struck from it. Resemblance presupposes a primary reference that prescribes and classes."[4]

Christian texts, as we shall see in this chapter, were no different in this respect from literary texts more generally. Among the some 5,400 Greek manuscripts of New Testament texts, for example, no two are identical; more relevant, perhaps, is the fact that some fifty-two extant manuscripts that can be dated to the period from the second century to the fourth exhibit more differences and variations than the thousands of later manuscripts.[5] The flexibility of Christian texts may well seem the logical corollary to the prominence of private modes of circulation we explored in the last chapter. For if text transmission was not orchestrated or controlled by centralized and institutionalized efforts, but rather was dependent upon private networks of friendships and associations, then it stands to reason that the scribes who copied early Christian texts did so with a certain freedom. Such an argument is supported by the view of New Testament textual critics, who have long noted that the "majority of textual variants that are preserved in the surviving documents, even the documents produced in a later age, originated during the first three Christian centuries."[6] Indeed, the second- and third-century text of the New Testament has been defined variously as "uncontrolled," "unstable," "wild," "free"—adjectives which suggest the unlimited flexibility, fluidity, and even randomness of the Christian texts preserved by scribes during the earliest period of text transmission.[7]

But is a simple and stark dichotomy—controlled versus wild—sufficient for understanding the textual history of Christian literature during the second and third centuries? Are we left to conclude from the lack of evidence for scriptoria during this period, that scribes were permitted total freedom? Did scribes, in fact, (re)produce, or (re)create, texts with wildness and unbounded freedom? If so, to what extent? And to what end? Such questions outline the contours of the present chapter, which centers on a more general theme: the nature of "control" over early Christian texts. My thesis is that the scribes who copied Christian literature during the second and third centuries were not "uncontrolled" nor were the texts that they (re)produced marked by "wildness." Rather, the (re)production of texts by early Christian scribes was bounded and constrained by the multifaceted and multilayered discursive practices of the second-and third-century church.

An exploration of the intersection of early Christian discourses and the copying of early Christian texts can be performed by outlining at least three interrelations. In chapter 3, for example, we explored how harmonizations in the earliest Christian papyri sometimes suggest the intersection of copying texts and liturgical practices—ritualized discourses—of the second and third centuries. In this chapter, we turn to two sets of discourses that intersected with and constrained the activity of copying literary texts. On one level, scribes were limited by what they knew to be the standards of text transmission; as we shall see, authors, readers, and scribes were well aware of the "mistakes" in their texts and often took great pains to "correct" these and prevent further mistakes. Yet on another level, one that is more precisely the concern of this chapter, scribes were limited by their geographic, social, religious, and ideological (con)texts; the freedom that they sometimes took with their texts was not unbounded but rather was shaped and formed by the various and discursive controversies that engaged the second- and third-century church. What early Christian manuscripts preserve, in effect, is a palimpsestic testimony to the overlay of oral/verbal "texts" upon written "texts."[8] By contextualizing these manuscripts within the arena of discursive contests over self-definition, questions of theology and Christology, as well as debates over the practice of Christianity, we illumine not only the role of scribes but also the role of texts in the various discourses of the second- and third-century church.[9]

ERASURES AND REINSCRIPTIONS

Ancient authors betray an awareness of the potential for erasure and reinscription of their texts. For authors, there appear to be two issues at hand: the recognition that scribes were bound to make errors and the awareness that sometimes scribes and readers intentionally, or deliberately, modified texts in the process of copying them.[10] Cicero, for example, is quite resigned to the realities of human transcriptional error: correction of copyists' mistakes is simply a part of the process of "publishing" a written work (*Att.* 13.23; 13.44).[11] But responses to the potential for deliberate modification were sharper, and varied from expressions of reluctance to write (as we saw with Clement above) to inclusions of curse formulas and sharp adjurations for any reader or copyist who would tamper with the text.[12] As is well known, the author of the Book of Revelation writes,

> I witness to all who hear the words of the prophecy of this book: If anyone should add to them, God will place upon him the plagues written in this book; and if anyone should take away from the words of the book of this prophecy, God will take away his portion in the tree of life and in the holy city, which are written in this book.

> Μαρτυρῶ ἐγὼ παντὶ τῷ ἀκούοντι τοὺς λόγους τῆς προφητείας τοῦ βιβλίου τούτου· ἐάν τις ἐπιθῇ ἐπ' αὐτά, ἐπιθήσει ὁ θεὸς ἐπ' αὐτὸν τὰς πληγὰς τὰς γεγραμμένας ἐν τῷ βιβλίου τούτῳ, καὶ ἐάν τις ἀφέλῃ ἀπὸ τῶν λόγων τοῦ βιβλίῳ τῆς προφητείας ταύτης, ἀφελεῖ ὁ Θεὸς τὸ μέρος αὐτοῦ ἀπὸ τοῦ ξύλου τῆς ζωῆς καὶ ἐκ τῆς πόλεως τῆς ἁγίας τῶν γεγραμμένων ἐν τῳ βιβλίῳ τούτῳ. (*Rev* 22: 18–19)

Similarly, Rufinus' translation of Origen's *Peri Archon* begins with the following adjuration:

> One request, however, I solemnly make of every one who shall either transcribe or read these books, in the sight of God the Father and the Son and the Holy Spirit, by his faith in the kingdom to come, by the mystery of the resurrection from the dead, by the 'everlasting fire which is prepared for the devil and his angels', that, as he would not possess for an eternal inheritance

that place where there is 'weeping and gnashing of teeth'. and where 'their fire is not quenched and their worm does not die', he shall neither add anything to this writing, nor take anything away, nor interpolate anything, nor change anything.

sane omnem, qui hos libros uel descripturus est uellecturus, in conspectu Dei Patris et Filii et Spiritus Sancti contestor atque conuenio per futuri regni fidem, per resurrectionis ex mortuis sacramentum, per illum 'qui praeparatus est diabolo et angelis eius aeternum ignem'; sic non illum locum aeterna hereditate possideat, ubi est 'fletus et stridor dentium,' et 'ubi ignis eorum non extinguetur et uermis eorum non morietur': ne addat aliquid huic scripturae, ne auferat, ne inserat, ne immutet, sed conferat cum exemplaribus unde scripserit, et emendet ad litteram et distinguat, et inemendatum uel non distinctum codicem non habeat, ne sensuum difficultas, si distinctus codex non sit, maiores obscuritates legentibus generet.

The author of Revelation and Rufinus alike testify both to the awareness of the potential for modification of texts and to the authorial attempts to combat modification by the inclusion of adjurations and curse formulas.

Like authors, readers knew firsthand the frequency with which texts, copied by hand, could have errors. In his treatise on anger, Seneca remarks on the book "we tear up because it is so full of mistakes" (liber . . . mendosum laceravimus) (*De ira* 2.26). Quintilian goes so far as to suggest that readers—"*unlearned readers*"—take it upon themselves to correct what they perceive to be scribes' errors in their copies; their "corrections," according to Quintilian, are not corrections at all, but rather additional mistakes: "Unlearned readers are apt to alter such forms when they come across them in old books, and in their desire to decry the ignorance of the scribes convict themselves of the same fault" (Quae in veteribus libris reperta mutare imperiti solent, et dum librariorum insectari volunt inscientiam, suam confitentur) (*Inst. Or.* 9.4.39). What Quintilian betrays here is testimony to the mistakes of copyists and simultaneously the fluidity of written texts with which we are concerned here, for his "unlearned readers" are explicitly accused of a tendency to "change" (*mutare*) the text before them. Additionally, Quintilian's remarks introduce us to the contests over texts; what he considers to be an error, some readers viewed as corrections. Such "corrections" are indeed found frequently in copies of literary texts, and occasionally we are able to recognize in the "corrections" the private and personal hand of a reader/ user of the text.[13]

We might think that since scribes were bound to make mistakes in the process of copying, there were prescriptive texts written to guide the work of scribes. There are indeed rules for scribes set out in later texts such as Cassiodorus' *Institutiones* (sixth century) or the rabbinic *Masseket Soferim* (eighth century). Yet we do not find such prescriptions for scribes during the second and third centuries. Even Quintilian's first century *Institutio Oratoria*, which we explored in chapter 3, does not offer guidelines or rules for scribes who set out to copy literary texts. The fact that we do not have prescriptive texts for scribal practices may in itself be a clue to the acceptance of the flexibility of texts. This point should probably not be pressed too far, however, for we do find implied in the copies that scribes produced an awareness of certain standards of text reproduction.

Scribes frequently reread and corrected their work, and in doing so they demonstrate an awareness of their own fallibility as well as an awareness of some "standard" of reproduction they are to meet. Corrections appear in extant manuscripts in a variety of forms: erasures with a sponge and then reinscription of the passage; deletions "indicated by enclosing a passage in round brackets," "by cancelling a letter or letters by means of a stroke drawn horizontally or obliquely through them," "by placing a dot . . . or a line above, or above and below, or to either side," or "by a combination of these methods."[14] Such corrections are common in literary papyri from the second and third centuries. Sometimes corrections were made after consulting another exemplar, but more often scribes simply reread the copy and corrected errors. Early Christian papyri are no different in this regard, as a few examples will suffice to illustrate: in P^{45}, for example, we find some 11 corrections, only two of which are by a second hand;[15] the majority of the 160 corrections in P^{46} were made by the initial scribe;[16] P^{47} contains 13 corrections, all of which appear to be made by the initial scribe;[17] among the 116 corrections found in P^{75}, only five appear to be by second hands.[18] Similarly, the various scribes involved in producing the Bodmer codex we explored in the previous chapter engaged in correcting their own work.

More than any other early Christian papyrus, the Bodmer codex of the Gospel of John (P^{66}) has been highlighted for its numerous corrections. Victor Martin noted that corrections were frequent; Gordon Fee counted some 450 corrections; and James Royse counted a total of 440.[19] In nearly all of the instances, it was the original scribe who made the corrections.[20] The frequency of nonsense readings (that are then corrected) has led some scholars to see the scribe of P^{66} as unattentive, careless, or ineffective.[21] But we might ask whether frequent corrections of errors actually demonstrates carelessness. To be sure, this scribe appears to have produced many readings that called for correction. But would a careless scribe take the trouble to correct his/her own work? Or do the corrections actually suggest the care the scribe took in attempting to produce a good copy? The scribe of P^{66} reread the copy and made corrections, and also made corrections according to a second exemplar. Such work does not indicate carelessness, it seems to me, but rather deliberate care and a desire to get the text right, a point made quite convincingly by James Royse.[22]

In addition to recognizing their own potential for error, scribes indicate an awareness for possible modification of their copies by readers, users, owners, or even other scribes. Evidence for such an awareness can be found in colophonic endings and marginal notes. I will bring here just two examples, which illustrate the themes of this chapter particularly well. Attached to a third-century copy of the *Iliad* is a note that reads as follows: "I am the coronis, guardian of letters. The reed pen wrote me, the right hand and the knee. If you should lend me to someone, take another in exchange. If you should erase me, I will slander you to Euripides. Keep off!" (ἐγὼ κορωνίς εἰμι, γραμμάτων φύλαξ. κάλαμος μ᾽ἔγραψε, δεξιὰ χεὶρ καὶ γόνυ. ἄν τινί με χρήσῃς, ἕτερον ἀντιλάμβανε, ἐὰν δέ με ἀλείφῃς, διαβαλῶ σ᾽ Εὐριπίδῃ. ἄπεχε).[23] This colophon is interesting in several respects. First, the "I" of the opening sentence refers to a coronis — an "elaborate structure of decorative curly lines" used to mark off sections or the end of a text — inscribed as a protection against tampering.[24] That written markings, here combined with written words, could guard a text testifies to the power of writing and relates to one of the themes of this chapter; we shall discuss momentarily the ways in which texts were resources of power and authority.

The remainder of the colophon appears to be spoken by the book to a potential owner and reader: the pen wrote the text, along with the hand and knee; if the owner should lend the copy, he/she should borrow a book in exchange; and most strikingly, if the owner/reader/user should erase the text, the text (or scribe?) shall slander the person "to Euripides." The final "keep off" serves as a warning to anyone who would tamper with the book and its text and speaks to the larger significance of this colophon: curse formulas and protective inscriptions, such as found here, testify to the potential for erasure and reinscription, reproduction, or creation of a new text.

Another useful illustration is found in a scribal libel in the margins of the fourth-century Codex Vaticanus, a passage that we noted briefly at the outset of chapter 3.[25] In a marginal note at Hebrews 1:3, we find the following: "Ignoramus and knave, leave the old [reading], and do not change it!" (ἀμαθέστατε καὶ κακέ, ἄφες τὸν παλαιόν, μὴ μεταποίει).[26] At issue for the scribe who wrote this marginal note is the precise reading of Hebrews 1:3b.[27] The original scribe apparently wrote of the Son of God, who is "revealing all things by the word of his power" (φανερῶν τε τὰ πάντα τῷ ῥήματα τῆς δυνάμεως αὐτοῦ); a "corrector," however, came along and changed the reading to one that was more customary: the Son of God, who is "bearing all things by the word of his power" (φέρων τε τὰ πάντα τῷ ῥήματι τῆς δυνάμεως αὐτοῦ). The change here entailed a very simple task: erasure of the αν in φανερῶν.[28] The marginal note was apparently by yet another scribe or reader who noticed the "correction" and changed the reading back to φανερῶν. Interestingly enough, the original reading in this passage is a singular one; in no other manuscripts do we find φανερῶν.[29] The first "corrector," then, has changed the reading to the reading that was more common, one that is found in every other extant manuscript as well as in quotations of the verse by church fathers, but the third scribe has reverted it back to a singular, and erroneous, reading. It is indeed ironic that the scribe who erases the reading φέρων and reinscribes the singular φανερῶν, attacks the second scribe for being an "ignoramus and knave." Essentially, what we find in this incident is a scribal contest over readings; the contest manifests itself here with a pattern of erasures and reinscriptions culminating in an inscribed attack on the work of a scribe.

This illustration highlights well the multiple senses in which I am using the term "reading." First, there is the text-critical understanding of a "reading," in which a "reading" simply means the wording of a particular passage in a particular papyrus or manuscript. For instance, in the example we have just discussed, the original "reading" of Codex Vaticanus at Hebrews 1:3 was φέρων τε τὰ πάντα τῷ ῥήματι τῆς δυνάμεως αὐτοῦ. This "reading," however, stands alone in opposing the entire textual tradition as well as the first corrector's change in the codex itself. The practice of textual criticism takes as its starting point such "variant readings" and attempts to determine which one is the "original reading."[30] There is, however, a second use of the term "reading" that is relevant here: to offer a "reading" of a text is analogous to presenting an interpretation of the text.

Recent interest in the intersection of reading and interpretation has alerted us to the inextricable link between these two activities. To engage in reading a text necessarily involves one in the practice of interpreting a text. As Roger Chartier has put it: "Readings and hearers, in point of fact, are never confronted with abstract or ideal texts detached from all materiality; they manipulate or perceive objects and forms whose structures and modalities govern their reading (or their hearing), thus the possible comprehension of the text read (or heard)."[31] To read, then, is to interpret. Scribes who copied texts, in a very real sense, were readers of the texts; and in the process of copying, they left the traces of their "readings" (interpretations). With a simple erasure, the scribes of Vaticanus have essentially inscribed two interpretations (two readings) of the same passage; in one, Jesus *bears* "all things by the power of his word," while in the other, he *reveals* "all things by the power of his word." Two wordings (readings), two interpretations (readings); or, more precisely, two interpretations (readings), two wordings (readings). The scribal changes in Codex Vaticanus indicate that scribes, as readers, were also interpreters; the manuscripts they produced bear the markings of their interpretations/readings of the texts and illustrate the scribal contests that took place over the interpretations/readings of texts.

CONTESTS OVER READINGS

The textual history of early Christian literature during the second and third centuries is one marked by the malleability of texts. As we have already seen, there is evidence aplenty for the frequency with which scribes made accidental mistakes in the process of copying; indeed, most of the variant readings in early Christian texts stem from simple errors. But there is also evidence that scribes deliberately modified texts in the process of copying. Such manipulations of texts suggest the extent to which scribes, as readers, were also simultaneously interpreters. The notion that early Christians might deliberately tamper with the text is not a new one. Origen, for example, was quite aware of the differences among copies of scripture: "The differences among copies have become many, either from the carelessness of some scribes or from the rascally audacity of others" (πολλὴ γέγονεν ἡ τῶν ἀντιγράφων διαφορά, εἴτε ἀπὸ ῥαθυμίας τινῶν γραφέων, εἴτε ἀπὸ τόλμης τινῶν μοχθηρᾶς) (*Comm.in Matt.* 15.14).[32] Early proto–orthodox heresiologists provide us with tirades against various "heretics" for tampering with scripture. Marcion's truncated Gospel of Luke and excision of unpalatable Pauline passages provide occasion for Irenaeus to lambaste him:

> Marcion of Pontus . . . advanced the most daring blasphemy against Him who is proclaimed as God by the law and the prophets. . . . besides this, he mutilates the Gospel which is according to Luke, removing all that is written respecting the generation of the Lord, and setting aside a great deal of the teaching of the Lord. . . . In like manner, too, he dismembered the Epistles of Paul, removing all that is said by the apostle respecting that God who made the world, to the effect that He is the Father of our Lord Jesus Christ, and also those passages from the prophetical writings which the apostle quotes, in order to teach us that they announced before-hand the coming of the Lord. (*Adv. Haer.* 1.27.2)

These accusations leveled against heretics are quite common in the midst of the debates over "heresy" and "orthodoxy" during the second and third centuries.[33] We can recall from chapter 1 the similar vein in which Eusebius attacks the Theodotians, who had "diligently written out copies corrected, but really corrupted by each of them" (*HE* 5.28). Eusebius's point also brings us back to the marginal note in Vaticanus, for it illustrates the slippage of the term "correction," and the extent to which this notion was interrelated with readings and interpretations.

The evidence from our literary texts for scribes, readers, and users modifying scripture is corroborated by close examination of our earliest Christian papyri. Scholars have become increasingly attuned to the ways in which variant readings suggest the intersection of ideology and text reproduction. For example, studies have shown that certain changes made by scribes in the process of copying appear to have been motivated by anti-Jewish sentiments;[34] others seem influenced by a certain animosity toward women;[35] others by apologetic concerns;[36] and still others can be explained by theological, especially, Christological, concerns.[37] Such studies have seriously countered Hort's famous statement: "even among the numerous unquestionably spurious readings of the New Testament there are no signs of deliberate falsification of the text for dogmatic purposes."[38] Moreover, the types of textual modifications exhibited point us toward the conclusion that in addition to the accusations of "orthodox" Christians against the "heretics" tampering with scripture, "orthodox" Christians themselves were involved in modifying scripture in accordance with what they believed. Finally, such changes in textual readings, as we shall see, become particularly sensible given the discursive contests of the second- and third-century church.

Since such scribal textual modifications have received extensive treatment in recent years, in what follows I wish simply to illustrate the range and type of changes that scribes made in the process of copying early Christian literature. Before turning to these illustrations, however, a word is necessary concerning method.

Determining where, when, how, and by whom certain variant readings — here, those that demonstrate ideological influence — entered into the textual history of early Christian literature is not altogether straightforward; several methods are possible, and each yields different results. First, one may isolate singular readings found in second-and third-century papyri of early Christian literature. We have already seen this method at work to determine "scribal habits" in our discussion of harmonizations. The benefit of this method is that it enables us to locate a variant reading with a fair amount of assurance to a particular papyrus and a particular scribe.[39] The disadvantage, as we shall see, is that the data that this method makes available to us are rather meager. This lack of data in itself would be significant if we had more papyri from the second and third centuries, and if it were not for the simultaneous fact that most of our deliberate changes to the text occurred in the earliest period of text transmission (i.e., the second and third centuries). This last point brings us to a second method, the one used most extensively by textual critics.

It is possible to determine what readings were introduced into the textual tradition by adopting the argument that later manuscripts actually reflect changes made in the earliest period of text transmission. As I have already stated, it is in the earliest centuries that we find the texts of early Christian literature most diverse; by contrast, later manuscripts are remarkably more stable.[40] When we find variant readings in later manuscripts, therefore, we can be reasonably sure that the readings were introduced into the textual tradition in the earliest period; this conclusion is corroborated by the fact that we frequently find support for a later reading in a second- or third-century papyrus.[41] The advantage of utilizing this method is that the quantity of data is significantly expanded. The drawback is that we cannot locate a particular scribe with whom the textual modification originated, although we can often determine the *terminus ad quem* of a particular reading.

There are other methods of determining the origins of various readings in the textual tradition of early Christian literature, but the two I have just outlined are the most useful for our study.[42] In the pages that follow, I will utilize first the method of singular readings and offer a sample of such readings that appear to be motivated by ideological influences, and then I will adopt the second method to present several illustrations of similarly motivated variant readings. My intent here is to summarize and illustrate the kinds of modifications that appear to indicate theological, social, or more generally ideological intentions on the part of scribes. With the exception of the last variant reading I discuss, the following readings lack any claim to originality, and their secondary nature remains uncontested.

Singular Readings Indicating Ideological Modifications

We can begin our discussion of singular readings that suggest ideologically motivated modifications by returning to the Bodmer codex, which we discussed extensively in the last chapter. There are several singular readings worth discussing briefly. First, at Jude 12, the scribe has replaced συνευωχούμενοι with συνευχό-μενοι. Now instead of reading, "these are spots on your love-feasts, for while they are feasting without fear, they are feeding themselves," the text reads: "these are spots on your love-feasts, for while they are *praying* without fear, they are feeding themselves" (οὗτοί εἰσιν οἱ ἐν ταῖς ἀγάπαις ὑμῶν σπιλάδες συνευχόμενοι ἀφόβως, ἑαυτοὺς ποιμαίνοντες). The substitution that the scribe makes at Jude 12 may well be a simple scribal blunder, but it produces a word that makes perfectly good sense in the context. Royse argued that it was an instance of harmonization to "general usage" on the grounds that εὐχή and εὔχομαι appear more frequently in New Testament texts.[43] When we note, however, that συνεύχο-μαι never appears in the New Testament, that εὐχή appears only three times (Acts 18:18; 21:23; Jas 5:15), and that εὔχομαι appears only seven times (Acts 26:29; 27:29; Rom 9:3; 2 Cor 13:7, 9; Jas 5:16; 3 Jn 2), it seems unlikely that the scribe here has harmonized the text to a word more familiar from other texts.

There may be other, more compelling, explanations for the change that make more sense given our exploration of the context of the Bodmer codex in the last chapter. If the codex as a whole, or some portions of it, is to be connected with some type of (Pachomian?) ascetic setting, then it is plausible to suppose that the scribe here has substituted a word that makes more sense given the context in which the text was to be used, an ascetic context that emphasized prayer rather than feasting.[44] Moreover, this word avoids the implication that Christians are "feasting together in love-feasts." This is particularly interesting given the fre-quency with which Christians were charged of "licentious behavior" and "de-bauchery" by pagans and the similar accusations made by "proto-orthodox" Christians against "heretics."[45] A rather simple change in the reading of a text, effects a reading that is more sensible within the scribe's milieu and has the additional advantage of erasing a reading that might be used to accuse Christians of immorality. We might well label such a change as apologetically driven in the context of second-and third-century charges against Christians in various regions of the empire.

We would do well to consider another textual change in this copy of Jude, a change that appears to be motivated by theological influences.[46] The contests over readings appear in Jude 5 in connection to the reference to the "Lord" who saved the people from Egypt. The reading "Lord" here is found in most manu-scripts; other manuscripts, however, read "Jesus" (e.g., A B 33 81), or "God" (C² 623 vg^ms). The scribe of the Bodmer Jude, however, is unique in reading that "the God Christ" saved the people from Egypt. Such a reading is not surprising given the fact that during the second and third centuries increasing attention was given to countering adoptionistic forms of Christianity; encapsulated within the identification of "the God Christ" is not only the equation God = Christ (which contrasts with a low Christology found among adoptionists) but also the affirmation of the existence of "Christ" prior to Jesus' baptism (which offers a counterpoint to adoptionistic views of Jesus' adoption by God at baptism).[47]

In the same Bodmer codex, we can turn to the texts of 1 and 2 Peter; although they have traditionally been attributed to the same scribe as that of Jude, we should recall the discussion from chapter 4 in which I argued for two different scribes. At 1 Peter 5:1 the text refers to Peter as "an elder and witness of the sufferings of Christ" (ὁ συμπρεσβύτερος καὶ μάρτυς τῶν τοῦ Χριστοῦ παθημάτων). The reading in the Bodmer codex, however, offers a substitution of "God" for "Christ"; Peter is now a witness to the "sufferings of God" (των του θυ παθηματων). Like the reading in Jude 5, this change serves a dual function: it affirms "that the one who suffered was God (against adoptionists)" and it stresses "that this God, Christ, really did suffer (against, e.g., various groups of Gnostics)."[48]

That the change in 1 Peter 5:1 is not simply accidental or insignificant is confirmed by the fact that we find a similar variant reading in the same papyrus at 2 Peter 1:2. Here, the omission of a καί effects a similar elevated Christological view. Rather than reading "may grace and peace be multiplied to you in the knowledge of God *and* our Lord Jesus," the text of the Bodmer codex reads "may grace and peace be multiplied to you in the knowledge of our God, the Lord Jesus (εν επειγνωση του θυ ιην του κυριου ημων).[49] The omission of the καὶ is a rather simple one, and if it were not for the fact that the omission produces a reading that is similar to another one produced in work of the same scribe, we might be inclined to think of it as a scribal blunder. What we find, however, is corroboration of this scribe's identification of Jesus with God, which makes particularly good sense in the context of second- and third-century Christological debates. Furthermore, such elevated Christological claims would fit well with what we know about Pachomian monasticism, a possible context for this codex. We find, for example, the elevation of Christ to God in the *Paralipomena*: "And since we see that you have from your fathers insensible idols, believing that the Godhead is worshipped through them, worship instead the One whom our master God begot, *true God become man for our sake, Jesus Christ* (καὶ ἐπειδὴ εἴδωλα ἀναίσθητα ὁρῶμεν ὅτι ἐκ πατέρων ἔχετε, ὡς δι' αὐτῶν τὸ θεῖον προσκυνεῖται πιστεύσαντες, μᾶλλον προσκυνεῖτε ὃν ἐγέννησεν ὁ δεσπότης ἡμῶν Θεός, Θεὸν ἀληθινόν, τὸν δι' ἡμᾶς γενόμενον ἄνθρωπον Ἰησοῦν Χριστόν); "And him whom they once did not know, God, son of God, Only begotten, become man for the sake of the human race" (καὶ ὅν ποτε ἠγνόουν Θεὸν Θεοῦ υἱὸν μονογενῆ ἐνανθρωπήσαντα διὰ τὸ ἴδιον πλάσμα, τὸ ἀνθρώπειον γένος) (*Paralipomena* 17.39).

Shifting our attention to other types of contests of readings, we can turn to a singular reading found at 1 Corinthians 16:19 in the third-century Chester Beatty codex of the Pauline Epistles (P⁴⁶). At the close of Paul's letter to the Corinthian church, we find the following: "Aquila and Prisca, together with the church in their house, greet you warmly in the Lord" (ἀσπάζεται ὑμᾶς ἐν κυρίῳ πολλὰ Ἀκύλας καὶ Πρίσκα σὺν τῇ κατ' οἶκον αὐτῶν ἐκκλησίᾳ). The couple Aquila and Prisca (Priscilla, in Acts 18:2–3, 18, 28) appear to have been Jewish converts to Christianity and are also referred to in Romans 16:3–5 and 2 Timothy

4:19. The text of P⁴⁶ at 1 Corinthians 16:19, however, is unique in reading Ἀκύλας καὶ Πρίσκας; the simple addition of a final sigma to Πρίσκα changes the name from a feminine form to a masculine one, thereby identifying in this passage two men, rather than a man and woman.[50] It must be admitted that such an addition may simply be due to the influence of the ending of Ἀκύλας. But there may be more at work in the change, for we know that the role of women was fiercely contested in early Christianity. Already in the pastoral Epistles, for example, we find the roles of women restricted and controlled; the move to limit the role and prominence of women in the early church became all the more active in the second and third centuries.[51] Furthermore, we have other instances in which textual changes appear to be motivated by antiwomen sentiments, and these provide a counterpart to the singular reading we find in P⁴⁶.

Ben Witherington and others have pointed in particular to the fifth-century Codex Bezae as preserving readings that diminish the roles and prominence of women in the early Christian movement.[52] In the book of Acts, for example, when Paul teaches in the synagogue at Thessalonica many were converted; among those converted are "not a few leading women" (γυναικῶν τε τῶν πρώτων οὐκ ὀλίγαι) (17:4). Codex Bezae, however, replaces "prominent women" with "wives of the leading men" (καὶ γυναῖκες τῶν πρώτων), thereby asserting a deliberate gender hierarchy. Similarly, just several verses later, where the text describes again the "Greek women and men of high standing" (τῶν Ἑλληνίδων γυναικῶν τῶν εὐσχημόνων καὶ ἀνδρῶν οὐκ ὀλίγοι) who were converted upon hearing Paul's words, Codex Bezae transposes the order of women and men: "and the leading men and women" (καὶ τῶν εὐσχημόνων ἄνδρες καὶ γυναῖκες). In another instance that appears to be motivated by the desire to lessen the stress upon women who converted to Christianity, Codex Bezae deletes the mention of the woman named Damaris in Acts 17:34. Bezae, of course, is beyond the time period with which I am concerned here, but I offer some of the examples of its textual variants because they confirm the existence of antiwomen influence on scribal modifications. Thus the change in P⁴⁶ becomes sensible, given the contours of debates over the role of women in the early church and the existence of textual changes manifesting these debates.

Although further examples of singular readings that suggest various ideological motivations on the part of scribes could be presented, the preceding cases suffice to illustrate the nature of our evidence.[53] That scribes could occasionally change the reading of their texts in accordance with various apologetic, Christological, and theological beliefs, as well as their views of women, emerges from the singular readings found among the earliest Christian papyri. Or, to put it differently, the discursive debates in the second and third century intersected with textual transcription in the activity of copying and the (re)production of texts and creation of new readings. Intentional scribal changes did not occur in a vacuum, nor were they random in nature; rather, they were constrained by the discursive contexts of the scribes themselves.

Variant Readings and Later Textual Tradition

The picture that the preceeding illustrations provides is corroborated by the evidence gleaned through the use of the second method I outlined above. Because this second method has been used so extensively, and the variant readings have received much attention, I will simply offer here a sample of three variants that illustrate again the range of scribal changes. The following variants offer, respectively, illumination of apologetic concerns, theological views, and anti-Jewish sentiments. Because the variant readings I discuss below, in contrast to those identified as singular, remain somewhat contested, I shall explore their history more fully.

Mark 6:3

I begin with a rather clear example of a textual modification motivated by apologetic reasons. The passage concerns Jesus' preaching in the synagogue in Nazareth, near the beginning of his ministry. Those who hear his teachings marvel, saying, "is this one not the carpenter (ὁ τέκτων), the son of Mary (ὁ υἱὸς τῆς Μαρίας), the brother of James and Joses and Judas and Simon?" (Mk 6:3). This reading is found in all of the Greek uncials, most of the minuscules, and many diverse versions.[54] In some manuscripts, however, the text identifies Jesus as "the son of the carpenter" (τοῦ τέκτονος υἱός) rather than "the carpenter" (ὁ τέκτων). Among the witnesses that attest this reading are the third-century P[45] (typically classified as proto-Alexandrian),[55] some "Caesarean" manuscripts, and some of the Bohairic and Old Latin versions. Despite this diverse attestation, the overwhelming external evidence in favor of ὁ τέκτων points to its originality.

How are we to account, then, for the variant reading "the son of the carpenter"? First, it is important to note that the Gospel parallels to this passage attest "the son of the carpenter" (ὁ τοῦ τέκτονος υἱός, Mt 13:55) and "Joseph's son" (υἱός ἐστιν Ἰωσὴφ, Lk 4:22). It may well be that the reading attested in P[45] and other witnesses represents a harmonization to the Matthean parallel.[56] But we still must explain the origin of the variant: Why do Matthew and Luke change their source? And why do some copyists of Mark 6:3 choose the longer reading? Is there something more at work than harmonization in the textual witnesses for the longer reading? Evidence exists that suggests indeed that the ὁ τέκτων reading was unpalatable to some early Christians.

We find, for example, in Origen an illuminating reference to this particular passage. In his response to the claims of Celsus, Origen writes,

> Celsus, moreover, has often mocked at the subject of a resurrection, a doctrine which he did not comprehend; and on the present occasion, not satisfied with what he has formerly said, he adds, 'And there is said to be a resurrection of the flesh by means of the tree.' . . . He next scoffs at the 'tree', assailing it on two grounds, and saying, 'For this reason is the tree introduced, either because our teacher was nailed to a cross, *or because he was a carpenter by trade*; not

observing that the tree of life is mentioned in the Mosaic writings, and being blind also to this, that in *none of the Gospels current in the Churches is Jesus himself ever described as being a carpenter.* (*Contra Celsum* 6.36)

Celsus here mocks the notion of a "resurrection of the flesh by means of the tree" on two grounds: because Christians follow a person who was nailed to a tree and because Christians follow a person who was a carpenter. Both reasons are cause for attack. Origen's response, however, is particularly puzzling given the extent to which the ὁ τέκτων reading is attested. Is it possible that Origen does not know of this reading? Among the early fathers, Origen distinguishes himself with his utmost care and concern for the words of the text.[57] Is it possible that he has simply forgotten the reading?[58] This too is unlikely. It seems most prudent to suppose that apologetic motivations are at work in Origen's statement. The notion of a carpenter as the founder of Christianity was an easy target for opponents and a troublesome passage for Christian apologists. To be sure, a similar attack on Christians is preserved in Tertullian's *Adversos Judaeos*: "Come, now, if you have read in the utterance of the prophet in the Psalms, 'God has reigned from the tree', [Ps 96:10] I wait to hear what you understand thereby; for fear you may perhaps think some carpenter-king is signified, and not Christ, who has reigned from that time onward when he overcame the death which ensued from His passion of 'the tree'" (10). Origen appears to have refuted Celsus' claim by simply arguing that the reading does not exist. In essence, Origen has corrupted the text for apologetic purposes.

Herein lies the most probable explanation for why Matthew and Luke change Mark, and why some scribes preserved the longer reading of "the son of the carpenter": in the face of opposition, the longer reading eliminates the charge against Christians following a carpenter. The importance of the text, here a matter of just two words, is displayed in this dispute over the passage in Mark 6:3.[59]

Mark 15:34

Here we take up a textual problem that demonstrates theologically motivated orthodox modification of scripture in response to certain "heretics" of the second and third centuries.[60] Mark 15:34 consists of Jesus' "cry of dereliction" just before his death. The Greek translation of Jesus' Aramaic cry (ελωι ελωι λεμα σαβαχ-Θανι), reads ὁ Θεός μου ὁ Θεός μου, εἰς τί ἐγκατέλιπές με. The problem here is the word ἐγκατέλιπες, taken by orthodox to mean "forsaken." Gnostics, however, took the word to mean "leave behind." Now Jesus cries out, "My God, my God why have you left me behind." We know that certain Gnostics considered Jesus separate from Christ. Christ entered Jesus at his baptism and left him here on the cross. Cerinthus was a primary proponent of such beliefs, and his ideas were cause for the heresiologists' attacks.[61] The debate over the interpretation of the verse can be well understood in light of what we know about Gnostic Christology.

What is most important for us, however, is that the hermeneutical debate clearly relates to the textual variant concerning this very word. In leading representatives of the Western text, instead of the word ἐγκατέλιπες, scribes have written ὠνείδισας. The reading becomes, "why have you reviled me?" Although von Harnack argued that the reading ὠνείδισας was original, his views have not been widely adopted.[62] Indeed, the external attestation for ἐγκατέλιπες is extensive: it is "found in every Greek manuscript of every textual group and subgroup, with the solitary exception of codex Bezae"; "the patristic sources attest this reading virtually without dissent, as do all of the versions."[63] Why would a scribe change the text from ἐγκατέλιπες to ὠνείδισας? The change appears to be interwoven with the contests between proto-orthodox and Gnostic Christians over interpretations of the verse. By changing the text, scribes have eliminated the possibility of the verse's "misinterpretation" and "misuse."[64] Moreover, scribes have exerted control upon the interpretation of scripture; changing the texts themselves provides orthodox Christians with another way to control and define orthodoxy in the face of "heresy" by means of the written word.[65] Once again, the discursive controversies that occupied the second- and third-century church intersect with the copying and transmission of early Christian literature.

Luke 23:34a

Our third and final textual variant stems from a slightly different motivation than our previous examples but is equally significant in light of our study. The question concerns the originality of Jesus' prayer on the cross, "Father, forgive them, for they do not know what they are doing" (ὁ δὲ Ἰησοῦς ἔλεγεν πάτερ, ἄφες αὐτοῖς, οὐ γὰρ οἴδασιν τί ποιοῦσιν [Lk 23:34]). Since the late nineteenth century scholars have debated the originality of these words.[66] The external evidence is divided. Our earliest and best proto-Alexandrian witnesses (P[75] and B) do not attest the reading. In addition, later Alexandrian (ℵ[1]), Western (D*), and Byzantine (W Θ) Greek manuscripts, along with the Syriac, Sahidic, Old Latin, and part of the Bohairic versions also exclude the prayer. On the other hand, the vast majority of the Greek manuscripts of Luke's Gospel do attest these words, including Alexandrian (ℵ*·[2]), Western (D[2]), Byzantine (A C L Ψ), and "Caesarean" (f[1.13]) text-types. The versional evidence for the longer reading is both diverse and early (lat sy[c.p.h.] bo[pt]). While at first the external evidence of P[75] and B may seem compelling, in fact, both readings are well attested in diverse Greek text-types and versions. Scholars who have argued against the originality of these words, have typically failed to note the compelling Patristic evidence.

The evidence of the church fathers who attest this verse is striking. While Cyril of Alexandria, in the fifth century, claims that the words are not original (*Julian* 13),[67] as early as the second-century the prayer is attested (in, e.g., such as Irenaeus [*Adv.Haer.* 3.18.5][68] and later Origen [*Peri Pascha* 43.33–36][69]). Moreover, the pseudo-Clementine literature (*Recognitions* 6.5; *Homily* 3.19 and 11.20), Hegesippus-Eusebius (*HE* 2.23), Archelaeus (*The Disputation with Manes* 44), *The*

Constitutions of the Holy Apostles (2.3.16; 5.3.14), *Gospel of Nicodemus* (10), and the *Acts of Philip* also cite this verse. Marcion's Luke and Tatian's *Diatessaron* include the prayer in Luke's Gospel.[70] These witnesses demonstrate that the prayer was known in the second century in Gaul, Alexandria, Palestine, Syria, and Rome. How can we account for this distribution? Are we to assume that it is only by coincidence that scribes in such diverse regions added the verse? Rather, we must conclude that all of these witnesses that attest the prayer go back to a common source. That this was a written source is corroborated by Origen's reference in *Homily* 2.1.5: "The Lord confirms this [i.e., that a congregation can sin through ignorance] in *the Gospel* when he says, 'Father, forgive them for they do not know what they are doing.'" This written source, if not original to Luke must be at least early second century, prior to Marcion's Luke (ca. 140 C.E.).

While the best Greek witness (P^{75}) does not attest the reading, the geographical distribution of the prayer is striking. The internal evidence, as I will demonstrate, clearly leans in favor of the originality of the prayer to Luke. The strongest internal argument against the longer reading is transcriptional. Some scholars have argued that the parallels between Stephen's prayer in Acts were harmonized to the account of Jesus' death in Luke.[71] While Stephen is being stoned he prays, "Lord, do not hold this sin against them" (κύριε, μὴ στήσῃς αὐτοῖς ταύτην τὴν ἁμαρτίαν) (Acts 7:60). Since this prayer echoes the words of Jesus in Luke 23:34a, scholars claim that the prayer in Luke is a harmonization. This argument, however, fails to take into account that when scribes harmonize they do so by repeating the same words *verbatim*, not by echoing a concept. Moreover, we know that Luke himself uses parallels between the Gospel and Acts to create narrative and thematic unity. He creates these parallels by mirroring parallel images, not by verbatim repetition.

Charles Talbert, for example, has highlighted the parallels within Luke's writings — parallels between the Gospel and Acts, between Peter and Paul, and in the "parallel panels" of Acts 1–5.[72] For our concerns the most important parallels are between the death of Jesus and that of Stephen. They are both brought before the authorities by the people (before Pilate in Lk 23:1; before the council in Acts 6:12), both are accused by the crowd (Lk 23:2; Acts 6:13–14), and both are questioned (Lk 23:3; Acts 7:1). Both Stephen and Jesus offer a final prayer (Lk 23:46; Acts 7:59). Stephen's prayer, κύριε Ἰησοῦ, δέξαι τὸ πνεῦμά μου ("Lord Jesus, receive my spirit") parallels Jesus' prayer in Luke 34:46, πάτερ, εἰς χεῖρας σου παρατίθεμαι τὸ πνεῦμά μου ("Father, into your hands I commend my spirit"). In the account of Jesus' death, Jesus himself predicts the coming of the Son of Man (21:27) and in Acts, Stephen sees a vision in which the Son of Man is seated at the right hand of God (7:55). Given these close parallels, the parallel between Jesus' prayer for his executioners must be regarded as a Lukan parallel to Stephen's prayer in Acts 7:60. In each case, Luke has paralleled narrative events not by using the same language but by mirroring the same idea. These parallels, along with others, are literary tools that Luke uses to create a sense of unity within his narrative. In addition, the parallels create a continuity between the period of Jesus and that of his disciples after his death. The martyr death of Jesus clearly sets an example for the first martyr death in the church.[73]

This leads us to another internal reason for the inclusion of the verse: Luke's presentation of Jesus as the suffering Messiah. The depiction of Jesus as a suffering martyr by Luke has long been recognized by scholars.[74] The question remains to what extent Luke constructed his Gospel on the basis of other martyrologies. It is interesting, for example, to compare Luke's description of Jesus' death with the presentation of Eleazar's death in 4 Maccabees. Luke presents a similar pattern: speeches on the lips of the dying person, the testing and torture, an encounter with the authorities, the willingness to die, and a parallel prayer. The intent of 4 Maccabees is admittedly different from that of Luke's Gospel. But the model for martyrdom remains the same. In 4 Maccabees, Eleazer prays as he is dying: "You know, O God, that though I could have saved myself I am dying in these fiery torments for the sake of the Law. Be merciful to your people and let our punishment be a satisfaction on their behalf" (6:27–28). So also Luke has Jesus pray first for those who are executing him ("Father, forgive them . . . ") and later, "Father, into your hands I commit my spirit" (23:46). Luke's passion narrative has been compared with other martyrologies such as 2 Maccabees, *The Martyrdom of Isaiah*, and Daniel 3 and 6.[75] While the extent of the parallels with other martyrologies continues to be debated, Brian Beck's study has demonstrated— to my mind conclusively—that Luke clearly is acquainted with the literature; Luke often uses the very same language and style to describe Jesus' death as found in other martyrologies.[76] Jesus' prayer in the context of his suffering is one more tool Luke has used to portray Jesus as the ideal suffering martyr.

There exist still other arguments for why Jesus' prayer from the cross was original to Luke. Jesus' prayer on the cross appears to contain an allusion to Isaiah 53:12: "Therefore he will inherit many things, and he will divide the spoil among the strong; because he surrendered his soul in death, and was reckoned among the transgressors; and he bore the sins of many, and *for their sins he was given over*" (διὰ τὰς ἁμαρτίας αὐτῶν παρεδόθη). What is most interesting is that Luke has a certain proclivity for Isaiah 53 and especially verse 12. In addition to Jesus' prayer, he alludes to this verse two other times (11:22, 22:37). Each time, the reference cites a portion of the Isaiah verse in chronological order. Verse 11:22 refers to dividing the spoils (Is 53:12a) and verse 22:37 quotes "and was reckoned among the transgressors" (Is 53:12b). Our passage in Luke 23:34a serves to complete the reference to Isaiah 53 with an allusion to the final clause. Given this proclivity of Luke for Isaiah 53,[77] it is more plausible to argue that the passage was original to the Gospel than to suppose that a scribe has inserted the words as an allusion to Isaiah 53.

We have seen thus far that Luke 23:34a exemplifies Lukan parallelisms, martyr-motifs, and proclivities toward Isaiah 53:12. In addition to these arguments, the central concept of Jesus' prayer captures the ignorance-forgiveness motif found throughout Lukan writings. Peter, in his speech at Solomon's portico, says, "And now, brethren, I know that you acted in ignorance (ἄγνοιαν), just as your rulers did" (Acts 3:17). Peter is referring here to the people acting in ignorance at the time of Jesus' death. Again in Luke's portrayal of Paul's Areopagus speech, ignorance is an excuse (Acts 17:27, 30). Now, however, the purpose is to convince people to repent. Conzelmann has argued that this forgiveness-ignorance motif arose out of missionary needs.[78] Particularly early in the ministry in Jewish synagogues, this motif provides an excuse to those who were in ignorance before Jesus' death. After Jesus' death and resurrection, ignorance is no longer an excuse for sin; now the command is to repent (Acts 17:30). What is crucial for our study of Luke 23:34a is not only that it represents a typically Lukan motif. More importantly, the references in Acts to ignorance prior to Jesus' death seem to *presuppose* the prayer of Jesus on the cross. Jesus prays on the behalf of those who *are* ignorant, and the Acts passages refer back to the time when ignorance *was* grounds for forgiveness.

One more argument can be added to those adduced thus far for the originality of Luke 23:34a. It is in Luke's gospel that Jesus prays with more frequency than in any other of the synoptic Gospels. Luke "depicts Jesus often at prayer, because this is to become one of the ways in which the disciple is to follow him."[79] Moreover, it is in Luke that the majority of Jesus' prayers begin with πατερ. In Matthew, the vocative form appears four times. Once it appears with the first-person plural possessive pronoun (6:9a), twice with the first-person singular possessive (26:39 and 26:42), and only once with the vocative form standing alone in a prayer (11:25). This form of address does not appear at all in Mark. In Luke, on the other hand Jesus uses the vocative form πατερ as an address eleven times. Once it parallels the verse in Matthew (Lk 10:21; cf. Mt 11:25) and once it parallels Matthew 6:9a but excludes the "our" so that πατερ stands on its own (11:2).[80] It is used a total of six times within parables (three in the parable of the Lost Son: 15:12,18,21; three times in the parable of the Rich Man and Lazarus: 16:24,27,30) where it refers to an earthly father. Including our contested passage, Jesus in Luke uses πατερ as a prayer address a total of three times in the passion narrative (22:42; 23:34, 46). The difference here between Matthew and Mark when compared with Luke is significant for the textual variant in Luke 23:34a. The grammar, language, and style agrees with Luke against the other Synoptics.[81]

I have argued on internal grounds that Luke 23:34a represents typically Lukan style and motifs. This argument is corroborated on transcriptional grounds. We know that scribal harmonization typically duplicates passages verbatim. Since what we have here between Luke 23:34a and Acts 7:60 is not verbal but conceptual agreement, it is unlikely that a scribe inserted this passage.[82]

The most striking evidence in favor of the originality of the prayer is that of transcriptional probabilities. Indeed, one is hard pressed to understand why the passage would be *inserted* in light of the early exegesis of the verse. The predominant interpretation of Luke 23:34a in the early church is that Jesus was praying for forgiveness for the Jews.[83] In the account of Hegesippus-Eusebius, the prayer spoken by James is clearly for the Jews. In his *Disputation with Manes*, Archelaus claims, "Our Lord prayed that the *Pharisees* might be pardoned, when He said, 'Father, forgive them, for they know not what they do'" (44).[84]

In light of observations concerning the early exegesis of Luke 23:34a, we must ask whether there is evidence to suggest that some scribes found it unpalatable that Jesus prayed for Jews as he was dying. In fact, we do know that in the early church the notion that God had not forgiven the Jews for crucifying Jesus, and therefore punished them by the destroying Jerusalem, was prevalent. Melito of Sardis makes precisely such a claim in his *Homily on the Passover* (99).[85] Origen likewise attests to the idea that the destruction of Jerusalem was punishment for the Jews' mistreatment of Jesus:

> For they [i.e., Jews] committed a crime of the most unhallowed kind, in conspiring against the Savior of the human race in that city where they offered up to God a worship containing the symbols of mighty mysteries. It accordingly behooved that city where Jesus underwent these sufferings to perish utterly, and the Jewish nation to be overthrown. (*Contra Celsum* 4.22)

On one hand, the exegesis of the verse typically takes Jesus' prayer to refer to Jews. On the other hand, the notion that God punished Jews for killing Jesus by destroying Jerusalem was prevalent in the early church. Is it possible, then, that scribes were motivated by anti-Jewish sentiments to excise Jesus' prayer that grants forgiveness to Jews? In fact, this is what several scholars have argued.[86] Scribes who took the destruction of Jerusalem as proof of God's punishment against Jews for killing Jesus found it impossible to retain Jesus' prayer of forgiveness. The excision of the verse was widespread and contemporary with the second-and third-century claims that Jews were responsible for the death of Jesus. The witness of the late second-or early third-century P[75] demonstrates that the variant emerged early on. Moreover, the argument that the words were omitted as a result of anti-Jewish sentiments is corroborated by a detailed study of Codex Bezae, the primary Western witness that omits the verse. Eldon Epp has convincingly demonstrated that Codex Bezae eliminates the ignorance-forgiveness motif from Acts. In this particular codex, the "element of excuse is virtually absent, while that of guilt [i.e., of Jews] finds more emphasis."[87] Bezae is just one example among many that has excised the verse out of anti-Judaic sentiments.[88]

We have dealt at length with the contests over readings in early Christian texts because they illustrate the degree to which deliberate modifications of texts stemmed from ideological concerns. In the case of Mark 6:3, we noted that the text was used to defend Christianity against its opponents. Excising the reference to Jesus being a carpenter, or changing the reading so Jesus becomes the *son* of the carpenter, were two ways in which scribes could avoid the confirmation of pagan attacks against Christians. We observed in Mark 15:34 that scribes, motivated by the doctrinal disputes of the second century, altered the text in response to the "heretical" usage of the passage. Finally, we explored quite extensively the prayer in Luke 23:34a, noting that it was omitted early and widely for anti-Jewish reasons. It is not merely coincidental that such scribal modifications occurred during Christianity's period of intense debates over theology, self-definition vis-à-vis Judaism and paganism, the roles of women in the church, and so forth. These very discursive controversies informed the textual modifications; or, to put it differently, controversies over readings were inextricably interwoven with controversies of ideology.

Why did scribes make such changes? Evidently because, as we know so well from other contexts, the very words ultimately mattered to scribes and church fathers. These words were to embody orthodox doctrine and orthodox self-definition. To ensure the "right" interpretation of the text, scribes and users occasionally modified the readings of various texts. Such scribal modifications demonstrate not the disregard for careful transcription of early Christian literature, but rather the unequivocal importance ascribed to the written text in early Christianity. Moreover, they illustrate that the scribes who copied early Christian texts were not "mere copyists" who sought to produce exact replicas; their texts leave the traces of their social, theological, and ideological embodiment within the context of nascent Christian questions of self-definition. Before concluding the present chapter, it may be useful to highlight briefly the authority of written texts in early Christianity.

THE AUTHORITY OF TEXTS IN EARLY CHRISTIANITY

The claims of Papias notwithstanding — "for I did not think that the things from books would help me as much as those from a living and surviving voice" (Eusebius, *HE* 3.29) — texts came to have an unqualified importance in the context of second- and third-century heresiological debates and more broadly in the questions of self-definition that occupied the church in this period. As we have already seen, variant readings attest to the debates over texts and their interpretations. The prominent heresiologists argue that their opponents (whether they be Gnostics, Montanists, Patripassianists, Docetists, or Adoptionists) are changing the words of Scripture to make them say what they want them to say; but simultaneously, "proto-orthodox" Christians were altering scripture. Such changes in the text are indicative of the larger hermeneutical and Christological debates taking place in the second century. In fact, it is through the written word that Christianity comes to define itself during the second and third centuries.

Christianity was rooted first in the oral teachings of Jesus. The "words of Jesus" and "testimony of the apostles" initially became formulated as a fulfillment of the Jewish scriptures.[89] Throughout the four gospels, Jesus' birth, ministry, and death are portrayed as continuous with and the fulfillment of written Jewish prophesies. This point hardly needs emphasis. Nor need it be emphasized that the Jewish Scriptures was the "Christian" Bible before the New Testament gradually came to formation. In addition, it is hard to miss the fact that nearly all of the church fathers appealed to scriptural texts as written authorities. The commentaries that were written in the third century, such as those of Origen, attest the increasing value of the written word. The work of heresiologists, such as Irenaeus, Tertullian, and Hippolytus, was invariably rooted in arguments based on the very words of scripture.[90] These writings demonstrate that at least a small portion of the Christian population—its upper echelons—was inextricably tied to the written word.

In addition to such textual controversies, we find evidence for the importance of written texts in early Christianity in the debates over the canon during the second and third centuries. Irenaeus is one of the first authors to attest the growing concern over issues of canon. Most interesting in this case, is that Irenaeus's emphasis on a four-gospel canon comes at the very time when Marcionism was flourishing (*Adv. Haer.* 3.11.8; 3.1.1). In the face of an archheretic—whose canon consisted of an edition of Luke and some Pauline letters—Irenaeus took the first steps toward establishing orthodoxy in terms of the texts that were to be considered authoritative.[91] Also critical is the implication of Irenaeus's four-gospel canon for the claims of other "heretics": Ebionites, Montanists, Valentinians, and Gnostics to cite four that Irenaeus explicitly mentions. Apparently, these Christians were appealing to single gospels as authority; Irenaeus recognized the danger in such claims. He saw, for example, that the Ebionites maintained their "heretical" Christology because they relied solely on Matthew; those Christians who claimed that Jesus was separate from Christ did so by appealing to the gospel of Mark; Marcion drew upon Luke alone; and Valentinians made copious use of John to illustrate their ideas (*Adv. Haer.* 3.11.7). To combat these various "heretics," Ireneaus argues for an inclusive but closed collection, numbering four, no more and no fewer, gospels. Thus, he limits the interpretive freedom of certain Christians by juxtaposing the four gospels in a canon *together*, thereby tempering the potential for "heretical" "misunderstandings" of scripture. In essence, Irenaeus's four-gospel canon prevents an appeal to one gospel as more authoritative than another.

Possibly contemporary with Irenaeus is the Muratorian Canon, traditionally dated between 170 and 190 C.E.[92] This list is invaluable for the information it provides concerning the criteria by which books were selected for inclusion. Although it appears that the antiquity and usage of a book were occasionally influential, by far the most prominent and important criteria were apostolicity and orthodoxy. For example, the Muratorian list explicitly denies a place in the canon for books forged in the name of Paul that further the "heresy of Marcion": "for it is not fitting that gall be mixed with honey."[93] Moreover, books in the names of Arsinous, Valentinus, Miltiades, and Basilides are to be excluded. According to this list, the *Shepherd* of Hermas, a widely circulated apocalyptic work, was not to be read publicly in churches because it was written recently and by Hermas, the brother of Pius (and hence it had no claim to apostolicity). We might also infer that the restriction on the *Shepherd* was possibly due to a concern with Montanism, a "heresy" rooted in an ecstatic and extreme apocalyptic form of Christianity.[94] The implicit argument concerning the exclusion of such books is linked to the notion of orthodoxy, for the "right belief" was certainly not to be found in the writings of those that have no claim to apostolicity.

Nowhere is the criterion of orthodoxy — or, "right belief" — more apparent and the power of literacy and authority of texts more striking than in the churches of Antioch during the bishopric of Serapion. As Eusebius tells us, Serapion originally allowed his congregations to read the *Gospel of Peter* (*HE* 6.12).[95] After *reading* the book for himself, however, Serapion claimed that it contained a heretical Christology and *wrote* to warn the Antiochene churches against the use of the book. This incident shows not only the power that literate Christians wielded in early Christianity (by excluding certain books from the canon and disallowing their use), but also the important ramifications of the debates and decisions of literate Christians (those who could read and write had the power to ensure longevity of their notion of "orthodoxy").

Even into the late third and early fourth centuries, we find orthodox writers debating the contents of the canon. Why does the issue of canon become so crucial for the early church? Perhaps in part for the same reasons that some scribes were inclined to modify their texts in the process of copying: because texts and their very words were of such importance to questions of self-definition (Christians vs. Jews; Christians vs. pagans), theology ("orthodoxy" vs. "heresy"), and various social issues facing the early Church (e.g., the role of women; asceticism). Written texts provided a foundation upon which to argue for particular beliefs, while simultaneously providing authoritative demonstration of the "correctness" of those beliefs. As Averil Cameron puts it, "Christians of whatever background in the early centuries formed their discourse on and around the Scriptures."[96]

The central concern of this chapter has been the nature of "control" over early Christian text transcription. Early Christian literature, like ancient literature more generally, was subject to unavoidable scribal errors and blunders. Authors, readers, and scribes share the awareness that scribes were bound to make mistakes, but also testify to the potential for deliberate tampering with texts. Moreover, their comments illumine the slippage of the term "corrections" in antiquity, for what was a "correction" to one author, reader, or scribe, may well have been viewed as an "error" to another. The controversies over what constituted a "correction" leads us directly into the contests over readings, and the intersection of reading and interpretation, in early Christianity. The question of "control," therefore, takes on a rather fluid meaning; nowhere, indeed, have we found ecclesiastically organized and hierarchically maintained efforts to control the process of text transmission. Rather, the "control" over texts was maintained by individual scribes, whose context influenced how they (re)produced their texts.

It was during the second and third centuries that various debates over "heresy" and "orthodoxy" circulated furiously, questions of self-definition became of crucial importance, issues of the role of women demanded attention, and diverse models of ascetic life required guidelines. Each of these discursive controversies was interwoven with texts; indeed, it is during the second and third centuries that texts — as proof texts, as demonstration of the validity of Christianity, as evidence of "right" versus "wrong" belief — became of vital importance. Although we can, through singular readings, occasionally locate a scribe who entered into the fray by creating a new text in the process of copying, more often our evidence is indirect and must be gleaned from the textual tradition we have at hand. Exploration of our earliest Christian papyri, as well as later manuscripts, testifies to the roles that scribes played in the (re)production of early Christian texts and to their setting within the intellectual discourses of early Christianity. Indeed, it was their very embodiedness within the multilayered discursive practices of second- and third-century Christianity that informed their modification of texts. Scribes' changes were not random, but marked by the constraints and pressures of their context. Simultaneously, their creation of new readings suggests that they held a certain power over these texts. Almost imperceptibly scribes were able to rewrite their texts and in doing so displayed an important role: "power exercised *over* texts allows power to be exercised *through* texts."[97] It was, in fact, these texts that came to the fore of the controversies of the second and third centuries. Finally, the fact that most scribes who copied early Christian texts remained anonymous had the paradoxical advantage of invisibly inscribing authority to the readings they produced.

CONCLUSION

There is therefore no such thing as "literacy" as a *universal* phenomenon with predetermined consequences; there are only *literacies*, each embedded in an ideological context from which it cannot be distinguished.

— Christopher Miller[1]

The central theme of the previous chapter — the malleability of written texts — brings our investigation of the scribes who copied early Christian texts full circle. I began this study with the observation that scribes have generally been overlooked by historians of antiquity; the neglect has in part been due to the assumption that scribes were simply mechanical reproducers, or replicators, of written texts. In holding these assumptions, scholars of early Christianity are no different from those of the larger Graeco-Roman world. If, however, we attach any significance to the ways in which scribes deliberately modified their texts in the process of copying them, we are drawn to the conclusion that the scribes who copied early Christian texts *did*, at least on occasion, do more than copy; these scribes, working from within the context of the discursive controversies that occupied the early Christian church, demonstrate how the contests over interpretations constrained the practices of copying. I take justification for a study of early Christian scribes in part from precisely this evidence that indicates that scribes were not "mere copyists," but rather flesh-and-blood human beings whose contexts — ideological, theological, social, geographical, and so forth — were unavoidably interwoven with their practices of copying written texts.

The present study has been driven by two central questions: Who were the scribes who copied early Christian literature during the second and third centuries? And what role(s) did these scribes play in the (re)production, transmission, and interpretation of these texts? These two questions are inextricably linked in my conception of the project as a whole. If, for instance, I had ended the story by simply replicating the Graeco-Roman denigration of the task of copying a literary text, or by concluding from the literary and epigraphic evidence that literary scribes were typically of the slave or freed classes and were not held in high regard, our story would have missed the implications of the function that these scribes performed. It is quite true that the scribes who copied Greek and Latin literary texts were usually slaves or freedpersons; but this is not the whole story. Literary scribes occupied a far more complex position; their work involved not only duplication of texts but also modification, correction, and interpretation. As (re)producers of literary texts, scribes held a certain control over the texts, and ancient authors were fully cognizant of the potential for scribal error, erasure, or emendation.

In the context of early Christianity, the questions of identity and function are also closely tied. Early Christian literature does not offer a uniform picture with regard to the identity of the scribes who copied the literature: they were not always scribes by profession nor do they appear consistently as slaves or freedpersons. When early Christian literature points to the religious identity of its scribes, however, the portrait is remarkably consistent: the scribes who copied early Christian texts were themselves Christians. This may well provide a sensible context from which to view Lucian's comments, which are puzzling for their lack of parallel: "It was then that he [Peregrinus] learned the marvellous wisdom of the Christians, by associating with their priests *and scribes*" (ὅτεπερ καὶ τὴν θαυμαστὴν σοφίαν τῶν Χριστιανῶν ἐξέμαθεν, περὶ τὴν Παλαιστίνην τοῖς ἱερεῦσιν καὶ γραμματεῦσιν αὐτῶν ξυγγενόμενος) (*de Morte Peregrini* 11). Similarly, when textual features of the second- and third-century Christian papyri offer clues to the religious identity of the scribes, these clues gesture in the same direction: harmonizations and theologically driven textual modifications, for example, point precisely to the location of scribes within early Christian communities. It may well seem that this point is self-evident; it stands in contrast, however, to the Graeco-Roman distance between the scribes who copied texts and the users of texts. Although it was customary in the Graeco-Roman world to hire a scribe or enlist the services of one's own slave-scribe to produce a copy of a literary text, a similar distinction between producers and users does not appear in the context of early Christian text transmission. What emerges from the historical record is precisely the opposite: the producers of copies of early Christian literature, the scribes, were also the users of this literature.

It is here that the connection between identity and function takes on acute significance. Early Christian scribes, who had a particular religious investment in the texts, undertook to copy these texts within the context of raging debates over heresy and orthodoxy, the limits of the canon, and questions of self-definition. All of these issues were inextricably bound to written texts. Indeed, the practice of (re)producing early Christian literature intersected with the discursive contests occupying the second-and third-century church; moreover, in (re)producing these texts, early Christian scribes staged a certain power over the texts they were copying.[2] On one level, this was a power over texts that all literary scribes in antiquity held: texts, in the hands of human scribes, were subject to various transcriptional errors as well as deliberate modification. But within the context of early Christian theological contests, the copying of early Christian texts offered a powerful resource. The literacy of scribes — and, more precisely, their ability to write — provided a means to enter into the debates over beliefs and practices through the medium of writing. In this instance, writing becomes a resource of power: the very texts that scribes (re)produced were those that had utmost significance and importance for questions of theology, self-definition, and praxis.[3]

Although such an argument contributes to the recent interest in the intersection of literacy and power in antiquity, I do not wish to universalize or overgeneralize the relationship between literacy and power. We should indeed be wary of applying totalizing statements — such as "literacy is always connected with power"[4] or "the primary function of written communication is to facilitate slavery"[5] — to the ancient context. Certainly our earliest Christian records do not preserve a uniform portrait of the power attached to writings. Papias, for example, remarks on his preference for *oral traditions*: "I did not suppose that the information from books would help me as much as that from a living and remaining voice" (οὐ γὰρ τὰ ἐκ τῶν βιβλίων τοσοῦτόν με ὠφελεῖν ὑπελάμβανον ὅσον τὰ παρὰ ζώσης φωνῆς καὶ μενούσης) (Eusebius, *HE* 3.39). It is clear that we still have much to learn about the interrelationships between written and oral in early Christianity, as well as in the Graeco-Roman world more generally. But at the moment when a scribe chooses to copy a particular text or modify a particular reading in accordance with what the scribe believes the passage to mean, the display of power over texts, and the intersection of power with literacy, becomes quite vivid. Indeed, these manipulations of texts offer evidence of a literacy that was, in Christopher Miller's words, "embedded in an ideological context from which it cannot be distinguished."

I highlight here a second difference between the Christian and Graeco-Roman contexts of text transmission: the few early Christian literary sources neither denigrate the practice of copying nor uniformly depict copyists as professional scribes or even as slaves and freedpersons. The work of Tertius, Evarestus, Hermas, Gaius, Socrates, and Pionius is nowhere denigrated; Hermas, a slave or freedman, is not identified as a professional scribe; and the Theodotians, who are lambasted by Eusebius for copying and "correcting" sacred scripture, are nowhere identified as slaves or freedpersons. This contrast becomes particularly stark if we juxtapose a source such as the first-century B.C.E. *Rhetorica ad Herennium*, which denigrates the task of copying, and Christian monastic sources of the fourth and fifth centuries, which are replete with references to reading, writing, and copying texts as demonstrative of piety and ascetic devotion. To be sure, my choices of texts here are separated by a wide five-hundred-year gap, but the paradigmatic shift from the menial slave-scribe to the elevated ascetic-copyist must somehow be accounted for.

Although an explanation of this change would require a separate study, it may well be that the appropriate place to begin would be within the Jewish context from which Christianity emerged. It would be important, for example, to explore the attitudes toward the task of copying — and perhaps writing more generally — in Jewish sources, as well as references to scribes per se. Materials are not lacking for such a study: Ezra, as the quintessential Jewish scribe, offers a starting point for any discussion of scribes in Jewish sources. Ben Sira provides a description of the ideal scribe (38:24–39:11). Jewish pseudepigrapha are replete with relevant material: Enoch is described as a "scribe of righteousness" (1 En 12:3–4; 15:1), and exalted figures, such as Enoch, Abraham, and Jacob, are depicted as copying texts (2 En 22:10–11; Jub 12:27). These sources, as well as others (e.g, *Letter of Aristeas*), offer a portrait of scribes that goes beyond merely copying texts: they are depicted as receivers of prophetic words, interpreters of the law, and wise men in general.[6] The early Christian Gospels offer a similar portrait of Jewish scribes, albeit filtered through a hostile lens. But this is only the beginning: the Dead Sea Scrolls, Philo, Josephus, Paul — there are a wealth of resources that can be mined for the identities and function of scribes per se, and the practice of copying literary texts more specifically. It may well be here that we will locate the antecedents of the late-antique Christian paradigm of the copying as a sign of one's religious devotion.

There may, of course, be other factors involved in the shifts: the political events of the fourth century, for example, warrant careful study with respect to text transmission. For a variety of reasons, I limited my study to pre-Constantinian Christianity. But it would be useful to examine what happens to the channels of private copying and transmission that appear prominently in the second and third centuries during the course of the fourth century. "Inaugurated by Constantine's recognition of Christianity"[7] and his subsequent request for fifty copies of sacred scripture, the fourth century finds the increased circulation of early Christian texts, not only among friends and associates but also, more significantly, within the confines of monastic institutions. By the turn of the fifth century, monastic scriptoria are in existence, where the practice of copying literary texts is carefully monitored and controlled (e.g., as we find in monasteries established by Rufinus). Such developments were closely linked to the legal and political legitimation of Christianity, which was followed by increasing organization and institutionalization, and clearly would bear close scrutiny.

To locate the identities and trace the functions of the scribes who copied Christian texts during the second and third centuries has been the primary aim of this study. I have intended to bring to center stage the characters that are normally left in the wings or, even worse, ignored altogether. We can now move beyond regarding literary scribes as unimportant to the processes of text transmission, denigrating them as menial low-class and low-status workers, and ignoring them as if they were invisible. When we listen carefully to our literary sources, and tease clues from features of our earliest Christian papyri, the (re)producers of our literary papyri emerge as actors who played important roles not only in the transmission of early Christian literature but also within the discourses that occupied the second- and third-century church. Placing the scribes who were behind the copies of early Christian texts into the foreground simultaneously advances our understanding of the processes of text transmission in the earliest church and restores the identities and functions of early Christian scribes to our historical narratives.

NOTES

INTRODUCTION

1. For the book trade more generally, see Raymond J. Starr, "The Circulation of Literary Texts in the Roman World," *CQ* 37 (1987) 213–223; Felix Reichmann, "The Book Trade at the Time of the Roman Empire," *Library Quarterly* 8 (1938) 40–76; A. F. Norman, "The Book Trade in Fourth-Century Antioch," *Journal of Hellenic Studies* 80 (1960) 122–126.

2. For discussions about this letter, see E. G. Turner, *Greek Papyri: An Introduction* (Princeton, N.J.: Princeton University Press, 1968) 87–88, and *Greek Manuscripts of the Ancient World*, 2d ed. (Princeton, N.J.: Princeton University Press, 1987 [1971]) 114; Julian Krüger, *Oxyrhynchos in der Kaiserzeit: Studien zur Topographie und Literaturrezeption* (Frankfurt am Main: Peter Lang, 1990) 205ff.

3. As the editor of the papyrus (J. D. Thomas) notes: "the slaves that are being distributed here were male slaves; but it is clear that a household of such size would have included female slaves as well. Therefore, we should suppose that the total number of slaves involved was much higher than fifty-nine" (see *The Oxyrhynchus Papyri* [London: Egypt Exploration Fund, 1976] 44:170).

4. Helpful discussions of this contract can be found in Greg Horsley, *NewDocs* 1 (1981) 69–70; Keith Bradley, *Slavery and Society at Rome* (Cambridge: Cambridge University Press, 1994) 63–64. Support for the implication that literate slaves were more valuable on the slave market is found in Suetonius, *de Gramm.* 4, where these slaves are labeled "litterator"; see also William H. Harris, *Ancient Literacy* (Cambridge, Mass.: Harvard University Press, 1989) 257–258.

5. Patricia Cox, *Biography in Late Antiquity: A Quest of the Holy Man* (Berkeley: University of California Press, 1983) 69.

6. On patronage, see Peter Garnsey and Richard Saller, *The Roman Empire: Economy, Society and Culture* (Berkeley: University of California Press, 1987) 148–159, especially 152–154; Richard Saller, *Personal Patronage under the Early Empire* (Cambridge: Cambridge University Press, 1982).

7. See J. W. Trigg, *Origen: The Bible and Philosophy in the Third-Century Church* (Atlanta, Ga.: John Knox Press, 1983) 81–82, 87, 147–148, 156–157; Pierre Nautin, *Origène: sa vie et son oeuvre* (Paris: Beauchesne, 1977) 74–75; Timothy D. Barnes, *Constantine and Eusebius* (Cambridge, Mass.: Harvard University Press, 1981) 84–85, 91.

8. For the text of the Muratorian Canon, see Bruce M. Metzger, *The Canon of the New Testament: Its Origin, Development, and Significance* (1987; repr., Oxford: Clarendon Press, 1997) 307; see also Geoffrey M. Hahneman, *The Muratorian Fragment and the Development of the Canon* (Oxford: Clarendon Press, 1992). The opening of *The*

Shepherd is instructive with regard to Hermas' slave status: "He who brought me up sold me to a certain Rhoda at Rome. After many years I made her acquaintance again, and began to love her as a sister" (*Shep., vis.* 1.1.1). The fact that Hermas lost touch with Rhoda may indicate that he was freed, but we do not know this for certain.

9. C. H. Roberts, *Greek Literary Hands 350 B.C.–A.D. 400* (Oxford: Clarendon Press, 1956) xi.

10. On the language of slavery, see especially Dale Martin, *Slavery as Salvation: The Metaphor of Slavery in Pauline Christianity* (New Haven, Conn.: Yale University Press, 1990); for the discussion of Christianity's attitude toward slavery as an institution, see Bradley, *Slavery and Society at Rome*, 145–153.

11. Roger Bagnall writes, "One might almost say that there was a direct correlation between the social standing that guaranteed literacy and the means to avoid writing. But this should not be taken to mean that men of this standing did not do a fair amount of writing all the same" (*Reading Papyri, Writing Ancient History* [London: Routledge, 1995] 25).

12. Since Harris's study appeared numerous scholars have taken up the issue of literacy in antiquity. See especially Rosalind Thomas, *Literacy and Orality in Ancient Greece* (Cambridge: Cambridge University Press, 1992), and *Oral Tradition and Written Record in Classical Athens* (Cambridge: Cambridge University Press, 1989); the essays in *Literacy and Power in the Ancient World*, ed. Alan K. Bowman and Greg Woolf (Cambridge: Cambridge University Press, 1994); and the special issue of the *Journal of Roman Archaeology* supp. ser. 3, entitled *Literacy in the Roman World* (1991).

13. *Ancient Literacy*, 13.

14. Indeed, he directs much of his work against previous scholarship on the subject of ancient education: he counters the notion that there was "a dense network of schools" (proposed by G. F. Gianotti and A. Pennacini, *Società e communicazione letteraria in Roma antica*, vol. 3 [Turin: Loescher, 1981] 128; quoted in Harris, *Ancient Literacy*, 235); he problematizes the use of evidence in the most widely accepted secondary study of ancient education—a study that argued, for instance, that "it remains true that the whole of the Empire was covered with a fairly dense network of academic institutions" (H.-I. Marrou, *A History of Education in Antiquity*, 3d ed., trans. George Lamb [New York: Sheed and Ward, 1956] 296; orig. pub. *Histoire de l'éducation dans l'antiquité* [Paris: Editions du Seuil, 1948]; for Harris' comments on Marrou's work see *Ancient Literacy*, 130, 134, 235, 244); for the Roman context, Stanley F. Bonner's work offers a portrait similar to Marrou's arguments for widespread ancient education (*Education in Ancient Rome: From the Elder Cato to the Younger Pliny* [Berkeley: University of California Press, 1977]).

15. Harris, of course, does address the question of literacy among slaves and argues that while the levels of slave literacy was limited, "it strongly influenced the shape of the entire educational system" (*Ancient Literacy*, 258).

16. That the legal regulations against slaves owning anything were often, in practice, not enforced is evident in emergence of the *peculium* (funds that the head of a household might set aside for children and slaves); many slaves had this money at their disposal, and they might earn additional money independently, but such funds

remained *legally* the property of the master (see Martin, *Slavery as Salvation*, 7–11; Bradley, *Slavery and Society at Rome*, 27).

17. On the terms "class" and "status" see Dale Martin, *The Corinthian Body* (New Haven, Conn.: Yale University Press, 1995) xvi; Wayne A. Meeks, *The First Urban Christians: The Social World of the Apostle Paul* (New Haven, Conn.: Yale University Press, 1983) 53–55; and the extensive discussion of such terms, particularly the Marxist understanding of "class," in G. E. M. de Ste. Croix, *The Class Struggle in the Ancient Greek World: From the Archaic Age to the Arab Conquests* (Ithaca, N.Y.: Cornell University Press, 1981) 43–44, 89–96, passim); see also Rosemary Crompton, *Class and Stratification: An Introduction to Currect Debates* (Cambridge: Polity Press, 1993).

18. For earlier periods see, for example, Aaron Demsky, "The Education of Canaanite Scribes in the Mesopotamian Cuneiform Traditions," in *Bar-Ilan Studies in Assyriology*, ed. Jacob Klein and Aaron Skaist (Ramat Gan, Israel: Bar-Ilan University Press, 1990) 156–170; Menahem Haran, "Archives, Libraries, and the Order of the Biblical Books," *JANES* 22 (1993) 51–61; idem, "Bookscrolls in Israel in Pre-Exilic Times," in *Essays in Honour of Yigael Yadin*, ed. Geza Vermes and Jacob Neusner (Totowa, N.J.: Allanheld, Osmun, 1983) 161–173; idem, "The Codex, the Pinax and the Wooden Slats" [Hebrew] *Tarbiz* 57 (1988) 151–164; idem, "More Concerning Book-Scrolls in Pre-Exilic Times," *JJS* 35 (1984) 84–85; the numerous studies on literacy and scribes in Ptolemaic period, cited below; for later periods, the literature is extensive, but see especially the following: Evaristo Arns, *La technique du livre d'après saint Jérôme* (Paris: E. de Boccard, 1953); Jonathan J. G. Alexander, *Medieval Illuminators and Their Methods of Work* (New Haven, Conn.: Yale University Press, 1992); Christopher de Hamel, *A History of Illuminated Manuscripts* (London: Phaidon Press, 1994 [1986]); Rosamond McKitterick, *Books, Scribes and Learning in the Frankish Kingdom, 6th–9th Centuries* (Aldershot, U.K.: Variorum Reprints, 1994); Malachi Beit-Arié, *Hebrew Manuscripts of the East and West: Towards a Comparative Codicology* (London: British Library, 1993), and "The Transmission of Texts by Scribes and Copyists: Unconscious and Critical Interferences," *Bulletin of the John Rylands University Library Manchester* 75 (1993) 33–51.

19. On palaeography, see most usefully, Ruth Barbour, *Greek Literary Hands A.D. 400–1600* (Oxford: Clarendon Press, 1981); C. H. Roberts, *Greek Literary Hands 350 B.C.–A.D. 400* (Oxford: Clarendon Press, 1956); and E. G. Turner, *Greek Manuscripts of the Ancient World*, 2d ed. (Princeton, N.J.: Princeton University Press, 1987 [1971]); on writing positions, see especially Bruce M. Metzger, "When Did Scribes Begin to Use Writing Desks?" in *New Testament Tools and Studies*, vol. 8, *Historical and Literary Studies, Pagan, Jewish, Christian* (Grand Rapids, Mich.: Eerdmans, 1968) 123–137; George M. Parássoglou, "ΔΕΞΙΑ ΧΕΙΡ ΚΑΙ ΓΟΝΥ: Some Thoughts on the Postures of the Ancient Greeks and Romans When Writing on Papyrus Rolls," *Scrittura e Civiltà* 3 (1979) 5–21, and "A Roll upon His Knees," *Yale Classical Studies* 28 (1985) 273–275; and Kenneth W. Clark, "Posture of the Ancient Scribe," *BA* 26 (1963) 63–72; on materials, see especially the work of Naphtali Lewis on the use of papyrus, *Papyrus in Classical Antiquity* (Oxford: Clarendon Press, 1974); and J. B. Poole and R. Reed, "The Preparation of Leather and Parchment by the Dead Sea Scrolls Community," *Technology and Culture* 3 (1962) 1–26; on the forms of books, especially related to the codex and roll, see particularly E. G. Turner, *Typology*

of the Early Codex (Philadelphia: University of Pennsylvania Press, 1977); C. H. Roberts and T. C. Skeat, *The Birth of the Codex* (London: Oxford University Press, 1987).

20. Beyond the work of Haran cited in note 18 above, see Saul Lieberman, *Greek in Jewish Palestine* (1965) and *Hellenism in Jewish Palestine* (1962), (reprinted as single volume (New York: Jewish Theological Seminary, 1994); John G. Gammie and Leo G. Perdue, eds., *The Sage in Israel and the Ancient Near East* (Winona Lake, Ind.: Eisenbrauns, 1990); Ellis Rivkin, "Scribes, Pharisees, Lawyers, Hypocrites: A *Study in Synonymity*," *HUCA* 49 (1978) 135–142; Daniel R. Schwartz, *Studies in the Jewish Background of Christianity* (Tübingen: J. C. B. Mohr, 1992) especially chapter 5, 89–101; Joseph H. Dampier, "The Scrolls and the Scribes of the New Testament," *Bulletin of the Evangelical Theological Society* 1 (1988) 8–19. The issues related to Jewish scribes, particularly as they are portrayed in the New Testament are enormously complex and will not be dealt with extensively in this study for reasons that will be discussed below. Fortunately, there is now available a more comprehensive study of second-temple Jewish scribes that attempts to deal carefully with the evidence from the synoptic Gospels: Christine Schams, *Jewish Scribes in the Second-Temple Period*, JSOT s.s. 291 (Sheffield: Sheffield Academic Press, 1998).

21. Most recently see John Oates, *The Ptolemaic Basilikos Grammateus* (Atlanta, Ga.: Scholars Press, 1995); also Guido Bastianini and John Whitehorne, *Strategi and Royal Scribes of Roman Egypt: Chronological List and Index* (Firenze: Edizioni Gonnelli, 1987); for literary scribes, see especially the work of Willy Clarysse, "Egyptian Scribes Writing Greek," *Chronique d'Égypt* 68 (1993) 186–201, and "Literary Papyri in Documentary 'Archives'," in *Egypt and the Hellenistic World: Proceedings of the International Colloquium, Leuven, 24–26 May 1982*, ed. E. van 'T Dack, P. van Dessel, and W. van Gucht (Lovanii: [Orientaliste], 1983) 43–61; E. G. Turner, "Roman Oxyrhynchus," *JEA* 38 (1952) 78–93, and "Scribes and Scholars of Oxyrhynchus," *MPER* 5 (1955) 141–149, and more recently see Julian Krüger, *Oxyrhynchos in der Kaiserzeit*.

22. On ancient libraries see T. Keith Dix, "'Public Libraries' in Ancient Rome: Ideology and Reality," *Libraries and Culture* 29 (1994) 282–296; Lorne Bruce, "Palace and Villa Libraries from Augustus to Hadrian," *Journal of Library History* 21 (1986) 510–552; J. W. Thompson, *Ancient Libraries* (Berkeley: University of California Press, 1940); on the circulation of literary texts and the book trade see especially, Felix Reichmann, "The Book Trade at the Time of the Roman Empire"; John J. Phillips, "Atticus and the Publication of Cicero's Works," *Classical World* 79 (1986) 227–237; Raymond J. Starr, "The Circulation of Literary Texts in the Roman World," *CQ* 37 (1987) 213–223; A. F. Norman, "The Book Trade in Fourth-Century Antioch," *Journal of Hellenic Studies* 80 (1960) 122–126; Richard Sommer, "T. Pomponius Atticus und die Verbreitung von Ciceros Werken," *Hermes* 61 (1926) 389–422; Kenneth Quinn, "The Poet and his Audience in the Augustan Age," *ANRW* 30.1 (1982) 75–180.

23. See especially David Diringer, *The Book Before Printing: Ancient, Medieval and Oriental* (New York: Dover Publications, 1982); and Leila Avrin, *Scribes, Script and Books: The Book Arts from Antiquity to the Renaissance* (Chicago and London: American

Library Association and the British Library, 1991); Theodor Birt, *Das Antike Buchwesen in seinem Verhältnis zur Literatur* (Berlin: Scienta Verlag Aalen, 1882).

24. Robin Lane Fox, "Literacy and Power in Early Christianity," in *Literacy and Power in the Ancient World*, 131, emphasis mine.

25. This will be explored fully in chapter 5, but I here highlight several studies that point to the ways in which scribes modified their texts in response to social, religious, or ideological issues: Bart D. Ehrman, *The Orthodox Corruption of Scripture: The Effect of Early Christological Controversies on the Text of the New Testament* (New York: Oxford University Press, 1993), and "The Text as Window: New Testament Manuscripts and the Social History of Early Christianity," in *The Text of the New Testament in Contemporary Research: Essays on the Status Quaestionis*, ed. Bart D. Ehrman and Michael W. Holmes (Grand Rapids, Mich.: W. B. Eerdmans, 1995) 361–379; J. Rendel Harris, "New Points of View in Textual Criticism," *The Expositor* 8/7 (1914) 316–334, and "Was the Diatessaron Anti-Judaic?" *HTR* 18 (1925) 103–109; Eldon Jay Epp, "The 'Ignorance Motif' in Acts and Anti-Judaic Tendencies in Codex Bezae," *HTR* 55 (1962) 51–62, and *The Theological Tendency of Codex Bezae Cantabrigiensis in Acts* (Cambridge: Cambridge University Press, 1966).

26. James E.G. Zetzel, *Latin Textual Criticism in Antiquity* (New York: Arno Press, 1981) 254.

27 "Morphology and the Book from an American Perspective," *Printing History* 17 (1990) 2–14; quoted by Roger Chartier, *The Order of Books* (Stanford, Calif.: Stanford University Press, 1994) 9.

28. *Egypt in Late Antiquity* (Princeton, N.J.: Princeton University Press, 1993) 47.

29. *Greek Literary Hands 350 B.C.–A.D. 400*, xvi.

30. *Greek Manuscripts*, 2d ed., 17. For a discussion of the hands of papyri found outside of Egypt, see especially Edoardo Crisci, "Scritture greche palestini e mesopotamiche (III secolo a.C.–III d.C.)," *Scrittura e Civiltà* 15 (1991) 125–183 & Plates I–XXVII; and a recent listing and survey of nonliterary papyri from the Roman Near East, see H. M. Cotton, W. E. H. Cockle, and F. G. B. Millar, "The Papyrology of the Roman Near East: A Survey," *JRS* 85 (1995) 214–235.

31. "Literary Papyri in Documentary 'Archives'," 49.

32. On linguistic diversity, see especially Harris, *Ancient Literacy*, 175–190; Ramsay MacMullen, "Provincial Languages in the Roman Empire," *American Journal of Philology* 87 (1966) 1–17.

33. E. R. Richards provides a useful introduction to secretaries in Graeco-Roman antiquity (*The Secretary in the Letters of Paul* [Tübingen: J. C. B. Mohr, 1991] especially 14–67).

34. Exceptions to this general tendency are the slaves and freed *librarii* that we find named in the correspondence of Cicero: Hilarus (*Att.* 12.37; 13.19); Spintharus (*Att.* 13.25); Philotimus (*Att.* 13.33); Pharnaces, Antaeus, and Salvius (*Att.* 13.44).

35. In the earliest period, *librarii* was the term used to describe the booksellers themselves; later, *librarii* becomes restricted to copyists and the Greek loan word *bibliopola* is used for booksellers (Federic G. Kenney, "Books and Readers in the Roman World," in *The Cambridge History of Classical Literature*, vol. 2 [Cambridge: Cambridge University Press, 1982] 19n.6). See further chapter 3.

36. See, for example, Strabo on Aristotle's library (13.1.54); see also the *Letter of Aristeas*; Seneca, *Tranq.* 9; Seneca, *Ep.* 27.5ff.

37. See especially L. D. Reynolds and N. G. Wilson, *Scribes and Scholars: A Guide to the Transmission of Greek and Latin Literature* (Oxford: Clarendon Press, 1968); Kenney, "Books and Readers," 3–32; and more recently, Elaine Fantham, *Roman Literary Culture from Cicero to Apuleius* (Baltimore, Md.: Johns Hopkins University Press, 1996).

38. *Scribes and Scholars*, 3–4, 8, and 22, respectively.

39. *Roman Literary Culture*, 2.

40. It is not my intent here to discuss the goals of "social history," particularly as set forth by the Annales school in conjunction with Marxism. Particularly useful are the discussions found in Joyce Appleby, Lynn Hunt, and Margaret Jacob, *Telling the Truth about History* (New York: W. W. Norton, 1994) 84; Lynn Hunt, ed., *The New Cultural History* (Berkeley: University of California Press, 1989) 1–6.

41. Fantham, *Roman Literary Culture*, 36.

42. Ibid., 36–37.

43. The best introduction to the study of the papyri is still E. G. Turner's *Greek Papyri*. See also Naphtali Lewis, *Papyrus in Classical Antiquity*; L. D. Reynolds and N. G. Wilson, *Scribes and Scholars*; C. H. Roberts and T. C. Skeat, *The Birth of the Codex*. For bibliographic interests in the papyri, the most useful resource is John F. Oates, Roger S. Bangall, William H. Willis, and Klaas A. Worp, *Checklist of Editions of Greek and Latin Papyri, Ostraca, and Tablets*, 4th ed. (Atlanta, Ga.: Scholars Press, 1992).

44. See especially the archives of Menches and Petaus. For discussion of Menches, who was a village scribe in Kerkeosiris in the late second century B.C.E., see P. W. Pestman, "The Official Archive of the Village Scribes of Kerkeosiris: Notes on the So-Called Archive of Menches," *Festschrift zum 100-jährigen Bestehen der Papyrussammlung der Österreichischen Nationalbibliothek, Papyrus Erzherzog Rainer* (Wien: Verlag Brüder Hollinek, 1983) 127–134; and Clarysse, "Literary Papyri in Documentary 'Archives'," 51; for Petaus see Ursula Hagedorn, Dieter Hagedorn, Louise C. Youtie, and Herbert C. Youtie, *Das Archiv des Petaus (P. Petaus)* (Köln: Westdeutscher Verlag, 1969).

45. *The Ptolemaic Basilikos Grammateus*. For brief overviews of these official scribes, see Friedrich Oertel, *Die Liturgie: Studien zur Ptolemäischen und kaiserlichen Verwaltung Ägyptens* (Leipzig: Teubner, 1917); for lists of named strategi and royal scribes, see Guido Bastianini and John Whitehorne, *Strategi and Royal Scribes of Roman Egypt: Chronological List and Index* (Florence: Gonnelli, 1987).

46. *Greek Literary Hands*, xi.

47. See especially the work of Roger Bagnall for these concerns: *Egypt in Late Antiquity* (Princeton, N.J.: Princeton University Press, 1993), *Reading Papyri*, and with B. W. Frier, *The Demography of Roman Egypt* (Cambridge: Cambridge University Press, 1994).

48. The distinction between "literary" (copies of literature) and "documentary" (everything else) papyri is a commonplace and is manifested in the standard publications' classifications of papyri according to this dichotomy, but this system of classification is not without serious problems. E. G. Turner's work in particular strives to avoid the pitfalls of a strict dichotomy, for in his opinion the "dichotomy of

the texts from Graeco-Roman Egypt into literary and documentary papyri has put scholarship in blinkers" (*Greek Papyri*, vi–vii). Pack offers an especially problematic definition of the distinction between "documentary" and "literary": "Pragmatic considerations have led me to use the term 'literary' in the sense prevalent among the papyrologists, who generally apply it to most or all of the texts that were intended to reach the eyes of a reading public or at least possessed a more than ephemeral interest or usefulness. In practice, this means that virtually nothing is excluded save documents and private letters, so that many of the fragments listed here are really 'quasi-literary', that is, they can lay only a dubious claim to literary merit" (Roger A. Pack, *The Greek and Latin Literary Texts from Greco-Roman Egypt*, 2d and revised ed. [Ann Arbor: University of Michigan Press, 1967] 1).

49. Turner, *Greek Papyri*, 94.

50. Subscriptions in the Roman period, the few that exist, usually only consist of stichometric calculations (see J. Rendel Harris, "Stichometry," *American Journal of Philology* 4 [1883] 133–157, 309–331). For subscriptions in a later period, see J. E. G. Zetzel, "The Subscriptions in the Manuscripts of Livy and Fronto and the Meaning of *Emendatio*," *Classical Philology* 75 (1980) 38–59; O. Jahn, "Über die Subscriptionen in den Handschriften römischer Classiker," *Berichte über die Verhandlungen der königlich-sächsischen Gesellschaft der Wissenschaften zu Leipzig, Philologisch-Historische Klasse* 3 (1851) 327–372; Reynolds and Wilson, *Scribes and Scholars*, esp. 33–37.

51. This may explain the frequency with which ancient authors complain about poor copies (e.g., Cicero, *Ep.Q.Fr.* 3.6; Seneca, *de Ira* 2.26.2).

52. See, for example, *P. Petaus* 121, in which the village scribe Petaus learns how to write by practicing his signature; *CPR* 5,2 also appears to be an example of an official scribe practicing writing. We also have letters of apprenticeship (e.g., to a shorthand writer, *P.Oxy.* 724).

53. On school texts, see most recently Raffaella Cribiore, *Writing, Teachers, and Students in Graeco-Roman Egypt* (Atlanta, Ga.: Scholars Press, 1996). Unfortunately, Cribiore's study does not include the training of scribes: "Since my principal aim is to investigate the acquisition of writing by beginners, I will not specifically treat the activity of scribes" (28).

54. The exception to this are E. G. Turner's *Greek Papyri* and *The Papyrologist at Work* (Durham, N.C.: Duke University Press, 1973).

55. Again the exception to this tendency is found in the work of E. G. Turner, but even Turner's most extensive discussions of scribes relates only to scholar-scribes ("Scribes and Scholars of Oxyrhynchus," *MPER* 5 [1955] 141–149; *Greek Papyri*, 92–96).

56. This will be addressed more fully in chapter 4; on the "scriptorium" at Qumran, see especially Ronny Reich, "A Note on the Function of Room 30 (the 'Scriptorium') at Khirbet Qumran," *JJS* 46 (1995) 157–160; Bruce M. Metzger, "When Did Scribes Begin to Use Writing Desks?" 134–137.

57. Leila Avrin, *Scribes, Script and Books*, 161.

58. For example, the third-century stele of a certain scribe named Timokrates included in Henri-Irénée Marrou, *Mousikos Aner: Étude sur les scènes de la vie intellectuelle figurant sur les monuments funéraires romains* (Rome: L'erma di Bretschneider, 1964) 149, number 189. See also the early second-century marble relief that depicts a female

clerk or record keeper in the shop of a butcher (Natalie Kampen, *Image and Status: Roman Working Women in Ostia* [Berlin: Gebr. Mann, 1981] 157 and figure 45).

59. "ΔΕΞΙΑ ΧΕΙΡ," 16.

60. For the first-century evidence, discussions of Paul's use of letter-writers/secretaries are particularly relevant: Richards, *The Secretary in the Letters of Paul*; Murphy-O'Conner, *Paul the Letter-Writer*. The writings of Eusebius, Jerome, and the desert Fathers are replete with references to manuscript production, copying, transmission, and dissemination of texts, as well as comments on the uses and significance of religious texts.

61. For a listing and discussion of early Christian papyri, see E. A. Judge and S. R. Pickering, "Biblical Papyri Prior to Constantine: Some Cultural Implications of Their Physical Form," *Prudentia* 10 (1970) 1–13; see also their "Papyrus Documentation of Church and Community in Egypt to the Mid-Fourth Century," *Jahrbuch Für antike und Christentum* 20 (1977) 47–71; K. Aland, ed., *Repertorium*; idem, *Liste*; J. van Haelst, *Catalogue*; J. K. Elliott, *Bibliography*; for the value of the early Christian papyri for social history, see especially Eldon Jay Epp, "The Significance of the Papyri for Determining the Nature of the New Testament Text in the Second Century: A Dynamic View of Textual Transmission," in *Gospel Traditions in the Second Century: Origins, Recensions, Text, and Transmission*, ed. William L. Petersen (Notre Dame, Ind.: University of Notre Dame Press, 1989) 71–103; and more extensively, see Colin H. Roberts, *Manuscript, Society and Belief in Early Christian Egypt* (London: Oxford University Press, 1979).

62. The feature most widely discussed is that of the codex form of the earliest Christian papyri: Colin H. Roberts and T. C. Skeat, *The Birth of the Codex*; Eric G. Turner, *The Typology of the Early Codex*; T. C. Skeat, "The Origin of the Christian Codex," *ZPE* 102 (1994) 263–298; William V. Harris, "Why Did the Codex Supplant the Book-Roll?" in *Renaissance Society and Culture: Essays in Honor of Eugene F. Rice, Jr.*, ed. John Monfasani and Ronald G. Musto (New York: Italica Press, 1991) 71–85; Harry Y. Gamble, "The Pauline Corpus and the Early Christian Book," in *Paul and the Legacies of Paul*, ed. William S. Babcock (Dallas, Tx.: Southern Methodist University Press, 1990) 265–398; Peter Katz, "The Early Christians' Use of Codices Instead of Rolls," *JTS* 46 (1945) 63–65; Irven M. Resnick, "The Codex in Early Jewish and Christian Communities," *Journal of Religious History* 17 (1992) 1–17; Alain Blanchard, ed., *Les débuts du codex* (Brepols: Turnhout, 1989).

63. See especially the pioneering work of Ernest C. Colwell, "Scribal Habits in Early Papyri: A Study in the Corruption of the Text," in *The Bible in Modern Scholarship*, ed. J. Philip Hyatt (Nashville, Tenn.: Abingdon Press, 1965) 370–389; republished as "Method in Evaluating Scribal Habits: A Study of P^{45}, P^{66}, P^{75}," in his *Studies in the Methodology in Textual Criticism of the New Testament* (Leiden: E. J. Brill, 1969) 106–124; James R. Royse has taken the discussion of scribal habits further: "Scribal Habits in Early Greek New Testament Papyri" (Ph.D. diss., Graduate Theological Union, Berkeley, Calif., 1981), and "Scribal Habits in the Transmission of New Testament Texts," in *The Critical Study of Sacred Texts*, ed. W. D. O'Flaherty (Berkeley: Berkeley Religious Studies Series, 1979) 139–161; see also Peter Head, "Observations on Early Papyri of the Synoptic Gospels, especially on the 'Scribal Habits'," *Biblica* 71 (1990) 240–247; and his more recent article, which offers an original and very

interesting study of how re-inking led to distraction and subsequently scribal errors, with M. Warren, "Re-Inking the Pen: Evidence from P.Oxy.657 (P^{13}) Concerning Unintentional Scribal Errors," *NTS* 43 (1997) 466–73; see further, Moisés Silva, "The Text of Galatians: Evidence from the Earliest Greek Manuscripts," in *Scribes and Scripture*, ed. D. A. Black (Winona Lake, Ind.: Eisenbrauns, 1992) 17–25.

64. See most comprehensively Bart D. Ehrman, *The Orthodox Corruption of Scripture*; Eldon Jay Epp, "The 'Ignorance Motif' in Acts and Anti-Judaic Tendencies in Codex Bezae," and *The Theological Tendency of Codex Bezae Cantabrigiensis in Acts*; Ben Witherington, "The Anti-Feminist Tendencies of the 'Western' Text in Acts," *JBL* 103 (1984) 82–84; Mikeal C. Parsons, "A Christological Tendence in P^{75}," *JBL* 105 (1986) 463–479; for older studies that deal with similar issues, see J. Rendel Harris, "New Points of View in Textual Criticism"; "Was the Diatessaron Anti-Judaic?"; C. S. C. Williams, *Alterations to the Text of the Synoptic Gospels and Acts* (Oxford: Basil Blackwell, 1951).

65. Judge and Pickering, "Biblical Papyri Prior to Constantine," 9.

66. Ibid., 8.

67. For an exception, see Colin H. Roberts, "P. Yale 1 and the Early Christian Book," in *American Studies in Papyrology*, vol. 1, *Essays in Honor of C. Bradford Welles* (New Haven, Conn.: American Society of Papyrologists, 1966) 26.

68. *The Text of the New Testament* (Grand Rapids, Mich.: Eerdmans, 1987) 70.

69. *The Text of the New Testament: Its Transmission, Corruption, and Restoration*, 3d ed. (New York: Oxford University Press, 1992) 14.

70. *Codex Bezae: An Early Christian Manuscript and Its Text* (Cambridge: Cambridge University Press, 1992) 2–3; similarly, see Jean Duplacy, "Histoire des manuscrits et histoire du texte du N.T.," *NTS* 13 (1965–1966) 124–139, especially 131.

71. The literature on "power," of course, is extensive. My use of "power" has been informed in part by Anthony Giddens, *Central Problems in Social Theory: Action, Structure, and Contradiction in Social Analysis* (Berkeley: University of California Press, 1979); Dorothy Emmet, "The Concept of Power," *Proceedings of the Aristotelian Society*, n.s. 54 (1953–1954) 1–26; Michael Mann, *The Sources of Social Power*, vol. 1, *A History of Power from the Beginning to A.D. 1760* (Cambridge: Cambridge University Press, 1986). On the third use of "power," the work of Michel Foucault has been most helpful: see especially, *The Archaeology of Knowledge*, trans. A. M. Sheridan Smith (New York: Pantheon, 1972; French original, 1969), and *Power/Knowledge: Selected Interviews and Other Writings, 1972–1977*, ed. and trans. Colin Gordon (New York: Pantheon, 1980). Simon Price, in part dependent upon Foucault's ideas, writes in his treatment of the Roman imperial cult: "power is a term for analysing complex strategic situations" (*Rituals and Power: The Roman Imperial Cult in Asia Minor* [Cambridge: Cambridge University Press, 1984] 242).

72. Particularly helpful is Robert Kraft's use and discussion of the phrase "scriptural consciousness" as "special reverential attitudes towards the localization and preservation of traditional authoritative materials in fixed written format" ("Scripture and Canon in Jewish Apocrypha and Pseudepigrapha," in *Hebrew Bible/Old Testament: The History of Its Interpretation*, vol. 1, *From the Beginnings to the Middle Ages [Until 1300]*, ed.

Magne Sæbø, pt. 1 [Göttingen: Vandenhoeck & Ruprecht, 1996] 199–216, esp. 201).

73. *MSB*, 46ff.

74. See especially, *The Order of Books: Readers, Authors, and Libraries in Europe between the Fourteenth and Eighteenth Centuries*, trans. Lydia G. Cochrane [Stanford, Calif.: Stanford University Press, 1994]; *Forms and Meanings: Texts, Performances, and Audiences from Codex to Computer* [Philadelphia: University of Pennsylvania Press, 1995]; "Texts, Printing, Readings," in *The New Cultural History*, ed. Lynn Hunt [Berkeley: University of California Press, 1989] 154–175; and *On the Edge of the Cliff: History, Language, and Practices*, trans. Lydia G. Cochrane [Baltimore, Md.: Johns Hopkins University Press, 1997).

75. I borrow here the term "textual culture" from Martin Irvine, whose own use of the term is closely related to Brian Stock's notion of a "textual community" (see Martin Irvine, *The Making of Textual Culture: 'Grammatica' and Literary Theory, 350–1100* [Cambridge: Cambridge University Press, 1994] especially 15; Brian Stock, *The Implications of Literacy: Written Language and Models of Interpretation in the Eleventh and Twelfth Centuries* [Princeton, N.J.: Princeton University Press, 1983]). I would depart from Irvine, however, in his argument that "textual culture," or "textual communities," did not emerge until the rise in late antiquity of *grammatica*, which (according to Irvine) "produced a culture that was explicitly *intertextual*" (15). We find already in the second century, indeed, Christians disputing the interpretation of *texts*; issues of doctrine hinge upon the precise words and meanings. Such a development marks the contours of an emerging "textual culture."

CHAPTER 1

1. Roger Bagnall, *Reading Papyri*, 25; see also Myles McDonnell, "Writing, Copying, and Autograph Manuscripts in Ancient Rome," *CQ* 46 (1996) 469–491.

2. For theoretical reflections on "boundaries," see especially Peter Stallybrass and Allon White, *The Politics and Poetics of Transgression* (Ithaca, N.Y.: Cornell University Press, 1986).

3. The locus classicus for discussion of various occupations is found in Cicero (*Off.* 1.150–151), who classifies doctors, architects, and teachers among the professionals (see the helpful discussion in Sandra R. Joshel, *Work, Identity, and Legal Status at Rome: A Study of the Occupational Inscriptions* [Norman: University of Oklahoma Press, 1992] 66–68).

4. According to the sample provided in OLD, s.v., "professio" and "professor."

5. The dichotomy between public versus private (found both in ancient sources and modern analyses) is a notoriously thorny one and has received recent criticism, particularly among feminist historians and theorists (see, e.g., Linda K. Kerber, "Separate Spheres, Female Worlds, Woman's Place: The Rhetoric of Women's History," *Journal of American History* 75 [1988] 9–39).

6. See OLD s.v., "publicus."

7. Raymond Starr makes a more stark distinction between a public book trade and private text circulation ("Circulation of Literary Texts," 213).

8. It is the term used by Libanius, however, for a copyist (see A. F. Norman, "Book Trade," 122–126; reprinted in *Libanios*, ed. Georgios Fatouros and Tilman Krischer [Darmstadt: Wissenschaftliche Buchgesellschaft, 1983] 267–280); on Libanius see further, Paul Petit, "Recherches sur la publication et la diffusion des discours de Libanius," *Historia* 5 (1956) 479–509. Furthermore, the term γραμματεύς normally designates a clerk or administrative official of some type (see below). For a helpful discussion of the ancient *librarius*, see H. Leclercq, "Librarius," *Dictionnaire d'archéologie Chrétienne et de liturgie*, vol. 9 (Paris: Librairie Letouzey et Ané., 1930) 553–557.

9. On the issue of dating, see J. J. Phillips, "The Publication of Books at Rome in the Classical Period" (Ph.D. diss., Yale University, 1981) 24. The reference from Catullus appears to be the earliest mention of a bookshop (although Birt, *Buchwesen*, 356–337, seems to think Cicero's *Phil.* 2.21 is earliest; according to Phillips, Catullus was written fourteen years before this particular Cicero passage [135 n. 38]).

10. Phillips, "Publication of Books," 25.

11. L. Richardson, Jr., *A New Topographical Dictionary of Rome* (Baltimore, Md.: Johns Hopkins University Press, 1992), s.v., "Emporium" (143–144; quotation taken from 143) and "Porta Trigemina" (310).

12. On the issues of dating inscriptions see especially introductory manuals such as Arthur E. Gordon, *Illustrated Introduction to Latin Epigraphy* (Berkeley: University of California Press, 1983); and John Edwin Sandys, *Latin Epigraphy* (Cambridge: Cambridge University Press, 1918; 2d ed. by S. G. Campbell 1927). As Gordon points out, the names in inscriptions are often useful clues to status and the date of the inscription (when, of course, no date is given within the inscription itself) (17–30). The name Celadus is used by both Suetonius and Josephus to refer to a certain freedman of Augustus by that name (see, respectively, Suet., *Aug.* 67.1; Jos., *Ant.* 17.332; *Bell.* 2.106–109); Juvenal also identifies a grammaticus by the name Celadus (7.215). For further references to the name see *PIR*² 2.146. On slaves taking their master's nomen and praenomen upon manumission, see Gordon, *Illustrated Introduction*, 27.

13. Horace, *Epist.* 1.20.2, *Ars* 345; Seneca, *Ben.* 7.6; Martial 1.113.5, 1.2.7–8, 13.3.4. Starr's summary of booksellers is quite helpful ("Circulation of Literary Texts," 219–223).

14. Martial 4.72.2; 13.3.4; 14.194.2; Pliny, *Ep.* 1.2.6; 9.11.2. As we shall see, the term *librarii* as copyist is found most frequently in the correspondence of Cicero. According to H.-I. Marrou, the term *antiquarius* as used to designate a copyist was supplanted by *librarii* by the Christian period ("La technique de l'edition a l'epoque patristique," *VC* 3 [1949] 213, especially n. 21).

15. See, e.g., *Noctes Atticae* 5.4.1, 13.31.1, 18.4.1.

16. See Starr's point: "most of the copies . . . were probably made at the specific request of a customer" ("Circulation of Literary Texts," 220).

17. "Circulation of Literary Texts," 220.

18. The literature on dictation is quite extensive. See most helpfully T. C. Skeat, "The Use of Dictation in Ancient Book-Production," *Proceedings of the British Academy* 42 (1956) 179–208; the work on reading practices in antiquity is also relevant here: Josef Balogh, "Voces Paginarum," *Philologus* 82 (1927) 84–109, 202–224 ; Bernard Knox, "Silent Reading in Antiquity," *GRBS* 9 (1968) 421–435.

19. Pseudo-Acro as quoted by Skeat, "Use of Dictation," 189.

20. "Publication of Books," 26.

21. On public and private libraries: in addition to the works cited above (Introduction, n.22), see *RE* s.v. "Bibliotheken"; Thomas Keith Dix, "Private and Public Libraries at Rome in the First Century B.C.: A Preliminary Study in the History of Roman Libraries" (Ph.D. diss., University of Michigan, 1986); Sandra Sider, "Herculaneum's Library in 79 A.D.: The Villa of the Papyri," *Libraries and Culture* 25 (1990) 534–542; Phyllis Culham, "Documents and *Domus* in Republican Rome," *Libraries and Culture* 26 (1991) 119–134; Thomas M. Tanner, "A History of Early Christian Libraries from Jesus to Jerome," *Journal of Library History* 14 (1979) 407–435; Moses Hadas, *Ancilla to Classical Reading* (New York: Columbia University Press, 1954) 21–27; Carl A. Hanson, "Were There Libraries in Roman Spain?" *Libraries and Culture* 24 (1989) 198–216. On the library at Alexandria, see Luciano Canfora, *The Vanished Library*, trans. Martin Ryle (London: Hutchinson Radius, 1989); Mostafa El-Abbadi, *The Life and Fate of the Ancient Library of Alexandria* (Paris: UNESCO, 1990); Rudolf Blum, *Kallimachos: The Alexandrian Library and the Origins of Bibliography*, trans. Hans H. Wellisch (Madison: University of Wisconsin Press, 1991; originally, *Kallimachos und die Literaturverzeichnung bei den Griechen*).

22. A nice summary of this progression is found in Menahem Haran, "Archives, Libraries, and the Order of Biblical Books," *JANES* 22 (1993) 51–61.

23. Dix, "Private and Public Libraries," 198.

24. Dix, "Private and Public Libraries," 203–211; according to Gellius both of these libraries had Greek and Latin sections and a reading room where conversation was permitted (*Noctes Atticae* 13.19; see Hadas, *Ancilla*, 24). See further on Pollio and Augustus, A. B. Bosworth, "Asinius Pollio and Augustus," *Historia* 21 (1972) 441–473; A. Dalzell, "C. Asinius Pollio and the Early History of Public Recitation at Rome," *Hermathena* 86 (1955) 20–28.

25. Anthony J. Marshall, "Library Resources and Creative Writing at Rome," *Phoenix* 30 (1976) 261.

26. See Dix, "Private and Public Libraries," 213–214; see also R. P. C. Weaver, *Familia Caesaris: A Social Study of the Emperor's Freedmen and Slaves* (Cambridge: Cambridge University Press, 1972) 7.

27. The quotation is from Marshall, "Library Resources at Rome," 254; the passage in Suetonius is *Domitian* 20.

28. Phillips, "The Publication of Books," 37.

29. Raymond Starr, "The Circulation of Literary Texts," 221.

30. See Sommer, "T. Pomponius Atticus," 389–422; Jérome Carcopino, *Les Secrets de la correspondance de Cicéron*, 2 vols. (Paris, 1947) especially 2, 305–363. These two earlier works — Sommer's, which argued for Atticus as a private producer of Cicero's works, and Carcopino's, which claimed that Atticus should properly be understood as originating the Roman publishing commercial industry — are usefully critiqued by Phillips, "Atticus and the Publication of Cicero's Works," 227–237.

31. For a lengthy introduction to the term γραμματεύς, see *RE* s.v. γραμματεῖς; on *scriba*, see further below.

32. Papyri that mention these various types of scribes are numerous. The discussion of F. Oertel on these various offices remains important: *Die Liturgie: Studien zur ptolemäischen und kaiserlichen Verwaltung Ägyptens* (Leipzig: B. G. Teubner, 1917).

33. On the administration of Roman Egypt, see especially P. A. Brunt, "The Administrators of Roman Egypt," *JRS* 65 (1975) 124–147; for the third–fifth centuries, see Roger S. Bagnall, *Egypt in Late Antiquity* (Princeton, N.J.: Princeton University Press, 1993).

34. See the representative sampling of texts in OLD, s.v., "scriba."

35. The distinction between *scribae* and *librarii* is apparent in Livy, 38.55, where the *librarii* are clearly copyists; and Cicero, *Agr.* 2.13.

36. On Petaus, see Ursula Hagerdorn, Dieter Hagerdorn, Louise C. Youtie, and Herbert C. Youtie, *Das Archiv des Petaus (P. Petaus)* (Köln: Westdeutscher Verlag, 1969; Herbert C. Youtie, "Pétaus, fils de Pétaus, ou le scribe qui ne savait pas écrire," in his *Scriptiunculae*, vol. 2 (Amsterdam: Adolf M. Hakkert, 1973) 677–693.

37. On the appointment of officials, see Naphtali Lewis, *Life in Egypt under Roman Rule* (Oxford: Clarendon Press, 1983) 177–181.

38. On the office of the village scribe, see F. Oertel, *Die Liturgie* 157ff; H. C. Youtie, "PUG 12: Τοπογραμματεις και κωμογραμματεις," *ZPE* 24 (1977) 138. For just a few examples of these responsibilities: they impose obligation on persons within the town to cultivate land (*P. Oxy.* 6.899); receiving declarations of unwatered land (*BGU* 13.2233; *SB* 16.12563); census returns (*BGU* 13.2220–2222); petitions (*BGU* 13.2243). Although this was not the case in this situation, the village scribe could also be called upon to write on behalf of those who were illiterate (*CPR* 7.18; October 379 C.E.).

39. For the use of this term in the papyri, see Maher-Leonard, ΑΓΡΑΜΜΑΤΟΙ: *In Aegypto qui litteras scriverint qui nesciverint ex papyris graecis quantum fieri potest exploratur* (Frankfurt-am-Main, 1913); updated by R. Calderini, "Gli ἀγράμματοι nell' Egitto greco-romano," *Aegyptus* 30 (1950) 14–41; H. C. Youtie, "ΑΓΡΑΜΜΑΤΟΣ: An Aspect of Greek Society in Egypt," *Harvard Studies in Classical Philology* 75 (1971) 161–176, reprinted in *Scriptiunculae* II (Amsterdam: Adolf M. Hakkert, 1973) 611–627.

40. For the papyri on which he affixes his own signature, see Hagerdorn and Youtie, *Das Archive*, 36.

41. Herbert C. Youtie, "Βραδέως γράφων: Between Literacy and Illiteracy," *GRBS* 12 (1971) 240.

42. For what appears to be a similar practice sheet perhaps by a relatively new scribe see *CPR* 5.2 (134–136 C.E.). On a papyrus from Karanis, we find the signature of a κωμογραμμτεύς about which the editors say, "the hand of the komogrammateus is that of a βραδέως γράφων — block letters, painstakingly formed" (*BGU* 13.2231).

43. Youtie, "Βραδέως γράφων," 240–241.

44. Lewis, *Life in Egypt*, 82; the elevated status of scribes of Pharaonic times is well known and the secondary literature substantial: see, for example, Ronald J. Williams, "Scribal Training in Ancient Egypt," *JAOS* 92 (1972) 214–221; Avrin, *Scribes, Script and Books*, 81–100; also helpful is Dorothy J. Thompson who attempts to answer the question, "What happens when the long-established tradition of Egyptian literacy, a priestly and scribal literacy which was both highly valued and closely confined, is brought into contact with the more open, secular tradition of Greek literacy?" ("Literacy and the Administration in Early Ptolemaic Egypt," in *Life in a Multi-Cultural Society: Egypt from Cambyses to Constantine and Beyond*, ed. Janet H. Johnson [Chicago: Oriental Institute, 1992] 323–326).

45. See Turner, *Greek Papyri*, 139.

46. Concerning the liturgists in Egypt, Roger Bagnall points out that they were "on the whole men of moderate means or better" (*Egypt in Late Antiquity* [Princeton, N.J.: Princeton University Press, 1993] 135).

47. *Greek Papyri*, 83.

48. See, for example, Susan Treggiari, "Jobs in the Household of Livia," *Papers of the British School at Rome* 43 (1975) 50. The term *librarius* is often combined with *a manu* in inscriptions that commemorate these private secretarial scribes (see, e.g., *CIL* 6.9523 = *ILS* 7399; *CIL* 6.9524 = *ILS* 7398).

49. Turner, *Greek Papyri*, 83.

50. Herbert C. Youtie, "ΥΠΟΓΡΑΦΕΥΣ: The Social Impact of Illiteracy in Graeco-Roman Egypt," *ZPE* 17 [1975] 209.

51. *Writing, Teachers, and Students*, 10–11.

52. The issue of handwriting will also be taken up in the chapter 3; I will here simply note some of the passages in which Cicero mentions either his own handwriting, or that of Atticus: *Att.* 2.23; 5.14; 6.9; 7.2; 7.3.

53. There is no doubt that there was a closeness between Cicero and Tiro—much like that apparently between Atticus and Alexis—that is different from Cicero's relationships with other copyists.

54. Martial 1.2.

55. Cicero, *Att.* 13.33.

56. For slaves, see, for example *CIL* 6.9616 (where a certain Benigno is designated as a *librarius*); *CIL* 6.9523 = *ILS* 7399 (for Iucundus, *librarius ad manum*); *CIL* (for Pitheros, a *librarius a manu*); for possible freedpersons, see *CIL* 6.9521 (which designates a certain L. Volusio Aegialeo Syrillio as a *librarius*).

57. Interestingly, we find a similar situation in the late ancient Jewish context: "The sofer was so indispensable that, according to R. Joshua b. Levi, the men of the Great Assembly observed twenty-four fast-days on which they prayed that the soferim might not become rich and therefore unwilling to write." (J. D. Eisenstein, "Scribes," *The Jewish Encyclopedia*, vol. 2 [New York: Funk and Wagnalls, 1905] 124).

58. Fantham admits that Cicero was exceptional, but proceeds to use this as the illustration for how texts were copied (*Roman Literary Culture*, 36); McDonnell argues the opposite: "Atticus cannot have been unique in owning more than a few skilled copyists" ("Writing in Ancient Rome," 486); see also Kenney's point: "Many well-to-do Romans must have had in their possession one or two slaves trained as clerks, who could be used as copyists of books when not otherwise employed and so build up the libraries of their employers and on occasion their employers' friends" ("Books and Readers," 20).

59. This separation of hands is quite standard, and we will discuss it extensively in chapter 3; (see E. G. Turner, *Greek Manuscripts*, 1; E. M. Thompson, *A Handbook of Greek and Latin Palaeography* (Chicago: Ares Publishers, 1975 [1901] 115ff).

60. See D. R. Jordan, "New Evidence for the Activity of Scribes in Roman Athens," *Abstracts of the American Philological Association, 120th Annual Meeting (Baltimore)* (Atlanta, Ga.: Scholars Press, 1989) 55; John G. Gager, *Curse Tablets and Binding Spells from the Ancient World* (New York: Oxford University Press, 1992) 118, 123 n. 12.

61. Youtie, "ΥΠΟΓΡΑΦΕΥΣ," 207–220.

62. G. P. Goold, ed., *Chariton: Callirhoe* (Cambridge: Harvard University Press, 1995); see trans. in B. P. Reardon, ed., *Collected Ancient Greek Novels* (Berkeley: University of California Press, 1989); on Chariton see further, B. E. Perry, "Chariton and His Romance from a Literary-Historical Point of View," *American Journal of Philology* 51 (1930) 93–134.

63. *Greek Papyri*, 77–78.

64. Willy Clarysse, "Literary Papyri in Documentary Archives," in *Egypt and the Hellenistic World: Proceedings of the International Colloquium, Leuven, 24–26 May 1982*, ed. E. van 'T Dack, P. van Dessel, and W. van Gucht (Lovanii: [Orientaliste], 1983) 43–61; William H. Willis, "Two Literary Papyri in an Archive from Panopolis," *Illinois Classical Studies* 3 (1978) 140–151; P. W. Pestman, "The Official Archive of the Village Scribes of Kerkeosiris: Notes on the So-Called Archive of Menches," *Festschrift zum 100-jährigen Bestehen der Papyrussammlung der Österreichischen Nationalbibliothek, Papyrus Erzherzog Rainer* (Vienna: Verlag Brüder Hollinek, 1983) 127–134.

65. For example, *P.Lond.* II, 256; on this papyrus, see most helpfully Willy Clarysse, "Literary Papyri," 46.

66. Clarysse, "Literary Papyri," 51, on *C.Ord.Ptol.* 53 and *P.Tebt.* I, 1 and 2, both of which come from the well-known Menches archive (which is somewhat early for our period, but still helpful).

67. Clarysse, "Literary Papyri," 52.

68. P. W. Pestman, "The Official Archive," 129–131, esp. 130–131.

69. "Roman Oxyrhynchus," *JEA* 38 [1952] 89–90; see also his "Recto and Verso," *JEA* 40 (1954) 102–106.

70. McDonnell, "Writing in Ancient Rome," 490.

71. Cribiore, *Writing, Teachers, and Students*, 5.

72. Turner, *Greek Papyri*, 95.

73. See most recently, Cribiore, *Writing, Teachers, and Students*; on identifying school texts, see Turner, *Greek Papyri*, 89–92; F. G. Kenyon, "Two Greek School-Tablets," *Journal of Hellenic Studies* 29 (1909) 29–40; P. J. Parsons, "A School-Book from the Sayce Collection," *ZPE* 6 (1970) 133–149.

74. See the examples provided in Turner, *Greek Manuscripts*, nos. 45, 85, 88.

75. See especially Richards, *The Secretary*; Murphy-O'Conner, *Paul the Letter-Writer*; Wayne A. Meeks, *The First Urban Christians: The Social World of the Apostle Paul* (New Haven, Conn.: Yale University Press, 1983) 57; Harry Y. Gamble, *Books and Readers in the Early Church: A History of Early Christian Texts* (New Haven, Conn.: Yale University Press, 1995) 95–96; Gerd Theissen, *Studien zur Soziologie des Urchristentums* (Tübingen: Mohr/Siebeck, 1979) 253ff.

76. James H. Charlesworth, ed., *The Old Testament Pseudepigrapha*, vol. 2 (Garden City, N.Y.: Doubleday, 1985).

77. On this particular passage, see especially, Bart D. Ehrman, "The Theodotians as Corruptors of Scripture," *Studia Patristica* 47 (1993) 105–113; Gamble, *Books and Readers*, 122–123.

78. Ambrose appears to be a patron of Origen. On patronage, see Peter Garnsey and Richard Saller, *The Roman Empire: Economy, Society and Culture* (Berkeley: University of California Press, 1987) 148–159, especially 152–154; Richard Saller,

Personal Patronage under the Early Empire (Cambridge: Cambridge University Press, 1982).

79. On the issues of a scriptorium and the "catechetical school," see G. Zuntz, *The Text of the Epistles: A Disquisition upon the Corpus Paulinum* (London: Oxford University Press, 1953) 271–276; Roelof van den Broek, "The Christian 'School' of Alexandria in the Second and Third Centuries," in *Centres of Learning: Learning and Location in Pre-Modern Europe and the Near East*, ed. Jan Willem Drijvers and Alasdair A. MacDonald (Leiden: E. J. Brill, 1995) 39–47; Robert M. Grant, "Theological Education at Alexandria," in *The Roots of Egyptian Christianity*, ed. Birger A. Pearson and James E. Goehring (Philadelphia: Fortress Press, 1986) 178–189; Robert L. Wilken, "Alexandria: A School for Training in Virtue," in *Schools of Thought in the Christian Tradition*, ed. Patrick Henry (Philadelphia: Fortress Press, 1984) 15–30; as well as the bibliography in Johannes Quasten's *Patrology*, vol. 2 (Westminster, Mass.: Newman Press, 1953) 2–4.

80. See *Lausiac History* 32.12; 38.10; 45.3; the letters of Jerome in which he urges female ascetics to read and copy texts (e.g., *Epp.* 22, 107, and 130); see also chapter 2 on the discussion of female scribes; on a related issue — the writing of hagiography as a practice of ascetic devotion — see Derek Krueger, "Hagiography as an Ascetic Practice in the Early Christian East," *Journal of Religion* 79 (1999) 216–232, and "Writing as Devotion: Hagiographical Composition and the Cult of the Saints in Theodoret of Cyrrhus and Cyril of Scythopolis," *Church History* 66 (1997) 707–719.

81. The translation is taken from P. Amidon, *The Panarion of St. Epiphanius, Bishop of Salamis (Selected Passages)* (New York: Oxford University Press, 1990) 244–246; for the Greek, see Epiphanius, *Haer.* 67 (3 GCS 37.132–140). On the issue of heresy and orthodoxy with relationship to Hieracas' role, see especially Susanna Elm, *'Virgins of God': The Making of Asceticism in Late Antiquity* (Oxford: Clarendon Press, 1994) 339–342, 346–347; A. von Harnack, "Hierakas und die Hierakiten," in *Realenzyklopädie für protestantische Theologie und Kirche* 8 (Leipzig, 1900) 38–39; Elizabeth A. Clark, *The Origenist Controversy: The Cultural Construction of an Early Christian Debate* (Princeton, N.J.: Princeton University Press, 1992) 97. We further find a certain scribe named Abraham at Scetis in the *Saying of the Fathers* (B. Ward, *The Sayings of the Desert Fathers* [London: A. R. Mowbrays, 1975]); for the Greek original of the alphabetic collection, see PG 65, 71–440.

82. Helen Waddell, trans., *The Desert Fathers* (Ann Arbor: University of Michigan Press, 1957) 115.

83. On the use of texts and prominence of literature in the Pachomian materials, see James M. Robinson, *The Pachomian Monastic Library at the Chester Beatty Library and the Bibliothèque Bodmer* (Claremont, Calif.: Institute for Antiquity and Christianity, 1990) especially 2–3; see more generally Derwas J. Chitty, *The Desert a City: An Introduction to the Study of Egyptian and Palestinian Monasticism under the Christian Empire* (London: A. R. Mowbrays, 1966); Douglas Burton-Christie, *The Word in the Desert: Scripture and the Quest for Holiness in Early Christian Monasticism* (New York: Oxford University Press, 1993) especially 111–114.

84. E.g., Meeks, *First Urban Christians*, 52.

85. In the *Apocryphal Acts*, we find both models of conversion: whole households convert on occasion, but sometimes just the individual converts (as in the case of

Thecla). The literature on conversion is extensive; see especially A. D. Nock, *Conversion* (Oxford: Oxford University Press, 1933); Ramsay MacMullen, *Christianizing the Roman Empire, A.D. 100–400* (New Haven, Conn.: Yale University Press, 1984); Robin Lane Fox, *Pagans and Christians* (San Francisco: Harper and Row, 1986).

CHAPTER 2

1. On the issue of essentializing the category "women" and a strict dichotomy between female and male, see especially, for example, Judith Butler, *Gender Trouble: Feminism and the Subversion of Identity* (London: Routledge, 1990); ibid., *Bodies that Matter: On the Discursive Limits of "Sex"* (New York: Routledge, 1993); Denise Riley, *"Am I That Name?" Feminism and the Category of "Women" in History* (Minneapolis: University of Minnesota, 1988).

2. On shorthand writing, see Foat, "On Old Greek Tachygraphy," 238–267; Thompson, *A Handbook*, 82–106; Richards, *The Secretary*, 26–43; see also chapter 3 on the contract dated to 155 C.E. in which a certain slave named Chaerammon is sent by his master to apprentice with Apollonius, a σημειογράφῳ (writer of signs, i.e., shorthand) (*P.Oxy.* 724).

3. Teresa de Lauretis, *Technologies of Gender: Essays on Theory, Film, and Fiction* (Bloomington: Indiana University Press, 1987) 2.

4. Albert Schramm, "Zur Geschichte der Stenographie in der alten Kirche," *Korrespondenzblatt, Amtliche Zeitschrift des königlichen stenographischen Instituts zu Dresden* 48 (1903) 66.

5. George Haven Putnam, *Books and Their Makers during the Middle Ages*, vol. 1 (New York: G. P. Putnam's Sons, 1896) 53, emphasis mine.

6. *Buried Books in Antiquity: Habent Sua Fata Libelli*, Arundell Esdaile Memorial Lecture, 1962 (London: Library Association, 1963) 15, emphasis mine.

7. "Books in the Graeco-Roman World and in the New Testament," *The Cambridge History of the Bible*, vol. 1: *From the Beginnings to Jerome* (Cambridge: Cambridge University Press, 1970) 65, emphasis mine.

8. This number is inevitably an estimate, since some of the inscriptions are too fragmentary to offer a definitive interpretation. The eleven that I have counted are: *CIL* 6.3979, 7373, 8882, 9301, 9525, 9540, 9541, 9542, 33892, 37757, 37802. This list is not meant to be comprehensive, simply illustrative. In compiling this list, I initially drew from the list in Susan Treggiari, "Jobs for Women," *American Journal of Ancient History* 1 (1976) 76–104, esp. 78; see also Natalie Kampen, *Image and Status: Roman Working Women in Ostia* (Berlin: Gebr. Mann, 1981) 118; and Lefkowitz and Fant, *Women's Life in Greece and Rome*, 223.

9. *Papers of the American School of Classical Studies at Athens* 2 (1888) no. 390.

10. *Mitteilungen des kaiserlich deutschen archäologischen Instituts* 35 (1910) no. 20.

11. Although Lefkowitz and Fant offer a translation of another text in which a woman is identified as "scribe" (*Women's Life in Greece and Rome*, no. 220), upon a closer look at the papyrus text it appears that they have too loosely translated βυβλιαφόρος (papyrus carrier) as "scribe." Furthermore, the editors of the papyrus itself claim that due to a lacuna we cannot even be certain that we have a female βυβλιαφόρος in the text (*CPR* XIII, G.T. IX, ed. H. Harrauer [1987] pp. 57–58).

12. On the presence of *contubernales* in Roman inscriptions, see especially Susan Treggiari, "*Contubernales* in *CIL* 6," *Phoenix* 35 (1981) 42–69; and her *Roman Marriage: Iusti Coniuges From the Time of Cicero to the Time of Ulpian* (Oxford: Clarendon Press, 1993 [c. 1991]) 52–54.

13. *Image and Status*, 118. Studies have shown that normally women married between the ages of 15 and 20; according to Augustan laws (especially the *Lex Papia Poppaea* of 9 C.E.) women were to start having children at the age of 20 (see Susan Treggiari, *Roman Marriage*, especially 60, 66, 398–403; see also Brent D. Shaw, "The Age of Roman Girls at Marriage: Some Reconsiderations," *JRS* 77 [1987] 30–46).

14. See the references to freedmen *librarii* throughout Cicero's letters (e.g., Tiro, of course, is Cicero's freedman who acted as his personal secretary and scribe; see also *Att.* 13.33 where the *librarius* Philotimus is identified as a freedman); Kenney, "Books and Readers, 3–32, especially 20; McDonnell, "Writing, Copying, and Autograph Manuscripts."

15. Treggiari, "Jobs for Women," 78.

16. In addition to the discussion in the previous chapter, see Cicero, *Agr.* 2.13; Cornelius Nepos, *Att.* 13.3; Martial 2.8.

17. The question of how representative epigraphic evidence is continues to be asked; see especially Ramsay MacMullen, "The Epigraphic Habit in the Roman Empire," *AJP* 103 (1982) 233–246; Elizabeth A. Meyer, "Explaining the Epigraphic Habit in the Roman Empire: The Evidence of Epitaphs,' *JRS* 80 (1990) 74–96; see also the comments of Ross S. Kraemer on the subject of epigraphic evidence for Jewish (and Christian) women's history: "Non-Literary Evidence for Jewish Women in Rome and Egypt," *Helios* 13 (1986) 85–101.

18. Harris, *Ancient Literacy*, 252, 270, 314; on the issue of resources available to the elites, see Bagnall, *Reading Papyri*, 25.

19. E. Courtney, *A Commentary on the Satires of Juvenal* (London: Athlone Press, 1980) 324.

20. John Ferguson, *Juvenal: The Satires* (New York: St. Martin's Press, 1979) 206.

21. R. F. Rossi offers a useful discussion of the Juvenal passage, but he is overconfident in his explanation of *libraria* as meaning *lanipendia* ("Librarius," *Dizionario Epigrafico di Antichita Romane*, 4 [Rome, 1958] 956). Part of his argument depends on a *lack of evidence* for female copyists, a point that I am contesting here: "Bisogna anche aggiungere che sembra meno sicuramente demonstrata l'esistenze di donne copiste o scrivane designate col termine libraria" (956).

22. John Ferguson admits this point, *Juvenal*, 206.

23. For the description of this relief: Kampen, *Image and Status*, 157 and figure 45. For other similar types of depictions, see, e.g., *Image and Status*, fig. 44; *A History of Private Life*, vol. 1, *From Pagan Rome to Byzantium*, ed. Paul Veyne (Cambridge, Mass.: Belknap Press of Harvard University Press, 1987) 85.

24. For Roman-period archaeological and artistic evidence for scribes, see especially H. I. Marrou, ΜΟΥΣΙΚΟΣ ΑΝΗΡ: *Étude sur les scènes de la vie intellectuelle figurant sur les monuments funéraires romains* (Roma: "L'Erma" di Bretschneider, 1964) 149, no. 189; Parássoglou, "ΔΕΞΙΑ ΧΕΙΡ," 5–21; "A Roll upon His Knees," 273–275; Metzger, "When Did Scribes Begin to Use Writing Desks?" 123–137.

25. Kampen, *Image and Status*, 118.

26. It may also be helpful to point out that we have later evidence of women copying medieval Hebrew manuscripts: the work of Malachi Beit-Arie, in particular, has demonstrated the existence of female scribes in medieval Ashkenaz ("The Codicological Data-Base of the Hebrew Palaeography Project: A Tool for Localising and Dating Hebrew Medieval Manuscripts," paper presented at the Center for Judaic Studies, Philadelphia, Pa., on 7 March 1996).

27. Samuel A. Meier mentions nine, "Women and Communication in the Ancient Near East," *JAOS* 111 (1991) 542; Laurie E. Pearce suggests "at least ten women scribes are known" at Mari ("The Scribes and Scholars of Ancient Mesopotamia," in *Civilizations of the Ancient Near East*, ed. Jack Sasson, vol. 4 [New York: Scribner, 1995] 2266).

28. The translation of the term *naditu* used here, as well as a list of eight female scribes by name along with the dates when they worked can be found in Rivkah Harris, "The Organization and Administration of the Cloister in Ancient Babylonia," *Journal of the Economic and Social History of the Orient* 6 (1963) 121, 138. The number fourteen is according to Meier's more recent count ("Women and Communication," 542).

29. Samuel A. Meier, "Women and Communication," 542.

30. See Betsy M. Bryan, "Evidence for Female Literacy from Theban Tombs of the New Kingdom," *Bulletin of the Egyptological Seminar* 6 (1985) 17–32; and John Baines and C. J. Eyre, "Four Notes on Literacy," *Göttinger Miszellen* 61 (1983) 65–96, esp. 81ff.

31. Betsy Bryan, for example, claims that the close connection with the person is underscored by the small number of females depicted with scribal outfits and the fact that two of these five women appear more than once with writing implements ("Evidence for Female Literacy," 20).

32. Bryan, "Evidence for Female Literacy," 18; on the 26th Dynasty (ca. 663–525 B.C.E.) tomb of Ireteru, which offers several instances of "female scribes" in service of the "divine adoratrice Nitokris," see further Baines and Eyre, "Four Notes," 82.

33. They served the "documentational needs of other women in their society" (Pearce, "The Scribes and Scholars of Ancient Mesopotamia," 2265).

34. Rivkah Harris, "The Female 'Sage' in Mesopotamian Literature (with an Appendix on Egypt)," in *The Sage in Israel and the Ancient Near East*, ed. John G. Gammie and Leo G. Perdue (Winona Lake, Ind.: Eisenbrauns, 1990) 7.

35. See the views of G. Posener, as discussed by Betsy Bryan, "Evidence for Female Literacy," passim.

36. Our richest source for Christian women reading and studying texts is the corpus of Jerome's letters; see especially the well-known letter to Laeta on the education of her daughter (*Ep.* 107). A lovely instance of a fourth-century ἀειπάρθενος (ever-virgin), whose apparent passion for reading has led to accusations that she has stolen books, can be seen in *P.Lips.* 43 (also found in *Women and Society in Greek and Roman Egypt: A Sourcebook*, ed. Jane Rowlandson [Cambridge: Cambridge University Press, 1998] no. 58). The recent study of Philip Rousseau on the subject of educated women in early Christianity offers a helpful summary of literary evidence, but does not engage with modern scholarship on the subject or offer any innovative arguments

("'Learned Women' and the Development of a Christian Culture in Late Antiquity," *Symbolae Osloenses* 70 [1995] 116–147). For a later period, see Susan Groag Bell, "Medieval Women Book Owners: Arbiters of Lay Piety and Ambassadors of Culture," *Signs* 7 [1982] 742–768; and the fascinating collection of essays in *Women and the Book: Assessing the Visual Evidence*, ed. Lesley Smith and Jane H. M. Taylor (London and Toronto: British Library and University of Toronto Press, 1996).

37. The Greek text and translation in taken from Elizabeth A. Clark, *The Life of Melania the Younger* (New York: Edwin Mellen Press, 1984) 12 and 46; I agree with Clark's argument for the priority of the Greek text (12).

38. On her building projects, see Clark, *The Life*, 115–119.

39. For a later period, see especially Bell, "Medieval Women Book Owners."

40. PL 67, 1022. On the issues of date and author, see William E. Klingshirn, trans., *Caesarius of Arles: Life, Testament, Letters* (Liverpool: Liverpool University Press, 1994) 1. I have here quoted from Klingshirn's translation.

41. Peter Dronke, *Women Writers of the Middle Ages: A Critical Study of Texts from Perpetua (203) to Marguerite Porete (1320)* (Cambridge: Cambridge University Press, 1984) 28.

42. This note is found on the first leaf of the codex; see the photographic facsimile by E. M. Thompson, *Facsimile of the Codex Alexandrinus*, 4 vols. (London, 1879–1883), volume 4 = New Testament.

43. The table of contents at the beginning lists the apocryphal Psalms of Solomon as concluding the volume and coming after II Clement.

44. It appears that Bentley was responsible for the translation inscribed just beneath the Arabic note: "Memorant hunc librum scriptus fuisse manu Thecla Martyris" (H. J. M. Milne and T. C. Skeat, *The Codex Sinaiticus and the Codex Alexandrinus* [London: British Museum, 1955] 36).

45. *A Dictionary of Christian Biography* vol. 4 (London: J. Murray, 1877–1887) 897.

46. *The Negotiations of Sir Thomas Roe, in his Embassy to Ottoman Porte, from the Year 1621–1628 inclusive* (London, 1740) p. 335, letter 241, and p. 618, letter 448, respectively.

47. Quoted by C. L. Hulbert-Powell, *John James Wettstein, 1693–1754* (London: S.P.C.K., 1938) 101.

48. The only reference I have found for this is in Agnes Smith Lewis, *Select Narratives of Holy Women*, Studia Sinaitica 10 (London: C. J. Clay and Sons, 1900) xiii. Although there is evidence that women were on the whole less literate and less educated than men throughout antiquity, there is nothing to suggest that when they were educated or trained to write, that their level of ability was inferior. On the general subject of women's education, see the next chapter, and F. A. Beck, "The Schooling of Girls in Ancient Greece," *Classicum* 9 (1978) 1–9; Susan Cole, "Could Greek Women Read and Write?" in *Reflections of Women in Antiquity*, ed. Helen P. Foley (New York: Gordon and Breach Science Publishers, 1981) 219–245; Susan Pomeroy, "Technikai kai Mousikai": The Education of Women in the Fourth Century and in the Hellenistic Period," *American Journal of Ancient History* 2 (1977) 51–68.

49. Scrivener, *Plain Introduction*, 102.

50. The examples discussed here do not exhaust the possibilities: an intriguing reference to a certain Litia of Thessalonica — "a scribe writing books and living in great asceticism in the manner of men" — is found in the Coptic version of the *Lausiac History* (Cuthbert Butler, *The Lausiac History of Palladius*, vol. 1 [Cambridge: Cambridge University Press, 1898) 150; for the Coptic, Cuthbert here cites M. Amélineau, *Monastères de la Basse-Égypte* (Paris: E. Leroux, 1894) 240ff.). I am especially grateful to Georgia Frank, who pointed me toward this reference.

CHAPTER 3

1. For a fascimile of the page on which this marginal note appears, as well as a brief discussion of the note, see Metzger, *Manuscripts of the Greek Bible*, 74–75.

2. On the colophons: Metzger, *The Text of the New Testament*, 17–18. We could also compare the scribe who concludes a copy of Menander's *Sikyonios* with the words "Do not laugh at the writing . . . How glad I am to rest my three fingers!" (A. Blanchard and A. Bataille, *Recherches de Papyrologie* 3 [1965] 103–176; Turner, *Greek Manuscripts*, no. 40).

3. See also, for example, Seneca, *de Ira* 2.26.2; Cicero, *Att.* 13.23; *Ep. Q. Fr.* 3.5.6. The cases where Cicero has his copyists correct a mistake that *he* made are clearly different from the copyists' own errors (*Att.* 12.6a; 13.21; 13.44); Aulus Gellius, paradoxically, attests to the existence of copyists' mistakes when he singles out for mention copies in bookstores that are said to be free from mistakes (5.3.4; 13.31.6). Strabo laments the poor quality of copies in Rome and Alexandria (13.609).

4. At least functionally illiterate as in the case of Petaus (see chapter above, pp. 39–41). It may well be, as Naphtali Lewis suggests, that Petaus was only illiterate in Greek, but we do not know this for certain (*Life in Egypt under Roman Rule* [Oxford: Clarendon Press, 1983] 81).

5. See, for example, the scribe who copied Callimachus into a copy of a tax register, whom Youtie described as a "érudite manqué" (noted by W. Clarysse, "Literary Papyri in Documentary 'Archives'," in *Egypt and the Hellenistic World*, 52).

6. Turner, *Greek Papyri*, 107–108; related to poor scribal copies are the school texts, which exhibit varying degrees of ability (on mistakes in school copies, e.g., see Cribiore, *Writing, Teachers, and Students*, 91–96).

7. Such as the "Hawara Homer" (W. M. F. Petrie, *Hawara, Biahmu and Arsinoe* [London: E. C. Tübner , 1889] 24–28; Turner, *Greek Manuscripts of the Ancient World*, no. 13). On the range of education among the scribes of Roman Egypt, see Lewis' statements: "The educational level of the scribes varied with the individual, but most leave the impression of being merely literate rather than highly educated. They wrote mostly in formulas and clichés" (*Life in Egypt*, 82).

8. Our most valuable primary source on ancient education is the *Institutiones Oratores* of Quintilian. Secondary studies of ancient education include the important but problematic (see above, Introduction, n. 14) work of H.-I. Marrou, *Histoire de l'Education dans l'Antiquité* (Paris: Editions du Seuil, 1948); trans. George Lamb as *A History of Education in Antiquity* (Madison: University of Wisconsin Press, 1982); see also Stanley F. Bonner, *Education in Ancient Rome: From the Elder Cato to the Younger Pliny* (Berkeley: University of California Press, 1977); M. L. Clarke, *Higher Education*

in the Ancient World (London: Routledge and Kegan Paul, 1971); and the collection of school texts in Arthur Laudien, *Griechische Papyri aus Oxyrhynchos für den Schulgebrauch ausegewählt* (Berlin: Weidmannsche Buchhandlung, 1912). William Harris's *Ancient Literacy* has shown much of the earlier work on education in antiquity to be overly optimistic in assuming widespread school systems and extensive literacy.

9. Harris, *Ancient Literacy*, 236; see also Bonner, *Education in Ancient Rome*, 120–125.

10. Harris, *Ancient Literacy*, 245.

11. *Writing, Teaching, and Students*, 6; cf. the definition in *MPER NS* XV, p. 1.

12. Harris, *Ancient Literacy*, 234.

13. "Literacy and Power in Ptolemaic Egypt," in *Literacy and Power*, ed. Bowman and Woolf, 76.

14. "The Schooling of Slaves in First-Century Rome," *TAPA* 109 (1979) 14–15.

15. Harris, *Ancient Literacy*, 236.

16. Alan Booth's comments, which imply that reading and writing were inextricably interwoven, are an oversimplification of the process of education ("Elementary and Secondary Education in the Roman Empire," *Florilegium* 1 [1979] 1–14, especially 3), and have not been widely accepted. On the distinction between learning to read and learning to write, see especially Cribiore, *Writing, Teachers, and Students*, 9–10 and 148–152.

17. On girls attending schools see Martial 8.3.15–16; 9.68.1–2. Evidence from papyri corroborates this: a second century C.E. letter, for example, from a certain Heraidous writes to her family to send "the necessary equipment for school, such as a book for Heraidous to read" (*P.Giss.* 80, 95; trans. Lefkowitz and Fant, *Women's Life in Greece and Rome*, no. 215); see further on the issue of women's education the sources cited in note 48 in chapter 2.

18. Booth takes Martial as evidence that "a common course [of training slaves in clerical skills] . . . was to enroll slaves at school" ("The Schooling of Slaves," 11, refering to Martial's comments in 10.62.1–5 and 3.58.30–31); Harris, on the other hand, argues against this view: "There is no reason to believe that all schools were socially equivalent in the ancient world any more than they are in class-ridden modern societies. Furthermore, Martial was writing about a place and time, *urbs Roma* in the first century, which had a far larger percentage of slaves, and a vastly greater need for educated slaves, than any other city in the Empire" (*Ancient Literacy*, 238).

19. On Christian attitudes toward the classics, see especially, Gerard L. Ellspermann, *The Attitude of the Early Christian Latin Writers toward Pagan Literature and Learning* (Washington, D.C.: Catholic University Press, 1949); H. I. Marrou, *A History of Education in Antiquity*, 424–438; Wendy E. Helleman, ed., *Christianity and the Classics* (New York: University Press of America, 1990). Harris has argued that the negative sentiments toward classical literature, the backbone of the Graeco-Roman school curriculum, among certain Christians helped to weaken the elementary educational system in the later third and fourth centuries (*Ancient Literacy*, 309).

20. M. L. Clarke, *Higher Education in the Ancient World* (London: Routledge and Kegan Paul, 1971) 127.

21. See, for example, *P.Cair.Isid.* 3.41, 4.21; *P.Cair.Isid.* 5.45 = *SB* V 7672.20; *P.Ryl.* IV 656.23 = *P.Sakaon 3*; *SB* VI 9191.24 = *SB* VI 9270.40 (see Cribiore, *Writing, Teachers, and Students*, 164–166).

22. On the imperial *paedagogia*, see especially S. L. Mohler, "Slave Education in the Roman Empire," *TAPA* 71 (1940) 262–280; Bonner, *Education in Ancient Rome*, 45–46; Harris, *Ancient Literacy*, 247–248.

23. See LSJ, s.v., "παιδαγωγεῖον"; see also OLD, s.v., "paedagogium."

24. See the sources cited by Harris, *Ancient Literacy*, 247 n. 389.

25. Forbes, "Education and Training," 335.

26. Concerning this practice of training slaves so as to sell them at a higher price, Bonner writes: "If any slave who could read and write should chance to be sold when the rest of his former master's estate was auctioned, he was described in the sale catalogue as *litterator*, [Suetonius, *De Gramm* 4] and the interesting point is that this was the term which, in addition to *ludi magister*, long remained in use to describe the Roman primary schoolmaster [Apuleis, *Flor* 20]. Of the numerous literate slaves who were taught in the home, or were self-taught, or who changed hands in the commercial world, many would eventually secure their freedom, and it was largely due to them that primary education spread, when they found their occupation as masters in their own schools" (*Education in Ancient Rome*, 59).

27. Forbes, "Education and Training," 341–342. Recall that this is the same term used of Caesaria, who was *magistra* of the "virgins of Christ" in her monastery (*Vita Caesarius* 1.58.

28. Titus too is said to have been expert in writing short hand (Thompson, *A Handbook*, 84). The *Notae Tironianae* is discussed in Foat, "On Old Greek Tachygraphy," 238–267; Arthur Mentz, "Die Entstehungsgeschichte der römischen Stenographie," *Hermas* 66 (1931) 371.

29. *Origen: The Bible and Philosophy in the Third-Century Church* (Atlanta, Ga.: John Knox Press, 1983) 81.

30. Harris, *Ancient Literacy*, 248.

31. For apprenticeship contracts in general, see A. Zambon, "Διδασκαλικαί," *Aegyptus* 15 (1935) 3–66. Zambon's lists of these contracts indicates that the most frequent form of apprenticeship was to weavers.

32. See Richards, *The Secretary*, for a few comments on shorthand writers being apprenticed (referring to *P.Oxy.* 724) and the suggestion that they used handbooks at a secondary stage (57).

33. On the apprenticing of the free, see Harris, *Ancient Literacy*, 68–69; Forbes, "Education and Training," 331.

34. The kosmetes (κοσμητής) was the magistrate of the *epheboi* (boys between the ages of 15 and 17) in the gymnasium (see LSJ, s.v. κοσμητής; OCD, s.v. "Epheboi"); see further Bagnall, *Egypt in Late Antiquity*, 58–60, 100; Oertel, *Die Liturgie* 329–332.

35. On the literary sources for the various stages of learning to write, see Cribiore's insightful discussion (*Writing, Teachers, and Students*, 139–152). Cribiore particularly criticizes the traditional scholarly fusion of the processes of learning to read with those of learning to write. She argues that it has become common to think of a progression of letters to syllables to words and then finally sentences, but that this progression only pertained to reading, not writing. For the traditional interpretation, see Marrou, *A History of Education*; F. David Harvey, "Greeks and Romans Learn to Write," in *Communication Arts in the Ancient World*, ed. Eric A. Havelock and Jackson P. Hershbell

(New York: Hastings House Publishers, 1978) 63–78, esp. 72; Bonner, *Education in Ancient Rome*, 165–180.

36. Cribiore, *Writing, Teachers, and Students*.

37. See *P.Charite* 8, 27, 36, 37, 38, and 41 as commented on by Cribiore, *Writing, Teachers, and Students*, 15.

38. On the difficulties of distinguishing between the exercises of school children and those of scribes, see Janine Debut, "Les documents scholaires," *ZPE* 63 (1986) 251; Cribiore, however, asserts that the differences between the two are quite obvious (*Writing, Teachers, and Students*, 38).

39. Cribiore, *Writing, Teachers, and Students*, 38.

40. Ibid., 149ff.

41. Turner, *Greek Manuscripts*, 3.

42. Ibid., 3.

43. Roberts, *Greek Literary Hands*, xi.

44. *A Handbook*, 118.

45. Ann Ellis Hanson, "Ancient Illiteracy," in *Literacy in the Roman World*, 173. For a very useful collection of documents that demonstrates both the range and the consistent feature of ligatures, see E. Boswinkel and P. J. Sijpesteijn, *Greek Papyri, Ostraka and Mummy Labels* (Amsterdam: Adolf M. Hakkert, 1968). See also the examples in Herbert C. Youtie, *The Textual Criticism of Documentary Papyri: Prolegomena*, 2d ed. (London: Institute of Classical Studies, 1974).

46. On this distinction, see especially Turner, *Greek Manuscripts*, 8 and 15; Turner, *Greek Papyri*, 95–96; Thompson, *A Handbook*, 86–104.

47. Cribiore, *Writing, Teachers, and Students*, 97.

48. Ibid., 98–99.

49. Ibid., 113.

50. For example, according to its editor, the writing in *P.Harr.* II.226 suggests the work of a "documentary scribe" who was in training; *P.Petaus* 121, as we have already seen, represents the writing practice of a village scribe; and *CPR* 5.2, as the editors suggest, may well contain the writing practice of "a relatively new recruit [in an office] trying rather unsuccessfully to copy the more formal hand of the other, but the better writer was probably practising too, since he wrote out the same incomplete text twice."

51. Cribiore, *Writing, Teachers, and Students*, 6–7, on *P.Flor.* II.259. For a comprehensive treatment of the Heroninos archive itself, see Dominic Rathbone, *Economic Rationalism and Rural Society in Third-Century A.D. Egypt: The Heroninos Archive and the Appianus Estate* (Cambridge: Cambridge University Press, 1991).

52. The quotation comes from Avrin, *Scribes, Script and Books*, 170.

53. I simply list here some of the more significant and widely quoted works: Roberts, *MSB*; Judge and Pickering, "Biblical Papyri," and "Papyrus Documentation of Church and Community in Egypt to the Mid-Fourth Century," *Jahrbuch für Antike und Christentum* 20 (1977) 47–71; T. C. Skeat, "Early Christian Book-Production: Papyri and Manuscripts," in *The Cambridge History of the Bible*, vol. 2, *The West from the Fathers to the Reformation*, ed. G. W. H. Lampe (Cambridge: Cambridge University Press, 1969) 54–79; and, most recently, Gamble, *Books and Readers*, esp. 42–81. The standard lists of Christian papyri are Kurt Aland's *Repertorium*, 2 vols., and his

Kurzgefasste Liste; and Joseph van Haelst's *Catalogue*. For New Testament manuscripts, the most helpful bibliographic tool is J. K. Elliott, *A Bibliography of Greek New Testament Manuscripts* (Cambridge: Cambridge University Press, 1989).

54. On the codex form see most importantly, Colin H. Roberts and T. C. Skeat, *The Birth of the Codex* (London: Oxford University Press, 1987); E. G. Turner, *The Typology of the Early Codex* (Philadelphia: University of Pennsylvania Press, 1977). On the *nomina sacra* see especially the foundational work of Ludwig Traube, *Nomina Sacra: Versuch einer Geschichte der christlichen Kürzung* (Munich: C. H. Beck, 1907); more recently, A.H.R.E. Paap, *Nomina Sacra in the Greek Papyri of the First Five Centuries A.D.: The Sources and Some Deductions* (Leiden: Lugdunum Batavorum, 1959); Roberts, *MSB*, 26–48; Schuyler Brown, "Concerning the Origin of the Nomina Sacra," *Studia Papyrologica* 9 (1970) 7–19; and George Howard, "The Tetragram and the New Testament," *JBL* 96 (1977) 63–83.

55. *MSB*, 14.

56. "Informal Uncial" is the term frequently used by the original editors of the earliest papyri (see Roberts, *MSB*, 12); on the professionalism of scribes, see Judge and Pickering, "Biblical Papyri prior to Constantine," 8.

57. Turner, *Greek Manuscripts*, 18; Roberts, drawing upon Turner, uses the abbreviations in early Christian papyri to point to their "independence" from the "secular tradition" and remarks "that this practice is confined to Christian literary manuscripts and is not found in Jewish manuscripts of the Greek verson of the Old Testament" (*MSB*, 18–19).

58. Roberts himself acknowledged the similarities between Christian and classical papyri, as I shall discuss further below (*MSB*, 15). S. Stevens, however, for all the insight she brings to the papyri of ancient novels, clearly misses the mark when she classifies literary papyri as "(1) standard works of the high culture, tradegy, comedy, history, and their commentaries, (2) writings that can be identified as Christian, and (3) works of the not-quite-literate, or the inexperienced, writer" ("Who Read Ancient Novels?" in *The Search for the Ancient Novel*, ed. James Tatum [Baltimore, Md.: Johns Hopkins University Press, 1994] 412).

59. Respectively, *P.Lond.* 126 and 3041 (for reproductions see Turner, *Greek Manuscripts*, nos. 14 and 32). P^{45} shares a general similarity to these papyri (an angular hand that slopes slightly to the right) as well as more specific similarities in letter formation (e.g., like *P.Lond.* 126, the α P^{45} is triangular, the ε is tall and has a square back, both hands are roughly bilinear with υ, φ, ρ extending below the line, the ξ is in book-hand type, and so forth). One may well suppose that the similarities are due to dating. Indeed, since literary papyri are notoriously difficult to date, they are dated by comparison to other literary papyri, whose date may for one reason or another be more certain. My point here is simply that one must be careful in generalizing about the "uniqueness" of the hands of early Christian papyri. On the issue of dating literary papyri, see the comments of Kirsopp and Silva Lake, "The Scribe Ephraim," *JBL* 62 (1943) 264; Metzger, *Manuscripts*, 49–51; Turner, *Greek Manuscripts*, 17–20.

60. Cribiore, *Writing, Teachers, and Students*, 97; for later chancery hands, see Thompson, *A Handbook*, 294ff.

61. It is not insignificant for his conclusion here that he includes Septuagint papyri that I have not included, for his most "documentary" hands are the Baden Exodus

and Deuteronomy (*MSB*, 14). When we limit ourselves to specifically Christian texts and include those papyri from the third century, the result is somewhat different.

62. Turner's description of the two traits is standard: "When a scribe joins the three consecutive movements of one letter in a single sequence he may be said to be writing a capital 'cursively' "; a "ligature" is when two or more letters are joined (i.e., when letters do not stand independently) (*Greek Manuscripts*, 1–2).

63. Turner, *Greek Manuscripts*, 15.

64. Turner, *Greek Manuscripts*, 15.

65. In this, again, they are not entirely unique. While we might assume from the letter regarding Chaerammon's apprenticeship (see above) that shorthand writers, and perhaps scribes more generally, were taught very rigid sets of abbreviations, Kathleen McNamee has discussed the idiosyncratic ways of scribes in Greek literary papryi (*Sigla and Select Marginalia in Greek Literary Papyri* [Bruselles: Fondation Égyptologique Reine Élisabeth, 1992] 23ff).

66. Neither of these cases can be attributed simply to abbreviations for the sake of even margins: the first instance exists at the beginning of a line, and the second in the middle of a line.

67. "The Date of the Magdalen Papyrus of Matthew [*P.Magd. Gr.* 17 = Response to C. P. Thiede," *Tyndale Bulletin* 46 (1995) 275. The interest in P^{64} has recently increased in energy, largely due to Thiede's (rather untenable) efforts to redate the papyrus to the first century; see C. P. Thiede, "Papyrus Magdalen Greek 17 (Gregory-Aland P^{64}): A Reappraisal," *ZPE* 105 (1995) 13–20; reprinted in *Tyndale Bulletin* 46 (1995) 29–42; see also his related "Notes on P^4 = Bibliothèque Nationale Paris, Supplementum Graece 1120/5," *Tyndale Bulletin* 46 (1995) 55–57; Philip W. Comfort, "Exploring the Common Identification of Three New Testament Manuscripts: P^4, P^{64} and P^{67}," *Tyndale Bulletin* 46 (1995) 43–54. Colin Roberts's late second-century dating still holds sway: "An Early Papyrus of the First Gospel," *HTR* 46 (1953) 233–237; see more recently, David C. Parker, *ET* 107 (1995) 40–43.

68. Indeed, part of our explanation for the overlap between literary and documentary styles in both classical and early Christian papyri must take into account the issue of date, for it is not until somewhat later that the two styles become *extremely* distant from one another. See the comments of G. Cavallo and H. Maehler, *Greek Bookhands of the Early Byzantine Period, A.D. 300–800*, Bulletin Supplement 47 (London: University of London, Institute of Classical Studies, 1987): "From the fourth century onwards, literary and documentary hands seem to develop along different paths and with increasing autonomy. The influence of documentary scripts on the forms of letters and ligatures, and on the general appearance, of contemporary bookhands, becomes far less evident than it had been in the preceding centuries; it can still be found in some formal literary hands but not, as a rule, in the formal and highly stylized scripts of this period" (1ff). While the gap widens during the fourth century and later, general distinctions between literary and documentary hands hold true for the centuries with which we are concerned here.

69. As, for example, we find in the case of the Hawara Homer; see below.

70. *MSB*, 15.

71. Cribiore admits this, though she uses "beauty" as a criterion for distinguishing teachers' hands from those of students (*Writing, Teachers, and Students*, 97–98).

72. *Edictum Diocletiani de pretiis rerum venalium,* col. 7, line 39–41 (*CIL* 3.831; ET: Turner, *Greek Manuscripts,* 1).

73. See Turner, *Greek Manuscripts,* 38, for this classification of the Hawara Homer; for the papyrus itself see W. M. F. Petrie, *Hawara, Biahmu and Arsinoe,* 24–28.

74. *CBBP,* vol. 3/1, ix; Henry Sanders noted the lack of ligatures in P[46] (*A Third-Century Papyrus Codex of the Epistles of Paul* [Ann Arbor: University of Michigan Press, 1935] 13); G. Zuntz's magisterial work on the text of the epistles, of course, devoted much time to the text preserved in P[46], and though he was little interested in the handwriting per se, he too highlighted its "neat appearance" (*The Text of the Epistles: A Disquistion upon the Corpus Paulinum* [London: Oxford University Press, 1953] 18).

75. *Papyrus Bodmer V* (Cologne-Genève: Bibliotheca Bodmeriana, 1958) 9; see also Émile de Strycker's identification of the writing as "exceptionally regular" (*La Forme le plus ancienne du Protévangile de Jacques* [Brussels: Societé des Bollandistes, 1961] 23).

76. Victor Martin, the editor of the text, noted the irregularity of the copy but understated, in my opinion, the significance of such irregularity (*Papyrus Bodmer VII–IX* [Cologne: Bibliotheca Bodmeriana, 1959] 15).

77. Most of the remaining papyri should be placed closer to the well-practiced and professional side of the spectrum. The hand of P[66], for instance, was described by Turner as a "medium-sized, rounded 'decorated' capital, slowly written" (*Greek Manuscripts,* 108, no. 63); Victor Martin, similarly, saw the hand as very stylistic and deserving of the "literary" epithet (*Papyrus Bodmer II: Evangile de Jean chap. 1–14* [Cologne: Biblioteca Bodmeriana, 1956] 15). Descriptions of P[75] vary: "the script is a clear and generally carefully executed uncial . . . " (Bruce M. Metzger, "The Bodmer Papyrus of Luke and John," *The Expository Times* 73 [1961–1962] 201–203); the hand is a "lovely vertical uncial, elegant and careful" (Victor Martin and Rodolphe Kasser, *Papyrus Bodmer XIV* [Cologne: Bibliotheca Bodmeriana, 1961] 13).

78. *A Papyrus Codex of the Shepherd of Hermas: (Similitudes 2–9) with a Fragment of the Mandates* (Ann Arbor: University of Michigan Press, 1934) 7 and 15). See more recently, in addition, the republication of *P.Oxy.* 179, a private letter whose "scribe had a very pleasing, almost literary hand, writing medium-sized rounded capitals slowly but fluently, and the literary appearance is heightened by the generous margins on all sides. The closest parallel is the hand of *P.Bodmer* II, the Gospel of St. John" (Dominic Montserrat, Georgina Fantoni, and Patrick Robinson, "Varia Descripta Oxyrhynchita," *BASP* 31 [1994] 42).

79. Harmonizations, it seems to me, are particularly ripe territory for an intertextual reading of early Christian literature. To do so here would require several chapters, however, for as we shall see there remain several definitional and methodological issues that complicate the investigation of harmonizations.

80. Aland and Aland, *Text of the New Testament,* 285.

81. Ernest Colwell, "Method in Evaluating Scribal Habits: A Study of P[45], P[66], P[75]," in his *Studies in Methodology in Textual Criticism of the New Testament* (Leiden: E. J. Brill, 1969) 113–114; Colwell's tripartite division has been adopted by others: see especially James Royse, "Scribal Habits in Early Greek New Testament Papyri," (Ph.D. diss., Graduate Theological Union, Berkeley, Calif., 1981). In the paragraphs

that follow, I depend heavily upon Royse's work, though at times I will argue against some of his precise points.

82. Metzger, *The Text of the New Testament*, 197.

83. *Books and Readers*, 71, 74.

84. On the use of the term "monk" (μοναχός) in the papyri see especially, E. A. Judge, "The Earliest Use of Monachos for 'Monk' (P. Coll. Youtie 77) and the Origins of Monasticism," *JAC* 20 (1977) 72–89; on monks as copyists, see Ludwig Koenen, "Ein Mönch als Berufsschreiber: Zur Buchproduktion im 5./6. Jahrhundert," in *Festschrift zum 150-Jährigen Bestehen des Berliner Ägyptischen Museums* (Berlin: Akademie Verlag, 1974) 347–354. It is not, of course, until the fourth century that Christian monasticism begins to develop and communties of monastics are organized, despite the fact that the impulse toward asceticism began much earlier: see Gerd Theissen, *Sociology of Early Palestianian Christianity*, trans. John Bowden (Philadelphia: Fortress Press, 1978; originally published as *Soziologie der Jesusbewegung* [München: Chr. Kaiser Verlag, 1977]) especially 8–16; Peter Brown, *The Body and Society: Men, Women and Sexual Renunciation in Early Christianity* (New York: Columbia University Press, 1988) especially 5–64; for later periods, of course, the literature is extensive, and here I cite only some of the more influential and recent works: Sebastian P. Brock, "Early Syrian Asceticism," *Numen* 20 (1973) 1–19; Elizabeth A. Clark, *Ascetic Piety and Women's Faith: Essays on Late Ancient Christianity* (New York: Edwin Mellen Press, 1986) and *Reading Renunciation: Asceticism and Scripture in Early Christianity* (Princeton, N.J.: Princeton University Press, 1999); Susanna Elm, *'Virgins of God': The Making of Asceticism in Late Antiquity* (Oxford: Clarendon Press, 1996 [1994]); Philip Rousseau, *Ascetics, Authority, and the Church in the Age of Jerome and Cassian* (Oxford: Oxford University Press, 1978); Aline Rousselle, *Porneia: On Desire and the Body in Antiquity* (Oxford: Basil Blackwell, 1988 [1983]); Derwas J. Chitty, *The Desert a City: An Introduction to the Study of Egyptian and Palestinian Monasticism under the Christian Empire* (London: A. R. Mowbrays, 1966).

85. On Antony, for example, see Athanasius's Vita Antonii (trans. R. C. Gregg, *The Life of Antony and the Letter to Marcellinus* [New York: Paulist Press, 1980]): "For he paid such close attention to what was read that nothing from Scripture did he fail to take in — rather he grasped everything, and in him the memory took the place of books" (3) PG 26.835–976. One may well wonder, however, about the accuracy of this record. In the fourth century, we find an explosion of references to memorizing scripture. For example, the fourth-century Pachomian literature is chock full of references to books, reading, and memorizing: "There shall be no one whatever in the monastery who does not learn to read and does not memorize something of the Scriptures. [One should learn by heart] at least the New Testament and the Psalter" (*Pachomian Koinonia: The Lives, Rules and Other Writings of Saint Pachomius and His Disciples*, vol. 2, *Pachomian Chronicles and Rules*, trans. A. Veilleux (Kalamazoo, Mich.: Cistercian Press, 1981) 166, 414–415, 260–262; see also James M. Robinson, *The Pachomian Monastic Library at the Chester Beatty Library and the Bibliothèque Bodmer* (Claremont, Calif.: Institute for Antiquity and Christianity, 1990) 2; Philip Rousseau, *Pachomius: The Making of a Community in Fourth-Century Egypt* (Berkeley: University of California Press, 1985) especially 81. Nowhere do find in our second- and third-century literature about catechetical instruction, however, any indication that Christian

initiates were taught how to read, nor is there indication that they were required to memorize "extensive portions" of scripture (see my "Hearing and Reading: Literacy and Power in the Early Christian Church," M.A. thesis [Chapel Hill, N.C.: University of North Carolina, 1993]).

86. Secondary literature on canonization is quite extensive; see especially, Bruce M. Metzger, *The Canon of the New Testament: Its Origin, Development, and Significance* (Oxford: Clarendon Press, 1997 [c. 1987]); Hans von Campenhausen, *The Formation of the Christian Bible*, trans. J. A. Baker (Philadelphia, Pa.: Fortress Press, 1972); Harry Y. Gamble, *The New Testament Canon: Its Making and Meaning* (Philadelphia, Pa.: Fortress Press, 1985), and "Christianity: Scripture and Canon," in *The Holy Book in Comparative Perspective* (Columbia: University of South Carolina Press, 1985) 36–62.

87. Tatian's Diatessaron, of course, is the most notable exception; but we should also mention Justin's gospel harmony. Both of these, however, are exceptional cases. On Tatian see especially the work of William L. Petersen, "New Evidence for the Question of the Original Language of the Diatessaron," in *Studien zum Text und Ethik des Neuen Testaments: Festschrift zum 80. Geburtstag Heinrich Greeven*, ed. W. Schrage (Berlin: de Gruyter, 1986) 325–343; *Tatian's Diatessaron: Its Creation, Dissemination, Significance, and History in Scholarship* (Leiden: E. J. Brill, 1994); "Textual Evidence of Tatian's Dependence upon Justin's ΑΠΟΜΝΗΜΟΝΕΥΜΑΤΑ," *NTS* 36 (1990) 512–534; and his history of the research on Tatian's Diatessaron, "The Diatessaron of Tatian," in *The Text of the New Testament in Contemporary Research: Essays on the Status Quaestionis*, ed. Bart D. Ehrman and Michael W. Holmes (Grand Rapids, Mich.: Eerdmans, 1995) 77–96.

88. My use of the term "text" here is reflective of recent work in cultural history, which offers an expansion of the notion of "text" (see especially, D. F. McKenzie, *Bibliography and the Sociology of Texts* [London: British Library, 1986] 5–6); on the oral influences on the text of the New Testament, see the comments of D. C. Parker, *The Living Text of the Gospels* (Cambridge: Cambridge University Press, 1997) 210ff.

89. "Method in Evaluating Scribal Habits"; see also his later article, "External Evidence and New Testament Textual Criticism," in *Studies in the History and Text of the New Testament in Honour of Kenneth Willis Clark*, ed. Boyd L. Daniels and M. Jack Suggs (Salt Lake City: University of Utah Press, 1967) 9.

90. *Novum Testamentum Graece ad Antiquos testes denuo recensuit*, 8th ed. (Leipzig: Giesecke and Devrient, 1869).

91. Colwell, "Scribal Habits," 108. Having defined singular readings, Colwell eliminated itacisms from inclusion as both impractical (the number being so great) and unnecessary (of no value in determining the original text of the New Testament). Singular readings were divided into two groups: nonsense readings ("include words unknown to grammar or lexicon, words that cannot be construed syntactically, or words that do not make sense in the context") and sensible readings (omissions, additions, transpositions, harmonizations) (111).

92. Colwell, for example, concluded that "P^{66} should not be cited as evidence for the omission of a short word, except where its kinship with a group that omits the word has been established"; "P^{45} should not be cited as evidence for a transposition, except where its kinship with a group that supports the transposition has been

established"; and "readings that are identifiable as harmonizations to immediate context should not be cited unless they characterize a group" ("Scribal Habits," 124).

93. James Royse, in particular, has extended Colwell's initial work; see his dissertation, entitled "Scribal Habits in Early Greek New Testament Papyri" (see n. 84 above) and his "Scribal Habits in the Transmission of New Testament Texts," in *The Critical Study of Sacred Texts*, ed. Wendy Doniger O'Flaherty (Berkeley, Calif.: Graduate Theological Union, 1979) 139–61. On scribal habits, see also the work of Peter Head, "Observations on Early Papyri of the Synoptic Gospels, especially on the 'Scribal Habits'," *Biblica* 71 (1990) 240–247; Moisés Silva, "The Text of Galatians: Evidence from the Earliest Greek Manuscripts," in *Scribes and Scripture*, ed. D. A. Black (Winona Lake, Ind.: Eisenbrauns, 1992) 17–25. Particularly surprising is that the work on scribal habits in our earliest papyri has called into question some of the very tools and assumptions of New Testament textual criticism, such as the shorter reading is to be preferred or the notion that harmonizations occur frequently in New Testament papyri and manuscripts.

94. And Peter Head, whose study on the scribal habits in the pre-fourth-century papyri of the synoptic Gospels that were not included in Royse's or Colwell's study, yielded similar results — only two cases of remote harmonization were found in the twelve manuscripts Head studied ("Observations on Early Papyri," 246).

95. "Scribal Habits," 263.

96. "Scribal Habits," 415.

97. "Scribal Habits," 415.

98. *Papyrus Bodmer XIV–XV*.

99. Royse, "Scribal Habits," 136–137.

100. Furthermore, if we assume the scribe is harmonizing in the passage, we are hard pressed to understand why the scribe did not harmonize the other word (λίθον) to the parallel passages.

101. One of our earliest passages regarding Christian services is that found in Justin's *Apology* I.67. Paul Achtemeier's study suggests that we look to the influence of memory upon the text ("*Omne Verbum Sonat*: The New Testament and the Oral Environment of Late Western Antiquity," *JBL* 109 [1990] 3–27, especially 27).

102. For a brief discussion of the passage, see Bruce M. Metzger, *A Textual Commentary on the Greek New Testament* (London: United Bible Societies, 1971) 533–536; the whole question is closely connected with Marcion's "edition" of the New Testament, which probably excluded chapters 15 and 16 from Romans; on Marcion's text see especially, Adolf von Harnack, *Marcion: Das Evangelium vom fremden Gott*, 2d edition (Leipzig: J. C. Hinrichs, 1924); on the role of Marcion's text in the text of Romans, see Zuntz, *The Text of the Epistles*, especially 226–241.

103. Admittedly, this remains a hypothesis; the distinction between the gospels and the prophets certainly goes back at least to the second century (Justin, *Apology* I.66). I am not entirely convinced by the explanation offered by W. Bauer: "P⁷²appears to distinguish prophecy and OT writing" (*BAG*, 722).

104. For the phrase's usage outside of the New Testament, see 2 Clem 5:5; 8: 4, 6; Ignatius, *Eph* 18:1; the *Shepherd*, *vis.* 2, 3, 2; *vis.* 3, 8, 4.

105. The versional issues are complex and are not explored in this study; the literature is extensive: see especially Bruce M. Metzger, *The Early Versions of the New*

Testament: Their Origin, Transmission and Limitations (Oxford: Clarendon Press, 1977); Arthur Vööbus, *Early Versions of the New Testament* (Stockholm: Estonian Theological Society in Exile, 1954); on Tatian's Diatessaron, see Petersen, *Tatian's Diatessaron*; Theodor Zahn, *Tatian's Diatessaron* (Erlangen: Deichert, 1881); the text preserved in Codex Bezae is also evidence of second-century harmonistic tendencies (see D. C. Parker, *Codex Bezae: An Early Christian Manuscript and Its Text* [Cambridge: Cambridge University Press, 1992] especially 279–280); see also the articles in *The Text of the New Testament in Contemporary Research: Essays on the Status Quaestionis*, ed. Bart D. Ehrman and Michael W. Holmes (Grand Rapids, Mich.: Eerdmans, 1995).

106. Turner, *Greek Papyri*, 58; Youtie, *Textual Criticism of Documentary Papyri*, 51.

107. Locating these tendencies, of course, has serious implications for the practice of New Testament textual criticism, as the work of Royse and Colwell demonstrated. Royse, for example, does draw a few conclusions about the individual manuscripts he studies regarding the scribal concern with style and grammar: for example, P^{45} dispenses with "unnecessary words" and smooths out readings; in P^{46} "some changes are somewhat more systematic or betray perhaps a conscious attempt to improve on his *Vorlage*" ("Scribal Habits," 269); P^{47}, on the other hand, does not appear to be "concerned with grammar and style" ("Scribal Habits," 355). One might also turn to the presence of Atticisms in the early Christian papryi; see G. D. Kilpatrick, "Atticism and the Text of the Greek New Testament," in *Neutestamentliche Aufsätze: Festschrift für Prof. Josef Schmid zum 10. Geburtstag*, ed. J. Blinzer, O. Kuss, and F. Mußner (Regensburg: Friedrich Pustet, 1963) 125–137; reprinted in *The Principals and Practice of New Testament Textual Criticism: Collected Essays of G. D. Kilpatrick*, ed. J. K. Elliott (Leuven: Leuven University Press, 1990) 19–24.

108. Similar to Turner's work on "scholars' copies" in which he found a correlation between less calligraphic hands (or, a range in calligraphy), more critical markings and annotations, and fewer errors (see Turner, *Greek Papyri*, 92–96).

109. Although the percentage of nonsense readings in P^{72} was rather high, according to Royse's study, almost all of the orthographic errors can be accounted for on the basis of Coptic influence: "The papyrus thus seems firmly located within the range of Coptic influence, and this influence is evidently responsible for many of the orthograhic singulars. Indeed, Testuz reports Kasser's opinion that the sound errors can be localized to the region around Thebes" ("Scribal Habits," 470).

CHAPTER 4

1. The earliest papyrus copy of the *Shepherd* is dated to "the third quarter of the second century" (*P.Mich.*130; for dating see Bonner, *A Papyrus Codex*, 129; Roberts, *MSB*, 14); Clement, *Stromata* II, 1, 9, 12; IV, 9; VI, 15; in Irenaeus, *Haer.* iv, 20, 2. On the Muratorian Canon, see especially Metzger, *The Canon*, 191–201; cf. Hahneman, *The Muratorian Fragment*. On the exchange of literature among early Christians, see especially Eldon Jay Epp, "New Testament Papyrus Manuscripts and Letter Carrying in Greco-Roman Times," in *The Future of Early Christianity*, ed. Birger A. Pearson (Minneapolis, Minn.: Fortress Press, 1991) 35–56; Stephen Robert

Llewelyn, "Sending Letters in the Ancient World: Paul and the Philippians," *Tyndale Bulletin* 46 (1995) 337–356.

2. For other examples, and a helpful discussion, see Gamble, *Books and Readers*, 96–99. On the ancient "postal system," the *cursus publicus* see most recently S. R. Llewelyn and R. A. Kearsley, "The Official Postal Systems of Antiquity," in *NewDocs* 7 (1994) 1–25.

3. On *P.Oxy.* 4365, see D. Hagedorn, "The Little Genesis," *ZPE* 116 (1997) 147–148; Hagedorn suggests that "the little Genesis" refers to the book of Jubilees. See also *Women and Society in Greek and Roman Egypt*, no. 59.

4. That these two modes are interwoven with the settings of a scriptorium in contrast to more private settings is clear from Metzger's discussion (*Manuscripts of the Greek Bible*, 21–22.

5. *The Book before Printing: Ancient, Medieval and Oriental* (New York: Dover, 1982; originally published as *The Hand-Produced Book*, 1953) 206.

6. See the series of articles by C. P. Hammond Bammel, "Products of Fifth-Century Scriptoria Preserving Conventions Used by Rufinus of Aquileia," *JTS* 29 (1978) 366–391, 30 (1979) 430–462, and 35 (1984) 345–393. In the earlier of these articles, Hammond Bammel argued that some of the features in a fifth-century manuscript of Rufinus' translation of Origen's *Commentary on Romans* are so similar to Rufinus' own practice that they suggest the possibility that it was copied in a monastery under his influence.

7. This is quite clearly the impetus behind the written account of Polycarp's martyrdom, though we know very little about the church in Philomelium (on the request see *Mart.Poly.* 22.1; on the location of Philomelium and the existence of a church there, see J. B. Lightfoot's edition, *The Apostolic Fathers*, part 2 [London 1889; repr., New York: Georg Olms, 1973] 363).

8. Marcianus, or Marcion, is not of course to be confused with the archheretic Marcion. Eusebius claims that one of Irenaeus' treatises was dedicated to a certain Christian named Marcion (*HE* 5.26), and Lightfoot thinks it "not improbably the same man" as we find here at the conclusion of the *Mart.Poly.* (*Apostolic Fathers*, 398). William R. Schoedel distinguishes between Marcianus as the composer and Evarestus as the scribe (*The Apostolic Fathers: A New Translation and Commentary*, vol. 5, *Polycarp, Martyrdom of Polycarp, Fragments of Papias* [London: Thomas Nelson and Sons, 1967] 78).

9. Irenaeus himself simply tells us he saw Polycarp when he was a youth in Smyrna (*Haer.* 3.3.4).

10. Numerous examples exist of disciples, or students, retaining copies of their teachers' works and/or notes of their lectures. See, for example, the mention of Damis' record book for the teachings of his teacher Apollonius of Tyana (Philostratus, *Apollonius of Tyana* 1.19); Tiro, whom Cicero claimed as a student, also kept records and copies of Cicero's letters, although his profession as personal secretary to Cicero makes this not an identical parallel to the relationship between Polycarp and Irenaeus (Cicero, *Att.* 16.5: "There is no collection [lit. gathering] of my letters, but Tiro has about seventy" [Mearum epistularum nulla est συναγωγή; sed habet Tiro instar septuaginta]).

11. L. W. Barnard thought the colophons to *Mart.of .Poly.* should not be dismissed entirely as "false or unreliable" ("In Defence of Pseudo-Pionius' Account of Saint Polycarp's Martyrdom," in *Kyriakon: Festschrift Johannes Quasten,* ed. Patrick Granfield and Josef A. Jungmann, vol. 1 [Münster: Aschendorff, 1970] 192; Schoedel identified this as an addition, but did not venture a guess as to the date when it was added (*Polycarp,* 78), although in his estimation the whole thing could be discounted as invention: "The effort to put even the copying of the letter in a sort of succession back to Polycarp is disquieting, and suggests that this appendix was reformulated (or even invented) by the editor who appended 22:3" (*Polycarp,* 80). I would agree with Gamble, however, in arguing that "it would be rash to dismiss for these reasons the entire transmission history indicated in the colophons of 22.2–4. It is possible and perhaps likely that the scribal notes in 22.2–3 give reliable information" (*Books and Readers,* 115).

12. Throughout this chapter, my interest in the networks of relationships between members of Christian communities and between individual scribes is informed by social network theory, which understands "a social network as a specific set of linkages among a defined set of persons, with the additional property that the characteristics of these linkages as a whole may be used to interpret the social behavior of the persons involved" (J. Clyde Mitchell, "The Concept and Use of Social Networks," in *Social Networks in Urban Situations: Analyses of Personal Relationships in Central African Towns,* ed. J. Clyde Mitchell [Manchester: Manchester University Press, 1969] 2; see also Jeremy Boissevain, *Friends of Friends: Networks, Manipulators and Coalitions* [Oxford: Basil Blackwell, 1974]). For the insightful application of such theories of social networks to studies of fourth- and fifth-century Christianity, see especially Elizabeth A. Clark, *The Origenist Controversy: The Cultural Construction of an Early Christian Debate* (Princeton, N.J.: Princeton University Press, 1992).

13. Starr, "Circulation of Literary Texts," 219–223, esp. 222.

14. On these requests see further, Sommer, "T. Pomponius Atticus," esp. 389.

15. For other examples, see Starr, "The Circulation of Literary Texts," 217.

16. The exception to this is, of course, Pliny's account of the one thousand copies that Regulus had made of his memoir for his son (*Ep.* 4.7.2.). It is precisely, however, the exceptionality of this incident that proves the rule of individualized copying (i.e., one copy made at a time in response to a specific request).

17. Skeat, "The Use of Dictation," 189. Here Skeat was drawing upon the foundational work of Theodor Birt, especially his *Antike Buchwesen,* published in 1882.

18. Cicero asks Atticus to send two copyists to work in the library with Tyrannio: Et velim mihi mittas de tuis librariolis duos aliquos (*Att.* 4.4a).

19. *Ancient Literacy,* 225. Harris, referring to the comments of Skeat that I have quoted above, writes: "It is futile to conjure up the alleged 'mass-production scriptoria of the big publishers of the ancient world', for neither 'mass-production' nor indeed 'publisher' is an appropriate notion" (*Ancient Literacy,* 224). Such sentiments find resonance in B. A. van Groningen, who emphasizes the role of friends and interested readers in the reproduction and transmission of literature: "Ce phénomène de distribution et de diffusion est la διάδοσις. Elle dépend uniquement de l'intéret

personnel des lecteurs; elle est arbitraire; elle n'a rien de systématique" ("ΕΚΔΟΣΙΣ," *Mnemosyne* 16 [1963] 3).

20. Diringer, *The Book Before Printing*, 159.

21. This was originally R. de Vaux's theory on the room; see on this issue Ronny Reich, "A Note on the Function of Room 30 (the 'Scriptorium') at Khirbet Qumran," *JJS* 46 (1995) 157–160. See also Bruce M. Metzger, "When Did Scribes Begin to Use Writing Desks?" in his *Historical and Literary Studies, Pagan, Jewish, and Christian* (Grand Rapids, Mich.: Eerdmans, 1968) 135–137; Stephen Goranson, "Further Qumran Archaeology Publications in Progress," *BA* 54 (1991) 110–111. Metzger appears to take for granted that the room was "the Scriptorium at Khirbet Qumran," but he is hard pressed to explain how the furniture in the room was used by scribes ("Whether the table was used for the preparation and repair of the skins and scrolls, or whether it was used to hold the necessary equipment for writing, such as the ink wells and perhaps the exemplar also, in any case there is very little likelihood that it served as a writing desk," 137).

22. The literature on the subject of scribal practices at Qumran is extensive, and much of the early scholarly literature was concerned with identifying scribal practices at Qumran with those prescribed by (late!) rabbinic literature on the subject; see, for example, J. B. Poole and R. Reed, "The Preparation of Leather and Parchment by the Dead Sea Scrolls Community," *Technology and Culture* 3 (1962) 1–26, and Jonathan Siegel, "The Scribes of Qumran: Studies in the Early History of Jewish Scribal Customs, with Special Reference to the Qumran Biblical Scrolls and to the Tannaitic Traditions of Massekheth Soferim" (Ph.D. diss., Brandeis University, 1972). The work of Emanuel Tov is particularly important on the subject of a "Qumranic scribal school," for it details closely both the diversity of scribal practices evident in the scrolls found at Qumran, while attempting to identify those scrolls that were produced outside of the community and those produced by scribes at Qumran (see especially his "Hebrew Biblical Manuscripts from the Judaean Desert: Their Contribution to Textual Criticism," *JJS* 39 [1988] 5–37; "The Textual Base of the Corrections in the Biblical Texts Found at Qumran," in *The Dead Sea Scrolls: Forty Years of Research*, ed. Devorah Dimant and Uriel Rappaport [Leiden: E. J. Brill, 1992] 299–314; and *Textual Criticism of the Hebrew Bible* [Minneapolis, Minn.: Fortress Press, 1992] especially 100–118).

23. I have found no instance of a woman *author* being asked for a copy of her works. To be sure, there appear to have been few women writers during the time period under consideration here, but they were not entirely absent; in the early Christian context, we might think of Perpetua, whose own written account of her imprisonment is supposedly preserved in the extant *Martyrdom of Saints Perpetua and Felicitas*, or the later Faltonia Betitia Proba, whose fourth-century *Cento* weaves together phrases from Virgil with biblical narratives, and Egeria, whose fifth-century travel narrative has received no small amount of scholarly attention. On women writers, see especially Jane McIntosh Snyder, *The Woman and the Lyre: Women Writers in Classical Greece and Rome* (Carbondale: Southern Illinois University Press, 1989); Peter Dronke, *Women Writers of the Middle Ages* (Cambridge: Cambridge University Press, 1984); Mary R. Lefkowitz, "Did Ancient Women Write Novels?" in *"Women Like This": New Perspectives on Jewish Women in the Greco-Roman World*, ed. Amy-Jill

Levine (Atlanta, Ga.: Scholars Press, 1991) 199–219; Ross Kraemer, "Women's Authorship of Jewish and Christian Literature in the Greco-Roman Period," in *"Women Like This,"* 221–242. Attempts to locate female authorship behind anonymous works have been quite vigorous, particularly with regard to the Apocryphal Acts, and here I simply list some of the more important studies: Virginia Burrus, *Chastity as Autonomy: Women in the Stories of the Apocryphal Acts* (Lewiston, N.Y.: Edwin Mellen Press, 1987); Stevan L. Davies, *The Revolt of the Widows: The Social World of the Apocryphal Acts* (Carbondale: Southern Illinois University Press, 1980); Dennis R. MacDonald, *The Legend and the Apostle* (Philadelphia: Westminster Press, 1983).

24. Nowhere is the connection between a particular papyrus and its context more clear than in the case of school papyri (see especially, Cribiore, *Writing, Teachers, and Students*); see also Turner, *Greek Papyri*, 89; *Greek Manuscripts*, 16; Turner's work on "scholars' texts" was an attempt to draw a connection between the physical characteristics of particular papyri and the context (or, persons) for which they were prepared ("Scribes and Scholars"; *Greek Papyri*, 92–96).

25. *The Text of the New Testament*, 14.

26. *Text of the Epistles*, 273. More recently, as we shall see below, E. Colwell, G. Fee, and C. H. Roberts have made similar statements. Roberts is most explicit in his acceptance of the claims of Zuntz and goes on to link Zuntz's Alexandrian scriptorium with the supposed "Catechetical School of Alexandria" (*MSB*, 24).

27. Colwell, "Method in Evaluating Scribal Habits," 118.

28. Gordon Fee, "The Myth of Early Textual Recension in Alexandria," in *Studies in the Theory and Method of New Testament Textual Criticism*, ed. Eldon Jay Epp and Gordon D. Fee (Grand Rapids, Mich.: Eerdmans, 1993) 258; see also his earlier *Papyrus Bodmer II (P[66])*, 82 n. 20.

29. The third-century fragment P[95] offers an example of a fairly calligraphic hand, although we could note that even here the α appears to be formed cursively (i.e., in one stroke); the late second-century P[4]-P[64]-P[67] is another example of a good hand, but here there is some irregularity in the evenness of lines.

30. On the first point, we may recall from chapter 3, that *P.Bodmer* V is closer to a strict bilinear hand than P[66]; see further the discussion below on the hand of *P.Bodmer* V as well as that of *P.Bodmer* XIII, which displays even more experience and calligraphic regularity (and these hands are found within the same codex, which was clearly a private copy). For the parallel to P[66], see *P.Oxy.* 179 and the following discussion: Dominic Montserrat, Georgina Fantoni, Patrick Robinson, "Varia Descripta Oxyrhynchita," *BASP* 31 (1994) 42–43.

31. See Metzger, *The Text of the New Testament*, 115 n.2, for this definition; this is also how the Alands appear to use the term (*The Text*, 22, 50); but they also use the term to mean, "thoroughgoing revisions of the New Testament" (87). Arguments for and against recensional activity are extremely complex, largely because they are interwoven with discussions of text types, text families, or textual clusters — that is, the "Alexandrian/Neutral," "Western," "Caesarean," and "Byzantine," and Metzger points out that the term "recension" is "often used in a loose sense as synonymous with 'family'" (*The Text of the New Testament*, 115 n. 2). Discussions of such textual groupings is vital to the practice of New Testament textual criticism, but there is

little consensus on the identification of textual families; the literature on the subject is extensive: see especially Eldon Jay Epp, "The Significance of the Papyri for Determining the Nature of the New Testament Text in the Second Century: A Dynamic View of Textual Transmission," in *Studies in the Theory and Method of New Testament Textual Criticism*, 274–297 (originally published as "Gospel Traditions in the Second Century: Origins, Recensions, Text, and Transmission," in *Gospel Traditions in the Second Century*, ed. William L. Petersen [Notre Dame, Ind.: University of Notre Dame Press, 1989] 71–103); Michael W. Holmes, "Codex Bezae as a Recension of the Gospels," in *Codex Bezae: Studies from the Lunel Colloquium, June 1994*, ed. D. C. Parker and C.-B. Amphoux (Leiden: E. J. Brill, 1996) 123–160, especially 142–150; Ernest Colwell, "Method in Grouping New Testament Manuscripts," in his *Studies in Methodology in Textual Criticism of the New Testament*, 1–25; more specific treatment of methodology in grouping New Testament manuscripts can be found in Ernest C. Colwell and Ernest W. Tune, "The Quantitative Relationships between MS Text-Types," in *Biblical and Patristic Studies*, ed. J. Neville Birdsall and Robert W. Thomson (Freiburg: Herder, 1963) 25–32; Gordon D. Fee, "Codex Sinaiticus in the Gospel of John: A Contribution to Methodology in Establishing Textual Relationships," *NTS* 15 (1968) 23–44; Bart D. Ehrman, "The Use of Group Profiles for the Classification of New Testament Documentary Evidence," *JBL* 106 (1987) 465–486.

32. Colwell, "Methods in Evaluating Scribal Habits," 118; Fee, *Papyrus Bodmer II*, 57–75, and especially 82.

33. Fee, *Papyrus Bodmer II*, 82; "The Myth of Early Textual Recension," 259–260.

34. See *The Text of the Epistles*, especially 252–262 on corrections, and 263–283 on the existence of a second-century Christian scriptorium at Alexandria, a scriptorium that strove for a standardization of the biblical text.

35. Royse, "Scribal Habits," 235–240 and 391–396. In P[66], as Royse has pointed out and highlighted, many of the corrections are made by the initial scribe, a not uncommon practice in the ancient world. The only exception to this is found in 13: 19a, where a second hand appears to have corrected a lengthy omission that produced nonsense ("Scribal Habits," 392). In his own study of P[66], Royse actually argues that "there is no clear evidence of any correction by a 'foreman' [Colwell's term], and the corrections to a second standard were all, with at most a few exceptions, by the scribe. Of course, it is conceivable that a scribe felt pressure from someone else to copy correctly. But this is a pressure which any scribe could feel. The fact is that the scribe makes his own corrections, whether of scribal slips or to a second *Vorlage*, and rather often makes them in the course of his copying" ("Scribal Habits," 403–404).

36. Metzger, *Manuscripts of the Greek Bible*, 22; Turner, *Greek Manuscripts*, 15–16.

37. See Turner's discussion of scholars texts and references there (*Greek Papyri*, 94).

38. For documents, see *BGU* 4.1114; for literary texts see again the Hawara Homer. On the role and presence of the corrector, see also Turner, *Greek Manuscripts*, 15–16.

39. *Greek Manuscripts*, 15 (emphasis mine).

40. *Greek Papyri*, 93.

41. Thompson, *A Handbook*, 78–82; Turner, *Greek Papyri*, 90 and 95. The most extensive treatment of stichometry is that of J. Rendel Harris, "Stichometry," *American Journal of Philology* 4 (1883) 133–157, 309–331.

42. *The Text of the Epistles*, 253.

43. Metzger, *The Text*, 15–16. See also the similar explanations and definitions in Thompson, *A Handbook*, 78–80.

44. As Turner admits in the case of *P. Oxy.* 852 (*Greek Manuscripts*, 16).

45. Metzger assumes the equation of commercial copies with a scriptorium environment, although there is no evidence to suggest that only scribes within the context of a scriptorium were paid. Turner indeed argued in publications prior to his *Greek Manuscripts* that they indicated a commercial copy, but he did not invoke a scriptorium environment: "if they are present in a text, we may be sure that the copy was professionally made and paid for" (*Greek Papyri*, 95).

46. Indeed, the most common mistake that scribes made in the process of copying was that of haplography, which was facilitated by *homoioteleuton* (sets or sequences of letters that were repeated) (Metzger, *The Text of the New Testament*, 189–190); that scribes more often omitted than added text is one of the more significant arguments made in recent studies of "scribal habits" (see especially, James Royse, "Scribal Habits," 593–608, passim).

47. The fact that P^{66} has such a high percentage and frequency of itacisms appears to have contributed to Colwell's theories about the scriptorium context behind this papyrus.

48. Metzger, *Manuscripts of the Greek Bible*, 21–22. That theories of scriptoria were interwoven with dictation theory, as it is commonly called, is the subject of much of Skeat's discussion of dictation: "The Use of Dictation," esp. 179–186; Milne and Skeat, *The Scribes and Correctors*, esp. 51–59; see also D. C. Parker, "A 'Dictation Theory' of Codex Bezae," *JSNT* 15 (1982) 97–112.

49. See the pioneering work of Joseph Balogh, "Voces Paginarum," *Philologus* 82 (1927) 84–109, 202–240; more recent works have explored the issue further and while generally agreeing with Balogh's argument that normally texts were read aloud in antiquity, they have emphasized that this was not the only mode of reading (i.e., silent reading was not "extraordinary"); see especially Bernard M. W. Knox, "Silent Reading in Antiquity," *GRBS* 9 (1968) 421–435; Paul Saenger, "Silent Reading: Its Impact on Late Medieval Script and Society," *Viator* 13 (1982) 367–414; Dirk M. Schenkeveld, "Prose Usages of AKOΥEIN 'To Read'," *CQ* 42 (1992) 129–141; and Frank D. Gilliard, "More Silent Reading in Antiquity: *Non Omne Verbum Sonabat*," *JBL* 112 (1993) 689–694.

50. Skeat, "The Use of Dictation," 187.

51. *MSB*, 24.

52. See, especially, *Greek Manuscripts*, no. 16, 55, 58, and 72.

53. On the subject of the Alexandrian school, see especially, Manfred Hornschuh, "Das Leben des Origenes und die Entstehung der alexandrinischen Schule," *Zeitschrift für Kirchengeschichte* 71 (1960) 1–25, 193–214; Roelof van den Broek, ".The Christian 'School' of Alexandria in the Second and Third Centuries," in *Centres of Learning: Learning and Location in Pre-Modern Europe and the Near East*, ed. Jan Willem Drijvers and Alasdair A. MacDonald (Leiden: E. J. Brill, 1995) 39–47; Robert L. Wilken, "Alexandria: A School for Training in Virtue," in *Schools of Thought in the Christian Tradition*, ed. Patrick Henry (Philadelphia, Pa.: Fortress Press, 1984) 15–30; Johannes Quasten, *Patrology*, vol. 2 (Utrecht: Spectrum, 1953) especially 2–6; Robert M. Grant,

"Theological Education at Alexandria," in *The Roots of Egyptian Christianity*, ed. Birger A. Pearson and James E. Goehring (Philadelphia, Pa.: Fortress Press, 1986) 178–189; for the school at Caesarea, see most recently Hayim Lapin, "Jewish and Christian Academies in Roman Palestine: Some Preliminary Observations," in *Caesarea Máritima: A Retrospective after Two Millenia*, ed. Avner Raban and Kenneth G. Holum (Leiden: E. J. Brill, 1996); and although it only touches upon Christian academies, see also Mark Hirshman, "The Preacher and his Public in Third-Century Palestine," *JJS* 42 (1991) 108–14.

54. *Books and Readers*, 120.

55. See *LSJ* for these definitions.

56. "The Titles of the Gospels and the Gospel of Mark," in his *Studies in the Gospel of Mark* (Philadelphia, Pa.: Fortress Press, 1985) 79.

57. On the *nomina sacra* see especially, the foundational work of Ludwig Traube, *Nomina Sacra: Versuch einer Geschichte der christlichen Kürzung* (Munich, 1907), which coined the term *nomina sacra* and argued that the practice originated among Hellenistic Jews who used contracted forms much like the Hebrew Tetragrammmaton; more recently, A.H.R.E. Paap, *Nomina Sacra in the Greek Papyri of the First Five Centuries A.D.: The Sources and Some Deductions* (Leiden: Lugdunum Batavorum, 1959), assembles all the evidence for the various contractions and abbreviations of the nomina sacra and argues that rather than originating among Hellenistic Jews, the practice originated among Jewish Christians and later was expanded. See also José O'Callaghan, *Nomina Sacra in Papyris Graecis Saeculi III Neotestamentariis* (Rome: Biblical Institute Press, 1970); Roberts, *MSB*, 26–48; Schuyler Brown, "Concerning the Origin of the Nomina Sacra," *Studia Papyrologica* 9 (1970) 7–19; and George Howard, "The Tetragram and the New Testament," *JBL* 96 (1977) 63–83. Hatch implies that the nomina sacra were somehow the result of scribal efficiency: "Certain frequently recurring words . . . are abbreviated in early as well as in later manuscripts" (*The Principal Uncial Manuscripts of the New Testament* [Chicago: University of Chicago Press, 1939] 25). On the use of *nomina sacra* in early Latin manuscripts, see especially C. H. Roberts, "The *Nomina Sacra* in Early Christian Latin Mss," *Miscellanea Francesco Ehrle* 4 (1924) 62–74.

58. Contractions properly describes the use of the first and last letters of a word and the elimination of the middle letters and use of a suprascript line above; suspension, on the other hand, consists of the first two letters of a word (and suprascript line) and the elimination of the rest.

59. Metzger, *Greek Manuscripts*, 36. For a convenient listing of the various *nomina sacra* that appear in early papyri (including pre-Christian LXX/OG copies), see Aland, *Repertorium* 1:420–428.

60. Roberts, *MSB*, 46.

61. This is not, of course, a new argument; indeed, inconsistent use of treatment of the *nomina sacra* has been used to date early Christian papyri. Henry A. Sanders, for example, used this to help date P^{46} (*A Third-Century Papyrus Codex of the Epistles of Paul* [Ann Arbor: University of Michigan Press, 1935] 16).

62. Royse, "Scribal Habits," 89. See Paap's table, *Nomina Sacra*, 12–13. In the discussion that follows, I have relied upon the original publications of individual

papyri, Paap's tables, and Aland's *Repertorium*; I have also checked my discussion of unique papyri against O'Callaghan's lists (*Nomina Sacra*, 41–70).

63. It is found also in *P.Oxy.* 1079 and 1224 (according to Kenyon, *Chester Beatty*, 2.1.ix); see also Roberts on this abbrevation (*MSB*, 36); and Paap, *Nomina Sacra*, 107; Aland's *Repertorium* offers five manuscripts where it is found (422). It also appears in *P.Egerton* 2 (see H. Idris Bell and T. C. Skeat, *Fragments of an Unknown Gospel and Other Early Christian Papyri* [London: Oxford University Press, 1935] especially 3) and appears to be known by the author of the Epistle of Barnabas (*Barn.* 9.8).

64. This was Kenyon's assessment (Kenyon 2:1:ix), and it is confirmed by Aland's list (*Repertorium* 1:425).

65. See Aland, *Repertorium* 1:428 where P^{45} is listed alone for this abbreviation; see also Paap, *Nomina Sacra*, 13, who indicates that this is a *nomen sacrum* in this manuscript (usage is "sacred" according to Paap).

66. Royse, "Scribal Habits," 248.

67. According to C. H. Roberts' reconstruction (*An Unpublished Fragment of the Fourth Gospel in the John Rylands Library* [Manchester: Manchester University Press, 1935] 17–18).

68. Kenyon identifies this as "a very unusual abbreviation, of which I know no other example" (Kenyon, *Chester Beatty*, 3:1:xii), but now it is also attested in *P. Bodmer* XIII, a third-century copy of Melito's *Homily on the Passover* (see below).

69. Victor Martin, *Papyrus Bodmer II: Evangile de Jean chap. 1–14* (Cologne: Bibliotheque Bodermiana, 1956) 27. Royse, in fact, uses the lack of consistency in the work of this scribe, to argue for the scribe's religious affiliation: "Furthermore, the scribe uses, without complete consistency, several of the usual abbreviations for *nomina sacra*. And it can be demonstrated that the scribe is not simply reproducing these from his *Vorlage*. For at 3:8a and 6:63a he started to write πνευμα *plene*, caught himself after writing πνευ, and then erased ευ and added α and the line; the result in each case is πνα. Even stronger evidence that the scribe himself is familiar with these abbreviations is provided by an error at 4:11b. Here the scribe wrote βαθυ and then (carelessly) added the line above θυ, so as to produce the abbreviation for θεου. The scribe was probably responsible for the subsequent erasure (imperfectly accomplished) of this line, but its initial presence is significant" (Royse, "Scribal Habits," 407).

70. P^{46} likewise has these last two nomina sacra; but these are the only two.

71. R. Kasser and V. Martin confirm the irregularity of the scribe with respect to the treatment of the *nomina sacra* (*Papyrus Bodmer XIV–XV* [Cologny-Genève: Bibliotheca Bodmeriana, 1961] 18).

72. See further on this subject, Roberts who briefly discusses eccentric forms of *nomina sacra* (*MSB*, 83–84).

73. *Fragments of an Unknown Gospel*, 4.

74. "Early Christian Book-Production: Papyri and Manuscripts," in *The Cambridge History of the Bible*, vol. 2, 72–73, emphasis mine.

75. See Gamble, *Books and Readers*, 80–81, for examples in the *Acts of Peter*, *Acts of the Scillitan Martyrs*, and pictorial examples.

76. Roberts and Skeat, *The Birth of the Codex*, 37.

77. On this subject scholarship is extensive, with little consensus on the explanations for the widespread use of the codex form among Christians. See especially, Roberts and Skeat, *The Birth of the Codex*; Turner, *Typology of the Early Codex*; T. C. Skeat, "The Origin of the Christian Codex," *ZPE* 102 (1994) 263–268; "Roll Versus Codex: A New Approach?" *ZPE* 84 (1990) 297–298; "The Length of the Standard Papyrus Roll and the Cost-Advantage of the Codex," *ZPE* 45 (1982) 169–175; William Harris, "Why Did the Codex Supplant the Book-Roll?" in *Renaissance Society and Culture: Essays in Honor of Eugene F. Rice, Jr.*, ed. John Monfasani and Ronald G. Musto (New York: Italica Press, 1991) 71–85; Irven M. Resnick, "The Codex in Early Jewish and Christian Communities," *Journal of Religious History* 17 (1992) 1–17; Harry Gamble, "The Pauline Corpus and the Early Christian Book," in *Paul and the Legacies of Paul*, ed. William S. Babcock (Dallas, Tx.: Southern Methodist University Press, 1990) 265–280; Peter Katz, "The Early Christians' Use of Codices Instead of Rolls," *JTS* 46 (1945) 63–65.

78. Roberts, *MSB*, 47.

79. *Typology*, 37.

80. The cost advantage of the codex form was proposed by Skeat ("The Length of the Standard Papyrus Roll," 175), but more recently Skeat has argued that "the net savings, if any, would be minimal" ("The Origin of the Christian Codex," 265); others have argued for religious motivations behind the use of the codex by Christians, principle among these the desire to differentiate Christian texts from Jewish (Peter Katz, "The Early Christians' Use of Codices," 63); practical arguments, such as the greater comprehensiveness of the codex over the roll, have also received some attention (Roberts and Skeat, *The Birth of the Codex*, 73; Harris, "Why did the Codex Supplant the Roll," 78–79); other practical considerations include the ease with which codices could be transported, and hence used by travelers (Harris, "Why did the Codex Supplant the Roll," 79); still other theories include the notion that the codex form was intimately tied to the emergence of the four-Gospel canon and whereas the four Gospels would not have fit onto a roll, a single codex could hold them (Skeat, "The Origin of the Christian Canon," 268, and "Irenaeus and the Four-Gospel Canon," *Novum Testamentum* 34 [1992] 194–199).

81. Portions of the following section were presented on 22 November 1997 at the AAR/SBL Annual Meeting in San Francisco; I am especially grateful to the respondent in that session, Mark Vessey, whose comments helped to refine my conception of this codex.

82. All of the editions were published in Cologny/Genève by the Bibliothèque Bodmer: Michel Testuz, *Papyrus Bodmer V* (1958), *Papyrus Bodmer X–XII* (1959), *Papyrus Bodmer VII–IX* (1959), *Papyrus Bodmer XIII* (1960); Victor Martin, *Papyrus Bodmer XX* (1964).

83. *Papyrus Bodmer VII–IX*, 9.

84. See especially, *The Pachomian Monastic Library at the Chester Beatty Library and the Bibliothèque Bodmer* (Institute for Antiquity and Christianity, Occasional Papers 19; Claremont, Calif.: Institute for Antiquity and Christianity, 1990).

85. The cache was found near Dishna (and subsequently given the name Dishna Papers). Robinson provides details of the location of the find, as well as the proximity to Pachomian monasteries. On Pachomian monasticism more generally, see Philip

Rousseau, *Pachomius: The Making of a Community in Fourth-Century Egypt* (Berkeley: University of California Press, 1985); Frederick Wisse, "Gnosticism and Early Monasticism in Egypt," in *Gnosis: Festschrift für Hans Jonas*, ed. Barbara Aland (Göttingen: Vandenhoeck and Ruprecht, 1978) 431–440; Susanna Elm, *'Virgins of God'*, 283–296; J. Goehring, "New Frontiers in Pachomian Studies," in *The Roots of Egyptian Christianity*, ed. B. A. Pearson and J. E. Goehring (Philadelphia, Pa.: Fortress Press, 1986) 236–257. Translation of the *Rules* is taken from Armand Veilleux, *Pachomian Koinonia*, vol. 2 [Kalamazoo, Mich.: Cistercian Publications, 1981]); for references to books in the monastery, see *Rules* 25, 82, 100, and 101; Palladius' *Lausiac History* corroborates the program of literacy training in Pachomian monasteries and further reports that there were copyists among the monks in Pachomius's monastery at Tabennisi (*Lausiac History* 12).

86. Respectively, these are *P. Bodmer* V, X, XI, VII, XIII, XII, XX, IX, and VIII.

87. Reliance on such plates, especially when they are not complete, is particularly problematic when arguments concern issues of paleography. E. G. Turner, as we shall see, was also frustrated by Testuz's incomplete information regarding his identification of scribal hands on paleographic grounds, and his visits to the Bodmer Library proved unproductive since he did not find "the relevant portions available for study" (*Typology of the Codex*, 80). I too contacted the Bodmer Library regarding the possibility of obtaining microfilm of the texts in this codex and was informed that that would not be possible; they did report, however, that a full photographic reproduction of this codex was planned.

88. *Typology of the Codex*, 79–80. Turner was not the first to call into question Testuz's identification of scribal hands: Jean Duplacy, already in the early 1960s, questioned the identification of the hands of Jude and 1 and 2 Peter (See "Bulletin de critique textuelle du NT," *RSR* 50 (1962) 253); Aland confirms Turner's identification of the Melito hand as different from that of the *Nativity* but is reluctant to ascribe the Epistles of Peter and that of Jude to two separate hands (*Repertorium* vol. 2, 374 n. 2 and 377 n. 14).

89. For this paleographical analysis, I have drawn particularly from Cribiore's helpful diagrams on stroke sequences in the educational process of learning how to write (*Writing, Teachers, and Students*, 107–111). Cribiore demonstrates that the more experienced a writer was, the fewer traces were left of the stroke sequences in letter formation. Such features alone would not necessarily make the case for two different scribes, since it could be argued that the appearance of gaps is due to the scribe's hastiness; but there are other arguments that can be adduced to support two scribes at work (see below).

90. On this feature and its use for determining provenance and scribe, see Testuz, *Papyrus Bodmer VII–IX*, 32–33. Testuz also uses some of the marginal notes in 2 Peter to point toward a Coptic scribe and his arguments are quite convincing. My point here is simply that the Epistle of Jude does not exhibit these same telltale features.

91. *Typology*, 79–81.

92. See Testuz, *Papyrus Bodmer X–XII*, 9; Turner, *Typology*, 79. A quire is a gathering of papyrus (or parchment) leaves that are stitched together: a single quire

refers to one papyrus sheet folded in half, which produces two leaves and four pages; a double quire would refer to two sheets of papyrus laid on top of each other and then folded and stitched at the fold, producing four leaves and eight pages; and so forth.

93. See the plates of the first page of the *Ode* (*Papyrus Bodmer X–XII*, 46) and the first page of Jude (*Papyrus Bodmer VII–IX*, 12).

94. See Turner, *Typology*, 80 who admits that he cannot decide whether this difference in size is "finally decisive" on the issue of whether this is a single composite codex or not.

95. Turner argued that the link here was secure, on the assumption that the title of the *Apology* would have appeared on the last leaf of the quire which concluded Melito and the hymn (*Typology*, 80). It seems to me, however, that the defective state of the opening of the *Apology* does not allow for such an assumption; furthermore, the fact that the *Apology* begins with new pagination, particularly when coupled with the size differential (the *Apology* measures 14 × 15.5cm), makes the link less secure.

96. See Turner's question regarding the opening quire of the Epistles (*Typology*, 80).

97. On the question of how long papyri lasted, see especially E. G. Turner, "Recto and Verso," *JEA* 40 (1954) 102–106, and "Roman Oxyrhynchus," *JEA* 38 (1952) especially 89–90.

98. The translations of these are taken from James M. Robinson, ed., *The Nag Hammadi Library*, rev. ed. (San Francisco: Harper and Row, 1988). The second of these colophons is particularly interesting, because it suggests again a relationship between two parties (an individual copyist) and a group or community (hence the plural) that desired copies of certain texts.

99. We still have much to learn about reading practices, and how the form of ancient papyri influenced reading practices; in this respect, our knowledge is far more inadequate than that for a later medieval period (on which see especially the work of Roger Chartier, *Forms and Meanings: Texts, Performances, and Audiences from Codex to Computer* [Philadelphia: University of Pennsylvania Press, 1995]). But we have here an instance that illustrates the scribe's awareness of readership.

100. Oscar Cullmann, in *New Testament Apocrypha*, ed. Wilhelm Schneelmelcher, vol. 1, trans. R. McL. Wilson (Louisville, Ky.: Westminster/John Knox, 1991) 425.

101. Trans. Stuart George Hall, *Melito of Sardis On Pascha and Fragments* (Oxford: Clarendon, 1979). See further on this passage Richard C. White, *Melito of Sardis Sermon "On the Passover"* (Lexington, Ky.: Lexington Theological Seminary, 1976) 76; A. E. Harvey, "Melito and Jerusalem," *JTS* 17 (1966) 402.

102. It rapidly becomes apparent, for example, that the author of the *Nativity* has little knowledge of Jewish customs and that the text itself seems rather to offer a response to Jewish claims of the illegitimacy of Jesus; thus the connection between this text and "Jewish-Christianity" falls away (see esp. Cullman's remarks in *New Testament Apocrypha*, 416–419, 423–425). The whole problem of "Jewish-Christianity" continues to thwart scholars (see especially, Joan E. Taylor, "The Phenomenon of Early Jewish-Christianity: Reality or Scholarly Invention?" *VC* 44 [1990] 313–334; Burton L. Visotzky, "Prolegomenon to the Study of Jewish-Christianities in Rabbinic Literature," *AJS Review* 14 [1989] 47–70).

103. *Papyrus Bodmer XX*, 9.

104. The appearance of the preposition περι (about) here without the genitive case that it normally would require was one of the arguments that Testuz used in favor of a Coptic scribe for 1 and 2 Peter (see above, n.106 and *Papyrus Bodmer VII–IX*, 33). Furthermore, the appearance of the Coptic ΠΜΕΙ at 2 Peter 2:22 and explanatory ορασις at 2 Peter 2:8 may also lend weight to the theory of a Coptic scribe (Testuz, *Papyrus Bodmer VII–IX*, 33).

105. Nowhere is this more relevant that in the Origenist controversy; see Clark, *The Origenist Controversy*. The scholarly interest in issues of the body in ancient society is becoming increasingly widespread: see Peter Brown, *The Body and Society: Men, Women, and Sexual Renunciation in Early Christianity* (New York: Columbia University Press, 1988); Aline Rousselle, *Porneia: On Desire and the Body in Antiquity* (Cambridge: Basil Blackwell, 1988); Elm, *'Virgins of God'*, esp. 376–381; see also now Elizabeth A. Clark, *Reading Renunciation: Asceticism and Scripture in Early Christianity* (Princeton, N.J.: Princeton University Press, 1999); the works of Caroline Walker Bynam, though pertaining to the medieval period, are important for their conceptualization of body issues: see especially, *The Resurrection of the Body in Western Christianity, 200–1336* (New York: Columbia University Press, 1995); *Fragmentation and Redemption: Essays on Gender and the Human Body in Medieval Religion* (New York: Zone Books, 1991).

106. See especially, Edward E. Malone, *The Monk and the Martyr: Monk as the Successor of the Martyr* (Washington, D.C.: Catholic University of America Press, 1950).

107. On the distinction between the two terms of "miscellany" (which represents a collection that is unified thematically), and "composite" (which was prepared over time, and may not be unified thematically) see especially Armando Petrucci, *Writers and Readers in Medieval Italy: Studies in the History of Written Culture*, ed. and trans. Charles M. Radding (New Haven, Conn.: Yale University Press, 1995) especially 1–18. Here I would slightly modify Petrucci's definitions for this particular codex: this codex may best be understood as a "miscellany" from the ancient *readers'* point of view, since the codex was not prepared in a single act of bookmaking (here I am drawing upon Mark Vessey's suggestions in his response to my use of the term "miscellany" in reference to this codex; see n. 81, this chapter).

CHAPTER 5

1. I am invoking here a host of various responses (and challenges) to W. K. Wimsatt Jr. and M. C. Beardsley's influential essay "The Affective Fallacy" (in their *The Verbal Icon* [Lexington: University of Kentucky Press, 1954]; originally published in *The Sewanee Review* 54 [1946] 468–488): the emergence of "reader-response criticism"; Derridian notions of citationality (see, e.g., Jacques Derrida, *Margins of Philosophy*, trans. Alan Bass [Chicago: University of Chicago Press, 1988] 309–330, especially 320–321); Stanley Fish's work on "interpretive communities" (*Is There a Text in This Class?* [Cambridge, Mass.: Harvard University Press, 1980]); and most importantly for the present project, the work of cultural historians and bibliographers on the subject of the intersection of form and meaning in the history of the book (see especially the interesting discussion of D. F. McKenzie, *Bibliography and the Sociology of Texts* [London: British Library, 1986] and the works of Roger Chartier).

2. Horace's remark is echoed in Sulpitius Severus' preface to his account of St. Martin (*Vita*, preface).

3. What I am saying here stands in direct contrast to the views of Adolf Deissmann, who wrote of the copyists of New Testament texts: "The copyists worked as a rule quite mechanically, like our compositors" (*Light from the Ancient East: The New Testament Illustrated by Recently Discovered Texts of the Graeco-Roman World*, trans. Lionel R. M. Strachan [New York: Harper and Brothers, 1927] 125). The arguments of this chapter also stand in tension to the extensive literature on orality and literacy, where oral modes of communication are defined as fluid and flexible in contrast to fixed and unchanging written modes. On the subject of literacy and orality, see especially the influential work of Jack Goody, *The Interface Between the Written and the Oral* (Cambridge: Cambridge University Press, 1987), and *The Logic of Writing and the Organization of Society* (Cambridge: Cambridge University Press, 1986); and Walter J. Ong, *Orality and Literacy: The Technologizing of the Word* (London: T. J. Press [Padstow] 1982), and *The Presence of the Word* (New Haven, N.J.: Yale University Press, 1967); issues of orality and literacy have been especially extensively explored by historians of ancient Greece: see especially the work of Eric A. Havelock, *The Literate Revolution in Greece and Its Cultural Consequences* (Princeton, N.J.: Princeton University Press, 1982), *The Muse Learns to Write: Reflections of Orality and Literacy from Antiquity to the Present* (New Haven, N.J.: Yale University Press, 1986), *Preface to Plato* (Cambridge: Belknap Press, 1963), *Prologue to Greek Literacy* (Cincinnati, Ohio: University of Cincinnati Press, 1971) and also Albert B. Lord, *The Singer of Tales* (Cambridge, Mass.: Harvard University Press, 1960), and *Epic Singers and Oral Tradition* (Ithaca, N.Y.: Cornell University Press, 1991); see also Øivind Anderson, "The Significance of Writing in Early Greece — A Critical Appraisal," in *Literacy and Society*, ed. Karen Schousboe and Mogens Trolle Larsen (Copenhagen: Akademisk Forlag, 1989) 73–90; Tony M. Lentz, *Orality and Literacy in Hellenic Greece* (Carbondale: Southern Illinois University Press, 1989); in the field of early Christianity, there has also been extensive interest in the subject, but see especially Werner H. Kelber, *The Oral and the Written Gospel* (Philadelphia, Pa.: Fortress Press, 1983).

4. Michel Foucault, *This Is Not a Pipe*, trans. James Harkness (Berkeley: University of California Press, 1983) 44.

5. The numbers of Greek manuscripts of New Testament texts are, of course, rough calculations, not simply because the number is constantly fluctuating as new manuscripts come to light but also because calculations are made according to differing methods. For example, in the case of the Bodmer papyrus codex I discussed in the last chapter, do we calculate 1 and 2 Peter and Jude as one manuscript or two? Currently, these are identified as one New Testament manuscript — P^{72} — but if there were two different scribes at work, then we may argue that these should be considered as separate manuscripts. For calculations of the number of manuscripts, see Aland and Aland, *The Text of the New Testament*, 81–82.

6. Ehrman, *Orthodox Corruption*, 28. This view was articulated earlier by H. Vogels, *Handbuch der Textkritik des Neuen Testaments*, 2d ed. (Bonn: P. Hanstein, 1955) 162; Hort claimed that the majority of variants were in existence by the fifth century (*Introduction to the New Testament*, 91–93); see also George D. Kilpatrick, "The Bodmer and Mississippi Collection of Biblical and Christian Texts," *GRBS* 4 (1963) 42, and

"Atticism and the Text of the Greek New Testament," in *Neutestamentliche Aufsätze: Festschrift für Prof. Josef Schmid zum 70. Geburtstag*, ed. J. Blinzler, O. Kuss, F. Mußner (Regensburg: Friedrich Pustet, 1963) especially 128–129; Ernest C. Colwell, "*Hort Redivivus*: A Plea and a Program," in *Transitions in Biblical Scholarship*, ed. J. Coert Rylaarsdam (Chicago: University of Chicago Press, 1968) 147–148; Royse, "Scribal Habits," 21.

7. For such adjectives, see especially Colwell, "*Hort Redivivus*," 150 n. 38; Jacobus H. Petzer, "The History of the New Testament — Its Reconstruction, Significance and Use in New Testament Textual Criticism," in *New Testament Textual Criticism, Exegesis and Church History: A Discussion of Methods*, ed. B. Aland and J. Delobel (Kampen: Pharos, 1994) 30–32; Aland and Aland, *The Text of the New Testament*, 56–71.

8. The reverse is also the case: written texts were important because they affected the oral texts of interpretation. Although the same written text might well evoke different interpretations, it was also the case in early Christianity that at least occasionally differing written renderings of the same text (i.e., textual variants) determined interpretation (see, e.g., Bart D. Ehrman, "Heracleon, Origen, and the Text of the Fourth Gospel," *VC* 47 [1993] 105–18). In employing the term "text" here to oral or verbal discourses as well as written symbols and words on a page, I am deliberately drawing upon D. F. McKenzie's expansion of "texts" "to include verbal, visual, oral, and numerical data" (*Bibliography*, 5–6). Furthermore, McKenzie's remarks on "text" as derivative of the Latin *textere* (to weave) are particularly relevant here, for what I am concerned with in this chapter is the ways in which a set of discourses were interwoven with written texts. For a particularly interesting discussion of McKenzie's work, see Roger Chartier, "Texts, Forms, and Interpretations," in his *On the Edge of the Cliff: History, Language, and Practices*, trans. Lydia G. Cochrane (Baltimore, Md.: Johns Hopkins University Press, 1997) 81–89.

9. Hayden White's comments on linking texts and discourses to contexts, as well as the benefits of "inscribing texts within 'discourses'," are helpful (see "The Context in the Text: Method and Ideology in Intellectual History," in his *The Content of the Form: Narrative Discourse and Historical Representation* [Baltimore, Md.: Johns Hopkins University Press, 1987] 185–213).

10. It is not always the case, of course, that we can differentiate between the accidental and deliberate, unconscious and conscious, or unintentional and intentional modifications, though the contrast between "unintentional" and "intentional" changes is a long-standing text-critical method of classification of variant readings (see, e.g., Metzger, *The Text of the New Testament*, 186–206; Ehrman, *Orthodox Corruption*, 27–28; and Larry Hurtado, *Text-Critical Methodology and the Pre-Caesarean Text: Codex W in the Gospel of Mark* [Grand Rapids, Mich.: Eerdmans, 1981] 68).

11. For other examples, see fn. 213; Martial 2.8; see also 7.11, 17; Varro, *De Lingua Latina* 8.51; see also 9.106.

12. See further on curse formulas Marc Drogin, *Anathema! Medieval Scribes and the History of Book Curses* (Totowa, N.J.: Allanheld, Osmun, 1983).

13. See, for example, Turner's identification of such hands in scholars copies ("Scribes and Scholars," 145).

14. See Turner, *Greek Manuscripts*, 16, for these forms of corrections and photographic reproductions of such forms in extant papyri from the period: examples of the sponge method include P[66], which will be discussed further below, and the third-century anonymous *Encomium on Theon* (*P.Oxy.* 1015); for deletions with brackets and dots see also P[66]; for lines through letters see *P.Oxy.* 2161; lines above and below deletions see *P.Oxy.* 1174.

15. See James Royse, "Scribal Habits," 122; the two corrections by a second hand appear at Mt 25:42 and Acts 7:12.

16. See Royse, "Scribal Habits," 235; Royse points out that the concentration of corrections at the beginning suggests that "the scribe and the later correctors devoted most of their attention to the earlier portion of the codex" (235); on the corrections in this particular manuscript, see also Günther Zuntz, *The Text of the Epistles* (Oxford: Oxford University Press, 1953) 252–262.

17. Royse, "Scribal Habits," 344.

18. Royse, "Scribal Habits," 539.

19. See, respectively, Martin, *Papyrus Bodmer II*, vol. 1, 30; Fee, *Papyrus Bodmer II*, 57; Royse, "Scribal Habits," 391–393.

20. Royse supports Fee's argument for a second hand at work in the correction of a lengthy omission at John 13:19a ("Scribal Habits," 391; Fee, *Papyrus Bodmer II*, 59–60), but argues that "this is the only case in the papyrus where a second hand is clearly at work" ("Scribal Habits," 392).

21. See especially Martin's (*Papyrus Bodmer II*, 30–31) and Fee's (*Papyrus Bodmer II*, 57) characterizations. Ernest Colwell similarly described P[66] as an example of "wildness in copying," although he was not speaking directly of the frequency of corrections ("Method in Evaluating Scribal Habits," 121).

22. "Scribal Habits," 403–404.

23. British Library, pap. inv. no. 136; see H. J. M. Milne, *Catalogue of the Literary Papyri in the British Museum* (London: British Library, 1927) 21–22 no. 11; A. Wifstrand, "Ein metrischer Kolophon in einem Homerpapyrus," *Hermas* 68 (1933) 468–472; B. Olsson, "Der Kolophon in den antiken Handschriften," *Zentralblatt für Bibliothekswesen* 51 (1934) 365–367; Skeat, "The Use of Dictation," 183–184; Parássoglou, "ΔΕΞΙΑ ΧΕΙΡ," 18–19; Metzger, "When Did Scribes Begin to Use Writing Desks?" 125.

24. Turner, *Greek Manuscripts*, 12.

25. On Codex Vaticanus see Milne and Skeat, *The Scribes and Correctors*, 87–91; T. C. Skeat, "The Codex Vaticanus in the Fifteenth Century," *JTS* 35 (1984) 454–465; Westcott and Hort, *The New Testament in the Original Greek*, 210–246, 250–270; Metzger, *The Text of the New Testament*, 47–48; Alands, *The Text of the New Testament*, esp. 107; Sakae Kubo, *P[72] and the Codex Vaticanus* (Salt Lake City: University of Utah Press, 1965).

26. See the facsimile of the page on which this marginal note appears in Metzger, *Manuscripts of the Greek Bible*, 74–75.

27. The textual history of the entire verse has several interesting textual variants, none of which is directly relevant to my discussion here; on these variants, and their implications, see especially, Ehrman, *Orthodox Corruption*, 96, 150–151; Zuntz, *The Text of the Epistles*, 43–45; Metzger, *A Textual Commentary*, 662; Paul Ellingworth,

The Epistle to the Hebrews: A Commentary on the Greek Text (Grand Rapids, Mich.: Eerdmans, 1993) 96–103.

28. It is unclear from available facsimiles whether the second scribe simply erased the αν (leaving the φ separated from the ending of the word); whether the scribe erased the φαν and then reinscribed the φ; or whether the scribes erased the whole word and replaced it with φέρων.

29. There is no support for the reading φέρων offered in Tischendorf's *Novum Testamentum Graece*, 8th ed., or Von Soden's *Die Schriften des Neuen Testaments*. Tischendorf notes that the "correction" that returned the reading to the original one was made in the thirteenth century, some nine hundred years after the codex was originally copied.

30. The questions of what an "original reading" means (is it the text that is the furthest back we can go? or what an author actually wrote?), as well as the question of whether the quest for the "original" should continue to be the primary focus of New Testament textual criticism (do we have a critical edition that is as close to the "original" as possible?), have only recently been asked; on such issues, see especially Bart D. Ehrman, "The Text as Window: New Testament Manuscripts and the Social History of Early Christianity," in *The Text of the New Testament in Contemporary Research: Essays on the Status Quaestionis*, ed. Bart D. Ehrman and Michael W. Holmes (Grand Rapids, Mich.: Eerdmans, 1995) 361–379; William L. Petersen, "What Text Can New Testament Textual Criticism Ultimately Reach?" in *New Testament Textual Criticism, Exegesis, and Early Church History: A Discussion of Methods*, ed. Barbara Aland and Joël Delobel (Kampen, The Netherlands: Pharos, 1994) 136–152.

31. *The Order of Books: Readers, Authors, and Libraries in Europe between the Fourteenth and Eighteenth Centuries*, trans. Lydia G. Cochrane (Stanford, Calif.: Stanford University Press, 1994) 3.

32. On Origen's references to variant readings, see esp. Metzger, "Explicit References in the Works of Origen" 78–95; see also Metzger's similar article on Jerome: "St. Jerome's Explicit References," 199–210.

33. See two studies: A. Bludau, *Die Schriftfälschungen der Häretiker: Ein Beitrag zur Textkritik der Bibel*, NTAbh, 11 (Münster: Aschendorf, 1925); C. S. C. Williams, *Alterations to the Text of the Synoptic Gospels and Acts* (Oxford: Basil Blackwell, 1951); see also Ehrman, *Orthodox Corruption*, 26–27. The literature on issues of orthodoxy and heresy is, of course, extensive: see most influentially, Walter Bauer, *Orthodoxy and Heresy in Earliest Christianity*, trans. Robert A. Kraft et al., ed. Robert Kraft and Gerhard Krodel (Philadelphia, Pa.: Fortress Press, 1971; originally, *Rechtglaübigkeit und Ketzerei im ältesten Christentum* [Tübingen: J. C. B. Mohn/Paul Siebeck, 1934]).

34. See, e.g., Eldon Jay Epp, "The 'Ignorance Motif' in Acts and Anti-Judaic Tendencies in Codex Bezae," *HTR* 55 (1962) 51–62, and *The Theological Tendency of Codex Bezae Cantabrigiensis in Acts* (Cambridge: Cambridge University Press, 1966); J. Rendel Harris, "New Points of View in Textual Criticism," *The Expositor* 8/7 (1914) 316–334, and "Was the Diatessaron Anti-Judaic?" *HTR* 18 (1925) 103–109; H. J. Vogels, *Handbuch der Textkritik des Neuen Testaments*, 2d ed. (Bonn: Hanstein, 1955 [c. 1923]) 178; and Bart D. Ehrman, "The Text as Window: New Testament Manuscripts and the Social History of Early Christianity," in *The Text of the New Testament in Contemporary Research*, 366–367, and "The Text of the Gospels at the

End of the Second Century," in *Codex Bezae: Studies from the Lunel Colloquium, June 1994*, ed. D. C. Parker and C.-B. Amphoux (Leiden: E. J. Brill, 1996) especially 109–114.

35. The literature here is less extensive, and one wonders whether this is due to lack of scholarly interest or lack of evidence; see especially, Ben Witherington, "The Anti-Feminist Tendencies of the 'Western' Text in Acts," *JBL* 103 (1984) 82–84; Elisabeth Schüssler Fiorenza, *In Memory of Her: A Feminist Theological Reconstruction of Christian Origins* (New York: Crossroad, 1988) 51–52; Ehrman, "The Text of the Gospels," 114–116, and "The Text as Window," 367–368.

36. Ehrman, "The Text of the Gospels," 117–121.

37. The most extensive treatment of such modifications of New Testament texts is Ehrman, *Orthodox Corruption*; idem, "1 John 4.3 and the Orthodox Corruption of Scripture," *ZNW* 79 (1988) 221–243; idem, "The Text of Mark in the Hands of the Orthodox," in *Biblical Hermeneutics in Historical Perspective*, ed. Mark Burrows and Paul Rorem (Grand Rapids, Mich.: Eerdmans, 1991) 19–31; idem with Mark A. Plunkett, "The Angel and the Agony: The Textual Problem of Luke 22:43–44," *CBQ* 45 (1983) 401–416; Alexander Globe, "Some Doctrinal Variants in Matthew 1 and Luke 2 and the Authority of the Neutral Text," *CBQ* 42 (1980) 52–72; Mikeal Parsons, "A Christological Tendency in P^{75}," *JBL* 105 (1986) 463–479; C. K. Barrett, "Is There a Theological Tendency in Codex Bezae?" in *Text and Interpretation: Studies in the New Testament Presented to Matthew Black*, ed. Ernest Best and R. McL. Wilson (Cambridge: Cambridge University Press, 1979) 15–27.

38. *Introduction*, 282.

39. Colwell, "Method in Evaluating Scribal Habits," 108.

40. On this point, see Ehrman, *Orthodox Corruption*, 28–29.

41. To state, however, "that in virtually no instance has the discovery of a new papyrus provided us with a reading that was altogether unknown from already available evidence" (Ehrman, "The Text of the Gospels," 100) seems to fly directly in the face of the singular readings found in six papyri that can be dated to the second or third centuries identified extensively by James Royse (see his "Scribal Habits").

42. Bart Ehrman discusses these methods as well as two others: (1) identifying variant readings as found in scriptural quotations of the early church fathers; (2) closely examining one particular manuscript to see what clues it might yield concerning variant readings (Ehrman, "The Text of the Gospels," 98–102). Examples of this latter method can be seen in the extensive scholarly work on Codex Bezae (Epp, Parker, and others), as well as in shorter studies such as that of Mikeal Parsons on P^{75} ("A Christological Tendency," 463–479).

43. Royse, "Scribal Habits," 481–482; the verb συνευωχέομαι occurs only at Jude 12 and 2 Peter 2:13. It is worth recalling that these two texts in the Bodmer codex have long been identified as the same scribe — an argument I countered in the last chapter. The scribe of 2 Peter 2:13 does not change the term, a fact that problematizes Royse's identification of a harmonization to general usage.

44. On the Pachomian emphasis on prayer, especially collective prayer (called *sunaxis* or *collecta*), see Rousseau, *Pachomius*, 80.

45. On pagan charges of immorality one thinks, for example, of Marcus Aurelius's *Octavius* 9.5–6; on charges against "heretics," see Epiphanius on the Phibionites

(*Panarion* 26); see Clement of Alexandria on the Carpocratians (*Stromata* 3.2.10); see Justin Martyr on those who "upset the lamp" (1 *Apology* 26.7). See further Robert L. Wilken, *The Christians As the Romans Saw Them* (New Haven, Conn.: Yale University Press, 1984) especially 16–21; Stephen Benko, "The Libertine Gnostic Sect of the Phibionites," *VC* 21 (1967) 103–119; R. M. Grant, "Charges of Immorality Against Various Religious Groups in Antiquity," in *Studies in Gnosticism and Hellenistic Religions*, ed. R. van der Broek and M. J. Vermaseren (Leiden: E. J. Brill, 1981); Burton L. Visotzky, "Overturning the Lamp," *Journal of Jewish Studies* 38 (1987) 72–80; Albert Henrichs, "Pagan Ritual and the Alleged Crimes of the Early Christians," in *Kyriakon: Festschrift Johannes Quatsten*, vol. 1, ed. Patrick Granfield and Josef A. Jungmann (Münster: Aschendorff, 1970) 18–35; and Bart D. Ehrman, "Those Lascivious Phibionites (and Other Christian Reprobates)," unpublished ms.

46. On this passage and its significance for theologically motivated scribal modifications, see especially, Ehrman, *Orthodox Corruption*, 84–85; Royse, "Scribal Habits," 486–487; Marchant A. King, "Notes on the Bodmer Manuscript of Jude and 1 and 2 Peter," *Bibliotheca Sacra* 121 (1964) 54–57.

47. On adoptionism, see Ehrman, *Orthodox Corruption*, 47–54; on "adoptionistic" notions in the New Testament, see James D. G. Dunn, *Unity and Diversity in the New Testament: An Inquiry into the Character of Earliest Christianity*, 2d ed. (Philadelphia, Pa.: Fortress; London: SCM Press, 1991 [c. 1977]) 235–266. On the variant reading here in Jude, see King, "Notes on the Bodmer Manuscript," 57.

48. Ehrman, *Orthodox Corruption*, 88; on this particular textual modification, see also the arguments for patripassionism behind this interchange in Frank W. Beare, "Some Remarks on the Text of 1 Peter in the Bodmer Papyrus (P[72])," in *Studia Evangelica*, 3.2, ed. F. L. Cross (Berlin: Akademie-Verlag, 1964) 263–265, and "The Text of 1 Peter in Papyrus 72," *JBL* 80 (1961) 253–260.

49. See Ehrman, *Orthodox Corruption*, 85; Royse, "Scribal Habits," 486–487.

50. As Royse points out, this same manuscript agrees with ℵ A B C D F G L P in reading the accusative πρεισκαν, "which could be either masculine or feminine" (Royse, "Scribal Habits," 274).

51. See, for example, Jouette M. Bassler, "The Widow's Take: A Fresh Look at 1 Timothy 5:3–16," *JBL* 103 (1984) 23–41; Stevan L. Davis, *The Revolt of the Widows: The Social World of the Apocryphal Acts* (Carbondale: Southern Illinois University Press, 1980); Karen Jo Torjesen, *When Women Were Priests: Women's Leadership in the Early Church and the Scandal of Their Subordination in the Rise of Christianity* (San Francisco: Harper, 1993).

52. Witherington, "The Anti-Feminist Tendencies of the 'Western' Text in Acts"; see also Ehrman, "The Text of the Gospels," 114–116, and "The Text as Window," 367–368.

53. For further similar discussion of the tendencies of early Christian papyri, see Mikeal Parson's study of christological changes in P[75] ("A Christological Tendency"); on P[46] see Howard Eshbaugh, "Textual Variants and Theology: A Study of the Galatians Text of Papyrus 46," *JSNT* 3 (1979) 60–72; Eshbaugh's conclusions are opposed by Royse ("Scribal Habits," 280–281).

54. Metzger, *A Textual Commentary*, 89.

55. Due to a lacuna, we can only say it appears that this was the reading in P[45].

56. Metzger, *Textual Commentary*, 89. See also F. J. A. Hort and B. F. Westcott, *The New Testament in the Original Greek*, appendix, 24.

57. See the discussion of Quasten concerning Origen's careful text critical work in writing his *Hexapla*, *Patrology* II, 44ff.

58. This was Hort's explanation for Origen's claim: "the natural inference is not that the reading of [this] text was unknown to Origen or rejected by him, but that he either forgot this passage or, perhaps more probably, did not hold Mark responsible for the words of the Galileans" (*Introduction*, appendix, 24). For the argument that Origen had a "lapse of memory," see Metzger, "Explicit References in the Works of Origen," 93.

59. Other examples of apologetically motivated textual corruptions could be adduced. For example, at Acts 4:13 Peter and John are identified as "unlettered" (ἀγράμματοί) and "untrained" (ἰδιῶται); Codex Bezae, however, has omitted the words "and untrained." Evidently this particular scribe (or a preceding scribe) found it unpalatable that John and Peter be labeled ἰδιῶται. This makes good sense given the accusations that Christians were "stupid," "unintelligent," "ignorant," or "unin-structed" (see Celsus' claims in Origen, *Contra Celsum*, 3.44). See also the textual problems in Mark 1:41 and 3:21. A helpful introduction to textual modifications made for reverential or apologetic reasons is the study of C. S. C. Williams, *Alterations to the Text of the Synoptic Gospels and Acts* (Oxford: Basil Blackwell, 1951) especially 4–9, 36–37.

60. For a full analysis of the textual issues at hand, see Ehrman, *Orthodox Corruption*, 143–144. See also Ehrman's article, "The Text of Mark in the Hands of the Orthodox," in *Biblical Hemeneutics in Historical Perspective: Studies in Honor of Karlfried Frochlich on His Sixtieth Birthday*, ed. by Mark Burrows and Paul Rorem (Grand Rapids, Mich.: Eerdmans, 1991) 19–31.

61. See, for example, Irenaeus, *Adv.Haer.* 1.26.1; Ephiphanius, *Haer.* 28.1.5–7; on Cerinthus see further, G. Bardy, "Cerinthe," *Revue Biblique* 30 (1921) 344–373; A. F. J. Klijn and G. J. Reinink, *Evidence for Jewish-Christian Sects* (Leiden: E. J. Brill, 1973) 3–19; Ehrman, *Orthodox Corruption*, 130–134.

62. Adolf von Harnack, "Probleme im Texte der Leidengeschichte Jesu," in *Studien zur Geschichte des Neuen Testaments und der alten Kirche*, vol. 1, *Zur neutestamentlichen Textkritik* (Berlin: W. de Gruyter, 1931) 86–104; see Ehrman, *Orthodox Corruption*, 145.

63. Ehrman, *Orthodox Corruption*, 145.

64. See Ehrman, *Orthodox Corruption*, 145.

65. More examples of theologically motivated corruptions of scripture could be mentioned. Instead, I refer the reader to the extensive discussions of various passages in Ehrman, *Orthodox Corruption*. See for example his treatment of Luke 3:22 (62–67), Luke 22:43–44 (187–194), Luke 24:51–52 (227–232), and John 1:18 (78–82).

66. In their *Introduction to the New Testament in the Original Greek*, Westcott and Hort placed the words in double brackets, indicating that they considered them not original to Luke. Since then, scholars have argued on both sides. On this verse, see most recently Joël Delobel, "Luke 23:34a: A Perpetual Text-Critical Crux?" in *Sayings of Jesus: Canonical and Non-Canonical: Essays in Honour of Tjitze Baarda*, ed. W. L.

Petersen, J. S. Vos, and H. J. de Jonge (Leiden: E. J. Brill, 1997); I have not been able, unfortunately, to see Delobel's article.

67. See H. C. Hoskier, "The Lost Commentary of Oecumenius on the Apocalypse," *AJP* 34 (1913) 303–304. Hoskier argues, on the basis of the references to Cyril in the thirteenth-century manuscript of Oecumenius's commentary, that the reading was known in Irenaeus's day, questioned between 350 and 500 C.E., and that by 600 C.E., it was once again accepted.

68. "And from this fact, that He exclaimed upon the cross, 'Father, forgive them, for they know not what they do', the long suffering, patience, compassion, and goodness of Christ are exhibited, since He both suffered, and did Himself exculpate those who had maltreated him."

69. "For this sacrifice [i.e., of Jesus] was performed by them in ignorance because they do not know (γινωσκειν) what they are doing—and that is why it is also forgiven them." See also Origen's reference in *Homily* 2.1.5.

70. For Marcion see E. C. Blackman, *Marcion and His Influence*, 50; Adolf Von Harnack, *Marcion: Das Evangelium vom fremden Gott* (Leipzig: J. C. Hinrichs, 1924) 248. On Tatian see, J. Rendel Harris, "Was the Diatessaron Anti-Judaic?" *HTR* 18 (1925) 108–109.

71. See Joseph A. Fitzmyer, *The Gospel According to Luke. The Anchor Bible* (Garden City, N.Y.: Doubleday, 1985) 1503; C. F. Evans, *Saint Luke* (London: SCM and Philadelphia: Trinity International, 1990) 867; I. Howard Marshall, *The Gospel of Luke: A Commentary on the Greek Text* (Exeter: Paternoster, 1978) 868.

72. *Literary Patterns, Theological Themes, and the Genre of Luke-Acts.* (JBLMS 20. Missoula, Mont.: Scholars' Press, 1974).

73. Talbert, *Literary Patterns*, 97.

74. Since M. Dibelius, *From Tradition to Gospel* (New York, 1935). More recently see Brian E. Beck, "'Imitatio Christi' and the Lucan Passion Narrative," in *Suffering and Martyrdom in the New Testament*, ed. William Horbury and Brian McNeil (Cambridge: Cambridge University Press, 1981) 28–47, and John T. Carroll, "Luke's Crucifixion Scene," in *Reimaging the Death of the Lukan Jesus*, ed. Dennis Sylva (Frankfurt: Anton Hain, 1990) 108–124.

75. See the literature Beck cites, "'Imitatio Christi'," esp. 28.

76. Beck, "'Imitatio Christi'," esp. 29ff.

77. See also Luke 24:25, Acts 8:32, and 3:13 for other Lukan references to Isaiah 53.

78. Hans Conzelmann, *The Theology of St. Luke* (London: Faber and Faber, 1961, 1953), 90. See also Eldon Jay Epp's interesting article, "The 'Ignorance Motif' in Acts and Anti-Judaic Tendencies in Codex Bezae," *HTR* 55 (1962) 53. Epp's argument is that Codex Bezae has intentionally removed the ignorance-forgiveness motif for anti-Jewish reasons.

79. Fitzmyer, *The Gospel According to Luke*, 244. See also the thorough discussion of Allison A. Trites, "The Prayer Motif in Luke-Acts," in *Perspectives on Luke-Acts*, ed. by Charles H. Talbert (Danville, Va.: Association of Baptist Professors of Religion; Edinburgh: T. and T. Clark, 1978) 168–186.

80. There is a textual variant here that seems to indicate that scribes have inserted ημων to harmonize the Lukan passage with the Lord's Prayer in Matthew.

81. The language used by Stephen in his prayer, which I have argued is parallel to Jesus' prayer, is even more distinctively Lukan than Jesus' prayer. The occurrence of κυριος in Matthew numbers 8 times, in Mark 18, in John 53, in Luke 104, and in Acts 107. Ιστημι occurs 21 times in Matthew, ten in Mark, 19 in John, 26 in Luke, and 35 in Acts.

82. Moreover, we could ask again, why would a scribe only harmonize the Lukan passage to Acts and nowhere else? Why not harmonize to Matthew or Mark?

83. See D. Daube, "'For they know not what they do': Luke 23,34," *Studia Patristica* 4 (1961) 59ff. Hippolytus is the only Father that Daube cites as interpreting Jesus' prayer to refer to the Roman soldiers (*Adversus Judaeos* 3).

84. For other documents that indicate Jesus' prayer was for the Jews, see the *Gospel of Nicodemus* 10 and the *Didascalia* 2.16.1.

85. For a commentary on this passage that argues Melito is referring to the destruction of Jerusalem as punishment, see Richard C. White, *Melito of Sardis Sermon "On the Passover"* (Lexington, Ky.: Lexington Theological Seminary, 1976) 76. On Melito's emphatic claim that Jesus' crucifixion happened "in the midst of Jerusalem" so as to sharpen the guilt, see A. E. Harvey, "Melito and Jerusalem," *JTS* 17 (1966) 402.

86. Harris, "New Points of View," 316–334. Even before Harris, Vogels suggested anti-Jewish tendencies in the second-century church (*Handbuch*). Harris discusses Vogels in his article "Was the Diatessaron Anti-Judaic?" More recently others have taken up this argument: see Burnett Hillman Streeter, *The Four Gospels: A Study of Origins* (London: Macmillan, 1936) 138, and David Flusser, "The Crucified One and the Jews," *Immanuel* 7 (1977) 27ff.; most recently, Ehrman, "The Text of the Gospels," 113.

87. Eldon Epp, "The 'Ignorance Motif'," 51–62.

88. In addition to this problem in Luke 23:34a, other passages attest similar anti-Jewish motivations for textual alterations. See, for example, Mt 1:21, Lk 6:5, Jn 4:22, and I Thess. 2:14–16.

89. Gamble, "Christianity: Scripture and Canon," 37–62. The issues involved in this change from oral to written are complex and have been dealt with in recent years. See, for example, Kelber, *The Oral and the Written Gospel*.

90. For a treatment of the heresiologists' use of scripture, see Walter Bauer, *Orthodoxy and Heresy in Earliest Christianity*, 195–228.

91. Campenhausen, *The Formation of the Christian Bible*, 203ff. See also T. C. Skeat, "Irenaeus and the Four-Gospel Canon," *Novum Testamentum* 35 (1992) 194–199.

92. Metzger, *The Canon*, 194. For the argument that the Muratorian Canon should be dated later, even into the fourth century, see Hahneman, *The Muratorian Fragment*.

93. The problem of forgery in antiquity was not, of course, unique to Christians forging writings in the name of apostles. On the prevalence of forgeries, see Bruce M. Metzger, "Literary Forgeries and Canonical Pseudepigrapha," *JBL* 91 (1972) 3–24. For the issues surrounding forgeries and the growth of literacy in the medieval period see M. T. Clanchy, *From Memory to Written Record: England 1066–1307* (1979; repr., Oxford: Basil Blackwell, 1993) 234ff.

94. See the Muratorian Canon, 73–80. For the influence of Montanism on the canon, see Campenhausen, *The Formation of the Christian Bible*, 244ff; Metzger, *The Canon*, 99–106.

95. Ehrman, *Orthodox Corruption*, 18; Quasten, *Patrology* 1:283; Metzger, *The Canon*, 119.

96. *Christianity and the Rhetoric of Empire: The Development of Christian Discourse* (Berkeley: University of California Press, 1991) 7.

97. Bowman and Woolf, "Literacy and Power," 8.

CONCLUSION

1. Taken from Miller's remarks in the "Selections from the Symposium on 'Literacy, Reading, and Power,'" Whitney Humanities Center, November 14, 1987 (published in the *Yale Journal of Criticism* 2 [1988] 193–232). Miller's comments are largely dependent upon the work of Brian Street (*Literacy in Theory and Practice* [Cambridge: Cambridge University Press, 1984]).

2. On such interrelationships between writing and power, see Bowman and Woolf, "Literacy and Power," 6.

3. My use of the phrase "resource of power" is partly dependent upon Anthony Gidden's definitions of power: "The exercise of power is not a type of act; rather power is instantiated in action, as a regular and routine phenomenon. It is mistaken moreover to treat power *itself* as a resource as many theorists of power do. Resources are the media through which power is exercised, and the structures of domination reproduced" (Giddens, *Central Problems in Social Theory*, 91).

4. R. Pattison, *On Literacy: The Politics of the Word from Homer to the Age of Rock*, viii (taken from Bowman and Woolf, *Literacy and Power in the Ancient World*, 1).

5. Claude Lévi-Strauss, *Tristes Tropiques*, trans. John and Doreen Weightman [New York: Athaneum, 1974] 299. The works of Jack Goody, while still influential, fall similarly into overly broad genderalizations: "[Writing] is a most powerful instrument, the use of which is rarely devoid of social, economic, and political significance, especially since its introduction usually involves the domination of the non-literate segment of the population by the literate one, or even the less literate by the more" (Jack Goody, *The Interface between the Written and the Oral* [Cambridge: Cambridge University Press, 1987] xv; see also Goody, *The Logic of Writing and the Organization of Society* (Cambridge: Cambridge University Press, 1986); and with Ian Watt, "The Consequences of Literacy," *Comparative Studies in Society and History* 5 (1963) 304–345.

6. I have not found any instances of Jewish women scribes in the Hellenistic or Graeco-Roman periods; we do, however, find Jewish women copying texts in the medieval context. On Second-Temple Jewish scribes, see now Christine Schams, *Jewish Scribes in the Second-Temple Period*, JSOT s.s. 291 (Sheffield: Sheffield Academic Press, 1998).

7. Susanna Elm, *'Virgins of God'*, 373.

SELECTED BIBLIOGRAPHY

Achtemeier, Paul J. "Omne Verbum Sonat: The New Testament and the Oral Environment of Late Western Antiquity." *JBL* 109 (1990) 3–27.

Aland, Barbara. "Die Rezeption des neutestamentlichen Textes in den ersten Jahrhunderten." In *The New Testament in Early Christianity*, ed. Jean-Marie Sevrin. Leuven: Leuven University Press, 1989, 55–70.

———, and Joël Delobel, eds. *New Testament Textual Criticism, Exegesis and Church History: A Discussion of Methods*. Kampen, The Netherlands: Pharos, 1994.

Aland, Kurt, and Barbara Aland. *The Text of the New Testament: An Introduction to the Critical Editions and to the Theory and Practice of Modern Textual Criticism*. Grand Rapids, Mich.: Eerdmans, 1987.

———, ed. *Repertorium der Griechischen Christlichen Papyri*. I, *Biblische Papyri, Patristische Texte und Studien* 18. Berlin: Walter de Groyter, 1976.

———. "The Significance of the Papyri for Progress in New Testament Research." In *The Bible in Modern Scholarship: Papers Read at the 100th Meeting of the Society of Biblical Literature Dec. 28–30, 1964*. Nashville, Tenn.: Abingdon, 1965, 325–346.

———. "The Twentieth-Century Interlude in New Testament Textual Criticism." In *Text and Interpretation: Studies in the New Testament Presented to Matthew Black*, ed. Ernest Best and R. McL. Wilson. Cambridge: Cambridge University Press, 1974, 1–14.

Alexander, Jonathan J. G. *Medieval Illuminators and Their Methods of Work*. New Haven, Conn.: Yale University Press, 1992.

Alexander, L. "The Living Voice: Scepticism Towards the Written Word in Early Christian and in Graeco-Roman Texts." In *The Bible in Three Dimensions*, ed. D. J. A. Clines and Stephen E. Porter. JSOT. Sheffield: Sheffield Academic Press, 1990, 221–247.

Allen, T. W. *Notes on Abbreviations in Greek Manuscripts*. Amsterdam: Adolf M. Hakkert, 1967.

Anderson, Øsivind. "The Significance of Writing in Early Greece — a Critical Appraisal." In *Literacy and Society*, ed. Karen Schousboe and Mogens Trolle Larsen. Copenhagen: Akademisk Forlag, 1989, 73–90.

Apophthegmata Patrum. PG 65, 72–440; PL 73, 739–1062. English translation: *The Saying of the Desert Fathers: The Alphabetic Collection*, trans. Benedicta Ward. London: A. R. Mowbrays, 1975.

Appleby, Joyce, Lynn Hunt, and Margaret Jacob. *Telling the Truth about History*. New York: W.W. Norton, 1994.

Arns, Evaristo. *La technique du livre d'après saint Jérôme*. Paris: E. de Boccard, 1953.

Auerbach, Erich. *Literary Language and Its Public in Late Latin Antiquity and in the Middle Ages*. Translated by Ralph Manheim. Princeton, N.J.: Princeton University Press, 1993. Originally published as *Literatursprache und Publikum in der lateinischen Spätantike und im Mittelalter* (Bern: Franke Verlag, 1958).

Avrin, Leila. *Scribes, Script and Books: The Book Arts from Antiquity to the Renaissance*. Chicago and London: American Library Association and the British Library, 1991.

Bagnall, Roger S. *Egypt in Late Antiquity*. Princeton, N.J.: Princeton University Press, 1993.

————. *Greek Historical Documents: The Hellenistic Period*. Chico, Calif.: Scholars' Press, 1981.

————. *Reading Papyri, Writing Ancient History*. London: Routledge, 1995.

Baines, John, and C. J. Eyre. "Four Notes on Literacy." *Göttinger Miszellen* 61 (1983) 65–96.

Balogh, Joseph. "Voces Paginarum." *Philologus* 82 (1927) 84–109, 202–240.

Barbour, Ruth. *Greek Literary Hands, A.D. 400–1600*. Oxford: Clarendon Press, 1981.

Barnes, Timothy D. *Constantine and Eusebius*. Cambridge, Mass.: Harvard University Press, 1981.

Bastianini, Guido, and John Whitehorne. *Strategi and Royal Scribes of Roman Egypt: Chronological List and Index*. Papyrologica Florentini 15. Firenze: Edizioni Gonnelli, 1987.

Bauer, Walter. *Das Leben Jesu im Zeitalter der neutestamentlichen Apocryphen*. Tübingen: Mohr/Siebeck, 1907.

————. *Rechtgläubigkeit und Ketzerei im ältesten Christentum*. BHT, 10; Tübingen: J. C. B. Mohr (Paul Siebeck), 1934; English translation of 2d ed. (1964, ed. by Georg Strecker), *Orthodoxy and Heresy in Earliest Christianity*, trans. Robert Kraft et al., ed. Robert Kraft and Gerhard Krodel. Philadelphia, Pa.: Fortress Press, 1971.

Beck, Brian E. "'Imitatio Christi' and the Lucan Passion Narrative." In *Suffering and Martyrdom in the New Testament*, ed. William Horbury and Brian McNeil. Cambridge: Cambridge University Press, 1981, 28–47

Beck, F. A. G. "The Schooling of Girls in Ancient Greece." *Classicum* [Sydney] 9 (1978) 1–9.

Beit-Arié, Malachi. *Hebrew Manuscripts of East and West: Towards a Comparative Codicology*. The Panizzi Lectures 1992. London: British Library, 1993.

————. "Transmission of Texts by Scribes and Copyists: Unconscious and Critical Interferences." *Bulletin of the John Rylands University Library of Manchester* 75 (1993) 33–51.

Bell, H. Idris. "The 'Thyestes' of Sophocles and an Egyptian Scriptorium." *Aegyptus* 2 (1921) 281–288.

————, and T. C. Skeat, eds. *Fragments of an Unknown Gospel and Other Early Christian Papyri*. Oxford: Oxford University Press, 1935.

Bell, Susan Groag. "Medieval Women Book Owners: Arbiters of Lay Piety and Ambassadors of Culture." *Signs* 7 (1982) 742–768.

Birdsall, J. Neville. "The New Testament Text." In *The Cambridge History of the Bible*, ed. by P. R. Ackroyd and C. F. Evans. Vol. 1: From the Beginnings to Jerome. Cambridge: Cambridge University Press, 1979, 308–377.

————. "Rational Criticism and the Oldest Manuscripts: A Comparative Study of the Bodmer and Chester Beatty Papyri of the Gospel of Luke." In *Studies in New Testament Language and Text*, ed. by J. K. Elliott. Supplements to Novum Testamentum XLIV. Leiden: E. J. Brill, 1976, 39–51.

Birt, Theodor. *Das Antike Buchwesen in seinem Verhältnis zur Literatur*. Berlin: Scientia Verlag Aalen, 1882.

Blackman, E. C. *Marcion and His Influence*. London: S.P.C.K., 1948.

Bludau, A. *Die Schriftfälschungen der Häretiker: Ein Beitrag zer Textkritik der Bibel*. Münster: Aschendorf, 1925.

Boge, H. "Die Überlieferung der griechischen Tachygraphie." *Studia Codicologica*. Texte und untersuchungen zur Geschichte der Altchristlichen Literatur 124. Berlin: Akademie-Verlag, 1977, 99–108.

Boissevain, Jeremy. *Friends of Friends: Networks, Manipulators and Coalitions*. Oxford: Basil Blackwell, 1974.

Bonner, Campbell. *A Payprus Codex of the Shepherd of Hermas (Similitudes 2–9) with a Fragment of the Mandates*. Ann Arbor, Mich.: University Of Michigan Press, 1934.

Bonner, Stanley F. *Education in Ancient Rome: From the Elder Cato to the Younger Pliny*. Berkeley: University of California Press, 1977.

Booth, A. D. "Elementary and Secondary Education in the Roman Empire." *Florilegium* 1 (1972) 1–14.

————. "Litterator." *Hermes* 109 (1981) 371–378.

————. "The Schooling of Slaves in First-Century Rome." *TAPA* 109 (1979) 11–19.

Bosworth, A. B. "Asinius Pollio and Augustus." *Historia* 21 (1972) 441–473.

Bower, E. W. "Some Technical Terms in Roman Education." *Hermes* 89 (1961) 462–477.

Bowman, Alan K, and Greg Woolf, ed. *Literacy and Power in the Ancient World*. Cambridge: Cambridge University Press, 1994.

Bowman, Alan K. *The Town Councils of Roman Egypt*. Toronto: A. M. Hakkert, 1971.

Boyarin, Jonathan, ed. *The Ethnography of Reading*. Berkeley: University of California Press, 1993.

Bradley, K. R. *Slavery and Society at Rome*. Cambridge: Cambridge University Press, 1994.

————. *Slaves and Masters in the Roman Empire: A Study in Social Control*. Bruxelles: Latomus Revue D'Etudes Latines, 1984.

Brown, Peter. *The Body and Society: Men, Women and Sexual Renunciation in Early Christianity*. New York: Columbia University Press, 1988.

————. *Power and Persuasion in Late Antiquity: Towards a Christian Empire*. Madison: University of Wisconsin Press, 1992.

Brown, Schuyler. "Concerning the Origin of the Nomina Sacra." *Studia Papyrologica* 9 (1970) 7–19.

Bruce, Lorne. "Palace and Villa Libraries from Augustus to Hadrian." *Journal of Library History* 21 (1986) 510–552.

Brunt, P. A. "The Administrators of Roman Egypt." *JRS* 65 (1975) 124–147.

Bryan, Betsy M. "Evidence for Female Literacy from Theban Tombs of the New Kingdom." *Bulletin of the Egyptological Seminar* 6 (1985) 17–32.

Burton-Christie, Douglas. *The Word in the Desert: Scripture and the Quest for Holiness in Early Christian Monasticism.* New York: Oxford University Press, 1993.

Calderini, "ἀγράμματοι nell' Egitto greco-romano," *Aegyptus* 30 (1950) 14–41.

Cameron, Alan. "Wandering Poets: A Literary Movement in Byzantine Egypt." *Historia* 14 (1965) 470–509.

Cameron, Averil. *Christianity and the Rhetoric of the Empire: The Development of Christian Discourse.* Berkeley: University of California Press, 1991.

Campenhausen, Hans von. *Ecclesiastical Authority and Spiritual Power in the Church of the First Three Centuries,* trans. by J. A. Baker. Stanford, Calif.: Stanford University Press, 1969.

———. *The Formation of the Christian Bible,* trans. J. A. Baker. Philadelphia: Fortress Press, 1972.

Cantarella, Eva. *Pandora's Daughters: The Role and Status of Women in Greek and Roman Antiquity.* Baltimore, Md.: Johns Hopkins University Press, 1987 [c. 1981].

Carroll, John T. "Luke's Crucifixion Scene." In *Reimaging the Death of the Lukan Jesus,* ed. Dennis Sylva. Frankfurt: Anton Hain, 1990, 108–124.

Carruthers, Mary. *The Book of Memory: A Study of Memory in Medieval Culture.* Cambridge: Cambridge University Press, 1990.

Chartier, Roger. *The Cultural Uses of Print in Early Modern France,* trans. Lydia G. Cochrane. Princeton, N.J.: Princeton University Press, 1987.

———. *Forms and Meanings: Texts, Performances, and Audiences from Codex to Computer.* Philadelphia: University of Pennsylvania Press, 1995.

———. *On the Edge of the Cliff: History, Language, and Practices,* trans. Lydia G. Cochrane. Baltimore, Md.: Johns Hopkins University Press, 1997.

———. *The Order of Books: Readers, Authors, and Libraries in Europe between the Fourteenth and Eighteenth Centuries,* trans. Lydia G. Cochrane. Stanford, Calif.: Stanford University Press, 1994 [1992].

———. "Texts, Printing, Readings." In *The New Cultural History,* ed. Lynn Hunt. Berkeley: University of California Press, 1989, 154–175.

Chitty, Derwas. *The Desert a City: An Introduction to the Study of Egyptian and Palestinian Monasticism under the Christian Empire.* London: A. R. Mowbrays, 1966.

Clanchy, Michael. *From Memory to Written Record, England 1066–1307.* 1979; repr., Oxford: Basil Blackwell, 1993.

Clark, Elizabeth A. *Ascetic Piety and Women's Faith: Essays on Late Ancient Christianity.* New York: Edwin Mellen Press, 1986.

———. *The Origenist Controversy: The Cultural Construction of an Early Christian Debate.* Princeton, N.J.: Princeton University Press, 1992.

———. *Reading Renunciation: Asceticism and Scripture in Early Christianity.* Princeton, N.J.: Princeton University Press, 1999.

Clark, Kenneth W. "Posture of the Ancient Scribe." *BA* 26 (1963) 63–72.

Clarke, G. W. "An Illiterate Lector?" *ZPE* 57 (1984) 103–104.

Clarke, M. L. *Higher Education in the Ancient World.* London: Routledge and Kegan Paul, 1971.

Clarysse, Willy. "Egyptian Scribes Writing Greek." *Chronique d'Égypt* 68 (1993) 186–201.

———. "Greeks and Egyptians in the Ptolemaic Army and Administration." *Aegyptus* 65 (1985) 57–66.

———. "Literary Papyri in Documentary 'Archives'." In *Egypt and the Hellenistic World: Proceedings of the International Colloquium, Leuven, 24–26 May 1982.* Ed. E. van 'T Dack, P. van Dessel, and W. van Gucht. Lovanii: [orientaliste] 1983, 43–61.

———. "Some Greeks in Egypt." *Life in a Multi-Cultural Society: Egypt from Cambyses to Constantine and Beyond*, ed. Janet H. Johnson. Chicago: Oriental Institute of the University of Chicago, 1992, 51–56.

Cole, Susan G. "Could Greek Women Read and Write?" In *Reflections of Women in Antiquity*, ed. Helene P. Foley. New York: Gordon and Breach Science Publishers, 1981, 219–245.

Colwell, Ernest C. "Genealogical Method: Its Achievements and Its Limitations." *JBL* 66 (1947) 109–33.

———. "Hort Redivivus: A Plea and a Program." *Transitions in Biblical Scholarship.* Ed. J. Coert Rylaarsdam. Chicago: University of Chicago Press, 1968, 131–155.

———. "The Origin of Texttypes of New Testament Manuscripts." *Early Christian Origins: Studies in Honour of Harold R. Willoughby*, ed. Allen Wikgren. Chicago: Quadrangle Books, 1961, 128–138.

———. *Studies in Methodology in Textual Criticism of the New Testament.* Grand Rapids, Mich.: Eerdmans, 1969.

———. "External Evidence and New Testament Textual Criticism." In *Studies in the History and Text of the New Testament in honor of Kenneth Willis Clark*, ed. Jacob Geerlings. Studies and Documents 29. Salt Lake City: University of Utah Press, 1967, 1–12.

———. "Scribal Habits in Early Papyri: A Study in the Corruption of the Text." In *The Bible in Modern Scholarship.* Ed. J. Philip Hyatt. Nashville, Tenn.: Abingdon Press, 1965, 370–389. Reprinted in Colwell's *Studies in Methodology in Textual Criticism of the New Testament*, 1969, 106–104.

——— with Ernest W. Tune. "The Quantitative Relationships between MS Text Types." In *Biblical and Patristic Studies: In Memory of Robert Pierce Casey*, eds. J. Neville Birdsall and Robert W. Thomson. Freiburg: Herder, 1963, 25–32.

Comfort, Philip W. "Exploring the Common Identification of Three New Testament Manuscripts: P^4, P^{64}, and P^{67}." *Tyndale Bulletin* 46 (1995) 43–54.

Cotton, H. M., W. E. H. Cockle, and F. G. B. Millar. "The Papyrology of the Roman Near East: A Survey." *JRS* 85 (1995) 214–235.

Cox Miller, Patricia. *Biography in Late Antiquity: A Quest of the Holy Man.* Berkeley: University of California Press, 1983.

Cribiore, Raffaella. *Writing, Teachers, and Students in Graeco-Roman Egypt.* Atlanta, Ga.: Scholars' Press, 1996.

Crisci, Edoardo. "Scritture greche palestini e mesopotamische (III secolo A.C.–III D.C.)." *Scritture e Civiltà* 15 (1991) 125–183 and plates I–XXVII.

Crompton, Rosemary. *Class and Stratification: An Introduction to Current Debates.* Cambridge: Polity Press, 1993.

Culham, Phyllis. "Documents and *Domus* in Republican Rome." *Libraries and Culture* 26 (1991) 119–134.

Curchin, Leonard A. "Literacy in the Roman Provinces: Qualitative and Quantitative Data from Central Spain." *American Journal of Philology* 116 (1995) 461–476.

Dalzell, A. "C. Asinius Pollio and the Early History of Public Recitation at Rome." *Hermathena* 86 (1955) 20–28.

Dampier, Joseph H. "The Scrolls and the Scribes of the New Testament." *Bulletin of the Evangelical Theological Society* 1 (1988) 8–19.

de Certeau, Michel. *The Writing of History*, trans. Tom Conley. New York: Columbia University Press, 1988 [c. 1975].

De Hamel, Christopher. *A History of Illuminated Manuscripts*. London: Phaidon Press, 1994 [1986].

Deissmann, Adolf. *Light from the Ancient East: The New Testament Illustrated by Recently Discovered Texts of the Graeco-Roman World*, trans. Lionel R. M. Strachan. 2d ed. London: Hodder and Stoughton, 1911.

Demsky, Aaron. "The Education of Canaanite Scribes in the Mesopotamian Cuneiform Tradition," ed. Jacob Klein and Aaron Skaist. *Bar-Ilan Studies in Assyriology*, dedicated to Pinhas Artze. Ramat Gan, Israel: Bar-Ilan University Press, 1990, 156–170.

Denny, Peter J. "Rational Thought in Oral Culture and Literate Decontextualization." In *Literacy and Orality*, ed. David R. Olson and Nancy Torrance. Cambridge: Cambridge University Press, 1991, 66–89.

De Ste. Croix, G. E. M. *The Class Struggle in the Ancient Greek World*. Ithaca, N.Y.: Cornell University Press, 1981.

De Strycker, É. *La Forme le plus ancienne du Protévangile de Jacques*. Brussels: Societé des Bollandistes, 1961.

———. "Notes sur l'abréviation des *nomina sacra* dans des manuscrits hagiographiques grecs." *Studia Codicologica*. Texte und Untersuchungen zur Geschichte der Altchristlichen Literatur 124. Berlin: Akademie-Verlag, 1977, 461–467.

Diringer, David. *The Book Before Printing: Ancient, Medieval and Oriental*. New York: Dover Publications, 1982.

Dix, T. Keith. "Private and Public Libraries at Rome in the First Century B.C.: A Preliminary Study in the History of Roman Libraries." Ph.D. diss., University of Michigan, 1986.

———. "'Public Libraries' in Ancient Rome: Ideology and Reality." *Libraries and Culture* 29 (1994) 282–296.

Drogin, Marc. *Anathema! Medieval Scribes and the History of Book Curses*. Totowa, N.J.: Allanheld, Osmun, 1983.

Dronke, Peter. *Women Writers of the Middle Ages: A Critical Study of Texts from Perpetua (203) to Marguerite Porete (1310)*. Cambridge: Cambridge University Press, 1984.

Duplacy, Jean. "Histoire des manuscrits et histoire du texte du N.T." *NTS* 13 (1965–1966) 124–139.

Edwards, S. A. "P75 under the Magnifying Glass." *NovT* 18 (1976) 190–212.

Ehrman, Bart D. "Heracleon, Origen, and the Text of the Fourth Gospel." *Vigiliae Christianae* 47 (1993) 105–118.

———. "1 Joh 4, 3 and the Orthodox Corruption of Scripture." *Zeitschrift Fur die Neutestamentliche Wissenschaft* 79 (1988) 221–243.

————. "Methodological Developments in the Analysis and Classification of New Testament Documentary Evidence." *NT* 29 (1987) 22–45.

————. *The Orthodox Corruption of Scripture: The Effect of Early Christological Controversies on the Text of the New Testament.* New York: Oxford University Press, 1993.

————. "A Problem of Textual Circularity: The Alands on the Classification of New Testament Manuscripts." *Biblica* 70 (1989) 377–388.

————. "The Text as Window: New Testament Manuscripts and the Social History of Early Christianity." *The Text of the New Testament in Contemporary Research: Essays on the Status Quaestionis,* ed. Bart D. Ehrman and Michael W. Homes. Grand Rapids, Mich.: Eerdmans, 1995. 361–379.

————. "The Text of Mark in the Hands of the Orthodox." In *Biblical Hemeneutics in Historical Perspective: Studies in Honor of Karlfried Froehlich on His Sixtieth Birthday,* ed. Mark Burrows and Paul Rorem. Grand Rapids, Mich.: Eerdmans, 1991. 19–31.

————. "The Text of the Gospels at the End of the Second Century." In *Codex Bezae: Studies from the Lunel Colloquium, June 1994,* ed. D. C. Parker and C.-B. Amphoux. Leiden: E. J. Brill, 1996, 95–122.

————. "The Theodotians as Corrupters of Scripture." *Studia Patristica* 47 (1993) 105–13.

————. "The Use of Group Profiles for the Classification of New Testament Documentary Evidence." *JBL* 106 (1987) 465–486.

————, and Michael W. Holmes, eds. *The Text of the New Testament in Contemporary Research: Essays on the Status Quaestionis.* Studies and Documents 46. Grand Rapids, Mich.: Eerdmans, 1995.

Elliott, J. K. *A Bibliography of Greek New Testament Manuscripts.* Cambridge: Cambridge University Press, 1989.

————. ed. *The Principles and Practice of New Testament Textual Criticism.* Collected Essays of G. D. Kilpatrick. Leuven: Leuven University Press, 1990.

Elliott, W. J. and D. C. Parker, eds. *The New Testament in Greek IV: The Gospel According to St. John.* Vol. 1. *The Papyri.* NTTS 20. Leiden: E. J. Brill, 1995.

Ellspermann, Gerard L. *The Attitude of the Early Christian Latin Writers toward Pagan Literature and Learning.* Washington: D. C.: Catholic University Press, 1949.

Elm, Susanna. *'Virgins of God': The Making of Asceticism in Late Antiquity.* 1994; repr., Oxford: Clarendon Press, 1996.

Emmet, Dorothy. "The Concept of Power." *Proceedings of the Aristotelian Society, N. S.* 54 (1953–1954) 1–26.

Epiphanius of Salamis. *Panarion,* ed. K. Holl. GCS 25, 31, 37 (1915, 1922, 1933). English translation: *The Panarion of St. Epiphanius, Bishop of Salamis (Selected Passages),* trans. P. Amidon. New York: Oxford University Press, 1990.

Epp, Eldon Jay. "The Significance of the Papyri for Determining the Nature of the New Testament Text in the Second Century: A Dynamic View of Textual Transmission." In *Gospel Traditions in the Second Century: Origins, Recensions, Text, and Transmission,* ed. W. L. Peterson. Notre Dame, Ind.: University of Notre Dame Press, 1989, 71–103.

————. "The Eclectic Method in New Testament Textual Criticism: Solution or Symptom?" *HTR* 69 (1976) 211–257.

————. "New Testament Papyrus Manuscripts and Letter Carrying in Graeco-Roman Times." In *The Future of Early Christianity*, ed. Birger A. Pearson. Minneapolis, Minn.: Fortress Press, 1991, 35–56.

————. "The New Testament Papyrus Manuscripts in Historical Perspective." In *To Touch the Text: Biblical and Related Studies in Honor of Joseph A. Fitzmyer, S. J.*, ed. Maurya P. Horgan and Paul J. Kobelski. New York: Crossroad, 1989, 261–88.

————. *The Theological Tendency of Codex Bezae Cantabrigiensis in Acts*. SNTS 3. Cambridge: Cambridge University Press, 1966.

————. "The Twentieth Century Interlude in New Testament Textual Criticism." *JBL* 93 (1974) 386–414.

————. "The 'Ignorance Motif' in Acts and Anti-Judaic Tendencies in Codex Bezae." *HTR* 55 (1962) 51–62.

————, and Gordon D. Fee. *Studies in the Theory and Method of New Testament Textual Criticism*. Studies and Documents 45. Grand Rapids, Mich.: Eerdmans, 1993.

Eshbaugh, Howard. "Textual Variants and Theology: A Study of the Galatians Text of Papyrus 46." *JSNT* 3 (1979) 60–72.

Eusebius of Caesarea, *Historia Ecclesiastica*, ed. G. Bardy. SC 31, 41, 55, 73.

————. *Vita Constantini*, ed. I. Heikel. GCS 7.

Falivene, Maria Rosaria. "Government, Management, Literacy: Aspects of Ptolemaic Administration in the Early Hellenistic Period." *Ancient Society* 22 (1991) 203–227.

Fantham, Elaine. *Roman Literary Culture from Cicero to Apuleius*. Baltimore, Md.: Johns Hopkins University Press, 1996.

Fee, Gordon D. "Codex Sinaiticus in the Gospel of John: A Contribution to Methodology in Establishing Textual Relationships." *New Testament Studies* 15 (1968) 23–44.

————. "Modern Textual Criticism and the Revival of the Textus Receptus." *JETS* 21 (1978) 19–33.

————. "The Myth of Early Textual Recension in Alexandria." In *Studies in the Theory and Method of New Testament Textual Criticism*, ed. Eldon Jay Epp and Gordon D. Fee. Grand Rapids, Mich.: Eerdmans, 1993, 247–273.

————. *Papyrus Bodmer II (P66): Its Textual Relationships and Scribal Characteristics*, ed. Jacob Geerlings. Studies and Documents 33. Salt Lake City: University of Utah Press, 1968.

————. "Rigorous or Reasoned Eclecticism — Which?" In *Studies in New Testament Language and Text: Essays in Honour of George D. Kilpatrick on the Occasion of His Sixty-Fifth Birthday*, ed. J. K. Elliott. Leiden: E. J. Brill, 1976. 174–97.

————. "The Text of John in Origen and Cyril of Alexandria: A Contribution to Methodology in the Recovery and Analysis of Patristic Citations." *Biblica* 52 (1971) 357–373.

Finegan, Jack. *Encountering New Testament Manuscripts: A Working Introduction to Textual Criticism*. Grand Rapids, Mich.: Eerdmans, 1974.

Fish, Stanley. *Is There a Text in This Class? The Authority of Interpretive Communities*. Cambridge, Mass.: Harvard University Press, 1980.

Forbes, Clarence A. "The Education and Training of Slaves in Antiquity." *TAPA* 86 (1955) 321–360.

Foucault, Michel. *The Archaeology of Knowledge*, trans. A. M. Sheridan Smith. New York: Pantheon, 1972. French original, 1969.

———. *Power/Knowledge: Selected Interviews and Other Writings, 1972–1977*, ed. and trans. Colin Gordon. New York: Pantheon, 1980.

———. *This is Not a Pipe*, trans. James Harkness. Berkeley: University of California Press, 1983.

Frantz, Alison. "Honors to a Librarian." *Hesperia* 35 (1966) 377–380.

Funghi, Maria Serena, and Gabriella Messeri Savorelli. "Note papirologiche e palaeografiche." *Tyche* 7 (1992) 75–88.

Gager, John G., ed. *Curse Tablets and Binding Spells from the Ancient World*. New York: Oxford University Press, 1992.

———. *The Origins of Anti-Semitism: Attitudes Toward Judaism in Pagan and Christian Antiquity*. New York: Oxford University Press, 1983.

Gallo, Italo. *Greek and Latin Papyrology*. Trans. Maria Rosaria Falivene and Jennifer R. March. London: Institute of Classical Studies, 1986.

Gamble, Harry Y. *Books and Readers in the Early Church: A History of Early Christian Texts*. New Haven, Conn.: Yale University Press, 1995.

———. "Christianity: Scripture and Canon." In *The Holy Book in Comparative Perspective*, 36–62. Columbia: University of South Carolina Press, 1985.

———. "The Pauline Corpus and the Early Christian Book." In *Paul and the Legacies of Paul*, ed. William S. Babcock. Dallas, Tx.: Southern Methodist University Press, 1990, 265–280.

Gameson, Richard, ed. *The Early Medieval Bible: Its Production, Decoration, and Use*. Cambridge: Cambridge University Press, 1994.

Gammie, John G., and Leo G. Perdue, eds. *The Sage in Israel and the Ancient Near East*. Winona Lake, Ind.: Eisenbrauns, 1990.

Gardiner, Alan H. "The House of Life." *JEA* 24 (1938) 157–179.

Garnsey, Peter, and Richard Saller. *The Roman Empire: Economy, Society and Culture*. Berkeley: University of California Press, 1987.

Gerontius. *Vie de Sainte Mealanie*, ed. D. Gorce. SC 90. English translation of the Greek text: Elizabeth A. Clark. *The Life of Melania the Younger*. New York: Edwin Mellen Press, 1984.

Ghellinck, Joseph de. *Patristique et Moyen Age*. 3 vols. Museum Lessianum, series historica Louvain. Bruxelles/Paris, 1946, 1947, 1948.

Gilliam, Elizabeth H. "The Archives of the Temple of Soknobraisis at Bacchias." *Yale Classical Studies* 10 (1947) 181–281.

Gilliard, Frank D. "More Silent Reading in Antiquity: *Non Omne Verbum Sonabat*." *JBL* 112 (1993) 689–694.

Globe, Alexander. "Some Doctrinal Variants in Matthew 1 and Luke 2 and the Authority of the Neutral Text." *CBQ* 42 (1980) 52–72.

Goehring, J. "New Frontiers in Pachomian Studies." In *The Roots of Egyptian Christianity*, ed. B. A. Pearson and J. E. Goehring. Philadelphia, Pa.: Fortress Press, 1986, 236–257.

Gold, Barbara K. *Literary Patronage in Greece and Rome*. Chapel Hill: University of North Carolina Press, 1987.

Goody, Jack. *The Interface between the Written and the Oral.* Cambridge: Cambridge University Press, 1987.

———. *The Logic of Writing and the Organization of Society.* Cambridge: Cambridge University Press, 1986.

Goody, Jack, and Ian Watt. "The Consequences of Literacy." *Comparative Studies in Society and History* 5 (1963) 304–345.

Goranson, Stephen. "Further Qumran Archaeology Publications in Progress." *BA* 54 (1991) 110–111.

Gordon, Arthur E. *Illustrated Introduction to Latin Epigraphy.* Berkeley: University of California Press, 1983.

Gordon, Richard, Mary Beard, Joyce Reynolds, and Charlotte Roueché. "Roman Inscriptions 1986–1990." *JRS* 83 (1993) 131–158.

Gould, G. P., ed. *Chariton: Callirhoe.* Cambridge, Mass.: Harvard University Press, 1995.

Grant, Robert M. "Charges of Immorality against Various Religious Groups in Antiquity." In *Studies in Gnosticism and Hellenistic Religions,* ed. R. van der Broek and M. J. Vermaseren. Leiden: E. J. Brill, 1981.

———. "Theological Education at Alexandria." In *The Roots of Egyptian Christianity,* eds. Birger A. Pearson and James E. Goehring. Philadelphia, Pa.: Fortress Press, 1986, 178–189.

Greene, W. C. "The Spoken and Written Word." *Harvard Studies in Classical Philology* 60 (1990) 267–278.

Greenfield, Jonas C. "'Because He/She Did Not Know Letters': Remarks on a First Millenium C. E. Legal Expression." *JANES* 22 (1993) 39–44.

Greenlee, J. Harold. *Introduction to New Testament Textual Criticism.* Grand Rapids, Mich.: Eerdmans, 1964.

Hadas, Moses. *Ancilla to Classical Reading.* New York: Columbia University Press, 1954.

Haelst, Joseph van. *Catalogue des Papyrus littéraires juifs et chrétiens.* Paris: Publications de la Sorbonne, 1976.

———. "Les origines du codex." In *Les débuts du codex,* ed. Alain Blanchard. Brepols: Turnhout, 1989, 13–35.

Hagedorn, Ursula, Dieter Hagedorn, Louise C. Youtie, and Herbert C. Youtie. *Das Archiv des Petaus (P. Petaus).* Papyrologica Coloniensia 4. Köln: Westdeutscher Verlag, 1969.

Hagendahl, Harald. "Die Bedeutung der Stenographie für die spätlateinische Christliche Literatur." *Jahrbuch für antike und Christentum* 14 (1971) 24–38.

Hägg, Tomas. *The Novel in Antiquity.* Berkeley: University of California Press, 1983.

Hahneman, Geoffrey Mark. *The Muratorian Fragment and the Development of the Canon.* Oxford: Clarendon Press, 1992.

Hanson, Ann Ellis. "Egyptians, Greeks, Romans, *Arabes,* and *Ioudaioi* in the First Century A.D. Tax Archive from Philadelphia: P. Mich. Inv. 880 Recto and *P. Princ.* III 152 Revised." *Life in a Multi-Cultural Society: Egypt from Cambyses to Constantine and Beyond,* ed. Janet H. Johnson. Chicago: Oriental Institute of the University of Chicago, 1992, 133–143.

Hanson, Carl A. "Were There Libraries in Roman Spain?" *Libraries and Culture* 24 (1989) 198–216.

Haran, Menahem. "Bookscrolls in Israel in Pre-Exilic Times." In *Essays in Honour of Yigael Yadin*, ed. Geza Vermes and Jacob Neusner. Totowa, N.J.: Allanheld, Osmun, 1983, 161–173.

———. "More Concerning Book-Scrolls in Pre-Exilic Times." *JJS* 35 (1984) 84–85.

———. "Archives, Libraries, and the Order of the Biblical Books." *JANES* 22 (1993) 51–61.

———. "The Codex, the Pinax and the Wooden Slats." *Tarbiz* 57 (1988) 151–164 [Hebrew].

Harnack, Adolf von. *Bible Reading in the Early Church*. New York: G. P. Putnam's sons, 1912.

———. *Marcion: Das Evangelium Vom Fremden Gott*. Leipzig: J. C. Hinrichs'sche Buchhandlung, 1924.

———. *The Mission and Expansion of Christianity in the First Three Centuries*, trans. James Moffatt. Goucester, Mass: Peter Smith, 1972, 1961.

Harris, J. Rendel. "New Points of View in Textual Criticism." *The Expositor* 8/7 (1914) 316–334.

———. "Was the Diatesseron Anti-Judaic?" *HTR* 18 (1925) 103–109.

———. "Stichometry." *American Journal of Philology* 4 (1883) 133–157, 309–331.

Harris, Rivkah. "The Female 'Sage' in Mesopotamian Literature (with an Appendix on Egypt)." In *The Sage in Israel and the Ancient Near East*, ed. John G. Gammie and Leo G. Perdue. Winona Lake, Ind.: Eisenbrauns, 1990, 3–17.

———. "The Organization and Administration of the Cloister in Ancient Babylonia." *Journal of the Economic and Social History of the Orient* 6 (1963) 121–157.

Harris, William. *Ancient Literacy*. Cambridge, Mass.: Harvard University Press, 1989.

———. "Literacy and Epigraphy, I." *ZPE* 52 (1983) 87–114.

———. "Why Did the Codex Supplant the Book-Roll?" In *Renaissance Society and Culture: Essays in Honor of Eugene F. Rice*, ed. John Monfasani and Ronald G. Musto. New York: Italica Press, 1991, 71–85.

Harvey, F. David. "Greeks and Romans Learn to Write." In *Communication Arts in the Ancient World*, ed. Eric A. Havelock and Jackson P. Hershbell. New York: Hastings House, 1978, 63–78.

Hatch, W. H. P. *The Principal Uncial Manuscripts of the New Testament*. Chicago: University of Chicago Press, 1939.

Havelock, Eric A. *Preface to Plato*. Cambridge, Mass.: Harvard University Press, 1963.

———. *The Literate Revolution in Greece and Its Cultural Consequences*. Princeton, N.J.: Princeton University Press, 1982.

———. *The Muse Learns to Write: Reflections on Orality and Literacy from Antiquity to the Present*. New Haven, Conn.: Yale University Press, 1986.

———, and Jackson P. Hershbell. *Communication Arts in the Ancient World*. New York: Hastings House, 1978.

Head, Peter M. "The Date of the Magdalen Papyrus of Matthew (*P. Magd. Gr.* 17 = P^{64}): A Response to C. P. Thiede." *Tyndale Bulletin* 46 (1995) 251–285.

———. "Observations on Early Papyri of the Synoptic Gospels, especially on the 'Scribal Habits'." *Biblica* 71 (1990) 240–247.

————. "Re-inking the Pen: Evidence from P. Oxy. 657 (P[13]) Concerning Unintentional Scribal Errors." *NTS* 43 (1997) 466–473.

Hengel, Martin. *Studies in the Gospel of Mark*. Philadelphia, Pa.: Fortress Press, 1985.

Henrichs, Albert. "Pagan Ritual and the Alleged Crimes of the Early Christians." In *Kyriakon: Festschrift Johannes Quatsten*, ed. Patrick Granfield and Josef A. Jungmann. Vol. 1. Münster: Aschendorff, 1970, 18–35.

Hippolytus. *La Tradition apostolique, d'après les ancienne versions*, ed. B. Botte. SC 11.

Hodges, Zane C. "Modern Textual Criticism and the Majority Text: A Response." *JETS* 21 (1978) 143–155.

Holmes, Michael W. "Codex Bezae as a Recension of the Gospels." In *Codex Bezae: Studies from the Lunel Colloquium, June 1994*, ed. D. C. Parker and C.-B. Amphoux. Leiden: E. J. Brill, 1996, 123–160.

Hopkins, Keith. "Élite Mobility in the Roman Empire." *Studies in Ancient Society*, ed. M. I. Finley. Past and Present Series. London: Routledge and Kegan Paul, 1974, 103–120.

Hornschuh, Manfred. "Das Leben des Origenes und die Entstehung der alexandrinischen Schule." *Zeitschrift für Kirchengeschichte* 71 (1960) 1–25, 193–214.

Horsley, Greg. *New Documents Illustrating Early Christianity*, Macquarie University. Vols. 1–7. 1981–1994.

Howard, George. "The Tetragram and the New Testament." *JBL* 96 (1977) 63–83.

Hulbert-Powell, C. L. *John James Wettstein 1693–1754: An Account of His Life, Work, and Some of His Contemporaries*. London: Society for Promoting Christian Knowledge, 1938.

Humphrey, J. H., ed. *Literacy in the Roman World: Journal of Roman Archaeology*. Supplementary Series 3 (1991).

Hunt, Lynn, ed. *The New Cultural History*. Berkeley: University of California Press, 1989.

Hussein, Mohamed. *Vom Papyrus zum Codex: Der Beitrag Ägyptens zur Buchkultur*. Leipzig, 1970.

Irvine, Martin. *The Making of Textual Culture: 'Grammatica' and Literary Theory, 350–1100*. Cambridge: Cambridge University Press, 1994.

Jahn, O. "Die Subscriptionen in den Handschriften Römischer Classiker." *Berichte eber die Verhandlungen der königlich-sachsischen Gesellschaft der wissenschaften zu Leipzig, Philologische-Historische Classe* 3 (1851) 327–372.

Johnson, W. A. "Pliny the Elder and Standardized Roll Heights in the Manufacture of Papyrus." *Classical Philology* 88 (1993) 46–50.

Joshel, Sandra R. *Work, Identity, and Legal Status at Rome: A Study of the Occupational Inscriptions*. Norman: University of Oklahoma Press, 1992.

Judge, E. A. "The Earliest Use of Monachos for 'Monk' (P. Coll. Youtie 77) and the Origins of Monasticism." *JAC* 20 (1977) 72–89.

————. "The Early Christians as a Scholastic Community." *JRH* 1 (1960) 4–15.

————. "The Magical Use of Scripture in the Papyri." In *Perspectives on Language and Text*, ed. Edgar W. Conrad and Edward G. Newing. Winona Lake, Ind.: Eisenbrauns, 1987, 339–349.

————. "Papyrus Documentation of Church and Community in Egypt to the Mid-Fourth Century." *JAC* 20 (1977) 47–71.

————, and S. R. Pickering. "Biblical Papyri Prior to Constantine: Some Cultural Implications of Their Physical Form." *Prudentia* 10 (1970) 1–13.

Junack, Klaus. "Abschreibpraktiken und Schreibergewohnheiten in ihrer Auswirkung auf die Textüberlieferung." In *New Testament Textual Criticism: Its Significance for Exegesis. Essays in Honor of Bruce M. Metzger,* ed. Eldon Jay Epp and Gordon D. Fee. Oxford: Clarendon Press, 1981, 277–295.

Kampen, Natalie. *Image and Status: Roman Working Women in Ostia.* Berlin: Gebr. Mann, 1981.

Kasser, R. and V. Martin. *Papyrus Bodmer XIV–XV.* Cologny-Genève: Bibliothèque Bodmer, 1961.

Kaster, Robert A. *Guardians of Language: The Grammarian and Society in Late Antiquity.* Berkeley: University of California Press, 1988.

Katz, Peter. "The Early Christians' Use of Codices Instead of Rolls." *JTS* 46 (1945) 63–65.

Kenney, E. J. "Books and Readers in the Roman World." In *The Cambridge History of Classical Literature. Vol. 2.* Cambridge: Cambridge University Press, 1982, 3–32.

Kenyon, Frederic G. *Books and Readers in Ancient Greece and Rome.* Oxford: Clarendon Press, 1951.

————. *The Chester Beatty Biblical Papyri: Descriptions and Texts of Twelve Manuscripts on Papyrus of the Greek Bible.* London: Oxford University Press, 1934.

————. "The Library of a Greek at Oxyrhynchus." *Journal of Egyptian Archaeology* 8 (1922) 129–138.

Kerber, Linda K. "Separate Spheres, Female Worlds, Woman's Place: The Rhetoric of Women's History." *Journal of American History* 75 (1988) 9–39.

Kilpatrick, George D. "Atticism and the Text of the Greek New Testament." In *Neutestamentliche Aufsätze: Festschrift für Prof. Josef Schmid zum 10. Geburtstag,* ed. J. Blinzer, O. Kuss, and F. Mußner. Regensburg: Friedrich Pustet, 1963, 125–137

————. "The Bodmer and Mississippi Collection of Biblical and Christian Texts." *Greek, Roman, and Byzantine Studies* 4 (1963) 33–47.

King, Marchant A. "Notes on the Bodmer Manuscript of Jude and 1 and 2 Peter." *Bibliotheca Sacra* 121 (1964) 54–57.

Klijn, A. F. J. "A Library of Scriptures in Jerusalem?" *Studia Codicologica.* Texte und Untersuchungen zur Geschichte der Altchristilichen Literatur 124. Berlin: Akademie-Verlag, 1977, 265–272.

Knox, Bernard M. W. "Silent Reading in Antiquity." *Greek, Roman, Byzantine Studies* 9 (1968) 421–435.

Koenen, Ludwig. "Ein Mönch als Berufsschreiber zur buchproduction im 5./6. Jahrhundert." *Festschrift zum 150 Jährigen Bestehen des Berliner Ägyptischen Museums.* Staatliche Museen zu Berlin Mitteilungen aus der Ägyptischen Sammlung Band 8. Berlin: Akademie-Verlag, 1974, 347–354.

Kraemer, Ross S. *Her Share of the Blessings: Women's Religions Among Pagans, Jews, and Christians in the Greco-Roman World.* New York: Oxford University Press, 1992.

————. "Women's Authorship of Jewish and Christian Literature in the Greco-Roman Period." In *"Women Like This": New Perspectives on Jewish Women in the*

Greco-Roman World, ed. by Amy-Jill Levine. Atlanta, Ga.: Scholars Press, 1991, 221–242.

Kraft, R. A. "An Unnoticed Papyrus Fragment of Barnabas." *VC* 21 (1967) 150–163.

———. "Scripture and Canon in Jewish Apocrypha and Pseudepigrapha." In *Hebrew Bible/Old Testament: The History of Its Interpretation*. Vol. 1: *From the Beginnings to the Middle Ages (Until 1300)*, ed. Magne Sæbøs, pt. 1. Göttingen: Vandenhoeck and Ruprecht, 1996, 199–216.

Krueger, Derek. "Hagiography as an Ascetic Practice in the Early Christian East." *Journal of Religion* 79 (1999) 216–232.

———. "Writing as Devotion: Hagiographhical Composition and the Cult of the Saints in Theodoret of Cyrrhus and Cyril of Scythopolis." *Church History* 66 (1997) 707–719.

Krüger, Julian. *Oxyrhynchos in der Kaiserzeit: Studien zur Topographie und Literaturrezeption*. Frankfurt am Main: Peter Lang, 1990.

LaCapra, Dominick. *Soundings in Critical Theory*. Ithaca, N.Y.: Cornell University Press, 1989.

Lake, Kirsopp, and Silva Lake. *Family 13 (The Ferrar Group): The Text According to Mark with a Collation of Codex 28 of the Gospels*. Studies and Documents 11. London and Philadelphia: Christophers and University of Philadelphia Press, 1941.

Lake, Kirsopp. "On the Italian Origin of Codex Bezae." *JTS* 1 (1900) 441–445.

Lane Fox, Robin. "Literacy and Power in Early Christianity." *Literacy and Power in the Ancient World*, ed. Alan K. Bowman and Greg Woolf. Cambridge: Cambridge University Press, 1994, 126–148.

Laudien, Arthur. *Griechische Papyri aus Oxyrhynchos für den Schulgebrauch Ausgewählt*. Berlin: Weidmannsche Buchhandlung, 1912.

Lefkowitz, Mary R. "Did Ancient Women Write Novels?" In *"Women Like This": New Perspectives on Jewish Women in the Greco-Roman World*, ed. Amy-Jill Levine. Atlanta, Ga.: Scholars' Press, 1991, 199–219.

Lefkowitz, Mary R., and Maureen B. Fant. *Women's Life in Greece and Rome: A Source Book in Translation*. Baltimore, Md.: Johns Hopkins University Press, 1992 [1982].

Lentz, Tony M. *Orality and Literacy in Hellenic Greece*. Carbondale: Southern Illinois University Press, 1989.

Leon, Harry J. *The Jews of Ancient Rome*. Peabody, Mass.: Hendrickson Publishers, 1960.

Lewis, Naphtali. *Life in Egypt under Roman Rule*. Oxford: Clarendon Press, 1983.

———. "Literati in the Service of Roman Emperors: Politics before Culture." *Coins, Culture, and History in the Ancient World: Numismatic and Other Studies in Honor of Bluma L. Trell*, ed. Lionel Casson and Martin Price. Detroit, Mich.: Wayne University Press, 1981, 149–166.

———. "The Non-Scholar Members of the Alexandrian Museum." *Mnemosyne* 16 (1963) 257–261.

———. *Papyrus in Classical Antiquity*. Oxford: Clarendon Press, 1974.

Lieberman, Saul. *Greek in Jewish Palestine [1965]/Hellenism in Jewish Palestine [1962]*. Repr. New York: Jewish Theological Seminary of American, 1994.

Linder, Amnon. *The Jews in Roman Imperial Legislation*. Detroit, Mich.: Wayne State University Press, 1987.

Llewelyn, Stephen Robert. "Sending Letters in the Ancient World: Paul and the Philippians." *Tyndale Bulletin* 46 (1995) 337–356.

Lord, Albert B. *The Singer of Tales*. Cambridge, Mass. Harvard University Press, 1960.

———. *Epic Singers and Oral Tradition*. Ithaca, N.Y.: Cornell University Press, 1991.

MacMullen, R. *Changes in the Roman Empire*. Princeton, N.J.: Princeton University Press, 1990.

———. *Christianizing the Roman Empire*. New Haven, Conn.: Yale University Press, 1984.

———. "The Epigraphic Habit in the Roman Empire." *AJP* 103 (1982) 233–246.

———. "The Preacher and His Audience." *JTS* 40 (1989) 503–511.

———. "Provincial Languages in the Roman Empire." *American Journal of Philology* 87 (1966) 1–17.

———. *Roman Social Relations, 50* B.C. to A.D. *284*. New Haven, Conn.: Yale University Press, 1974.

Magie, David. *Roman Rule in Asia Minor to the End of the Third Century after Christ*. Princeton, N.J.: Princeton University Press, 1959.

Maher-Leonhard, E. ΑΓΡΑΜΜΑΤΟΙ. In Aegypto qui litteras sciverint qui nesciverint ex papyris graecis quantum fieri potest exploratur. Frankfurt am Main: A. Diekmann, 1913.

Manfredi, Manfredo. "Cultura Letteraria nell'Egitto Greco e Romano." *Egitto e Società Antica*. Milan: Vita e Pensiero, 1985, 271–285.

Mann, Michael. *The Sources of Social Power*. Vol. 1: *A History of Power from the Beginning to A.D. 1760*. Cambridge: Cambridge University Press, 1986.

Marrou, H.-I. *Histoire de l'éducation dans l'antiquité*. Paris: Editions du Seuil, 1948; *A History of Education in Antiquity*, trans. George Lamb. New York: Sheed and Ward, 1956.

———. ΜΟΥΣΙΚΟΣ ΑΝΗΡ: *Étude sur les scènes de la vie intellectuelle figurant sur les monuments funéraires romains*. Roma: "L'Erma" di Bretschneider, 1964.

———. "La technique de l'edition a l'epoque patristique." *VC* 3 (1949) 208–224.

Marshall, Anthony J. "Library Resources and Creative Writing at Rome." *Phoenix* 30 (1976) 252–264.

Martin, Dale B. *The Corinthian Body*. New Haven, Conn.: Yale University Press, 1995.

———. *Slavery as Salvation: The Metaphor of Slavery in Pauline Christianity*. New Haven, Conn.: Yale University Press, 1990.

Martin, Henri-Jean. *The History and Power of Writing*, trans. Lydia G. Cochrane. Chicago: University of Chicago Press, 1994. Originally published as *Histoire et pouvoirs de l'écrit* (Paris: Librairie Académique Perrin, 1988).

Martin, Victor. *Papyrus Bodmer II: Evangile de Jean*. Cologny-Genève: Bibliothèque Bodmer, 1956.

———. *Papyrus Bodmer XX*. Cologny-Genève: Bibliothèque Bodmer, 1964.

Martini, Carlo M. "Is There a Late Alexandrian Text of the Gospels?" *NTS* 24 (1978) 285–296.

Maxey, Mima. "Occupations of the Lower Classes in Roman Society." Ph.D. dissertation, University of Chicago, 1938.

McDonnell, Myles. "Writing, Copying, and Autograph Manuscripts in Ancient Rome." *CQ* 46 (1996) 469–491.

McKenzie, D. F. *Bibliography and the Sociology of Texts*. Panizzi Lectures 1985. London: British Library, 1986.

McKitterick, Rosamond. *Books, Scribes and Learning in the Frankish Kingdom, 6th-9th Centuries*. Aldershot, U.K.: Variorum Reprints, 1994.

McKitterick, Rosamond, ed. *The Uses of Literacy in Early Mediaeval Europe*. Cambridge: Cambridge University Press, 1990.

McNamee, Kathleen. *Sigla and Select Marginalia in Greek Literary Papyri*. Papyrologica Bruxellensia 26. Bruxelles: Fondation Égyptologique Reine Élisabeth, 1992.

Meeks, Wayne A. *The First Urban Christians: The Social World of the Apostle Paul*. New Haven, Conn.: Yale University Press, 1983.

Meier, Samuel A. "Women and Communication in the Ancient Near East." *JAOS* 111 (1991) 540–547.

Metzger, Bruce. "The Caesarean Text of the Gospels." *JBL* 64 (1945) 457–489.

———. *The Early Versions of the New Testament: Their Origin, Transmission, and Limitations*. Oxford: Clarendon Press, 1977.

———. "Explicit References in the Works of Origen to Variant Readings in New Testament Manuscripts." *Biblical and Patristic Studies in Memory of Robert Pierce Casey*, ed. J. Neville Birdsall and Robert W. Thomson. Freiburg: Herder, 1963, 78–95.

———. "Greek Manuscripts of John's Gospel with 'Hermeneiai'." In *Text and Testimony*, ed. by T. Baarda, A Hilhorst, G.P. Luttikhuizen, and A. S. van der Woude. Kampen: Uitgeversmaatschappij L. H. Kok, 1988.

———. "Literary Forgeries and Canonical Pseudepigrapha." *JBL* 91 (1972) 3–24.

———. "Handing Down the Bible through the Ages: The Role of Scribe and Translator." *Reformed Review* 43 (1990) 171–170.

———. *Manuscripts of the Greek Bible: An Introduction to Greek Palaeography*. New York: Oxford University Press, 1981.

———. "Recent Trends in the Textual Criticism of the Iliad and the Mahabharata." In *Chapters in the History of New Testament Textual Criticism*, vol. 4 of *New Testament Tools and Studies*, ed. Bruce M. Metzger. Leiden: E. J. Brill, 1963, 142–154.

———. "St. Jerome's Explicit References to Variant Readings in Manuscripts of the New Testament." In his *New Testament Studies: Philological, Versional, and Patristic*. Leiden: E. J. Brill, 1980, 199–210.

———. *The Text of the New Testament: Its Transmission, Corruption, and Restoration*. New York: Oxford University Press, 1992.

———. *A Textual Commentary on the Greek New Testament*. 2d ed. London: United Bible Societies, 1995.

———. "When Did Scribes Begin to Use Writing Desks?" In *New Testament Tools and Studies*, vol. 8 of *Historical and Literary Studies, Pagan, Jewish, Christian*. Grand Rapids, Mich.: 1968, 123–137.

Meyer, E. A. "Explaining the Epigraphic Habit in the Roman Empire: The Evidence of Epitaphs." *JRS* 80 (1990) 74–96.

———. "Literacy, Literate Practice, and the Law in the Roman Empire, A.D. 100–600." Ph.D. dissertation, Yale University, 1988.

Milne, H. J. M., and T. C. Skeat. *Scribes and Correctors of the Codex Sinaiticus*. London: British Museum, 1938.

Mitchell, J. Clyde. "The Concept and Use of Social Networks." In *Social Networks in Urban Situations: Analyses of Personal Relationships in Central African Towns*, ed. J. Clyde Mitchell. Manchester: Manchester University Press, 1969, 1–50.

Mohler, S. L. "Slave Education in the Roman Empire." *TAPA* 71 (1940) 262–280.

Musurillo, Herbert. "Early Christian Economy: A Reconsideration of P. Amherst 3 (a) (= Wilcken, Chrest. 126)." *Chronique D'Egypte* 36 (1956) 124–134.

Nautin, Pierre. *Origène: sa vie et son oeuvre*. Paris: Beauchesne, 1977.

Norman, A. F. "The Book Trade in Fourth-Century Antioch." *Journal of Hellenic Studies* 80 (1960) 122–126.

Oates, John F. "The Basilikos Grammateus." *Life in a Multi-Cultural Society: Egypt from Cambyses to Constantine and Beyond*, ed. Janet H. Johnson. Chicago: Oriental Institute of the University of Chicago, 1992, 255–258 .

—————. *The Ptolemaic Basilikos Grammateus*. BASP Supplement 8. Atlanta, Ga.: Scholars Press, 1995.

O'Callaghan, José. *Nomina Sacra in Papyris Graecis Saeculi III Neotestamentariis*. Rome: Biblical Institute Press, 1970.

Oertel, F. *Die Liturgie*. Leipzig: E. G. Teubner, 1917.

O'Neill, J. C. "The Rules Followed by the Editors of the Text Found in the Codex Vaticanus." *NTS* 35 (1989) 219–228.

Ong, Walter. *Orality and Literacy: The Technologizing of the Word*. London: Methuen, 1982.

—————. *The Presence of the Word*. New Haven, Conn.: Yale University Press, 1967.

Paap, A.H.R.E. *Nomina Sacra in the Greek Papyri of the First Five Centuries A.D.: The Sources and Some Deductions*. Leiden: E. J. Brill, 1959.

Pachomius. *Vitae Graecae*, ed. F. Halkin. Subsidia Hagiographica 19. English translation of Pachomian materials: A. Veilleux. *Pachomian Koinonia: The Lives, Rules and Other Writings of Saint Pachomius and His Disciples*, 3 vols.: 1, *The Lives of Saint Pachomius and His Disciples*; 2, *Pachomian Chronicles and Rules*; 3, *Instructions, Letters, and Other Writings of Saint Pachomius and His Disciples*. Kalamazoo, Mich.: Cistercian, 1980–1982.

Pack, Roger A. *The Greek and Latin Literary Texts from Greco-Roman Egypt*. Ann Arbor, Mich.: University of Michigan Press, 1965.

Parássoglou, George M. "ΔΕΞΙΑ ΧΕΙΡ ΚΑΙ ΓΟΝΥ: Some Thoughts on the Postures of the Ancient Greeks and Romans when Writing on Papyrus Rolls." *Scrittura e Civiltà* 3 (1979) 5–21.

—————. "A Roll upon His Knees." *Yale Classical Studies* 28 (1985) 273–275.

Parker, D. C. *Codex Bezae: An Early Christian Manuscript and Its Text*. Cambridge: Cambridge University Press, 1992.

—————. "A 'Dictation Theory' of Codex Bezae." *JSNT* 15 (1982) 97–112.

Parsons, Mikeal C. "A Christological Tendency in P[75]." *JBL* 105 (1986) 463–479.

Pestman, P. W. "L'agoranomie: un avant-poste de l'administration grecque enlevé par les Égyptiens?" *Das ptolemäische Ägypten, Akten des Internationalen Symposions 27.–29. September 1976 in Berlin*, ed. V. M. Strocka and H. Maehler. Mainz: Philipp von Zabern, 203–210.

————. "The Official Archive of the Village Scribes of Kerkeosiris: Notes on the So-Called Archive of Menches." In *Festschrift zum 100-Jahrigen Bestehen der Papyrussamlung der österreichisschen nationalBilbiothek, Papyrus Erzherzog Rainer (P.Rainer Cent)*. Wien: Verlang Brüder Hollinek, 1983, 127–134.

————. "Who Were the Owners, in the 'Community of Workmen', of the Chester Beatty Papyri." *Gleanings from Deir el-Medina*, ed. R. J. Demarée and Jac. J. Janssen. Leiden: Nederlands Instituut voor Het Habije Oosten, 1982, 155–172.

Petersen, William L. *Tatian's Diatessaron: Its Creation, Dissemination, Significance, and History in Scholarship*. Leiden: E. J. Brill, 1994.

Petit, Paul. "Recherches sur la Publication et la Diffusion des Discours de Libanius." *Historia* 5 (1956) 479–509.

Petzer, Jacobus H. "The History of the New Testament — Its Reconstruction, Significance, and Use in New Testament Textual Criticism." In *New Testament Textual Criticism, Exegesis and Church History: A Discussion of Methods*, ed. B. Aland and J. Delobel. Kampen, The Netherlands: Pharos, 1994, 30–32.

Phillips, John J. "Atticus and the Publication of Cicero's Works." *Classical World* 79 (1986) 227–237.

Pollard, Alfred. *An Essay on Colophons with Specimens and Translations*. New York: Burt Franklin, 1905.

Pomeroy, Sarah B. *Goddesses, Whores, Wives, and Slaves: Women in Classical Antiquity*. New York: Schocken Books, 1975.

————,. ed. *Women's History and Ancient History*. Chapel Hill: University of North Carolina Press, 1991.

————. "Technikai kai Mousikai": The Education of Women in the Fourth Century and in the Hellenistic Period." *American Journal of Ancient History* 2 (1977) 51–68.

Poole, J. B., and R. Reed. "The Preparation of Leather and Parchment by the Dead Sea Scrolls Community." *Technology and Culture* 3 (1962) 1–26.

Porter, Calvin L. "Papyrus Bodmer XV (P^{75}) and the Text of Codex Vaticanus." *JBL* 81 (1962) 363–376.

————. "An Analysis of the Textual Variations between Pap 75 and Codex Vaticanus in the Text of John." In *Studies in the History and Text of the New Testament in Honor of K. W. Clark. S & D* 29. Salt Lake City: University of Utah Press, 1967, 71–80.

Preuschen, Erwin. "Die Stenographie im Leben des Origenes." *Archiv für Stenographie*. Berlin 56 (1905) 6–15, 49–55.

Price, Simon. *Rituals and Power: The Roman Imperial Cult in Asia Minor*. Cambridge: Cambridge University Press, 1984.

Quaegebeur, Jan. "Greco-Egyptian Double Names as a Feature of a Bi-Cultural Society: The Case Ψοσνευς ο κὰι Τριάδελφος." In *Life in a Multi-Cultural Society: Egypt from Cambyses to Constantine and Beyond*, ed. Janet H. Johnson. Chicago: Oriental Institute of the University of Chicago, 1992, 265–272.

Quinn, Kenneth. "The Poet and His Audience in the Augustan Age." *ANRW* 30.1 (1982) 75–180.

Reich, Ronny. "A Note on the Function of Room 30 (the 'Scriptorium') at Khirbet Qumran." *JJS* 46 (1995) 157–160.

Reichmann, Felix. "The Book Trade at the Time of the Roman Empire." *Library Quarterly* 8 (1938) 40–76.

Resnick, I. M. "The Codex in Early Jewish and Christian Communities." *Journal of Religious History* 17 (1992) 1–17.

Reynolds, L. D., and N. G. Wilson. *Scribes and Scholars: A Guide to the Transmission of Greek and Latin Literature*, 2d edition. Oxford: Clarendon Press, 1974 [1968].

———. "Scribes and Scholars: A Guide to the Transmission of Greek and Latin Literature." *JTS* 20 (1969) 666–667.

Richards, E. Randolph. *The Secretary in the Letters of Paul*. Tübingen: J. C. B. Mohr (Paul Siebeck), 1991.

Richardson, L. *A New Topographical Dictionary of Rome*. Baltimore, Md.: Johns Hopkins University Press, 1992.

Ricoeur, Paul. "Epilogue: The 'Sacred' Text and the Community," in *The Critical Study of Sacred Texts*, ed. Wendy O'Flaherty. Berkeley, Calif.: Graduate Theological Union, 1979, 271–276.

Roberts, C. H. "Books in the Graeco-Roman World and in the New Testament." In *The Cambridge History of the Bible*. Vol. 1. Cambridge: Cambridge University Press, 1970, 48–66.

———. *Buried Books in Antiquity: Habent Sua Fata Libelli*. Arundell Esdaile Memorial Lecture, 1962. London: Library Association, 1963.

———. "The Christian Book and the Greek Papyri." *JTS* 50 (1949) 155–168.

———. *Greek Literary Hands, 350* B.C.–A.D. *400*. Oxford: Clarendon Press, 1956.

———. *Manuscript, Society and Belief in Early Christian Egypt*. London: Oxford University Press, 1979.

———. "The *Nomina Sacra* in Early Latin Christian MSS." *Micellanea Francesco Ehrle* 4 (1924) 62–74.

———. "P. Yale 1 and the Early Christian Book." In *American Studies in Papyrology*. Vol. 1: *Essays in Honor of C. Bradford Welles*. New Haven, Conn.: American Society of Papyrologists, 1966, 25–28.

———, and T. C. Skeat. *The Birth of the Codex*. London: Oxford University Press, 1987.

Robinson, James M. *The Pachomian Monastic Library at the Chester Beatty Library and the Bibliothèque Bodmer*. Institute for Antiquity and Christianity Occasional Papers 19. Claremont, Calif.: Institute for Antiquity and Christianity, 1990.

Roccati, Alessandro. "Writing Egyptian: Scripts and Speeches at the End of Pharaonic Civilization." *Life in a Multi-Cultural Society: Egypt from Cambyses to Constantine and Beyond*, ed. Janet H. Johnson. Chicago: Oriental Institute of the University of Chicago, 1992, 291–294.

Rodgers, Peter R. "The New Eclecticism." *NovT* 33 (1992) 388–397.

Ross, J. M. "Floating Words: Their Significance for Textual Criticism." *NTS* 38 (1992) 153–156.

Rousseau, Philip. "'Learned Women' and the Development of a Christian Culture in Late Antiquity." *Symbolae Osloenses* 70 (1995) 116–147.

———. *Pachomius: The Making of a Community in Fourth-Century Egypt*. Berkeley: University of California Press, 1985.

Rousselle, Aline. *Porneia: On Desire and the Body in Antiquity*. Cambridge: Basil Blackwell, 1988.

Rowlandson, Jane, ed. *Women and Society in Greek and Roman Egypt: A Sourcebook.* Cambridge: Cambridge University Press, 1998.

Royse, J. R. "Scribal Habits in Early Greek New Testament Papyri." Ph.D. diss., Graduate Theological Union, Berkeley, Calif., 1981.

———. "Scribal Habits in the Transmission of New Testament Texts." In *The Critical Study of Sacred Texts*, ed. W. D. O'Flaherty. Berkeley, Calif.: Graduate Theological Union, 1979, 139–161.

———. "Von Soden's Accuracy." *JTS* 30 (1979) 166–171.

Ryan, D. P. "Papyrus." *BA* 51 (1988) 132–140.

Saenger, Paul. "Silent Reading: Its Impact on Late Medieval Script and Society." *Viator* 13 (1982) 367–414.

Saller, Richard. *Personal Patronage under the Early Empire.* Cambridge: Cambridge University Press, 1982.

Sanders, Henry A. *A Third Century Papyrus Codex of the Epistles of Paul.* Ann Arbor: University of Michigan Press, 1935.

Sanders, James A. "Text and Canon: Concepts and Method." *JBL* 98 (1979) 5–29.

Schams, Christine. *Jewish Scribes in the Second-Temple Period.* JSOT s.s. 291 Sheffield: Sheffield Academic Press, 1998.

Schenkveld, Dirk M. "Prose Usages of Ακουειν 'To Read'," *Classical Quarterly* 42 (1992) 129–141.

Schofield, E. M. "The Papyrus Fragments of the Greek New Testament." Ph.D. diss., Southern Baptist Theological Seminary, 1936.

Schramm, Albert. "Zur Geschichte der Stenographie in der alten Kirche." *KorrB* 48 (1903): *Origenes* 62–66, 98–105; *Die drei grossen Kappadozier* 221–223, 241, 246, 265–268.

Sherwin-White, A. N. *The Letters of Pliny: A Historical and Social Commentary.* Oxford: Clarendon Press, 1966.

Sider, Sandra, "Herculaneum's Library in 79 A.D.: The Villa of the Papyri." *Libraries and Culture* 25 (1990) 534–542.

Silva, Moises. "The Text of Galations: Evidence from the Earliest Greek Manuscripts." In *Scribes and Scripture, Festschrift for H. Greenlee*, ed. D. A. Black. Winona Lake, Ind.: Eisenbrauns, 1992, 17–25.

Skeat, T. C. "Early Christian Book-Production: Papyri and Manuscripts." In *The Cambridge History of the Bible.* Vol. 2. Cambridge: Cambridge University Press, 1969, 54–79.

———. "Irenaeus and the Four-Gospel Canon." *NT* 34 (1992) 194–199.

———. "The Length of the Standard Papyrus Roll and the Cost-Advantage of the Codex." *ZPE* 45 (1982) 169–175.

———. "The Origin of the Christian Codex." *ZPE* 102 (1994) 263–268.

———. "The Use of Dictation in Ancient Book-Production." *Proceedings of the British Academy* 42 (1956) 179–208.

———. "Roll Versus Codex: A New Approach?" *ZPE* 84 (1990) 297–298.

Slusser, Michael. "Reading Silently in Antiquity." *JBL* 111 (1992) 499.

Snyder, Jane McIntosh. *The Woman and the Lyre: Women Writers in Classical Greece and Rome.* Carbondale: Southern Illinois University Press, 1989.

Soden, Hermann von. *Die Schriften des Neuen Testaments in ihrer ältensten Erreichbaren Textgestalt.* Göttingen: Vandenhoeck and Reprecht, 1913.

Sommer, Richard. "T. Pomponius Atticus und die Verbreitung von Ciceros Werken." *Hermes* 61 (1926) 389–422.

Stallybrass, Peter, and Allon White. *The Politics and Poetics of Transgression.* Ithaca, N.Y.: Cornell University Press, 1986.

Starr, Raymond J. "The Circulation of Literary Texts in the Roman World." *CQ* 37 (1987) 213–223.

Stock, Brian. *The Implications of Literacy: Written Language and Models of Interpretation in the Eleventh and Twelfth Centuries.* Princeton, N.J.: Princeton University Press, 1983.

———. *Listening for the Text: On the Uses of the Past.* Baltimore, Md.: Johns Hopkins University Press, 1990.

Stoddard, Roger E. "Morphology and the Book from an American Perspective." *Printing History* 17 (1990) 2–14.

Streeter, Burnett Hillman. *The Four Gospels: A Study of Origins.* London: Macmillan, 1936.

Susini, Giancarlo. *The Roman Stonecutter: An Introduction to Latin Epigraphy,* trans. A. M. Dabrowski. Totowa, N.J.: Rowman and Littlefield, 1973. Published first as *Il Lapicida Romano,* 1967.

Tanner, Thomas M. "A History of Early Christian Libraries from Jesus to Jerome." *Journal of Library History* 14 (1979) 407–435.

Tassier, Emmanuel. "Greek and Demotic School-Exercises." *Life in a Multi-Cultural Society: Egypt from Cambyses to Constantine and Beyond,* ed. Janet H. Johnson. Chicago: Oriental Institute of the University of Chicago, 1992, 311–315.

Taylor, Joan E. "The Phenomenon of Early Jewish-Christianity: Reality or Scholarly Invention?" *VC* 44 (1990) 313–334.

Testuz, Michel. *Papyrus Bodmer V.* Cologny-Genève: Bibliothèque Bodmer, 1958.

———. *Papyrus Bodmer X–XII.* Cologny-Genève: Bibliothèque Bodmer, 1959.

———. *Papyrus Bodmer VII–IX.* Cologny-Genève: Bibliothèque Bodmer, 1959.

———. *Papyrus Bodmer XIII.* Cologny-Genève: Bibliothèque Bodmer, 1960.

Thiede, Carsten Peter. "Notes on P4 = Bibliothèque Nationale Paris, Supplementum Graece 1120/5." *Tyndale Bulletin* 46 (1995) 55–57.

———. "Papyrus Magdalen Greek 17 (Gregory-Aland P64): A Reappraisal." *Tyndale Bulletin* 46 (1995) 29–42.

Thomas, Rosalind. *Literacy and Orality in Ancient Greece.* Cambridge: Cambridge University Press, 1992.

———. *Oral Tradition and Written Record in Classical Athens.* Cambridge: Cambridge University Press, 1989.

Thompson, Dorothy J. "Literacy and the Administration in Early Ptolemaic Egypt." *Life in a Multi-Cultural Society: Egypt from Cambyses to Contantine and Beyond,* ed. Janet H. Johnson. Chicago: Oriental Institute of the University of Chicago, 1992, 323–326.

Thompson, Edward Maunde. *A Handbook of Greek and Latin Palaeography.* Chicago: Argonaut, 1966.

Tischendorf, Constantinus. *Novum Testamentum Graece: Ad Antiquissimos Testes Denuo Recensuit.* 8th ed. Lipsiae: Giesecke and Devrient, 1869.

Tov, Emanuel. "Hebrew Biblical Manuscripts from the Judaean Desert: Their Contribution to Textual Criticism." *JJS* 39 (1988) 5–37.

———. "The Textual Base of the Corrections in the Biblical Texts Found at Qumran." *The Dead Sea Scrolls: Forty Years of Research*, ed. Devorah Dimant and Uriel Rappaport. Leiden: E. J. Brill, 1992, 299–314.

———. *Textual Criticism of the Hebrew Bible.* Minneapolis, Minn.: Fortress Press; Asses: Van Gorcum, 1992.

Traube, Ludwig. *Nomina Sacra: Versuch einer Geschichte der christlichen Kürzung.* Munich, 1907.

Treggiari, Susan. "Contubernalis in *CIL* 6." *Phoenix* 35 (1981) 42–69.

———. "Jobs for Women." *American Journal of Ancient History* 1 (1976) 76–104.

———. "Jobs in the Household of Livia." *Papers of the British School at Rome*, n.s. 43 (1975) 48–77.

———. *Roman Marriage: Iusti Coniuges from the Time of Cicero to the Time of Ulpian.* Oxford: Clarendon Press, 1993 [c. 1991].

Treu, Kurt. "Antike Literatur im byzantinischen Ägypten im Lichte der Papyri." *Byzantinoslavica* 47 (1986) 1–7.

Trigg, J. W. *Origen: The Bible and Philosophy in the Third-Century Church.* Atlanta, Ga.: John Knox Press, 1983.

Turner, Eric G. *Greek Manuscripts of the Ancient World.* Princeton, N.J.: Princeton University Press, 1971.

———. *Greek Papyri: An Introduction.* Oxford: Clarendon Press, 1980, 1968.

———. "Recto and Verso." *Jorunal of Egyptian Archaeology* 40 (1954) 102–106.

———. "Roman Oxyrhynchus." *Journal of Egyptian Archaeology* 38 (1952) 78–93.

———. "Scribes and Scholars of Oxyrhynchus." *MPER* 5 (1955) 141–149.

———. *Typology of the Early Codex.* Philadelphia: University of Pennsylvania Press, 1977.

Vaganay, Leon, and Christian-Bernard Amphoux. *An Introduction to New Testament Textual Criticism.* Cambridge: Cambridge University Press, 1991.

Van Groningen, B. A. "ΕΚΔΟΣΙΣ." *Mnemosyne* 16 (1963) 1–17.

Vassall-Phillips, O. R., trans. *The Work of St. Optatus, Bishop of Milevis, Against the Donatists.* London: Longmans, Green, 1917.

Visotzky, Burton L. "Overturning the Lamp." *JJS* 38 (1987) 72–80.

———. "Prolegomenon to the Study of Jewish-Christianities in Rabbinic Literature." *AJS Review* 14 (1989) 47–70.

Vööbus, Arthur. *Early Versions of the New Testament.* Stockholm: Estonian Theological Society in Exile, 1954.

Weaver, P. R. C. *Familia Caesaris: A Social Study of the Emperor's Freedmen and Slaves.* Cambridge: Cambridge University Press, 1972.

———. "Social Mobility in the Early Roman Empire: The Evidence of the Imperial Freedmen and Slaves." *Studies in Ancient Society*, ed. M. I. Finley. Past and Present Series. London: Routledge and Kegan Paul, 1974, 121–140.

Wellisch, Hans H. *Kallimachos: The Alexandrian Library and the Origins of Bibliography.* Madison, Wis.: University of Wisconsin Press, 1991.

Westcott, B. F., and F. J. A. Hort. *Introduction to the New Testament in the Original Greek*. 1882; repr. Peabody, Mass.: Hendrickson Publishers, 1988.

Wilken, Robert L. "Alexandria: A School for Training in Virtue." In *Schools of Thought in the Christian Tradition*, ed. Patrick Henry. Philadelphia, Pa.: Fortress Press, 1984, 15–30.

———. *The Christians as the Romans Saw Them*. New Haven, Conn.: Yale University Press, 1984.

Williams, C. S. C. *Alterations to the Text of the Synoptic Gospels and Acts*. Oxford: Basil Blackwell, 1951.

Williams, Ronald J. "Scribal Training in Ancient Egypt." *JAOS* 92 (1972) 214–221.

Willis, James. *Latin Textual Criticism*. Urbana: University of Illinois Press, 1972.

Willis, William H. "Two Literary Papyri in an Archive from Panopolis." *Illinois Classical Studies* 3 (1978) 140–151.

Wills, Lawrence M. *The Jewish Novel in the Ancient World*. Ithaca, N.Y.: Cornell University Press, 1995.

Wilson, N. G. *Scholars of Byzantium*. London: Duckworth, 1983.

Wipszycka, Ewa. "Un Lecteur Qui Ne Sait Pas Ecrire Ou un Chretien Qui Ne Veut Pas Se Souiller?" *ZPE* 50 (1983) 117–121.

Wisse, Frederick W. "Gnosticism and Early Monasticism in Egypt." In *Gnosis: Festschrift für Hans Jonas*, ed. Barbara Aland. Göttingen: Vandenhoeck and Ruprecht, 1978, 431–440.

———. "Language Mysticism in the Nag Hammadi Texts and in Early Coptic Monasticism I: Cryptography." *Enchoria* 9 (1979) 101–120.

———. "The Use of Early Christian Literature as Evidence for Inner Diversity and Conflict." In *Nag Hammadi, Gnosticism and Early Christianity*, ed. by C. W. Hedrick and R. Hodgson, Jr. Peabody, Mass.: Hendrickson, 1986, 177–190.

Witherington, Ben. "The Anti-Feminist Tendencies of the 'Western' Text in Acts." *JBL* 103 (1984) 82–84.

Wright, Leon E. *Alterations of the Words of Jesus as Quoted in the Literature of the Second Century*. Cambridge, Mass.: Harvard University Press, 1952.

Young, Norman H. "The Figure of the Paidogogos in Art and Literature." *BA* 54 (1990) 80–86.

Youtie, Herbert C. "Avoidance of Theta in Dating by Regnal Years: Superstition or Scribal Caution?" *ZPE* 28 (1978) 269–270. Reprinted in *Scriptiunculae Posteriores*. Part 1. Bonn: Rudolf Habelt Verlag GMBH, 1981, 455–456.

———. "ΑΓΡΑΜΜΑΤΟΣ: An Aspect of Greek Society in Egypt." *Scriptiunculae* II. Amsterdam: Adolf M. Hakkert, 1973, 611–627.

———. "Because They Do Not Know Letters." *ZPE* 19 (1975) 101–108.

———. 'Βραδέως γράφων: Between Literacy and Illiteracy." *GRBS* 12 (1971) 239–261.

———. "Pétaus, fils de Pétaus, ou le scribe qui ne savait pas écrire." *Scriptiunculae* II. Amsterdam: Adolf M. Hakkert, 1973, 677–693.

———. "Τοπογραμματεις και Κωμογραμματεις." *ZPE* 24 (1977) 138–139. Reprinted in *Scriptiunculae Posteriores*, part 1. Bonn: Rudolf Habelt Verlag GMBH, 1981, 400–401.

————. "ΥΠΟΓΡΑΚΦΕΥΣ: The Social Impact of Illiteracy in Graeco-Roman Egypt," *ZPE* 17 (1975) 201–221.

Zahn, Theodor. *Tatian's Diatessaron*. Erlangen: Deichert, 1881.

Zetzel, James E. G. *Latin Textual Criticism in Antiquity*. New York: Arno Press, 1981.

————. 'The Subscriptions in the Manuscripts of Livy and Fronto and the Meaning of *Emendatio*." *Classical Philology* 75 (1980) 38–59.

Zuntz, G. *The Test of the Epistles: A Disquisition upon the Corpus Paulinum*. London: Oxford University Press, 1953

INDEX